To my three guys—Jack, Ian, and Aaron—who give me so much joy.

Contents

5. Detailed Design and Choosing a Programming Language   192

8. More about Software Engineering: Now and in the Future   319

Preface

What Is Special About This Book

This textbook is an introduction to the study and practice of software engineering. There are a number of textbooks available, many of which provide a good introduction to software engineering. What is special about this book, however, is that it is specifically designed to be used in a course in which the study of software engineering is combined with the application of software engineering principles and techniques to an actual, ongoing project. The project is assumed to involve the development of a nontrivial software system by a team of students. (An instructor's manual with suggestions for project planning, organization, and grading is available from the publisher.)

To support the project component of the course, the topics covered in the text follow the stages in the development of a software system. For each stage, a small number of methods and techniques from those widely known in software engineering are introduced. Each method is then described in sufficient detail that it can be applied to the students' projects. Both simple and more advanced examples are provided to illustrate the techniques and to serve as guidelines. When appropriate, suggestions are given for applying the methods using resources readily available to most students. Throughout the text, the student's project goals form a unifying theme and tie the chapters together. Exercises at the end of each chapter allow the students to practice the methods on a small scale before applying them to their projects. In addition, a case study is included. The case study is an actual project carried out by a group of students as part of a software engineering course. At the end of each chapter, the relevant portion of the case study project is discussed, and excerpts from the documentation are provided. Appendix A includes additional excerpts from the case study documentation. The case study allows readers to see how the principles and techniques discussed can be applied to an actual project similar in scope to their own projects.

Another special feature of this book is the coverage of user interface design. It has been estimated that up to 70 percent of the source code for a typical application is directly concerned with user interface. In recognition of this fact, software engineering practitioners are focusing more attention on the design and implementation of such an important component of applications systems. An entire chapter is devoted to interface issues and interface design. Furthermore, the topic is presented as part of the preliminary design phase. Software design proceeds from the outside to the inside — from the user interface to the functionality. This approach combines the best features of prototyping with the power of traditional design methods.

To round out the students' knowledge of software engineering, a number of topics not directly related to the advancement of the project are covered. Chapter 1 provides an introduction and overview of software engineering and the software development cycle. Chapter 8 covers alternate analysis and design methods, automated methods and tools, software development environments, software maintenance, and object-oriented programming. The current status of and future trends in software engineering are discussed as well.

While writing a computer user's manual is not strictly a topic in software engineering, many students are faced with the task of producing one in the course of carrying out a software development project. Appendix B is a condensed guide to writing user's manuals written by Katherine N. Macfarlane, a documentalist with Borland International, Inc.

The book assumes the readers have had experience programming in at least one high-level language, and have had an introduction to algorithms and data structures. While most software engineering courses are intended for college juniors and seniors, there is some indication that the courses are moving to lower levels in the curriculum. Due to the style and project-focused approach used in this book, it is suitable for any student who has the necessary background, regardless of college class.

Why a Student-Project Orientation Is Used

The impetus for the approach taken in this text came from two different personal experiences. The first experience was my own efforts in teaching software engineering. While preparing to teach the course, I gained much from reading books and journals and from attending conferences and training seminars. When actually teaching, however, I found I had some difficulty in meshing the knowledge with the student projects. In many cases, the written and oral descriptions of the techniques and methods were lacking in sufficient detail to make it clear exactly how to apply the technique to an actual software development task. In some cases, topics that I needed to cover, such as user interface and writing user's manuals, were not mentioned in software engineering texts. Furthermore, there was only limited guidance available on document content and format, document evaluation, and project organization. I strongly felt the need for a book oriented toward student projects rather than toward large-scale commercial or government projects, and which presented the material in a truly student-usable way.

The second experience that influenced the choice of the approach used in this text was seeing the results of a survey conducted by my colleague, Laura M. Leventhal, and myself. The Leventhal and Mynatt survey (1987) was designed to profile undergraduate software engineering education in North America. The survey covered issues of course content, course organization, and project characteristics. The results showed that the typical software engineering course includes in-depth to moderate coverage of the major stages in the software life cycle: requirements and analysis, system design, detailed design, coding, and testing. In addition, the topic of user interface receives in-depth to moderate coverage in nearly 60 percent of software engineering courses. Topics such as software metrics, project management, maintenance, and legal and ethical issues receive more limited coverage. The survey also indicated that the course very often requires written and oral reports from the students, and is frequently plagued by staffing problems and the acquisition of suitable software.

Ninety-five percent of the courses described in the survey included project components. These projects are often significant software projects intended for actual use. They are not "toy" projects. In most cases, the students work in groups with student leaders. Typically, the class is working on several different projects and the instructor acts as the user for the projects. Finally, in the majority of cases, the project counts for more than 40 percent of the student's grade.

The results of this survey highlight the importance of the project component in most software engineering courses. Not only does the project count for a large proportion of the student's grade, but it influences the choice of subject matter and the types of demands put on the student, such as oral and written reports. In short, the typical software engineering course is certainly *not* a typical college course, nor is it a typical computer science course.

Given the profile of the typical software engineering course, it is not surprising that a textbook written in the standard college textbook style is often not appropriate for such a course. The typical software engineering text is a survey text. It attempts to cover all of the significant areas of software engineering. Within each area, it attempts to discuss all of the major topics. Its orientation is toward large-scale commercial or government software development. Each author tends to stress some areas more than others, but the basic intent of these texts is the same: to survey the topic of software engineering. While this approach is fine for courses that intend to provide a broad or theory-oriented introduction to software engineering, it has drawbacks when used as a source of information to guide a student project. One drawback is that the coverage of every technique or method may be at such a high or cursory level that the student is unable to gain a working understanding of any one method. Although the teacher may direct the students to use one particular method in a project, the textbook may not provide sufficient detailed description or enough examples to allow the students to actually apply the method to their own cases. A second drawback of the survey approach is that it does not provide step-by-step guidance on carrying out a project. This text attempts to remedy these problems by taking a different approach. The chapters covering the software development cycle present only a few selected techniques. These techniques are presented in enough detail that the students should be able to use them in their projects. Specific suggestions concerning documentation content and format are included to provide project guidance. Criteria for evaluation are provided. A checklist of project activities is given at the end of each chapter.

Other Guidelines Used in Writing the Book

The choice of which techniques to cover was based on a number of criteria. These included the popularity of a technique, its ease of learning, ease of use, and use as a basis for later learning either on the job or in future classes. Another consideration was the degree of automation of the technique. A criterion for the techniques chosen was that they can be implemented using paper and pencil, if necessary. The chapters on requirements analysis and specification and on preliminary design, for example, are based on the structured design and analysis methods of Constantine and Yourdon (1979) and DeMarco (1978). These methods are widely used and are fairly easy to learn and apply. Documentation can be done with paper and pencil, or with general application software such as a word processor and/or a drawing program. In addition, several software packages are available that directly implement these methods or parts of these methods. Other chapters also introduce techniques that can be implemented with paper and pencil, general application software or, when available, with automated software engineering tools. This criterion was set up to promote the greatest flexibility for the teacher, and because the Leventhal and Mynatt survey indicated that obtaining software was a problem for many teachers.

An important new trend in software engineering is object-oriented design and object-oriented programming. The object-oriented approach to software development is a paradigmatic shift from the more traditional methods based on data flow or data structure. While the approach offers great promise for increased productivity in software development, there is not yet a mature and tested engineering methodology associated with it. The development of such a methodology will take time. Meanwhile, this book attempts to weave in some of the more central ideas of the object-oriented approach with the intention of preparing the reader for the future.

Another guiding principle that was used in writing the book was to leave out a number of topics related to the "business side" of software development. Financial and management issues are an important part of any software development project done outside of a classroom. However, there is not enough time in one course on software engineering to cover all of the relevant topics in any detail. Because these particular topics do not relate directly to the implementation of student projects, they were left out.

In presenting the material, I have attempted to use a style that makes complex concepts understandable, without oversimplification. In many cases, simple examples and illustrations are provided and discussed first, followed by more complicated examples. I have endeavored to choose examples that are common computing problems (most often with an application orientation) so that the reader can focus on the use of the technique, rather than on understanding the problem domain.

When feasible, the same problem is used at several places throughout the book to provide continuity.

Some readers may feel that the level of presentation is somewhat low. While the style may initially give this impression, the students (mostly seniors) that have used the book in draft form have not found this to be true. Furthermore, their answers to essay exam questions requiring integration and application of the concepts show a good knowledge of the material. They are able to demonstrate that they truly understand the material, and have not just memorized a number of isolated facts. If the students learn and understand the material, does it matter whether it was initially easy or hard for them to acquire this knowledge? I think not. The feedback received from prior students now in the workforce and from their employers has been quite positive, as well. The students know and can apply software engineering principles on the job.

Acknowledgments

I would like to thank some of those people who have provided help and encouragement on writing this book. Katherine Macfarlane, always a wizard with words, came through with the appendix on writing a user manual. Mildred Lintner had the kindness to try out an earlier version of the book on her students and provide feedback, as did Laura Leventhal. Laura has also been a valuable sounding board for ideas and a reassuring optimist. Diane Crow, efficient and meticulous as always, has been a great help in preparing the manuscript. She has been ably assisted in her efforts by Cathy Frankfather. Thanks also go to Yew Chian Teh for writing the exercise answers included in the instructor's guide and to Kelly Ann Vogel, who ably and enthusiastically undertook the task of editing the instructor's guide and creating the camera-ready copy. Larry Dunning provided many helpful comments during the editing stages. Jack Mynatt took mouse in hand to clean up many of the figures. Considerable aid was also provided by my reviewers: Doug Bickerstaff, Eastern Washington University; Henry A. Etlinger, Rochester Institute of Technology; Robert L. Glass, Carnegie-Mellon University; David A Gustafson, Kansas State University; and Ronald J. Leach, Howard University. Their comments and insights were invaluable, and I thank them.

References

DeMarco, T. (1979) *Structured Analysis and System Specification*. Englewood Cliffs, NJ: Prentice-Hall.

Leventhal, L. M., and Mynatt, B. T. (1987) Components of typical undergraduate software engineering courses: Results from a survey. *IEEE Transactions on Software Engineering*, SE-13 (11), 1193–1198.

Yourdon, E., and Constantine, L. (1979) *Structured Design*. Englewood Cliffs, NJ: Prentice-Hall.

1. What Is Software Engineering?

The following multiple-choice questions all concern software development. Just for fun, try to answer these questions. (The answers are given on page 2.)

1. The typical software development project takes _____ months.

   a. 1 to 5

   b. 6 to 11

   c. 12 to 23

   d. 24 to 48

2. For a medium-sized software system, _____ lines of executable source code are typically produced per day per person during the entire period of development of the system.

   a. less than 10   b. 10 to 20

   c. 21 to 30   d. more than 30

3. The approximate number of errors found in every 1000 lines of executable source code *during development* of a software system is _____ .

   a. less than 30

   b. 30 to 40

   c. 40 to 50

   d. 50 to 60

4. The approximate number of errors found in every 1000 lines of executable source code in a *delivered* software system is _____ .

   a. less than 4 errors in each 1000 lines

   b. 4 to 8 errors in each 1000 lines

    c. 8 to 12 errors in each 1000 lines

    d. more than 12 errors in each 1000 lines

5. Approximately what percentage of software systems that begin development are finally completed?

    a. 90 to 100%   b. 80 to 89%

    c. 70 to 79%   d. 60 to 69%

6. The cost of owning and maintaining software is typically _____ times as expensive as developing the software.

    a. 0.5 (one half as expensive)

    b. 1 (just as expensive)

    c. 2 (twice as expensive)

7. Most errors found by users in software are the result of _____ .

    a. programmer error

    b. problems in the problem statement or understanding the problem statement

    c. clerical errors

    d. errors in the design

8. In software development today, a system would be considered large if it contained at least _____ lines of executable source code.

    a. 10,000

    b. 30,000

    c. 50,000

How did you do? Did you find some of the answers surprising? Software engineering deals with the issues raised by these questions and many other facets of software development and maintenance. Software engineering is, simply stated, a systematic approach to the creation and ownership of software. Part of what makes the study of software engineering so fascinating is that many aspects of software development and ownership have been found to be counterintuitive. The discipline of software engineering, in fact, emerged to a large extent because the people who were developing software systems in the 1960s and 1970s were consistently wrong in their estimates of the time, effort, and costs involved in development. These estimates were not just a little wrong either, but were spectacularly

---

Answers to the questions on page 1, with references.
1. c (Parikh and Zvegintzov, 1983) 2. a (Boehm, 1981) 3. d (Boehm, 1981; Mills, Dyer, and Linger, 1987) 4. a (Lipow, 1982; Hamilton, 1986) 5. c (Jones, 1981) 6. c (Lientz and Swanson, 1980) 7. b (Jones, 1978; Basili and Perricone, 1984) 8. c (Fairley, 1985; Yourdon, 1975)

wrong. It was not uncommon for systems to cost more than twice the estimated cost and to take months and even years longer than projected (Brooks, 1975). Furthermore, reliability and maintainability were serious problems for the sponsors and developers of software in the 1960s and 1970s. Systems delivered to sponsors frequently did not work correctly. Often, every attempt to fix a problem in a delivered system produced only more problems because of the lack of documentation and the poorly designed nature of the system. A study in the late 1970s looked at a small number of government software projects that were in trouble (Comptroller General, 1979). Of the projects examined, 2 percent worked on delivery, 3 percent could work after some corrections, over 45 percent were delivered but never successfully used, and 20 percent were used but either extensively reworked or abandoned. The remaining 30 percent of the projects were paid for, but never delivered.

1.1 Forces Behind the Emergence of Software Engineering

The inability of organizations to predict the time, effort, and cost in software development and the poor quality of the software that was produced were only two of the driving forces behind the emergence of software engineering as a discipline. Other factors contributed to the emergence of software engineering and continue to exert influence on the development and refinement of software engineering. Among these factors, which are examined next, are:

- Changes in the ratio of hardware to software costs
- The increasingly important role of maintenance
- Advances in hardware
- Advances in software techniques
- Increased demands for software
- The demand for larger and more complex software systems

Changes in the Ratio of Hardware to Software Costs. In the early part of the 1960s, hardware costs represented 80 percent of expenditures for hardware and software combined. The primary concern was with acquiring and maintaining hardware. Software was almost considered an afterthought. After all, software is "soft" and easy to change, while hardware is "hard" and more difficult to change. Most people planned carefully for hardware development, but gave little thought to software. Furthermore, because the cost of software amounted to only a small fraction of the cost of the hardware, it did not seem very important to manage its development and costs. On the other hand, it was considered important to develop programs that made efficient use of computer time and memory resources in order to save on hardware expenses. Programmer time was used to save computer time. Making the software development process efficient was a low priority.

However, by the middle of the 1960s, a decided change occurred in the ratio of hardware to software costs: software costs were taking up approximately 40 to 50 percent of the total costs. This trend has continued. Today, hardware represents only 20 percent of the total hardware/software costs (Boehm, 1983). It is not difficult to find reasons for this reversal in costs. Certainly the reduced cost of hardware is a very important factor. Increased cost of personnel is another important factor. Demand for computing professionals was extremely high for many years, continues to be strong, and is projected to be strong into the 1990s (Musa, 1985). Scarcity creates higher prices, and computing personnel are a scarce resource.

The Increasingly Important Role of Maintenance. The responsibility of the software developer does not end when a piece of software is implemented and installed. While the software is in use, errors will be discovered. In addition, the sponsors will want to make changes in the software. This may be the result of changes in procedures or circumstances, or because the sponsors want the software to perform additional functions. These activities—fixing errors, making modifications, and adding enhancements—are all considered software maintenance. As more and more software has been created, there has been an increasing need for personnel to maintain existing software. Furthermore, the cost of maintenance is high. The cost and effort involved in adding code to perform a new function to an old system is many times the cost involved in writing the same number of lines of code when the system was created. Today, maintenance costs represent twice the costs of developing a piece of software.

Advances in Hardware. The 1960s saw the introduction of the third generation of computers, those based on integrated circuit technology. Tubes had been replaced by transistors and transistors replaced by integrated circuits. The third generation of computers offered increased speed and memory capacity. In addition, as semiconductor technology advanced, the cost of computers came down. More organizations could afford to buy computers and to use them in new ways. This, in turn, increased demands for software. Another significant development was the introduction of magnetic disk storage. Because disks allow random access, any item from a mass of data is readily available. The disk allowed the development of many on-line systems that were not feasible using sequential storage devices. To add more fuel to the fires of the hardware boom, the microcomputer was introduced. Here was a computer costing a few thousand dollars that was more powerful than older mainframes costing several million dollars. Integrated circuits also opened up whole new worlds of applications. It now became feasible and affordable to put "a computer on a chip" into such things as manufacturing equipment, consumer products, and even toys. Demand for software increased even more. Programmers could not begin to keep up with the demand.

Advances in Software Techniques. The 1960s also saw the advent of the techniques of multiprogramming and timesharing. These techniques, in turn, supported such applications as interactive systems, multiuser systems, and on-line and real-time computing. With these techniques, entirely new ways of using computers that had never been envisioned before were available. The computer was beginning to come out of the back room and into the hands of users. For example, businesses could use computer terminals to process a customer's transaction on the spot, with quicker and more accurate service.

Increased Demand for Software. It has already been noted that advances in hardware capabilities and availability fueled a demand for software. Increasing demand came from another source as well. As computer use became more widespread, organizations discovered the usefulness of computers and the increased productivity that usually resulted from their use. They became interested in using computers in new and more varied ways and demanded software for new applications. Computers in education, medicine, manufacturing, entertainment, and publishing are only a few of the many new areas of applications that began to spring up.

Demand for Larger and More Complex Software. The technological advances of the decade allowed for the development of larger and more complex software systems than was possible in the past. Larger systems are capable of doing more than smaller systems, resulting in increased productivity. This, in turn, created even more demand for sophisticated software, and so on. Technological advances foster software advances. Software advances foster demand for more software, and foster technological advances as well. Furthermore, systems were being developed to handle more critical tasks than had past systems. Systems to monitor life-support equipment, guide a rocket launch, or control the braking system of a car have to be completely reliable. As developers attempted to build larger, more complex, more critical systems, they discovered that the developmental techniques used in the past on smaller systems simply did not work. Cost overruns, missed deadlines, unreliable software, and abandoned projects were common occurrences. The need for a disciplined approach to the development of large and/or complex projects became evident.

1.2 What Is Software Engineering?

As the costs of creating and owning software skyrocketed due to the factors discussed, there was increased interest in learning how to control costs. Current practices in software development and maintenance were examined to pinpoint the areas that could be made more cost effective. It soon became obvious that a systematic approach to software development and maintenance was needed, and the idea of a software engineering discipline emerged. As defined by the *IEEE Standard Glossary of Software Engineering Terminology* (IEEE, 1983), software engineering is "The systematic approach to the development, operation, maintenance and retirement of software."

Before pursuing the definition of software engineering further, consider what is meant by the terms software and engineering. *Software* certainly includes the source code for a program or system. The source code is, in a sense, the only tangible evidence that a program exists. Once a program is translated and loaded and begins executing, there is no tangible "thing" that can be pointed to as being software. In addition to referencing programs, the term software has come to take on a broader meaning in the context of software engineering. Software also includes the documentation for a system. This includes not only the documentation for the source code, but the various documents needed for the development, installation, utilization, and maintenance of a system. These documents are just as important products of the software development process as the source code itself. In fact, Jones (1986) points out that the cost of documentation is now often one of the top two or three most expensive items. (Travel and defect removal are typically the other two most costly items.)

Engineering refers to the application of a systematic approach, based on science and mathematics, toward the production of a structure, machine, product, process, or system. Civil engineers, for example, apply engineering principles and techniques in building structures such as roads, dams, and bridges. They follow standard procedures in designing and building the structure. Guidelines are followed that give design loads for seismic and wind conditions. Allowable stresses for steel, concrete, and other materials are provided. Models are built and in some cases subjected to tests. Because engineers have been building bridges and other complex structures for centuries, their techniques, procedures, and tools are highly developed (Spector and Gifford, 1986). Their products are usually quite successful. Although software engineering is a very young discipline, the goal is to make it into a true engineering discipline.

Another way to understand what is meant by software engineering is to look at its goals. Broadly speaking, the methods and systematic application of software engineering aim to:

- produce a quality software system
- at a low cost,
- on time.

The phrase "low cost" does not necessarily mean that it will be cheap to produce a system. It simply means that the system should be produced in a cost-effective manner and within its estimated budget. The system should be delivered and installed on time, as well. Intermediate deadlines must be met to make sure the project is progressing as it should and to allow the sponsor to evaluate the quality of the product being produced. The descriptor "quality software system" is central to the understanding of software engineering and deserves special discussion.

1.2.1 Quality Software Is a Primary Goal of Software Engineering

A primary goal of software engineering is to produce quality software systems. What is meant by a "quality" system? There is no simple answer to this question. In fact, the answer depends on who is answering the question. Once a software system has been developed and installed (put into use), there are three different categories of people to whom good quality software is important, as shown in Figure 1.1. The first category is the sponsor of the system. The *sponsor* is the individual or organization that has paid for the development or procurement of the software system and who is typically responsible for any further costs involved in owning the software. The second category is the user of the system. A *user* is anyone who directly interacts with executing software, who provides direct input to a computer system, or who uses direct output from a computer. The third category is the maintainer/modifier of the system. Installed software *will* have errors in it, and these errors must be fixed to keep the software operational. Circumstances *will* change, and the software must be modified to handle new or different situations. Furthermore, sponsors and users of the software *will* want enhancements to be made to the system to provide new functions and new ways of using the system. Typically, all three of these activities — error correction, modifications, and enhancements — are included under the title of *software maintenance*. Many people think that the term "maintenance" implies only error correction. The term "maintainer/modifier" will be used in this chapter to emphasize the other important functions of software maintenance: modifications and enhancements.

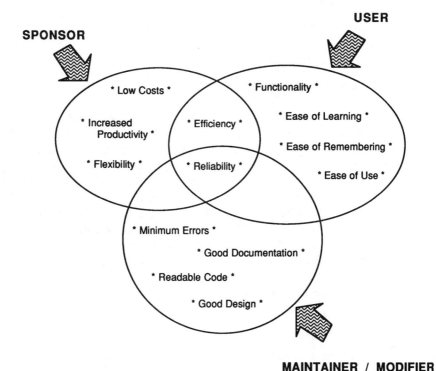

Figure 1.1 The Qualities Looked for in Software Depend on the Point of View

Each of these three categories of people—sponsors, users, and maintainer/ modifiers—views a software system from a different perspective. Each has a different set of criteria concerning what makes a good software system. Each set of criteria will be discussed next.

The Sponsor. The sponsor's main objective is typically in making and/or saving money. The sponsor's initial interest in obtaining and using a computer system stems from a wish to increase the organization's productivity. The sponsor hopes to produce more goods or services at a lower cost. To this end, the cost of acquiring or developing the computer system must be reasonable. The system itself must be reliable. A *reliable* system is one that is consistently available and produces correct output. Flexibility is important because it allows the users to use the system across a spectrum of situations. An *efficient* system is important to the sponsor, too. An efficient system is one that utilizes minimal computer resources by being fast and using less storage. Finally, the cost of owning the software, that is, the cost of maintenance, modifications, and enhancements, should be as low as possible. In summary, the sponsor is looking for:

- Low cost for acquisition
- Increased productivity
- Reliability
- Flexibility
- Efficiency
- Low ownership costs

The User. To users, a computer system is a tool to aid them in carrying out the functions of their jobs. To be a good tool, the computer system must provide *functionality* to the users. Reliability and efficiency are important to a user, just as they are to the sponsor of a system. The system must consistently produce correct output, and it must do so in a timely manner. Other important qualities from the user's point of view are ease of learning, ease of use, and ease of remembering how to use the system. This latter quality is particularly important if the system is used intermittently. All these factors make the computer system not just a tool that can be used to do a job, but a *good* tool—one that is a pleasure to use. To summarize, the qualities that are particularly important to the user of a system are:

- Functionality
- Reliability
- Efficiency
- Ease of learning
- Ease of use
- Easy to remember

The Maintainer/Modifier. To the maintainer/modifier, it is important that the system contain relatively few errors when it is initially installed. It is often a hopeless task to maintain a bug-ridden system. The second most important characteristic is that the system be well documented. Documentation includes not only source code and source code comments, but the documents created during the development of the software system. These documents are essential to the maintainer/modifier. The source code should be easy to read. The system should be well designed and well structured. A good design and a good structure go hand in hand. Modularity is an important component of both good design and good structure. In summary, the qualities the maintainer/modifier looks for are:

- Minimum errors

- Good documentation

- Well-designed, well-structured software, based on modularity

- Reliability

Although each of these people — the sponsor, the user and the maintainer/modifier — have different criteria for quality, these criteria are not independent. Notice how these different quality characteristics interact with one another. A bug-ridden system will not be reliable. An unreliable system will not be functional. A nonfunctional system will not be effective in increasing productivity, and so on. This interaction of the different quality characteristics of a system makes an important point concerning the creation of a software system. The point is that a good software system is one that possesses all these characteristics, not just one or two. To obtain this sort of multifaceted quality is not easy. Quality must be built into the system from the very first day of development. Quality is not a feature that can be added to software after it is created. It must be planned for, checked for, and worked on at every single step in the development process.

1.3   Software Life Cycle

To understand what software engineering is about, it is essential to become familiar with the idea of the *software life cycle*. The term software life cycle is used to draw an instructive analogy between the life cycle of animals and the progression of states gone through by a software system. Broadly, software can be seen to have a childhood, adulthood, and retirement, just as humans do. During childhood, the software is developed and tested. Once the software has sufficiently matured, it is ready to go out into the world and serve its function as an adult. As with humans, being an adult does not mean development and change stop. Additional functions can be added and refinements can be made during adulthood. Finally, the software is retired.

The childhood of software involves all the activities in the production of a software system. These activities, taken together, form what is often called the *soft-*

ware development cycle. The software development cycle is divided into the following stages:

- Requirements analysis and specifications
- Design
- Implementation
- System testing
- Installation

Each stage involves its own particular set of activities. The description of these stages and their associated activities form the major content of this book.

The adulthood of software is that period during which the software is operational. During this period, maintenance of the software takes place. Maintenance includes fixing errors, making modifications, and adding enhancements. This period of the software life cycle is more formally called the *operational and maintenance phase*.

The retirement of a piece of software can have any one of several causes. In some cases, software becomes functionally obsolete. That is, there is no longer any need to have the software perform the functions it once performed, perhaps due to a change in procedures or goals within an organization. For example, if sales personnel were switched from a commission basis to hourly wages, the software that kept track of each salesperson's sales and commissions would be obsolete. In other cases, old software is replaced by software that performs the same function in better ways, usually adding an extended range of functions as well. The generations of word processors that have come and gone are good examples of retirement due to replacement. Some software is retired due to hardware constraints. A faithful old piece of software may be retired only because the hardware that it runs on has become obsolete or must be replaced. Retirement can come to software during its childhood as well. Jones (cited in Burton, 1984) estimates that up to 25 percent of large software projects is abandoned before delivery. New software that is advertised and announced in the media but has not yet been released to the public has a special name: *vaporware*. While the name may be amusing, the fact that such a word has been coined reflects poorly on the software development techniques used by some companies.

1.3.1 A Closer Look at the Stages in the Software Development Cycle

The major focus of this book is on the development of software. But it is important to understand that software does not exist in isolation. Software interacts with other entities as part of a larger system. A *system* is a collection of interacting elements that perform some function or functions aimed at achieving some objective. A system includes not only software and hardware, but people, machines, data, procedures and documentation. In computer-based systems, software is the major component of the system. A word processing system is an example of such a system. In other systems, the software may be only a minor component. The claims processing system for an insurance company or a car that includes electronic components are examples of systems where the software is only one of many components of a complex system. If a large system is being developed, *systems engineers* are involved. They are responsible for analyzing the problem and breaking the system down into its appropriate components. When one or more of these components are software components, the responsibility for the creation of these components is passed on to *software engineers*. It is at this point that the software development cycle begins. In the case of computer-based systems, the software engineer is involved from the beginning.

As the major focus of this book is on the development of software, we will assume throughout that a single computer-based system is being developed. This computer-based system may be the entire system, or it may be one component of a larger system. Let us now look at the development cycle in somewhat more detail. Subsequent chapters of this text deal with these stages in greater depth, and a brief overview of the development stages should help provide a framework for later learning. Table 1.1 presents the major stages and activities of the development cycle. Each stage is discussed in the following sections.

Requirements Analysis and Specifications. The first step in system development is to analyze, understand, and record the problem that the sponsor is trying to solve. The functions, goals, and contraints on the proposed system must be precisely specified. Both the sponsor and the developers must agree on the specifications, as they form the basis for the design of the system.

Design. The design phase of the development cycle involves creating a solution that meets the specifications outlined in the analysis and specification phase.

Table 1.1 Major Stages and Activities of the Software Development Cycle

Requirements analysis and specification

Design

    User interface design

    Preliminary design

    Detailed design

Implementation

    Coding

    Unit testing

    Integration

System testing

Delivery and Installation

Design is a complex process and is often broken down into three different types of design: user interface design, preliminary design, and detailed design. *User interface design* is the design of the software system as it will be seen by the users. In user interface design, the styles of interface are chosen (for example, menu-driven input, screen output, sound feedback) and the semantics of the interface is designed as well. The user interface must be designed so that all system functions described in the requirements and specification, both input and output, are handled. The user interface design process can often be carried out in parallel with the *preliminary design*. In preliminary design, the structure of the software system is defined. The structure of a software system is its modular components and the relationship among these components. The major data structures are also defined at this time. In *detailed design,* decisions are made concerning how to implement each of the components specified in the preliminary design.

Implementation. The major product of the implementation phase of the software development cycle is the source code for the system. The three activities of implementation — *coding, unit testing,* and *integration* — are repeated over and over as units of the source code are implemented. *Coding* involves writing the source code for some predefined modular unit of the system. Each modular unit is then unit tested. In *unit testing,* each unit is subjected to a number of tests for reliability and validity. Groups of unit-tested modules are interfaced and tested as subsystems during *integration*.

System Testing. The entire software system is subjected to a variety of tests during system testing. The major goals of system testing are to make sure that the subsystems created and tested during implementation function together as a system and to make sure that the system meets the requirements and specifications set forth at the beginning of the project.

Delivery/Installation. For most microcomputer software products, the final stage is delivery of the product. The user is responsible for whatever installation that is necessary and is guided in the installation and use of the product by user guides. In the case of minicomputer or mainframe products, the software system is delivered to the sponsor and installed on the sponsor's hardware. Installation may be done by the developer or by the customer or sponsor. The sponsor is responsible for testing the software to make sure it is acceptable. Once the system has been accepted by the sponsor, the software development cycle has ended, and the operational and maintenance phase of the software life cycle begins.

1.3.2 Models, Approaches, and Methods in Software Engineering

There is no general agreement in the field of software engineering on exactly which phases should be included in the software development cycle and in exactly what order they should occur (see Agresti, 1986, for a review). To some extent, this disagreement is due to the variety of approaches and methods used to produce software systems by different organizations. Different approaches emphasize different phases in the cycle or combine software development activities in unique ways. Some object to the concept of phases in the software development cycle because it suggests that each phase has a definite beginning and a definite end and that phases are nonoverlapping. For example, the classic life cycle described previously is sometimes referred to as the "waterfall model." The picture conjured up by this label is that software development goes in definite steps, with all the products from one stage being passed on to the next level and with no chance to go back, just as water flows from one level to the next in a waterfall, with no flow back up the waterfall. Such is certainly not the case in software development. Activities from one phase can, to a certain extent, be carried out in parallel with activities from another phase. Furthermore, the discovery of a problem in one phase often leads to backtracking to earlier phases in the cycle. Activities within a phase need not be undertaken in a strict sequential order and can overlap. Parallelism and iteration are common within phases as well as between phases. The cover of this book—a picture of an impossible waterfall created by M. C. Escher—is a more accurate depiction of the software life cycle. Although one phase logically follows another, the cycle may be repeated many times and in the form of many epicycles during the life of a software system.

Once again, a constructive analogy can be drawn between software development and human development. In the development of a child there are no sharp distinctions between the different stages of growth—infancy, toddler, childhood, adolescent, and so on—just as there are no sharp boundaries between the phases in the software development cycle. Likewise, different parents use different methods to raise and educate their children, just as different software development methods are used. For example, some parents are stricter in their discipline than other parents. Finally, the order in which certain milestones are achieved in human development is often irrelevant, just as in software development. For example, it does not matter whether a baby learns to speak a few words or learns to walk first, as long as both milestones are achieved.

As Wileden and Dowson (1986) point out, the software development cycle is basically a descriptive representation—a *software process model*—of the processes involved in the production of a software system. The software development cycle described here provides only one model of how software might be produced. Other software process models are possible. In addition to the software process models, software engineers are interested in *approaches to software development* and *methods*. *Approaches to software development* are strategies for achieving the production of a software system in a way that conforms to some software process model. For example, if an organization based its approach to software development on the classical life cycle model described previously, management and production activities would proceed according to the phases described in the model. More specifically, management might establish a set of milestones based on the model, see that production followed the stages prescribed by the model, and conduct critical reviews at certain points suggested by the model. *Methods* are explicit ways of achieving an activity or set of activities required by an approach to software development. For example, a variety of different methods has been proposed for carrying out the preliminary design of a software system. An organization must choose which of these methods to use.

While it is important for an organization to choose a software process model and the appropriate approaches and methods to implement the chosen model, it is also important to keep in mind the essential nature of the task software engineers face. That task is basically problem solving. The stages of problem solving are well known. To solve any problem involves four fundamental steps:

1. Problem recognition and definition

2. Designing a solution

3. Implementing the solution

4. Evaluating the solution

Problem recognition involves admitting or noticing that there is a problem with the current state of affairs and deciding that a solution should be sought for the problem. Problem definition involves figuring out exactly what the problem is and defining it by understanding what would constitute a successful solution of the problem. In the second step, the problem solver produces ideas concerning one or more possible solutions to the problem. After choosing the best solution, the problem solver applies the solution to the problem. The solution is then evaluated. Has the problem been solved? Is the solution acceptable? Will another solution have to be sought?

Problems such as a malfunctioning car, a calculus problem, deciding what school to attend, writing a term paper, and so on, all appear to be very different sorts of problems, but are all solved by following the steps outlined. As a simple example, consider the problem of the "bad" roommate. Perhaps you are unhappy with your roommate. In thinking it through, you realize that what annoys you most is that your roommate uses your things without asking. You have now recognized that you have a problem and have defined it fairly precisely: a roommate who uses your things without permission. The next step is to design a solution. No doubt a number of ideas come to mind, ranging from changing schools, to using your roommates things without asking, to first-degree murder. Then a light dawns. Maybe you could just *ask* your roommate not to use your things! After coming up with this solution, you apply it to the problem. You have a serious talk with your roommate in which you assure the roommate that you think that she or he is terrific, that you are happy to share most of your possessions, but that she or he must ask permission first. Next, you evaluate the solution. Did it work? Did the bad roommate become more considerate? Does the solution need some refinement (maybe the roommate needs to be thanked when she or he does ask permission)? Are more drastic measures called for?

Software engineers follow exactly these same four steps: only the nature of the problems being solved is different, and the terminology is somewhat different.

Problem recognition and definition are important components of the software development process. In software development, the sponsor must recognize that a problem exists, specify exactly what the problem is, and specify what would constitute a solution to the problem. In the design stage, various possible solutions to the problem are considered, and one solution is picked as the best. The design is turned into a problem solution during implementation. Finally, the solution is evaluated during system testing and the operational and maintenance phases.

1.3.3 An Alternative Development Model: Prototyping

In many situations, the general objectives of a software system can be determined, but the sponsor may not be able to give precise specifications concerning the input, output, and processing. In other situations, the feasibility of a project may be questionable. In these cases and others, a prototyping approach may be better than the classical life cycle model.

Prototyping involves building a working model of a system or part of a system. The model may be a *scenario, a demonstration* or a *version 0* (Carey and Mason, 1983). A *scenario* is a simulation or mock-up of the system usage. The system actions are only simulated, and what the user sees is basically a script of the typical interaction. Screen mock-ups are often used. These can be done with paper and pencil, or using various types of software. If a computer is used, it need not be the target computer for the final system. A *demonstration* system processes a limited range of user activities. The demonstration portions of the system are usually linked together by skeletal code. The portions of code created may be carried over to the final system. Special software development tools, such as screen generators and prototyping software, can be useful in creating demonstrations. Alternatively, a demonstration system can be considered strictly a throwaway. In the *version 0* approach to prototyping, the prototype is a working release of the system intended to be used under conditions similar to the final system environment. The final product builds on version 0, adding more functions, changing existing functions, and creating documentation.

Clearly, different situations would call for different sorts of prototypes, depending on the intent of the prototype and its expected benefits. A scenario can be used to evolve user interface requirements and some functional requirements, although it cannot test application logic or feasibility. A demonstration provides more insight into processing logic, but may not cover the full range of user interface and functional requirements. The version 0 approach is most useful when the functions of the system are clearly separable.

The use of prototyping alters the classical life cycle in a number of ways. The primary change is that the distinctions among requirements, design, and implementation activities become blurred. Prototyping begins with analysis, just as in the classical approach. However, because the sponsor is unable to complete the specification, a prototype is used. The prototype is then designed and created. In the case of demonstrations and version 0 prototypes, the prototyping activity may involve implementing some of the final system code. The prototype is then evaluated by the sponsor and the developer. The evaluation results in revisions of the system requirements. The new requirements are then used to either revise and expand the prototype or as a basis for the design and creation of the system using the classical approach.

There are a number of advantages to using prototypes (Alavi, 1984). Prototypes have the advantage of being real and tangible. The sponsor has a system she or he can look at and try out, and the system forms a basis for concrete comparisons and specific requirements. Many times, a sponsor cannot express exactly what he or she wants, but feels that "I will know it when I see it." Providing a prototype lets the sponsor "see it." Prototypes create a common reference point for both the sponsor and the developers. Sponsors are enthusiastic about prototypes, and they cultivate sponsor participation and commitment to the project. The sponsors feel that their needs are being listened to, and that they have some real influence in the design process. Most importantly, prototyping makes sure the job is done right — that the sponsors get the system they want.

A major disadvantage of prototypes is that the sponsor may believe the prototype *is* the system and expect delivery of the final system almost immediately. They do not realize that the prototype is only the icing on the cake, so to speak, and that the cake itself takes a long time to bake. Furthermore, the icing may not even be real icing at all, only shaving cream or some other substance that simply looks like icing. Sponsors may push the developers to deliver the system, resulting in compromises on the quality of the system. The delivered system may lack functionality and be hard to maintain. Another disadvantage of using prototypes is that the prototype may be oversold, leading the sponsor to expect more from the final system than can be delivered. While it may be easy to suggest that a system will provide functions *w, x, y,* and *z* in a prototype, functions *y* and *z* may turn out to be infeasible. Disappointment results. A third disadvantage of prototyping is that the management and control of the prototyping process is more difficult than for the classical method. The specific phases, milestones, and deliverables used in the classical method are lacking in prototyping. It is difficult to assess how much progress is actually being made on the project. Planning is more difficult, as well. Finally, it is difficult to maintain sponsor enthusiasm and involvement throughout the project. After a sponsor has seen and approved a prototype, they believe their work is done. They are reluctant to spend time on the details and additional decisions that inevitably crop up during the design and implementation of the actual system.

Nonetheless, prototyping offers a compelling alternative to the classical life cycle methods when requirements are unclear or fuzzy. It should also be considered in situations where there is a need for experimentation and learning before resources are committed to developing a full-scale system. Such situations may arise when innovative technical approaches are being used.

An experiment by Boehm, Gray, and Seewaldt (1984) compared teams of programmers building the same application product using either prototyping or specifying (classic) methods. The products developed using prototyping had approximately equal performance, but had about 40 percent less code and took 45 percent less effort. The prototyped products were rated as somewhat lower on functionality and robustness, but were higher on ease of use and ease of learning. On the other hand, the specifying approach yielded more coherent designs and software that was easier to integrate. This implies that the specified products would be somewhat easier to maintain.

1.4   Costs of Software Development and Ownership

It has already been mentioned that a primary goal of software engineering is to make software development and ownership cost effective. Let us see just where the money goes. Figure 1.2 shows the cost of software ownership compared to software development. Software ownership is generally twice as expensive as development (Lientz and Swanson, 1980). In part, the cost of ownership is due simply to the length of time the software is in use. For example, a typical software system takes 1 to 2 years to be developed and is used for 5 to 10 years or so (Fairley, 1985). The cost of ownership, however, is primarily the cost of maintenance. Within maintenance activities, 20 percent of the effort goes toward error correction, 20 percent for modifications, and 60 percent for enhancements (Lientz and Swanson, 1980). These cost and effort figures emphasize once again that the end of the development phase of software does not mean the end of the development, in the broader sense, of the software. Software is not a static entity, but an evolving entity. These figures also clearly show that if one's goal is to reduce software ownership costs then the focus should be on reducing maintenance costs. In prac-

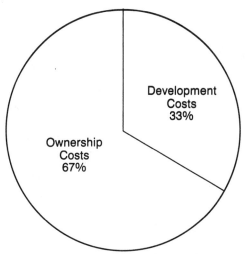

Figure 1.2 The Relative Cost of Software Ownership and Software Development (from Lientz and Swanson, 1980)

tice, the attack on maintenance costs is two pronged. First, the system must be developed in such a way that it is easy to maintain. As discussed previously, a quality product is one with good documentation, readable code and a good design — all factors that make a system easier to understand. The development principles described throughout this text are aimed toward producing a quality software product, and thus one that is maintainable. The second prong of attack on maintenance costs is to reduce the cost of the maintenance activities themselves. Maintenance will be discussed in detail in Chapter 8. To generalize, however, the basic approach to cost-effective maintenance is to follow the software development cycle in miniature.

Figure 1.3 shows the typical distribution of costs of the stages of software development. Sometimes this distribution is referred to as the 40–20–40 rule. Forty percent of the cost and effort is expended in analysis and design, 20 percent in coding and unit testing, and 40 percent in integration and system testing (Boehm, 1973; Brooks, 1975). The exact proportions of effort will differ depending on the characteristics of the system being developed. A radically new system might require much more analysis and design effort than a system that is a new variation on an old idea. A highly critical system, such as a space shuttle control program or a patient-monitoring program, would require more extensive testing than a typical system. Notice that the proportions of effort are very different than what they would be for the typical computer science student working on a programming assignment. In most cases, students are not required to do much in the way of analysis. The teacher explains to the students what the program should do, what the input will be, and what the expected output is. The majority of a student's effort is expended on the design and writing of the program. Design is usually informally done, with no documentation. Testing is also informally and nonsystematically

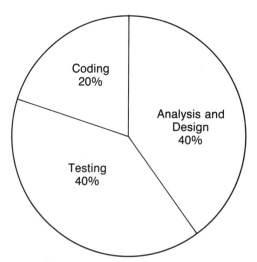

Figure 1.3 The Distribution of Costs across Software Development Stages

done. Most students run a program only until it accepts the input provided by the teacher and produces the expected output. No systematic attempt is made to try additional sorts of input. While this approach can produce reasonably good small programs, it does not work for programs requiring the efforts of more than one person or for very complex programs. As soon as even one other person is involved or the complexity of the program becomes great, the need for a systematic approach and written communication becomes evident. The larger or more complex the project is, the greater the need for software engineering. The larger or more complex the project is, the greater the need for increased effort in the analysis and design phases and the more critical testing becomes.

Because the costs of testing often consume 40 percent or more of a project budget, testing is an obvious candidate for cost-cutting efforts. The purpose of testing is to discover errors in the software. Everytime an error is discovered, the software must be fixed and then tested again. Anything that can be done to prevent errors from occurring will reduce testing costs. Understanding where errors are made is the first step toward eliminating errors. Figure 1.4 shows the distribution of errors across various activities of software development. As you can see, the majority of errors are *not* coding errors. Most errors are attributable to missing, incorrect, or misunderstood specifications and design (Jones, 1978; Basili and Perricone, 1984; Yeh, 1984).

Before drawing any conclusions concerning the distribution of errors across the development cycle, consider the data presented in Figure 1.5. Figure 1.5 shows the relative costs of fixing an error depending on when the error is discovered. The cost of fixing an error discovered during the requirements analysis and specification stage is used as a base line. Compared to this base figure, the cost of fixing an error (of whatever type) discovered during the coding stage is about eight

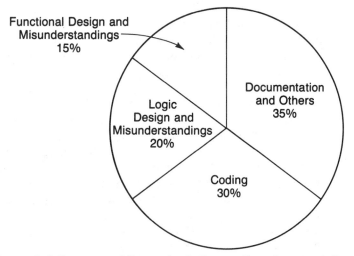

Figure 1.4 Sources of Errors in Software Development (from Jones, 1978)

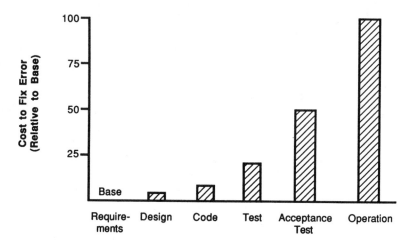

Figure 1.5 The Relative Cost of Fixing an Error Depending on When It Is Discovered in the Software Life Cycle (Barry W. Boehm, SOFTWARE ENGINEERING ECONOMICS, ©1981, p. 40. Adapted by permission of Prentice-Hall, Inc., Englewood Cliffs, New Jersey)

times as expensive, and an error discovered during the operational and maintenance phase is 100 times more costly to fix. Clearly, the sooner an error is discovered, the better. The reasons for these huge increases in cost are not hard to pinpoint. During the requirements analysis and specification stage the problem is being studied, and most errors are errors on paper with few or limited ramifications. Errors made and/or discovered within the design stage are somewhat more costly to fix. This is because a design represents a commitment to build the software in a certain way. When an error is discovered, it requires that the commitment be reevaluated. Changes may then have to be made that significantly alter the initial design. Errors discovered at the design stage may also require that additional analyses be carried out—a step backward to an earlier stage. Errors discovered during the coding stage are still more expensive to fix, because they may require backtracking to design, or backtracking all the way to analysis with a reevaluation of design. The most expensive errors to fix during the development process are those discovered during testing. This is due to potential backtracking and to the retesting that must take place after the error is fixed. Errors discovered during the operational and maintenance phase are the most expensive of all errors. Such errors require not only backtracking and retesting, but they may require maintenance personnel to work on a project that they may have never seen before, thus requiring considerable start-up time and effort.

Another factor that has a significant impact on the cost of errors in software is when and by whom errors are found. More errors are found by outside testers and users than by the developers (Boehm, 1973). Thus, more errors are found in the two later stages — acceptance testing and operation and maintenance — than in the earlier stages. Errors found in the later stages are the most expensive to fix. Overall, then, most errors are found later rather than earlier and are thus of the sort that is expensive to fix.

The message should be clear: *early detection of errors saves money*. Software engineering emphasizes the importance of checking and testing not only the source code itself, but all the intermediate products, such as the requirements and specifications, the preliminary design, the detailed design, and so on. Checks are made not only for accuracy, but also for quality. Errors are corrected and modifications are made throughout the development of the system. These checks and corrections take time and may appear to be slowing down progress in creating a system. However, experience has shown that the extra time spent up front has payoffs in all the later stages (Jones, 1978; Hecht and Houghton, 1982; Parnas, 1985).

1.5   Why Is Software Development So Difficult?

The preceding sections have made the point that software development is a complex and costly process. What are the factors that make software development so difficult? There are many, but a few deserve special mention and discussion:

- Communications
- Sequential nature of system development
- Project characteristics
- Characteristics of personnel
- Management issues

1.5.1   Factor 1: Communications

If all software were developed by single individuals for their own private use, communication would not be a problem. As soon as one individual has even a single programmer create a program for him or her, communication becomes a serious problem. The sponsor has a general idea of what he or she wants the program to do, but may not really understand how computers work or what is involved in programming. The programmer, on the other hand, knows a lot about computers and programming, but typically does not know very much about the task from the sponsor's point of view. Even when both parties speak the same language, their vocabularies of technical words are different. Terms in English like "drive shaft torque," "tax deferred annuities," and "ceiling R-values" may as well be in Tatooinese as far as the programmer is concerned. Computer terms such as "data base," "baud," and "ROM" are just as confusing to the sponsor. Time must be taken for each to learn and understand the other's vocabulary to the extent necessary to carry out the project. Misunderstandings are bound to occur, and errors will be caused by these misunderstandings. A mutual recognition of the communication problem and a systematic approach to the project go a long way toward solving the inherent problems.

The larger and more complex the project, the more difficult the communication becomes between the sponsor and the developers. A more formal approach becomes a necessity. Software engineering, particularly in the area of requirements analysis and specification, offers a variety of techniques for dealing with communications. None of the techniques is foolproof, but they do provide standards and guidelines that reduce communication problems.

Communication among team members is another major difficulty in software development and maintenance. As soon as more than one programmer is involved in a project, accurate and frequent communication among team members is essential. To make communications accurate and readily available, written communication is required. Brooks (1975) has observed that, beyond a certain level, every programmer added to a development team greatly increases the number of possible paths of communication. With two people involved, there is one path of communication. With three people involved, there are three paths; with four people, six paths; and with ten people, there are forty-five paths. (The expression for determining the number of paths is $n(n-1)/2$.) These figures clearly show that communication takes more and more of the members' efforts as the number of people on a project increases. Yet communication becomes even more essential as the number of people increases. Furthermore, the possibilities for misunderstanding increase as well. Therefore, communication must become even more extensive and even more precise and accurate as numbers increase.

On any nontrivial software development project, communication is accomplished through documentation. Each stage in the development cycle results in a new set of documents. These documents are the tangible evidence of the project. People may come and go, but the project remains, embodied in documents. Documentation is often one of the two or three most expensive items in the development process. Clearly, documentation is a major portion of any project. This does not mean the goal of the project is just to produce documents. The documentation must support and facilitate the development process, and not become a meaningless exercise. Nonetheless, the point remains: communication is essential to any project, and communication is done through documentation.

1.5.2 Factor 2: Sequential Nature of System Development

A central and sometimes frustrating fact about software system development is that it is basically sequential in nature. Many of the tasks involved in development are interdependent and must occur in a fixed order. For example, analysis must come before design, design must come before coding, coding must come before testing, and so on. Even within these stages, certain processes must occur before others. A ramification of this fact is that adding more personnel to a project may not increase productivity, but may actually have a detrimental effect on the progress of the project. Brooks (1975) has dubbed this phenomenon the *mythical man-month* and summarized the problem as follows: "Men and months are interchangeable commodities only when a task can be partitioned among many workers with communication among them. This is true of reaping wheat and picking cotton; it is not even approximately true . . . of programming." Brooks likens the program development process to having a baby: there is no way that a baby can be produced in one month by using nine women.

Even in cases where parts of a software development project are independent, adding more personnel can be counterproductive. The loss of productivity is due to the increase in communications overhead. Every person added to a project results in a dramatic increase in the number of paths of communication. The increase in, for example, lines of code produced per day caused by adding people to a project may be more than offset by the additional effort needed to train the new people, to bring them up to speed on the project, and to include them in the communications networks within the existing project group. Brooks' now famous law sums up the effect as follows: "Adding manpower to a late project makes it later" (Brooks, 1975, p. 25).

1.5.3 Factor 3: Project Characteristics

As a programmer you have probably already discovered a central truth about developing software: no software development task is ever as easy as it appears to be. Aside from the eternal optimism of programmers, a number of other factors can contribute to the difficulty of a development project (Pfleeger, 1987). Foremost is the sheer *size* of the project. Size is determined mainly by the number of functions the software is to perform. The greater the number of functions is, the more difficult the project will be. The amount of data to be processed and the complexity of the data structures also contribute to the size of the project. Another major contributor to difficulty is the *novelty* of the system. A system that is to implement functions that are well-understood or that have been implemented before is easier to build than one that implements novel functions or uses new methods of implementation. In general, systems and utility programs are more difficult to program than applications programs. Systems programs include operating system routines, input/output control, and data communications. Utility programs include such software as compilers, assemblers, and linkage editors. The increased difficulty is often due to the novelty of the programs.

A surprisingly frequent problem is that the sponsor's *requirements may keep changing* as the project progresses. Ideally, all specifications will be spelled out at the beginning of a project. In some cases, however, the novelty of the project may lead to constant revisions of the specifications, changes in hardware availability may affect the specifications, or factors beyond the sponsor's control may require changes in specifications. The more frequent the changes in specifications, the more difficult the project will be.

Factors related to the *hardware/software configuration* being built also contribute to difficulty. These factors include the number of simultaneous users, the use of remote access, the degree of interaction with other systems, and the degree of hardware dependence. The simplest system to build is a single-user system to be run on a dedicated machine, with no hardware constraints. A much more difficult system would require simultaneous access by many users with the use of remote access and would be constrained to specific hardware, such as particular input/output devices or sensors.

Additional factors that affect difficulty include security, response time requirements, and reliability and criticalness requirements. Security relates to the need to control access to programs, files, records, and/or data communications. Designing systems to handle security can become quite complex, depending on the degree and types of security needed. In some systems, rapid response times are essential. Airline reservation systems, bank teller machines, and other on-line systems that service customers must have quick response times. In such cases, slow system response times could result in lost customers. Real-time systems are systems in which the computer is expected to respond essentially instantaneously to outside stimuli. Examples of real-time systems include brake-control systems on cars and airplane control systems. Special design techniques may be required to ensure rapid response times. Other systems may have special reliability requirements. For such systems, downtime cannot be tolerated or must be very limited. Point-of-sale terminals, satellite launching systems, and stock-market monitoring systems are all examples of systems where high reliability would be of especial importance. Criticalness is another facet of reliability. A critical system is one in which errors cannot be tolerated due to the potentially disastrous consequences. The U.S. Air Forces' F-16 jet fighter, for example, is aerodynamically designed in such a way that it *cannot* be flown solely by manual operation. Human reaction times are not fast enough to respond to the various forces that affect the plane during flight. Computer intervention is a necessity and the software *must* be reliable. (The budget for software development for the F-16 is $85 million. The cost for software maintenance is estimated at $250 million; Suydam, 1987. Clearly, there is a high price tag for reliability.)

1.5.4   Factor 4: Characteristics of Personnel

As soon as more than one person begins working on a software development task, a whole realm of issues dealing with group processes opens up. The central role of communications in the development process has already been emphasized. In addition, characteristics of individuals within the group become important. These characteristics include:

- Ability to perform the work
- Prior experience or training
- Ability to communicate
- Ability to work in a group

Ability to perform the work of a software development project is related to the general capabilities of the individual. Individuals vary in their general capabilities.

However, there appears to be an especially high degree of variation among computer professionals. Sackman, Erikson, and Grant (1968) conducted an experiment to compare productivity levels in a batch environment versus an interactive environment. Programmers were asked to code and debug programs and various measures of productivity were recorded. Unexpectedly, there was much more variation in the results due to individual differences than due to the programming environment used. The ratio of differences in number of coding hours for the worst to the best programmer was 25 to 1, and the number of debugging hours varied from 28 to 1. In a subsequent experiment, Sackman found differences of 16 to 1 in programming productivity. Even with the most extreme cases eliminated, ratios of 5 to 1 were found. These variations were not due to a lack of familiarity with the application area, as all programmers in the experiments were familiar with the area.

With such great variability in programming productivity, the average development team is bound to contain some less productive members. Although no experiments have been reported that assess variability in the quality of programs produced by different programmers, such variability must exist. Thus, most teams must be prepared to compensate for weaker team members. Small teams could be particularly affected by a weak member. Common wisdom among managers says that, if you want to have quality software developed in a reasonable amount of time, you find the best development team possible. Unfortunately, there are not enough topnotch computer professionals around to satisfy the demand. Just as in sports, there are only so many superstars. One of the purposes and strengths of software engineering is to provide guidelines, tools, and techniques that enable competent, if not outstanding, programmers to perform quality work. The idea of using software engineering techniques is similar to a person using a cookbook. If the person has some basic cooking skills, he or she will be able to produce a meal by following the instructions in a cookbook. While the meal may not be of the same quality or prepared as rapidly as one made by a gourmet cook, the meal will nonetheless be tasty and well prepared.

A second relevant characteristic of personnel is prior experience or training with similar applications, tools, or methods. Many large organizations and a number of smaller organizations provide formal training for new employees to acquaint them with the development tools and techniques they use. The training makes the employees more productive when they are assigned to a project. When formal training is not provided, a person may take a certain amount of time before becoming an asset to their development team. A knowledge of the application area for which the system is being developed is always a great advantage. It facilitates all phases of the development, including communication with the sponsor, design, and testing. Prior experience with similar projects is also quite useful. A person who has been involved in developing a point-of-sales terminal system for one store will be a great resource in developing a similar system for another store. Even prior experience with the target programming language is a plus.

The central role of communication in the software development process has already been stressed. The developers must be able to communicate with the sponsor, with users, with management, and with each other. For communication to proceed smoothly, it is necessary that every member of the development team has good communication skills. These skills include the ability to speak clearly in English in formal and informal situations, the ability to listen to what someone else is saying and to ask the right questions, the ability to write formally and informally in English, and the ability to understand and use technical and formal notations of various sorts.

The final characteristic of personnel that closely affects the software development process is the ability to work in a group. In a study of programmers at IBM, McCue (1978) found that 50 percent of a typical programmer's time was spent interacting with other team members, 30 percent was spent working alone, and 20 percent was spent on activities that were not directly productive, such as training or travel. The high percentage of time that programmers interact with each other emphasizes once again the important role of communication, but also suggests that the ability to work well in a group is essential. What makes one person able to work well in a group and another not is mostly speculation. While personality factors would seem to be important, studies done on the relationship of different personality factors to group productivity and cohesion have not been very enlightening. Of greater help is research that has looked at the size and structure of groups and the role of the group leader in the success or failure of groups (Leavitt, 1951; Porter and Lawler, 1965; Shaw, 1971). Without going into the details of this research, the best strategy appears to be to keep the size of the groups small, to provide clear roles for each member of the group, and to have democratic leadership. Personality clashes are best resolved by redefining the roles of the conflicting members or restructuring the team.

1.5.5 Factor 5: Management Issues

Software development is affected by management both within the development project and outside the project. Of importance is the issue of finding competent managers. In some cases, managers are brought in from other areas to manage a development project. However, many of the problems in software development are unique, and managers experienced in other areas of management may not have the necessary knowledge or skills. On the other hand, the practice of promoting managers from among the ranks of former project-team members is not always successful, either. These individuals may have many technical skills, but no managerial skills. Management training programs may not be successful in these cases due to lack of interest and/or the appropriate social skills among the promoted technicians.

A central problem in software engineering is the imbalance that exists between the development of the technical aspects of software engineering and the development of the managerial aspects. Great advances have been made in the technical aspects, and lesser advances have been made in the managerial aspects. Nonetheless, both are important.

When the sponsors of a software system are also the higher-level management of a development team, there are management issues external to the development project itself. These issues have to do with the goals of the project, its funding, and its scheduling. It is important that realistic goals be set for any project. Unfortunately, setting realistic goals is especially tricky in the area of software development. It is hard for sponsors to understand that adding one or two more features to a project proposal can add quite significantly to the complexity of the project. Furthermore, the expectations and demands of managers keep rising as the sophistication of software and hardware rises. Most fail to realize that the dramatic increases in sophistication have been accompanied by dramatic increases in development costs. While software engineering has helped to make increased sophistication possible and has helped to keep costs in line, there is a question of just how much software engineering can accomplish (Parnas, 1985; Brooks, 1987).

Managers-as-sponsors often have unrealistic expectations concerning the cost and scheduling of a software development project. It has already been noted that software development professionals themselves have been notoriously bad at estimating development times and costs in the past. While experience and the software engineering discipline have taught them how to make better time and cost estimates, sponsors may find the estimates hard to accept. In particular, they may believe in the mythical man-month fallacy discussed previously. Management that is willing to listen and learn about the special problems of system development is important. Their support in implementing software engineering standards and procedures and in the purchase of software engineering tools is also important. They must understand that some cost and effort put forth early can result in long-term payoffs in the form of increased productivity and quality.

1.6 Understanding Systems

To begin understanding a computer-based system, we must understand its objectives and functions. The objectives of a system are what the sponsors want the system to do for their organization. These objectives usually relate to increased productivity. The functions of the system must be described. The functions are closely tied to input, output, and procedures or processing. Input describes what information, data, or materials the system takes in. The format or form of the input must be described. The source of the input, whether it be from human data entry, sensors, or electronic media, must be specified. Output describes what information or control the system produces. The format and nature of the output must be described. Is the output to be in the form of graphics, printed form, electronic form, or control signals? Who or what uses the output? While the descriptions of the input and output tell a lot about the processing and functions performed by the system, additional questions must be asked to clarify the system's functions.

A second area of concern for the analyst is the constraints that are imposed on the system. Economic considerations can impose constraints. The amount of economic resources available to solve the problem is limited to some degree. The analyst must determine the extent of these limits. Another constraint may be the other systems that the system must interact with, whether these be human, hardware, procedural, or software systems. Still another source of constraints is the environment the new system will function in.

Once these initial questions have been asked and answered, the analyst has an overall understanding of the system. This understanding is best expressed in plain language as a *statement of system scope* (Pressman, 1988). The statement of system scope will eventually become part of the requirements and specification documentation that results from the analysis stage and serves as a starting point for problem solving. The statement should describe the high-level objectives and functions of the system, but should not contain detailed requirements or design details. The statement represents an abstraction of the system. It provides a succinct overview of the system and hides many, many details. As analysis progresses, this abstract picture of the system is expanded, details are added to the picture, and the description becomes less abstract.

1.6.1   Understanding a System by Identifying Objects and Operations

Once the statement of system scope has been refined and clarified, the analyst continues the analysis process. An effective approach that can be used is to identify *objects* and *operations* in the system and their relationships. An *object* is an entity in a system. When a computer-based system is being described, objects can include people, hardware, materials, information, software, processes, and procedures. When a software system is being described, objects are data structures that represent abstractions of real-world objects. Each object, whether it is a physical, real-world or abstract object, has associated with it certain behaviors. That is, each object is capable of responding to stimuli in certain known or defined ways. These behaviors are called *operations*. For example, an oven is a physical object that has a number of operations associated with it. Ovens can be turned on to a specified temperature, turned off, loaded, and unloaded. A queue is an abstract object often used in computer programs that has enqueue, dequeue, check-if-empty, and check-if-full operations associated with it. Identifying the objects and operations in a system enables us to better understand the structure, logic, and functions of the system.

The steps to be followed in carrying out this analysis include:

- Identifying the objects in the system
- Identifying the type of each object, thus specifying its role in the system
- Identifying each operation in the system
- Associating each operation with its object

Let us apply these steps to a couple of examples. Here is a statement of system scope for a blueberry muffin factory.

> The Blueberry Muffin Factory gets raw ingredients, including flour, milk, eggs, and blueberries, from a supplier. All the ingredients except the blueberries are made into a batter. The blueberries are washed and sorted (to remove any bad berries or foreign objects) and then added to the batter. The batter is then poured into baking tins and baked. The baked muffins are cooled and packaged. The packages are put in boxes and shipped to distributors.

First, the objects in the system are listed. Each noun or noun phrase in the statement of system scope represents an object in the system. Thus we have the following list: suppliers, raw ingredients, flour, milk, eggs, blueberries, batter, baking tins, baked blueberry muffins, packages of muffins, distributors. Looking over the list of objects and the verbal description, we can see that flour, milk, eggs, and blueberries all fall under the category of raw ingredients. This category or group of objects forms what is called a *class* of objects. Flour, milk, eggs, and so on, are each a *subclass* of the class raw ingredients. It is often useful to form classes and subclasses of objects. Many times the operations associated with one member of a class apply to other members of the class as well. By combining the objects into one class, the complexity of the system is reduced. The other objects in the system — batter, baking tins, baked muffins, packages of muffins and boxes of muffins — each stand as distinct objects.

The Blueberry Muffin Factory is a system consisting of physical objects. Let us consider another system that consists of nonphysical objects. Here is a statement of system scope describing a computerized concordance system. (A *concordance* is a list of all the words that appear in a document, along with a word count for each word, and, optionally, an indication of where in the document each word occurs.)

> In the computerized concordance system the user indicates a text file to be processed. The file is analyzed one line at a time. Words are extracted from the line and edited. If the word is not already in the concordance, it is added. If the word is already in the concordance, the word count is incremented. A record is kept of the line where each word was found. When the file has been completely analyzed, the user inputs a choice of displaying the concordance on the screen and/or printing the concordance on a printer.

The objects in this system include text file, user, line, word, concordance, word count, line record, choice input, screen, and printer.

The next step in the analysis is to identify the type of each object. There are five different categories of object types. Each category can apply to physical, material, or abstract entities. Abstract entities are usually referred to as data entities. The categories will be described here using data object types, but physical objects can be classified in exactly the same way. The first category is a *data source*. Data sources are objects that supply input to the system. A *data item* is any system input or output that has information content and is (or has been) somehow processed or transformed by the system. A *control item* is input that signals an action or event or the occurrence of an action or event. A control item triggers other events. The control item itself is not processed or transformed. For example, in a telephone system, the ringing of your phone is a control item. It signals that a call is pending. Once you answer the telephone, the caller speaks a message to you, which you process and respond to. The message is a data item. A *data sink* is an object that absorbs or collects the output from a system. And a *data store* is an object that holds data items for later use.

The first two columns of Table 1.2 show each object from the Blueberry Muffin Factory and its type. Notice that the supplier is a data source, because the supplier supplies the raw materials that are input into the system. The distributors are a data sink, because the final output goes to them. The baking tins might be thought of as a data store, because the "data" are deposited into them for later use. All the remaining objects are data items. The first two columns of Table 1.3 show each object from the Computerized Concordance System and its type. By identifying the type of each object in the system, the nature and role of the object become clearer.

The next step is to identify operations in the system. Operations are processes in the system and are indicated by verbs and verb phrases. Operations also include decisions. In the Blueberry Muffin Factory system, the operations include gets, made, washed, sorted, added, poured, baked, cooled, packaged, put in boxes, and shipped. In the final step, these operations are paired with their associated actions. The last column of Table 1.2 shows the actions assigned to the objects in the Blueberry Muffin Factory system. Notice that one operation, "made," is associated with all the raw materials. This is because the raw materials form a class of objects. The raw material object, blueberries, however, also has the "washed" and "sorted" actions associated with it. Blueberries are a special case within the category of raw materials. The actions for the Computerized Concordance System include

Table 1.2 Objects, Object Types, and Operations for the Blueberry Muffin Factory System

Object	Object Type	Operations
Suppliers	Data source	Gets
Raw materials	Data item	Made
Flour	Data item	Made
Milk	Data item	Made
Eggs	Data item	Made
Blueberries	Data item	Made, sorted, washed
Batter	Data item	Added, baked
Baking tins	Data store	Poured
Baked muffins	Data item	Cooled
Packaged muffins	Data item	Packaged
Boxed muffins	Data item	Boxed
Distributors	Data sink	Shipped

Table 1.3 Objects, Object Types, and Operations from the Computerized Concordance System

Object	Object Type	Operations
User	Data source	Indicates
Text file	Data source	Indicates
Line	Data item	Analyzed
Word	Data item	Extracted, edited
Concordance	Data store	Is-not-in, added, if-already-in
Word count	Item	Incremented
Line record	Item	Kept
Choice input	Control item	Inputs
Screen	Data sink	Displaying
Printer	Data sink	Printing

indicates, processed, analyzed, extracted, edited, is-not-in, added, if-already-in, incremented, kept, inputs, display, printing. The last column of Table 1.3 shows the actions assigned to the appropriate objects.

The four-step approach just described is called an *object-oriented approach* to system understanding. Object-oriented programming and object-oriented design are important new influences in software engineering (see Chapter 8). However, these approaches are not yet mature enough to provide a holistic and generalizable approach to all phases of software development. If an object-oriented programming language is to be used to implement a system, the analysis approach described here can feed directly into the design and programming phases of the software development cycle. But the object-oriented approach is also useful when more traditional analysis and design methods are to be used. In particular, the approach provides a framework and guidance in performing Structured Analysis, as described in Chapter 2. The enumeration and classification of data objects lay the groundwork for defining the data flow and creating the data dictionary that are parts of the Structured Analysis method. The enumeration of the operations lays the groundwork for defining activities in the Structured Analysis models. In the design phase, object-oriented analysis provides guidance for creating data abstractions, another important recent idea in software engineering. The use of data abstractions in design will be discussed in Chapter 4.

1.7 Project Component of a Software Engineering Course

The majority of software engineering courses being taught today include a group-project component (Leventhal and Mynatt, 1987). It is very likely, then, that your course includes such a group project. Your instructor will be providing considerable guidance on carrying out the project. In addition, this textbook is designed specifically to facilitate the execution of a project, as well as to provide an introduction to the study of software engineering. This approach is somewhat different than that taken in most software engineering textbooks currently available. Most software engineering textbooks are survey texts. Such books attempt to provide an overview of many topics in software engineering and to give the reader a broad understanding of software engineering. In the present text the goal is to focus primarily on those topics and techniques that can facilitate an ongoing student software development project and to cover these topics in depth. In particular, the organization and contents of Chapters 2 through 7 are designed to be used in parallel with the ongoing project. Each chapter is related to the software development cycle and focuses on a limited number of techniques, covering those techniques in some detail. The purpose of the in-depth coverage is to give you enough of an understanding of the technique that it can be immediately applied to the project. In choosing which techniques to cover, consideration was given to the popularity of the various techniques, ease of learning, ease of use, and their use as a basis for later learning, either on the job or in future classes. In addition to describing techniques, specific suggestions are given for carrying out the phase of the project being discussed and for document contents and format. Finally, evaluation criteria and methods are discussed. When feasible, alternative techniques and methods are discussed to allow you and your instructor to select the most appropriate or appealing approach to your particular project or to provide a comparison. The chapters on requirements analysis and specification and on preliminary design, for example, are based on the structured analysis and structured design techniques of Constantine and Yourdon (1979) and DeMarco (1978). These methods are widely known and widely used and are fairly easy to learn and to apply.

To give an idea of the progression of topics and project events, here is a brief overview of the book organization. Chapter 2 covers the first stage: requirements analysis and program specification. In this stage the problem to be solved is studied and the nature of the problem solution is outlined. In particular, the exact functions to be performed by the software system are identified and documented in detail. Chapters 3 and 4 cover the preliminary design of the software system. The preliminary design is broken down into its two major facets: the design of the user interface, and the design of the software and data structures. The user interface represents the software system as it will be seen and used by the user. The user interface gives the user access to the various functions that the system provides. The ease and facility with which the user is able to utilize the system's functions are of major importance in the overall success and quality of the system. Once the system has been designed from the user's point of view, the supporting functional core must be designed. In Chapter 4 the design of the software structure and data structures — the functional core of the system — is discussed.

In Chapter 5 the tasks involved in the detailed design of the system are covered. In detailed design, what is essentially a set of blueprints for building the system is created. Various considerations in choosing a programming language for implementation of the system are also discussed. Once detailed design is underway, coding and integration can commence. Chapter 6 deals with these topics. Coding involves translating the detailed designs into actual source code for individual modules or components of the system. In integration, modules are combined and tested in systematic ways. Testing is discussed in Chapter 7. Techniques for the testing of individual modules, groups of modules, and the entire system are covered. Chapter 8 differs from earlier chapters in that it is not project oriented. In Chapter 8 a survey of a number of topics in software engineering is made. In particular, several other well-known analysis and design methods are covered. Software development tools and software development environments are defined and described. Possible future trends in software engineering are discussed. This chapter is included to round out the picture of software engineering presented in the earlier chapters.

1.7.1 Getting Started on the Project

A number of approaches can be used in the project component of a software engineering course. One approach is to have a number of miniprojects or assignments throughout the term, each of which might be worked on by an individual or a team. A more common approach is to have one major project that spans the entire term. Typically, the project involves a team of students assigned to see the development of a software system through from requirements and specification to installation. In most cases, your instructor will have decided which project or projects will be attempted. In some situations, you might get to choose your own project. In any case, your instructor has probably decided on the scope of the project you will be working on and on the size of the teams.

It is extremely important that you begin working on the project as soon as it is assigned. As previously mentioned, the history of software development is strewn with stories of incomplete, unusable, and abandoned software projects. Such failures do not reflect on the programming skill of any individual; they reflect a failure to organize, to communicate, to evaluate, to take account of the sequential nature of software development—in short, a failure to apply good software engineering principles. If you do not want your project to join this undistinguished list, you must give yourself all the time possible. Waiting until later to start is like planting corn in August and hoping to get a crop harvested in time for winter. Corn, like software, grows more or less at its own rate, and there is only so much one can do to speed up the process.

The first order of business for any team is to agree on and set up its team organization. Your instructor may impose an organization on the team, or you may be free to choose your own organization. The following section describes three different sorts of team structures. The size of the team, the nature of the project, and the talents of your team members should all be considered in setting up the team organization. Other considerations, such as time commitments and ease of communication among the members, should also be taken into account.

1.7.2 Team Organization

Working on a team is probably not a new experience for you. Anyone who has worked on a family project, been a member of an athletic team, played in a band, or been a member of a club has worked as part of a team. Nonetheless, because teams are the essential component of a software engineering project, it is a good idea to think about team structure and organization.

Teams are based on two principle ideas: the achievement of a goal and division of labor. A team is formed in the first place with the idea of achieving some specific goal. Division of labor is central to the idea of a team because the goal cannot be achieved without the efforts of several people or because the goal can be achieved more quickly or efficiently with a group effort. What makes a team successful is having obtainable goals, having a clear understanding of its goal or goals, and having a wise and workable division of labor. Team organization refers to how the labor is divided and delegated.

In some cases, it is possible to have a democratic team. A democratic team is a team with no leader where decisions are reached by voting or by reaching a consensus. This type of team organization is feasible under limited circumstances. These circumstances include a readily attainable goal, a small number of team members (for example, two to five), approximately equal ability among the members (although these abilities may be in different areas of expertise), and a real ability to give and take. Unfortunately, democratic teams, especially those formed from groups of peers, can waste a lot of time simply carrying out the democratic process. Many hours may be spent in discussions and in trying to come to a consensus. Furthermore, while it may be easy to decide who is responsible for what aspect of the project, it is hard to hold an individual group member responsible for his or her portion of the work without the appearance of the group "ganging up" on the individual.

Having a leader can greatly expedite matters. A leader is responsible for defining and setting goals, for establishing the group organization and delegating responsibilities, for setting deadlines and monitoring progress, for making sure the necessary resources are available to the team, and for motivating the team. One team structure that has been widely used in industry is the *chief programmer team* (Brooks, 1975). In such teams, one person is the chief programmer or leader. The chief programmer designs the software, implements critical parts of the software, makes all the major technical decisions, and delegates work to the team members. In addition to the chief programmer, the team members consist of:

- An *assistant programmer,* whose job is to consult the chief programmer on technical matters, provide liaison with the sponsor and other groups, and serve as a backup to the chief programmer when the chief is unavailable or leaves the project. The assistant may also aid in the design or coding.

- Two to five *programmers,* who implement the design, document the source code, and do testing.

- An *administrator,* who takes care of the day-to-day administrative detail, thus allowing the chief programmer to focus on technical duties.

- A *librarian,* who maintains program listings, documentation, test plans, test runs, and so on, and handles the duties of configuration management.

- A *toolsmith,* whose duties are to adapt existing tools to the needs of the team and to write customized tools for the team. A detailed knowledge of the operating system being used is necessary for this member.

Chief programmer teams have the advantage of centralizing decision making and providing strong team structure. However, the overall effectiveness of the team is quite dependent on the technical and managerial skills of the chief programmer. Furthermore, the morale of the team may suffer because everyone but the chief appears to be second-class citizens (Mantei, 1981).

A compromise between democratic and chief programmer teams is a hierarchical team structure. In a hierarchical structure the project leader makes the major decisions, assigns tasks, participates in evaluations, and performs technical duties as well. Under the project leader are a few technical leaders. Each technical leader is in charge of one or more separate aspects of system development and has in her or his charge no more than five to seven programmers and other staff members. The technical leaders report directly to the project leader and also communicate among themselves. This approach allows for some democracy among the leaders or among the team members working with each technical leader. On the other hand, the leaders have authority and are responsible for making sure assigned tasks get done.

The hierarchical team structure can work well with student teams. One person can be named the project leader. This person can call meetings, set goals, delegate responsibilities, and otherwise push the project along. Other team members can be the technical leaders for various aspects of the project. They are responsible for administrating their parts of the project. When necessary, the project leader can serve as a member of a technical team and come under the charge of the technical leaders. Likewise, a person who is a technical leader on one aspect of the project can serve as a member of a different technical team. An easy way to divide a software development project into parts is by phases in the development cycle. A technical leader can be named for each phase.

1.7.3 Guidelines for Holding Meetings

Although much of the communication among the members of a group can be done on a one-to-one basis, there are many times when three or more of the members need to get together at one time to talk things over. Whenever three or more people gather to communicate, it is a meeting. There is no doubt that meetings will play a central role in the course of carrying out a group project. Meetings can be more or less formal, can be on any topic, and can certainly be more or less successful. There are few things more frustrating than spending a lot of time in a meeting that serves no purpose and is a waste of time. The discussion presented here is intended to help make both informal and formal meetings more productive.

All meetings should have a leader. The leader of a meeting does not necessarily have to be the project leader or a technical leader. The leader of a meeting has two major categories of responsibilities: task responsibilities and people-oriented responsibilities. Task responsibilities relate to getting the job done. The goals of the meeting must be met, and good solutions should be produced. People-oriented responsibilities relate to keeping the people involved interacting in a productive, goal-oriented, and motivated way. More specifically, the leader's responsibilities include creating an agenda (see later), determining who should attend, notifying potential attendees, leading the meeting session, and making sure the meeting is followed up. If possible, the leader should take a facilitative role, not a dictatorial role. That is, the leader should make sure the meeting goes smoothly and that everyone who wishes to participate has the opportunity to contribute without simply imposing his or her will on the group.

Every meeting involves three phases: preparation, the meeting session itself, and follow-up. Preparation is probably the most important and most neglected area of holding a meeting. Preparation involves a number of activities. First, and foremost, preparation involves deciding on the function and purpose of the meeting. Palmer and Palmer (1983) suggest that meetings can serve a number of functions and purposes, including:

Planning and preparation. To define issues, investigate or study an issue; to advise or propose

Policy making. To set goals, develop procedures, rules or policies; to set priorities

Managing. To organize, assign duties, allocate resources, or supervise

Taking action. To sell an idea or product; to implement or produce something

Facilitating action. To instruct or train; to build morale

Solving problems. To define problems and causes; to identify and evaluate proposed solutions; to review and evaluate; to resolve disputes

Any meeting can have more than one of these purposes, but at a well-designed meeting the attendees will know exactly which of these purposes are to be served for each topic in the meeting. Specifically, the meeting leader should make an *agenda* for the meeting: a list of all topics or subjects that are to be covered in the meeting. For each topic, the exact actions or decisions that should result from the meeting should be listed. For example, one topic for a meeting might be when to schedule future meetings. This topic is a management issue. The agenda should state what a discussion of this issue should yield; for example, "The group will decide on a regular weekly meeting time." Another topic might be choosing a programming language to implement the project in. This is a problem-solving issue. The agenda might state that "The group will consider the pros and cons of different programming languages and select a language for the project."

Once an agenda for the meeting has been established, the next step of preparation is notifying the people who should attend the meeting and giving them a copy of the agenda. It is possible that not all members of a project team will need to attend every meeting, but it is important that no one who should be involved is left out. Early notification is essential to allow preparation. Too often, poor meetings are blamed on poor leadership, when in fact it is the fault of the participants. If the participants have not "done their homework," then all they have to offer are opinions and poorly thought out ideas. Consider the problem-solving issue of choosing a programming language for a project. To make this decision in a sound and fruitful manner requires facts and knowledge. Knowledge of what languages exist, what their features are that make them more or less suitable for the particular project, what language compilers are available locally, and so on, are all necessary to make an informed decision. The potential attendees at a meeting should be notified well in advance what knowledge or facts they are responsible for and should be made accountable for having that knowledge by the time of the meeting.

The leader of the meeting is responsible for running the actual meeting session. The meeting should stick to the agenda. If a topic is started that the participants are not adequately prepared to discuss, then shelve the topic until a later meeting if possible. Try to keep the meeting focused on goals. Do not let it degenerate into personal attacks or let one or two people dominate the meeting at the expense of contributions from others. The participants should really listen to what other people say and respond directly to what was said before offering another opinion. Start the meeting on time and end it on time. Starting meetings late only encourages lateness and wastes time. Ending meetings late causes frustration, lack of attention, and often a loss of participants due to other commitments. Meetings should rarely last more than two hours. An hour to an hour and a half is a more realistic limit.

The last phase of meetings is the follow-up. Meetings should end with a clear understanding of the outcomes. What exactly were the conclusions that were reached and how? What follow-up duties are there? Were any specific assignments made at the meeting? Participants should leave the meeting fully aware of what their responsibilities are and should take care of these responsibilities in a timely fashion. To facilitate the follow-up process, a recorder should be appointed for each meeting to take minutes. Minutes help to make duties and assignments clear and prevent later misunderstandings.

Table 1.4 presents a portion of a meeting diagnosis checklist developed by Palmer and Palmer (1983) to be used in assessing the planning, execution, and effectiveness of meetings. This checklist presents a concise guide to the qualities a good meeting should have. Read the list and consider each item carefully.

Table 1.4 A Meeting Diagnosis Checklist

	Yes	No
Meeting Goals and Objectives		
Were the issues or topics of the meeting clear to all in attendance?	___	___
Did everyone know what decisions or actions were to be taken?	___	___
Were hidden agendas ferreted out and dealt with forthrightly?		
Were the meeting's objectives reasonable, given available time and resources?	___	___
Was a good sense of priorities established to guide deliberations?	___	___
Notification		
Was the agenda made clear by the meeting organizer before the meeting (verbally or in writing)?	___	___
Were participants told of the meeting sufficiently in advance to allow adequate preparation?	___	___
Were they prepared to make decisions or act?	___	___
Were all necessary materials distributed sufficiently in advance to allow review?	___	___
Was the distribution of unnecessary materials avoided?	___	___
Was the time of the meeting convenient?	___	___
Participation		
Was everyone needed to take action present?	___	___
Were the interests of all whom meeting outcomes might affect represented?	___	___
Was your contribution to or benefit from the meeting sufficient to warrant your attendance?	___	___
Were people there whose presence was unnecessary?	___	___
Was sufficient time allocated to each item on the agenda?	___	___
Were all people given an opportunity and encouraged to participate?	___	___
Was a spirit of cooperation fostered?	___	___
Was domination of the group by one or two persons avoided?	___	___
Were people presenting information well prepared and organized?	___	___
Did the group adhere to the agenda?	___	___
Was the meeting leader effective in:		
instilling a sense of common purpose?	___	___
keeping the group on track?	___	___
creating an atmosphere conducive to the free exchange of ideas and information?	___	___

resolving conflict? _____ _____
providing positive feedback when warranted? _____ _____
maintaining interest and enthusiasm? _____ _____
summarizing periodically and/or at the end of the meeting? _____ _____
moving the group toward closure on agenda items? _____ _____

Was parliamentary procedure employed when necessary? _____ _____

Was it employed properly? _____ _____

Were previously adopted bylaws applied properly? _____ _____

Was the meeting concluded reasonably close to the scheduled ending
time? _____ _____

Meeting Follow-up

At the close of the meeting, was there consensus on decisions or
actions? _____ _____

Were follow-up assignments and responsibilities clear? _____ _____

Were minutes, follow-up correspondence, or actions executed in
a timely fashion? _____ _____

Source; From the book, THE SUCCESSFUL MEETING MASTER GUIDE by Barbara C. Palmer and Kenneth R. Palmer. ©1983. Used by permission of the publisher, Prentice-Hall, Inc., Englewood Cliffs, New Jersey.

While you may feel that having a meeting leader, an agenda, and keeping minutes is far too formal for students meeting together to work on a project, consider the following quote:

> Some people tell us that "This system is fine for formal meetings, but many of mine are among friends. I don't need to go through all this." We couldn't disagree more. In fact, it's meetings of people who know each other, who meet regularly and within the same work context, that most frequently go sour. And they use that closeness as their excuse for not preparing. The fact that those attending a meeting know each other well and work together on a daily basis, if anything, should argue for more concern and consideration rather than less. (Tropman and Morningstar, 1985, p. 41)

The lesson is that the very use of formality can save friendships rather than ruin them. Do not be afraid to insist on organization, personal responsibility, and a certain degree of formality in meetings.

Finally, one technique that can be useful at problem-solving meetings is brainstorming. The purpose of brainstorming is to come up with a variety of solutions to a problem. The idea of using brainstorming in a group is that one person's idea may spark other ideas from different people, thus producing a greater number of ideas and more creative ideas than might be produced by an individual working on his or her own. For a brainstorming session to be productive, a couple of guidelines should be followed. First, evaluation of ideas should take place in a separate evaluation phase, not during the brainstorming phase. This rule is to encourage people to put forward all suggestions, without worrying about being criticized or put down by other participants. Second, do not reject ideas too soon. Think about each idea that is offered. Even if an idea seems clearly unworkable, there may be some facet of the idea that will work or will inspire other, more workable ideas. To encourage true acceptance of each idea, make sure each idea is restated by another person before going on to the next idea, or write down each idea and make sure all ideas receive attention during the evaluation phase. In the evaluation phase, the ideas proposed during brainstorming are used as a basis for the problem solution. A small number of candidate solutions should be formulated from the pool of brainstormed ideas. These solutions can then be evaluated again and a final solution chosen.

Summary

Chapter 1 presents an introduction to the study of software engineering. The historical forces that led to the development of a discipline called software engineering were discussed. Software engineering was defined, and the central role of quality in software development was discussed. Many topics in software engineering are closely tied to the software life cycle. The life cycle of a software system includes the software development cycle, the operational and maintenance phase, and retirement. The classical software development cycle was outlined. The classical cycle includes the requirements analysis and specification stage, the design stage, the implementation stage, the system testing phase, and the delivery/installation phase. Software engineering encompasses a variety of approaches and methods that can be used within the framework of the software life cycle. The costs of software development and software ownership were discussed. A study of these costs highlights the savings that can be made throughout the software life cycle through the conscientious use of software engineering. A number of factors that make software development difficult were highlighted. These included communications, the essentially sequential nature of system development, various project characteristics, characteristics of the personnel involved in system development, and management issues.

Software always exists as part of a system. Therefore, it is important to understand what a system is and how to analyze systems. A system is a collection of interacting elements that performs functions aimed at achieving some objective. One way to approach the problem of understanding a system is to first write down an overview of the system goals and constraints in a statement of system scope. The next step is to identify objects and operations in the system. This is done by listing the objects in the system, identifying the type of each object, identifying each operation, and assigning each operation to an object.

Group projects are often a central component of a software engineering course. This book has been written to facilitate and parallel the carrying out of a group project, as well as to provide an overview of software engineering. Working as a group means working as a team. Team organization was discussed. Possible organizations include democratic, chief programmer, or hierarchical. Guidelines for holding meetings were also discussed. Every meeting has a preparation phase, a meeting session, and a follow-up. For the leader of a meeting, preparation involves deciding on the function and purpose of the meeting, creating an agenda, and notifying participants. For participants, preparation involves reading the agenda and becoming prepared to deal with and participate meaningfully in each agenda item. The meeting session should closely follow the agenda, stay on track, and start and end on time. Meeting follow-up should include a written record of meeting outcomes. If duties and assignments were made during the meeting, the participants should be clearly aware of them and should perform them in a timely fashion. Brainstorming is one technique that can be used in problem-solving meetings.

Checklist of Project Activities

_____ Meet with your project group and decide on a team organization.

_____ If the group is using something other than a democratic organization, select a leader for the group.

_____ Set up a formal communication network for the group. For example, a telephone chain might be set up where each member is responsible for contacting the next member on a list.

_____ Decide on meeting procedures to be used: who will call the meetings, where the meetings will be held, who the meeting leader will be (for at least the next meeting), what the format of the meetings will be, and how long typical meetings will last.

_____ Consider establishing a regular meeting time so that people can build their schedules around the regular time.

_____ Choose a recorder to take minutes of meetings.

_____ If the group has not been assigned a project, choose a project according to the instructor's guidelines.

Terms and Concepts Introduced

software engineering	software life cycle
software	software development cycle
software quality	software process model
sponsor	the "mythical man-month"
user	chief programmer team
software maintenance	agenda
software reliability	system
efficiency	statement of system scope
functionality	object
operation	class
subclass	data source
data sink	data item
data store	control item
object-oriented approach	

Exercises

1. Find a description of a computer foul-up in a publication such as a newspaper, magazine, or journal. One good source is the "Risks to the Public" section in *ACM Sigsoft Notes*. What was the cause of the foul-up? From what you know about software engineering so far, what could have been done to prevent the foul-up?

2. Consider some category of software that you have used or been familiar with for a number of years, such as video games, word processors, compilers, or operating systems. Make a list of the software, arranged in its chronological age. What sorts of changes in complexity can you see? Which systems offer the most functions and features? What sort of added features might you expect to see in the future? If known, consider the cost of these systems. Do you see a trend in the costs?

3. Not so long ago, the source code for a computer program was created and edited on physical input media, such as cards. In using cards, each statement in the source language was typed on a single card using a card punch machine. If a typographical error was made, a new card had to be punched. When completed, the program was submitted to the computer through a card reader. The computer then compiled and executed the program, and produced listings and output on a line printer. Compare this system of program development to a system you have used recently. What are the disadvantages of the card-oriented approach to programming? How does it compare to your system?

4. An automobile company has recently used the advertising slogan "Quality is Job 1." What are the qualities an owner or driver looks for in a car? What are the qualities the automobile company looks for? What about the perspective of the automobile salesperson? What about the mechanic's perspective? Do all these perspectives agree on what is quality in an automobile? How do they differ? Is it possible to produce an automobile of high quality from all perspectives?

5. The software life cycle is often compared to the processes involved in building and owning a house. For each stage in the software life cycle, list and describe the comparable processes in building a house. How good is the analogy? Are there any stages in the software life cycle that do not have analogies in building a house, or vice versa?

6. Write a statement of system scope for an egg-producing operation. Perform an object-oriented analysis of the system. Identify the objects and their types. Identify operations and assign them to the objects.

7. Write a statement of system scope for a computerized tic-tac-toe game, where a human plays against the computer. Perform an object-oriented analysis of the system. Identify the objects and their types. Identify operations and assign them to the objects.

8. Describe a situation where you have worked with others on a group or family project. Describe the structure of the group (for example, was there a formal

leader?). How were communications handled during the project? How successfully was the project completed? How satisfied were you with the group experience?

9. Use the meeting diagnosis checklist in Table 1.4 after you attend your next meeting. What things were done right? What things were not handled so well? What could have been done to improve the meeting?

10. Consider the life cycle costs of owning a piece of equipment such as a television or an automobile. Which costs more, buying the item in the first place or the cost of ownership? What are the reasons for the ownership costs? What are the causes of retirement of the equipment? Compare these life cycle facts to the life cycle of software. How and why are they different? How and why are they the same?

11. (a) Draw a diagram of all the paths of communication among five people in a completely democratic organization. Use a single line to indicate a two-way path of communication. How many lines are there?

    (b) Now assume one person is the chief and the other four people are team members and on a lower level. Draw all paths of communication, assuming communications flow up and down and also among all members on one level. How many lines are there?

    (c) Now assume a three-level system with the chief programmer at the top, the assistant at the next level, and three team members at the bottom. Communications can only pass up and down one level, but flow among all members of a level. Draw all the communication lines. How many are there?

    (d) Repeat the process for a four- and a five-level organization.

    (e) What are your conclusions concerning how to organize a team to reduce the burden of communications?

12. List a number of other endeavors from every day life, besides pregnancy and software development, that have an essentially sequential nature.

13. Give some reasons why systems and utility programs are more difficult to build than applications software.

2. Requirements Analysis and Specification

> The hardest single part of building a software system is deciding precisely what to build. No other part of the conceptual work is as difficult as establishing the detailed technical requirements, including all the interfaces to people and machines, and to other software systems. No other part of the work so cripples the resulting system if done wrong. No other part is more difficult to rectify later. (Brooks, 1987)

As this quote suggests, the most difficult and critical step in software development is the first one: understanding what the project is all about. A software project is basically a problem-solving task on a grand scale. And the first step toward solving any problem is understanding what the problem is. The nature and bounds of the problem must be understood and constraints on how the problem can be solved must be known. In software development, the developer begins by talking to the potential sponsor to discover exactly what the sponsor's problems are and what sort of solution is envisioned. The goal is to identify and understand the problem for which a solution is sought and to determine what is to be done. This stage is called the *requirements analysis and specification* stage. Sometimes this stage is referred to more informally as the *analysis stage*. The people who are responsible for carrying out this first stage of the software development process are called *systems analysts*.

As the longer name—requirements analysis and specification—implies, the analysis stage actually has two components. The first, *requirements analysis,* involves stating the problem to be solved and the requirements that exist that define a successful solution to the problem. The present situation should be analyzed and understood, and goals for the new system should be clearly stated. The second component is *specification*. The goal of specification is to completely specify the technical requirements for the system, including precisely what the system is supposed to do and the operational constraints. The specification often serves as a performance contract between the developers and the sponsor. The specifications are used by the system designers as their guide and must contain everything they need to know about the proposed system. The analysis stage is extremely critical in the development of successful software. If the analysts do not completely understand the sponsor's requirements and communicate them correctly to the designers through the specifications, the designers cannot be expected to develop the sort of system the sponsor needs.

The results of the analysis process are embodied in a *requirements specification document*. This document serves, either formally or informally, as a contract between the sponsor and the developers. It is important that the document communicate clearly, accurately, and completely to both parties involved. A number of guidelines and techniques have been developed for use in the analysis stage. One particular technique, structured analysis, will be described later. First, however, let us consider what is involved in the general process of analysis in a little more detail.

2.1 Requirements Analysis

One of the most challenging aspects of requirements analysis is to understand the sponsor's problem. The analyst must be able to see the current situation from the sponsor's point of view and to understand what sort of solution the sponsor envisions. In many ways, the analyst is similar to a newspaper or television reporter who is sent out into the field to get a story. Reporters must interview the people involved in the story, collect facts, and then organize the collected information into a coherent story. When reporters are trained, they are taught to repeatedly ask "the five W questions"—who, what, when, where, and why—to guide them in collecting and organizing their information. If we add "how" to this list of questions, they are an ideal guideline for an analyst as well.

- **Who** is involved in the situation we are analyzing? What role is played by each of these people? Who will actually be using the proposed software? Will the users be highly trained individuals, computer novices, or both?

- **What** is the current situation? What is it about the current situation that is posing a problem? What is the proposed system to be? What functions are to be performed by the proposed system?

- **When** must the new system be in place? When will the changeover to the new system take place? When will the sponsor be ready to install and test the new system on site?

- **Where** will the new system fit into the old environment? Where will the current personnel fit into the new system?

- **Why** is a new system being sought? Why do the users believe they need a new system? What is it about the current situation that requires a change to a new system?

- **How** will the new system function? Are there constraints on how the proposed system can operate? Are there constraints, for example, on the hardware, the cost of the system, or the programming language to be used?

All these questions, and many more, must be answered during analysis in order to adequately understand the sponsor's problem and to begin defining an acceptable solution. Techniques that the analyst can use to understand the sponsor's problem include interviews with the personnel in the problem domain, observation of the problem tasks, and actual performance of the problem tasks by the analyst. The analyst must be a critical listener, however, because different personnel will have different perspectives, biases, and opinions concerning the problem. The analyst must be able to pull out the true and complete story, as much as possible, from the different fragments given to him or her by each person interviewed.

A second facet of the analyst's job is to find out from the sponsor exactly what goals are to be achieved by the new system and what constraints there are on the sorts of solutions that would be acceptable to the sponsor. An example of a goal might be that the sponsor wants the system to save the company money by cutting the time necessary to process certain transactions or by reducing the number of errors that occur. Other goals might relate to employee satisfaction, increased volume demands, or changes in company policies or procedures. Constraints include environmental factors that might affect the design and development of the new system. Perhaps the new system must run on existing hardware or be able to interface with existing software. Or perhaps the system must be designed so that the operational procedures are similar to those currently in use. By understanding the goals and constraints on a system, it is possible to view the proposed system in its proper perspective and guide the design of the system effectively.

2.1.1   Requirements Specification

Once the sponsor's problem has been analyzed and the goals for the project have been made clear, the system specifications are created. The specifications should clearly, completely, and consistently specify the technical requirements for the system, including software, hardware and manual components. All the features to be included in the software should be listed, along with any constraints or limitations. All the functions to be performed by the software should be noted. The specifications must also state what is to be done in exceptional cases, such as when there are errors in the data or when unusually large data sets are encountered. Any requirements related to performance characteristics, such as speed, accuracy, or ease of use, must also be included.

2.1.2   Requirements Specification Document

The information collected during the requirements analysis and specification stage is presented in the requirements specification document. It is a very important document because it represents the major link between the sponsor and the developer. On the one hand, there is the sponsor, who knows that there is a problem with the current system but has little or none of the technical knowledge needed to solve that problem. On the other hand, there is the developer, who has lots of technical know-how but very little idea of what goes on in the sponsor's world. These two points of view must be brought together. The analyst must be able to enter into the sponsor's world and understand the problems and constraints operating there. The sponsor must communicate his or her needs precisely to the analyst and recognize that there are practical limits on the sorts of solutions that can be implemented. To a very large extent, the analysis stage is centered around overcoming barriers to communication. Neither side can ever assume that the other side knows precisely what they are talking about. All terms and procedures must be clearly and unambiguously defined. All constraints and assumptions must be fully spelled out. The requirements specification document is where everything *is* spelled out.

To give an idea of what is involved, here are some general criteria, taken from Gilbert (1983), that the requirements specification document should meet:

The requirements specification document should be readily understandable to both the sponsor and the developer. Because the requirements specification serves as a contract between the sponsor and the developer, each side should clearly understand what they have agreed to. Furthermore, the requirements specification is used throughout the development of the system. It is used during the design phase as a base of information for solving the problem and producing the design solution. It is used during testing as a comparison or standard against which the final product is judged. Because the document serves so many needs, it should be readily understood by a variety of readers.

The conditions stated in the requirements specification should be mutually agreeable to both the developer and the sponsor. Each side must realize that it must operate under certain constraints. The sponsor cannot demand a system that is impossible to produce or that will cost more to produce than the sponsor is willing to pay. The developer must provide a realistic statement of what functions the system will be able to perform, when the system will be finished, and how much it will cost to produce it. Furthermore, both sides in the agreement must realize that they cannot change their minds to a great extent once the requirements specification document has been signed.

The requirements specification must precisely state all functions to be performed by the proposed system. The functions to be carried out by the proposed system are at the heart of the requirements specification document. What exactly is the proposed system supposed to do for the sponsor? What activities and processes will be carried out by the system? Each of these functions must be spelled out in detail. At this stage, no attempt is made to say how or in what particular order these functions will be carried out, but the functions must be described as clearly and completely as possible.

The requirements specification must state all constraints that affect the proposed system. Must the proposed system have fast response times? What is the target hardware for the system? Is there a limit to the memory available for the software? What are the characteristics of the potential users of the system? Does the sponsor require that a particular programming language be used? Factors such as these impose constraints on the set of possible designs for the proposed system. It is important that both sides be aware of these constraints from the beginning.

The requirements specification must provide testable criteria for acceptance of the system. When sponsors request that a system be developed, they should have some ideas concerning what they expect that system to be. How will they know when they have the system they want? A sponsor cannot just say, "I will know it when I see it." Sponsors must instead state, up front, what features, characteristics, and qualities they will be judging the system on once it is created. Furthermore, these criteria must be stated in testable form. If a sponsor wants a system with fast response times, this requirement must be specified in testable form, for example, "The system will respond to a command within 3 seconds."

The requirements specification should list the qualities of the desired system, their relative importance, and how these qualities will be measured or tested. In some systems, such as medical systems or satellite control systems, accuracy and reliability are paramount qualities. Other qualities, such as ease of use or reusability, might be of lesser importance. In other cases, speed or user-friendliness might be of primary importance to the sponsor. In each case, the sponsor should consider the relative importance of these different software qualities and provide the developers with a ranking. Furthermore, testable criteria should be established against which the system can be measured to see if it has the desired qualities. For example, if a system is supposed to be easy to use, a measure of "ease of use" might be how long it takes to train the average high-school graduate to use the system.

Default and error conditions should be stated whenever necessary. If a data value of "$4" occurs, is it permissible to assume that "$4.00" was intended? In other words, is zero cents the default value? What if a data value of "$59.V2" occurs? How should it be handled? For every function of the proposed system that handles raw data, there is a possibility of errors in the data. For every function that performs a calculation on data, there is a possibility that unacceptable values may be computed. Specifications concerning what is to be done in all these cases must be included.

2.2 Using Structured Analysis

The requirements analysis stage is an important and difficult stage in the development of software. There is much information that must be gathered and organized and many communication barriers to overcome. Unfortunately, there is no foolproof way to complete this task. Several techniques or guidelines have been proposed in the past, and new ways are being developed even now. The choice of which technique to use is an important one. Some techniques have been developed which are useful for modeling real-time systems (e.g., SREM. See Alford, 1977.). Other techniques were created to assist in the development of systems where the structure and interrelationship of the data elements in the system is the central problem. Examples of these techniques include the JSD method (Jackson System of Design) and the LCP method (Logical Construction of Programs). Both are discussed in Chapter 8. The method to be discussed here is the structured analysis method, developed by DeMarco (1978). The structured analysis method is most useful for more traditional data processing systems. Such systems can be characterized as ones where data flows among activities or functions in the system. The activities create or output data, or transform the data into new forms and pass along the changed data. We will focus on the structured analysis method here for several reasons. First, it is one of the most widely-used methods. Second, the majority of system development involves data processing systems. And finally, a number of automated software engineering tools have been developed based on this method (see Chapter 8).

In the structured analysis method, the main goal is to produce various models of the current system and the proposed system. Models are used in many different endeavors as a way of compacting and organizing ideas and information. Architects, for example, often create models of proposed buildings to help them see what the building might look like. They can then look at the model from different perspectives and ask important questions concerning its design. How well will people be able to move about in the building? How will the plumbing and electrical components fit into the proposed structure? How well will the building harmonize with surrounding buildings? These questions would be hard to answer if the architect were simply looking at a set of blueprints. They would be virtually impossible to answer from reading a prose description of the proposed building.

In structured analysis, the models that are built are models of systems, rather than of physical objects. As defined in Chapter 1, a system is a collection of interacting elements that perform some function or functions aimed at achieving some objective. The systems studied during software development involve software, hardware, people, physical entities, data, procedures, and documents. Because so much detail is involved in even a simple system, it is useful to come up with a model or several models of the system to help organize the details. In structured analysis the system model consists of three components: *data-flow diagrams,* a *data dictionary,* and *activity specifications. Data-flow diagrams* are large-scale graphs that diagram activities, data stores, and the flow of information or entities within the system. Activities and data stores are represented as labeled nodes in the diagrams. The activities are connected by lines that represent the relationships among the various activities. The lines are labeled to show what pieces of information (data) or entities are moving among the activities in the system. A *data dictionary* is a list of all the data elements shown in the data-flow diagram, along with a definition or description of the data elements. *Activity specifications* are detailed descriptions of each of the activities (nodes) indicated in the data-flow diagram. Each of these components will be described in more detail next.

2.2.1 Data-flow Diagram Notation

The component structures for data-flow diagrams are shown in Figure 2.1. Activities or processes are represented as circles. A title or phrase is written inside the

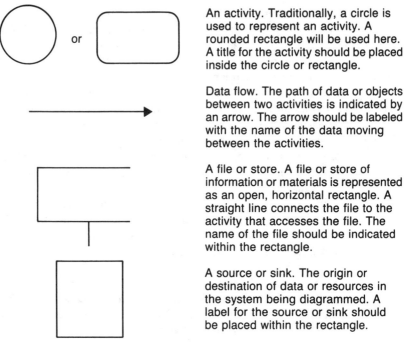

An activity. Traditionally, a circle is used to represent an activity. A rounded rectangle will be used here. A title for the activity should be placed inside the circle or rectangle.

Data flow. The path of data or objects between two activities is indicated by an arrow. The arrow should be labeled with the name of the data moving between the activities.

A file or store. A file or store of information or materials is represented as an open, horizontal rectangle. A straight line connects the file to the activity that accesses the file. The name of the file should be indicated within the rectangle.

A source or sink. The origin or destination of data or resources in the system being diagrammed. A label for the source or sink should be placed within the rectangle.

Figure 2.1 Data-flow Diagram Components

circle to describe the activity being represented. In this text, rounded rectangles will be used. As a convention, activity titles will be written here using all capital letters. An arrow is used to indicate the directed flow of data or materials between two activities. Arrows are labeled with the names of the data entities or materials that are traveling along them. As a convention, data entities will be represented using capital and lowercase letters. In addition, data names that consist of multiple words will be hyphenated to indicate that a single entity is being named. A file or store of information or materials is represented using an open, horizontal rectangle surrounding the name of the file or store. The ultimate destination of the information or materials produced by the system (the data sink) and the originating source of the information or materials used by the system, but that are outside the system (data sources), are represented as tall rectangles.

At the most abstract level, any system can be reduced to a data-flow diagram of the type shown in Figure 2.2a. Every system has some sort of input from a source outside the system, processes or transforms the input in some way, and produces output that is passed outside the system to a destination. As a simple example of a system, consider the Blueberry Muffin Factory system introduced in Chapter 1. A high-level data-flow diagram of the system is shown in Figure 2.2b. The Blueberry Muffin Factory is a system that procures ingredients from its suppliers. The suppliers are outside the system and provide input into the system. The suppliers, therefore, are a data source, and ingredients are input into the system from the

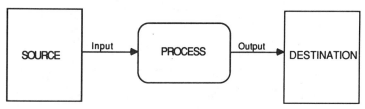

Figure 2.2(a) Data-flow Diagram of All Typical Systems

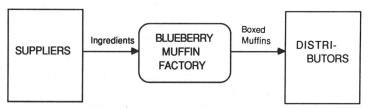

Figure 2.2(b) High-level Data-flow Diagram of the Blueberry Muffin Factory

source. The major activity of the system is to create packages of blueberry muffins for shipment to distributors. The rectangle in the middle of Figure 2.2b is labeled BLUEBERRY MUFFIN FACTORY to indicate all the processes and activities of the system. The finished product, boxed muffins, is sent out to distributors and is the output from the system. The distributors are the ultimate destination of the output from the system (the data sink) and are also considered to be outside the system of interest.

Clearly, not enough information is given in Figure 2.2b to clarify what is really involved in producing blueberry muffins. More detail must be presented. A data-flow diagram can be refined into *lower-level data-flow diagrams*. In a *lower-level data-flow diagram,* one activity of a higher-level data-flow diagram is expanded or exploded to reveal more details concerning that activity. Figure 2.3a shows a lower-level data-flow diagram of the BLUEBERRY MUFFIN FACTORY activity from Figure 2.2b. The BLUEBERRY MUFFIN FACTORY activity has been expanded to show the three major subactivities involved: MAKE MUFFINS, PACKAGE MUFFINS, and SHIP MUFFINS TO DISTRIBUTORS. Notice that the source and destination are not indicated in this data-flow diagram. Typically, the source and destination need to be shown only in the highest-level data-flow diagram. Their presence is assumed in lower-level diagrams. Notice also that the activities have been given identifying letters. These letters are used to relate any lower-level diagrams to this diagram. For example, the details concerning the MAKE MUFFINS activity are shown in Figure 2.3b. Each of these subactivities is given the same letter name, A, as its parent activity and is given a unique number. Thus the activities have descriptive names, such as CREATE BATTER, and also have an identification number, such as A.1, A.2, . . . , A.4. (If it were necessary to refine one of the activities in Figure 2.3b, the activities in the lower-level data-

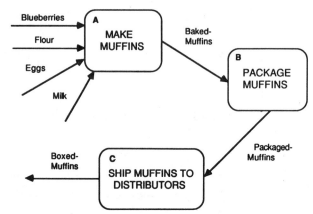

Figure 2.3(a) Lower Level Data-flow Diagram of the Blueberry Muffin Factory

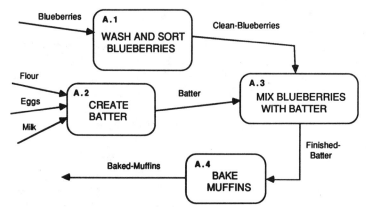

Figure 2.3(b) Refinement of the Make Muffins Activity in the Second-level Data-flow Diagram of the Blueberry Muffin Factory

flow diagram could be labeled using an additional numeric suffix, for example, A.2.1, A.2.2, and so on.)

As another example, consider a data-flow diagram for the computerized concordance system introduced in Chapter 1. A concordance is an alphabetized list of all the unique words that appear in a text along with the location of their occurrence. In our version, the user can enter the name of a text file (stored on a disk) for which a concordance is to be created. The concordance system will pull words from the text and edit them. For example, if a word begins with a capital letter because it occurs at the beginning of a sentence, the first letter will be changed to lowercase. If a word is hyphenated because it occurs at the end of a line, the hyphen will be removed in the concordance entry. Each line of text will be numbered as the concordance is created and a record kept of the line numbers where each

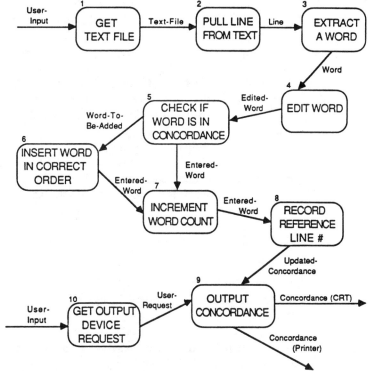

Figure 2.4 Data-flow Diagram of a Computerized Concordance System

unique word occurs. In addition, a running count of the total number of occurrences of each word will be kept. The user will have the option of printing the concordance on a line printer or listing it on the computer screen. The data-flow diagram for the concordance system is shown in Figure 2.4.

2.2.2 Abstraction and Decomposition in Systems Analysis

The simple example of the modeling of the muffin factory system using data-flow diagrams at different levels of refinement illustrates two important ideas in software engineering that will be recurring themes throughout this textbook. These ideas are *abstraction* and *decomposition*. *Abstraction* is the process of reducing the complexity of something by mapping many details into one meaningful higher-level entity or concept. By using abstraction, we can change the level of detail being considered. An abstract painting of a house, for example, may consist of a few colored rectangles and lines. It does not contain the detail that a photograph of the house would have, yet the viewer is (usually) able to identify the simplified forms as a house. When abstraction is used in problem solving, certain details are ignored along the way in order to convert the original, highly complex problem to a simpler one. Viewing a system as being made up of objects and procedures as described in Chapter 1 is one way to make a more abstract description of the system. Each object and its associated behaviors form a packet of information about one component of the system. In diagramming the blueberry muffin factory the highest-level data-flow diagram (Figure 2.2b) represents the most abstract view of the system. Many details of the system are hidden or ignored in this diagram. The lower-level data-flow diagrams begin to expose more of the details of the system and are less abstract.

Decomposition (sometimes called *stepwise refinement*) is the idea that a problem, such as understanding a complex system, can best be tackled by dividing (decomposing) the problem into subproblems. The division into subproblems is not arbitrary. How the problem is divided is important, and should be done in such a way that:

- Each subproblem is at the same level of detail as the other subproblems it goes with.

- Each subproblem can be solved as an individual problem.

- The solutions to the subproblems can be combined to solve the original problem.

In the case of the muffin factory data-flow diagrams, the highest-level diagram (Figure 2.2b) represents the overall problem: the system as a whole. Figure 2.3a shows the decomposition of the system into major components or subproblems. Notice that the three activities represented in the diagram, MAKE MUFFINS, PACKAGE MUFFINS, and SHIP MUFFINS TO DISTRIBUTORS, are all at about the same level of detail—in this case, still a fairly abstract or high level of detail. Finally, Figure 2.3b shows a decomposition of the MAKE MUFFINS activity. That is, Figure 2.3b is a solution to a subproblem from the higher-level diagram. Figure 2.3b itself contains subproblems.

The processes of decomposition and abstraction are useful in systems analysis. Decomposition is used to divide the system into components that make the system understandable; abstraction is used to make a reasonable choice of components. The processes stop when the original problem has been reduced to a set of problems with known or trivial solutions.

2.2.3   System Evolution

In analysis, it is necessary to first understand the sponsor's present situation completely. The analyst must know exactly what people, objects, machines, procedures, and documents comprise the system and must understand the interrelationships among them. Second, the analyst must determine what activities and functions the new system is to perform and must relate these new activities and functions to the people, machines, and so on, that will be interacting with the new system. As an aid in carrying out these different aspects of the analysis process, it may be necessary to produce up to four different sets of data-flow diagrams: one set each for the *current physical system,* the *current logical system,* the *proposed logical system,* and the *proposed physical system.*

The *current physical system* is the system currently in place. It includes the people involved and their roles (for example, secretary, accountant, restocker) and any machines, objects, or documents that are part of the system. In creating a data-flow diagram of the current physical system, the object is to "take a snapshot" of the system as it is. Each person or machine becomes an activity in the data-flow diagram, and the objects, documents, or verbal information that pass among them comprise the data flow.

To create a diagram of the *current logical system,* the analyst must be able to isolate the functional or logical components of the current system from its physical components. Often one person in the current system may actually be performing duties that involve two or more logically separate parts of the system. For example, a secretary who sorts and distributes incoming mail and also sets up appointments is performing two logically different activities. On the data-flow diagram of the current physical system, the secretary would be represented as one activity. In the data-flow diagram of the current logical system, the two functions, distributing mail and setting up appointments, would be represented as separate activities. These two types of diagrams together paint a complete and detailed picture of the current system. These diagrams are useful in pinpointing problems with the current system and in determining how the transition to the new system might be accomplished.

Note that in some situations, a current system may not exist. The proposed system may provide a completely new function that was not available before. Examples of smaller systems of this type might be an online tutorial or demonstration, an electronic mail system, a spelling checker or a music-composition system. Larger systems where no current system may exist include a telecommunications system, a process control system or a large, central database system.

The next data-flow diagram to be created represents the *proposed logical system.* In this diagram, the analyst represents how the activities to be performed in the new system will relate to each other and how the data will flow among these activities. The sponsor's desires concerning the new system are incorporated into the proposed logical system. In addition, the analyst may discover patterns of activities in the old system that can be arranged or ordered in more effective patterns in the new system.

Once the proposed logical system has been created, the proposed physical system can be described. In the *proposed physical system,* the activities shown in the proposed logical system are related to physical entities that will carry out the proposed activities under the new system. For example, a decision must be made concerning which of the proposed activities will be carried out by computer and which will be manually or mechanically done, and the job descriptions for people in the new system must be defined.

2.2.4   An Example: The Noncredit Courses Office

To illustrate some of the concepts just discussed, a small problem will be presented and analyzed. The sample system will be an office in the continuing education college of some university. The office of noncredit courses handles courses such as cooking, computer skills, arts and crafts, or recreational pastimes that might be offered to anyone in the community on a noncredit basis. A small fee is charged for participation in the courses. The noncredit courses office handles all matters, including registration of students, cancellations, inquiries from students or potential students, and payments.

The office operates as follows:

The receptionist, Mr. T, processes all incoming mail and all telephone calls. The incoming mail can include registrations, cancellations, inquiries, or payments. Registrations, cancellations, and inquiries can also come over the telephone. Mr. T routes all inquiries, registrations, and cancellations to the noncredit courses coordinator, Ms. Spock. Ms. Spock answers all inquiries. Registrations are recorded on a blue registration form (in duplicate) that can be mailed in by a student or filled in by Mr. T when a student enrolls by telephone. The blue forms are passed on to Ms. Spock. Ms. Spock keeps one copy of these forms in a file, sorted by course (the Course File). She also checks to see if the student has a record in the Student File. If not, they are added to the Student File. In addition, Ms. Spock sends the duplicate copy of the blue form to the accounting office. Accounting produces an invoice from the blue form and sends the invoice back to Mr. T, who mails the invoice to the student along with further information about the course. A copy of the invoice is sent to Ms. Spock, who files it in an Invoice File. When Ms. Spock receives a cancellation, she pulls the blue enrollment slip from the Course File and the invoice from the Invoice File, and fills out a cancellation form in duplicate. The cancellation form and the invoice are sent to accounting. Accounting credits the student's account using one copy of the cancellation form. The other copy goes to Mr. T, who sends it to the student. Payments come in to Mr. T, who pulls the student's invoice from the file and sends the payment and the invoice to accounting. Accounting credits the student and makes out a receipt. The receipt is given to Mr. T to be mailed to the student.

(As a useful exercise, you should try drawing up the data-flow diagram describing the current physical system of the noncredit courses office on your own before reading any further.)

Figure 2.5 is the data-flow diagram for the current physical system in the noncredit courses office. Notice that Mr. T, Ms. Spock, students, and the accounting office are represented as activity rectangles in the data-flow diagram. In the current physical system, they represent centers of activity. They initiate actions; transform, retrieve, or store data; or make decisions. All the information that flows among these activities is also shown in the diagram. In some cases the infor-

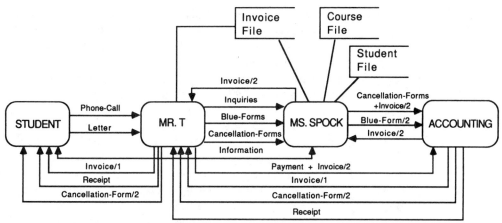

Figure 2.5 Data-flow Diagram of the Current Physical System of the Non-credit Courses Office

mation has a physical manifestation, such as the blue registration forms or the receipts. In other cases, such as the phone calls and inquiries, the information may be intangible. Nonetheless, its flow should be shown in the diagram.

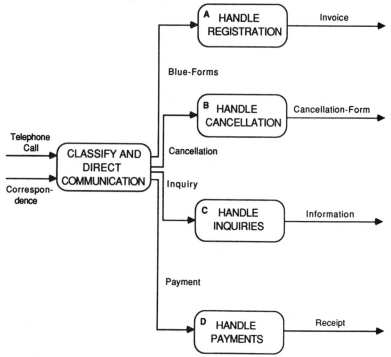

Figure 2.6 High-level Data-flow Diagram of the Current Logical System of the Noncredit Courses Office

After the current physical system has been diagrammed and checked with the sponsor, a diagram of the current logical system is created. It is at this point that the process of abstraction comes into play. The analyst should study the diagram of the current physical system carefully and look for "themes" or clusters of activities that can be abstracted. As much as possible, the flow of information should be analyzed separately from the activities to look for patterns of flow that relate to these abstract themes. In the noncredit courses office, for example, the data flow contains four distinct themes: inquiries, registrations, cancellations, and payment. The current logical system data-flow diagrams should be built around these four abstractions. Figure 2.6 is the high-level data-flow diagram for the current logical system. Figures 2.7a, b, and c show the three lower-level data-flow diagrams representing three of the activities shown in Figure 2.6. (Because the functions performed in HANDLE INQUIRIES are fairly simple, it needs no further refinements.) Notice that Mr. T and Ms. Spock are no longer represented in the data-flow diagrams. The point of creating the current logical system data-flow diagrams is to obtain a more abstract view of the functions and activities within the system, independent of the people, software, or machines that perform the functions. With a clear understanding of the functions and activities that the current system includes, the analyst is in a better position to understand the problems

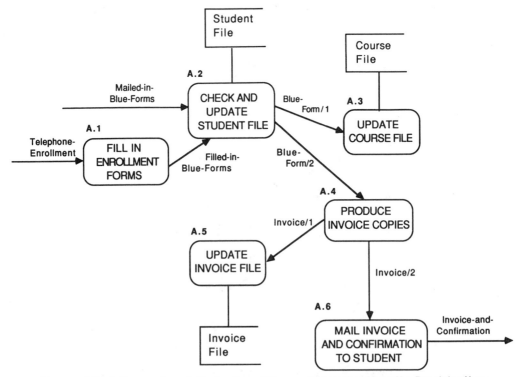

Figure 2.7(a) Lower Level Data-flow Diagram for the Handle Registration Activity Shown in Figure 2.6

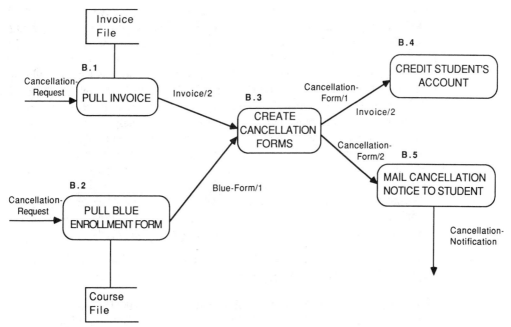

Figure 2.7(b) Data-flow Diagram for the Handle Cancellation Activity Shown in Figure 2.6

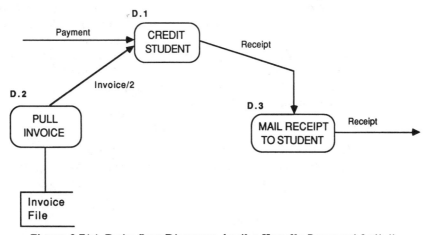

Figure 2.7(c) Data-flow Diagram for the Handle Payment Activity Shown in Figure 2.6

with the current system and to see the relationship of the old system to the new system that the sponsor desires.

Another feature of data-flow diagrams, which is evident in the diagrams in Figure 2.7, is the lack of a rigid time line. In general, the flow of activities and the order in which they logically must proceed is from left to right across the diagrams. However, whenever two or more activities are logically independent, this should be indicated in the diagrams. Notice, for example, the two activities PULL INVOICE and PULL BLUE ENROLLMENT FORM in Figure 2.7b. Although PULL INVOICE is shown above the other activity, it need not be performed before PULL BLUE ENROLLMENT FORM. The activities are independent, and it does not matter which is performed first. Likewise, it does not matter whether CREDIT STUDENT'S ACCOUNT or MAIL CANCELLATION NOTICE TO STUDENT is performed first. If a computer were performing these activities, one activity would have to precede the other. However, the analyst is *not* the designer or the programmer. This is an important point to keep in mind. The analyst's job is to simply describe the functions performed in current and proposed systems, not to decide the order in which they are to be executed. Data-flow diagrams are *not* flowcharts.

The noncredit courses office example will not be carried further. However, if the office were being automated, the next step would be to create data-flow diagrams of the proposed logical system and the proposed physical system.

2.3 Creating the Data Dictionary

The second major component of the structured analysis model of the system is the *data dictionary*. The data dictionary contains formal definitions of all the data items shown in the data-flow diagrams. It is used to provide precise detail concerning the data entities.

The general format of a data dictionary is similar to a standard dictionary; it contains an alphabetically ordered list of entries. In a data dictionary, each entry consists of a formal definition and verbal description. The verbal description is simply a sentence or two describing what the data element is. The formal description provides detail concerning the syntax and composition of the data element. A mathematical sort of notation is used to force the author to provide detail. The general format of the formal description is:

> data-element-name = expression

If the data element name consists of several words, the words should be joined by hyphens in the data dictionary entry. Expressions are composed of strings of data elements and operators. The vocabulary of operators and their meaning is:

+ A plus sign indicates one element is followed by or concatenated with another element.

| A vertical line stands for "or" and is used to indicate alternatives.

' ' Single quote marks are used to surround and indicate literals.

[ ] Square brackets are used to enclose one or more optional elements.

{ } Curly braces indicate that the element being defined is made up of a series of repetitions of the element(s) enclosed in the brackets.

$\{\}_x$ A lower limit on the number of allowable repetitions can be indicated by including an integer subscript on the right bracket. Here x represents an integer and indicates that the number of repetitions cannot be lower than x.

$\}^y$ The upper limit on the number of allowable repetitions can be indicated by including an integer superscript on the right bracket. Here y represents an integer and indicates that the number of repetitions cannot be greater than y.

$\}_x^y$ Both the upper and lower limits on the number of repetitions can be indicated. A fixed number of repetitions can be indicated by setting the superscript and subscript at the same value.

In the data dictionary, higher-level elements (those actually appearing in the data-flow diagram) may be defined in terms of lower-level elements. At the lowest level, elements are described as a set of literals or in some unambiguous base terms.

As an example, assume a data-flow diagram for a magazine subscription system included a data element, Payment, that is input into some activity in the system. Payment might be defined in the data dictionary as follows:

Payment = '$' + dollar-amount + '.' + cents-amount

Notice that Payment will consist of a literal character, $, followed by some dollar amount, followed by a character decimal point, followed by some cents amount. The terms dollar-amount and cents-amount must now be defined. Assume the sponsor states that no payment amount will ever exceed $9999.99 and that it is possible that payments of less than a dollar might be received. The data dictionary definitions might read as follows:

dollar-amount = $\{$digit$\}_0^4$
cents-amount = digit + digit

The first definition states that dollar-amount will be expressed as a series of digits and that the series can contain anywhere from zero to four digits. The definition of cents-amount makes it clear that exactly two integers are needed to specify a cents amount. The term digit probably does not need to be defined. If a definition were needed, however, it might look like this:

digit = 0|1|2|3|4|5|6|7|8|9

As a useful convention, the first letter of the term Payment is capitalized to signify that it actually appears in the data-flow diagram. Because the terms dollar-amount and cents-amount are used in defining Payment and do not appear in a data-flow diagram, they are written using lowercase letters.

Remember that the data dictionary entries include not only the formal definition created using the technique just described, but a verbal description as well. Thus, the complete entry for Payment and its associated terms might read as follows:

Payment = '$' + dollar-amount + '.' + cents-amount
        Payment is the income received from subscribers. It is
        entered as dollars and cents.
dollar-amount = $\{$digit$\}_0^4$
        Dollar amounts may range from 0 to 9999, inclusive.
cents-amount = digit + digit
        Cents amounts may range from 00 to 99, inclusive.

This example shows the definition of a familiar type of data element, dollars and cents. Formal data dictionary entries can easily be created for more unusual sorts of data elements as well. For example, a magazine subscription system might contain category-type information, as follows:

```
Transaction = Renewal | New-Subscription | Cancellation
Payment-Method = cash | check | money-order | charge-card
```

Furthermore, details concerning input or output formats can be specified in the data dictionary. Suppose the subscription system will print a monthly report of new subscribers. In the data-flow diagram, one activity is shown that produces a data element as output, New-Subscribers-Report. In the data dictionary, the format of the report could be defined as follows:

```
New-Subscribers-Report = report-header + new-subscriber-list
                         + report-summary
report-header = report-title + current-date
report-title = 'Monthly Report of New Subscribers'
new-subscriber-list = {subscriber-name + subscriber-address}
report-summary = 'The total number of new subscribers:' +
                 Number-of-new-subscribers
```

Any non-terminal terms used in these definitions must be defined elsewhere in the data dictionary.

2.4 Activity Specifications Complete the Model

To complete a model of the system, descriptions of the *basic activities* shown in the data-flow diagrams must be provided. *Basic activities* are those activities for which no lower-level data-flow diagrams exist. For each basic activity, an *activity specification* is created that describes exactly what functions are being performed by the activity and what decisions or classifications are made by the activity. Several different techniques can be used for creating activity specifications. Three will be discussed here: *prose, pseudocode,* and *decision tables*.

One approach to writing activity specifications is to write a paragraph or two of *prose* (English sentences) for each activity in the data-flow diagram describing the functions of the activity in detail. The advantage of using prose is that there is no new technique to be learned to begin using prose. Another advantage is that the activity specifications can be created using a word-processing system. However, prose can be a poor way of communicating the sort of information that often must be included in a specification. Consider, for example, how difficult it would be to read recipes if they were written in strict prose style, as paragraphs. Recipes include combinations of different sorts of information: lists of ingredients, descriptions of operations to be performed ("Pour into greased muffin tins") and decisions to be made ("Beat butter and sugar until fluffy"). Styles for writing recipes have evolved that are much better for communicating these sorts of information than prose. Activity specifications must include similar sorts of information: lists of data elements involved, descriptions of operations to be performed, and decisions to be made. A representational scheme that helps to organize the information visually as well as verbally is usually more successful than a purely verbal scheme.

2.4.1 Using Pseudocode for Activity Specifications

Another method for creating activity specifications is to use structured pseudocode. As the name implies, *pseudocode* is "fake code"; it is like a programming language, but lacks the strict formality. Pseudocode is less formal than a programming language and closer to English prose. In using structured pseudocode, the analyst has a limited vocabulary of actions and decision structures available to describe the activity. Although this may sound like a disadvantage, it is not. On the contrary, it is the primary advantage of using pseudocode. All activities must be broken down into a set of subactivities that can be stated in the pseudocode vocabulary. This forces the analyst to think through the details of the activity and to state them in a standard form. The pseudocode used should be structured; that is, the activities should be specified in a hierarchical, nested format.

One disadvantage of pseudocode is that there is no widely accepted set of standards. If no standards are followed, different analysts are free to produce their own versions of pseudocode. This causes misunderstandings when the activity specifications are used by the designers or reviewed by the sponsor. Which version of pseudocode is used is not important as long as a standard is agreed upon and as long as the pseudocode uses structured program constructs.

One set of standards will be presented here. They may be modified to cover your own particular needs. The vocabulary of structured pseudocode is built around the three basic processes of any structured language: *sequence, decision,* and *iteration*.

Sequence. In the sequence process, one action is followed by another. Sequence is represented in pseudocode as successive lines of text, each line representing one action:

```
action1
action2
```

For example,

```
Compute Total-Sales
Compute Sales-Tax
Add Sales-Tax to Total-Sales to compute Total-Bill
```

Decision. Decisions can be embodied as *if-then, if-then-else,* or *case* pseudocode statements. In any decision some condition is tested, and then one of one or more alternative actions is performed, depending on the condition state. In a pseudocode *if-then,* the condition is stated in the first line of the decision block. The action or actions to be performed if the condition is true are stated below the condition, indented to the right several spaces. The end of the decision block is marked by an *end-if* line, which is not indented:

```
if condition then
    action
end-if
```

For example,

```
if Payment less than Amount-Owed then
    calculate Amount-Overdue
    calculate Late-Payment-Fee
end-if
```

An *if-then-else* construct includes two action parts, one to be performed if the condition is true and a second to be performed if the condition tested is false. Each action part is indented, and the entire decision block is followed by an *end-if* line:

```
if condition then
    action1
else
    action2
end-if
```

For example,

```
if NumberOfScores <= 0 then
    print "No scores were entered."
else
    Mean ← SumsOfScores/NumberOfScores
    print Mean
end-if
```

The last pseudocode decision structure is a *case* statement. The first line of a pseudocode case construct identifies the item being tested, the selector. Then each possible condition or value of the selector is listed below and indented, with its associated actions. An *end-case* marks the end of the case block:

```
case selector of
    condition1: action1
    condition2: action2
    condition3: action3
end case
```

For example,

```
case Subscriber-Type of
        Lifetime:    RenewalNotice ← false
        OneYear:   RenewalNotice ← true
                     DiscountOffer ← 10%
        ThreeYear: RenewalNotice ← true
                     DiscountOffer ← 20%
end case
```

Iteration. There are two different iteration constructs: *while-do* and *repeat-until*. In the *while-do* construct, the first line contains the condition to be tested at the beginning of each iteration through the action portion of the block. The action or actions to be executed are indented below the first line, and the end of the block is marked with an *end-while* line:

```
while condition do
        action
end-while
```

For example,

```
while there are more Scores do
        SumOfScores ← SumOfScores + Score
        Increment NumberOfScores
        read next Score
end-while
```

In the *repeat-until* construct, the keyword *repeat* appears at the beginning of the repeat-until block to mark the start of the block. The actions are listed and indented below the *repeat* line. The last line in the block contains the condition to be tested to determine if the actions within the iteration block should be repeated:

```
repeat
        action
until condition
```

For example,

```
repeat
        read User-Password
        if User-Password is not valid then
                print Invalid-Password-Message
                add 1 to NumberOfTries
        end-if
until User-Password is valid or NumberOfTries = 3
```

Note that, in this last example, the structure being illustrated, the *repeat-until* structure, contained a structure described earlier, an *if-then*. It is perfectly permissible, and in fact necessary, that the structures described be nested in this manner. Whenever an action part is indicated in the structure, another structure of the same or of a different sort may be inserted. The action part of the inserted structure may likewise be expanded with another structure, and so on.

2.4.2 Using Decision Tables for Activity Specifications

Decision tables are a useful tool in describing the basic activities in data-flow diagrams that involve relating different processes to a variety of different conditions (Hurley, 1983). *Decision tables* provide a method for systematically noting all the different variables that affect a decision, all the values these variables can take on, and all the rules that apply in the different cases. Furthermore, by organizing the information provided by the sponsor into a decision table, any gaps or inconsistencies in the sponsor's specifications become apparent and can be corrected.

Consider a simple decision that might be involved in a billing system. When the monthly bills are processed, it is noted whether each customer has made a payment. The payment may or may not equal what is owed. Or perhaps a customer owed money, but made no payment at all. For a customer that sent in money, a receipt must be sent. For a customer who owes money, a bill must be sent. Furthermore, a customer not owing money is to receive a special preferred-customer sales flyer. In other words, a decision must be made concerning what action or actions to take (send bill and/or receipt and/or flyer), based on certain conditions (payment amount).

Figure 2.8 shows a decision table that represents the conditions and rules just described. Notice that the table is divided into four quadrants by heavy lines. The two quadrants in the top half of the table represent the conditions that apply. The top left quadrant lists the two variables being examined (Payment and Balance Owed) and the possible values these variables can take on (Made and Not Made for Payment and Yes and No for Balance Owed). The ×'s in the top right quadrant indicate each possible combination of these conditions that can occur. To determine the total number of possible outcomes, multiply the number of values each variable can take on by the number (or numbers) of values each of the other variables involved can take on. In our example, there are two variables and each variable can take on two values. Two times two equals four; there are four possible conditions. If a different case involved three variables, each of which could take on one of two different values, there would be $2 \times 2 \times 2 = 8$ different possible conditions. Notice that each possible condition is represented as a separate column in the right side of the table.

The bottom half of the table represents the alternative actions or results that apply for the given conditions. A description of each action is given in the lower left quadrant, and the O's in the lower right quadrant indicate under what conditions that action is to occur. Notice how straightforward it is to scan down the right-hand columns to see exactly how each customer is to be handled, depending on their payment and balance status.

Payment	Made	X	X		
	Not Made			X	X
Balance Owed	Yes	X		X	
	No		X		X
Send Receipt		O	O		
Send Bill		O		O	
Send Flyer			O		O

Figure 2.8 Decision Table for a Simple Billing System

Let us try a more complex example. Suppose a system is being designed to handle the membership information for a public television station. One basic activity in the data-flow diagram for the proposed logical system is shown in Figure 2.9. The activity is labeled Determine Membership Characteristics. The data flowing into this activity are Amount-of-Contribution and Age-Class, and the output is to be Membership-Characteristics. The sponsor has explained to us that viewers can become members of the public television station by sending in money. If a person is a student or retiree, then only $25 is needed to become a regular member. All others must send in at least $40 to become a member. Anyone contributing $120 or more becomes a Studio Club member. All members receive the monthly television guide publication. As additional incentive, premiums are provided for different levels of contributions. For amounts between $40 and $59, the donor receives a coffee mug. For amounts between $60 and $119, the donor receives an umbrella. And for amounts greater than $119, the donor receives an autographed picture of Big Bird.

The output from the activity, then, is the membership category of the donor, the premium type the donor is to receive, and an indication of whether or not the donor is to receive the publication. There are three member categories (nonmember, member, and Studio Club member), four premium levels (none, mug, umbrella, picture), and two publication categories (yes or no). There are two input variables: Age Class and Amount Contributed. There are two values of the variable Age Class: Regular or Student/Retiree.

Contribution Amount	$0–$24		$25–$39		$40–$59		$60–$119		>$119	
Age Class	Reg.	S/R	Reg.	S/R	Reg.	S/R	Reg.	S/R	Reg.	S/R
Nonmember	O	O	O							
Member				O	O	O	O	O		
Studio Club									O	O
No premium	O	O	O	O						
Mug					O	O				
Umbrella							O	O		
Picture									O	O
Publication				O	O	O	O	O	O	O
No Publication	O	O	O							

Figure 2.9 Decision Table for the Determine-Membership-Characteristics Activity

By studying the specifications, it can be seen that five different categories of contribution amount are relevant to the membership characteristics. Amounts in the ranges from $0 to $24, $25 to $39, $40 to $59, $60 to $119, and $120 and up are all significant. Two times five equals ten different possible combinations of input conditions that must be handled. Figure 2.9 shows the decision table that represents these decisions. Examine the table to make sure you understand how it was created.

2.4.3 Comparison of Decision Tables to Pseudocode

As a comparison, Figure 2.10 shows the same Determine Membership activity written up using pseudocode. Which do you prefer? Which seems clearer to you? Decision tables have an advantage in that they make all possible combinations of input conditions obvious. The sponsor can then check over the decision table to make sure all categories will be handled in an appropriate manner. In pseudocode,

```
while there are members in New-Member-File do
    get next record containing Member-Info
    if Age-Class is Regular then
        case Contribution-Amount of
                (1) $1 - $39            Member-Status <- Nonmember
                                        Premium <- None
                                        Publication <- No
                (2) $40 - $59           Member-Status <- Member
                                        Premium <- Mug
                                        Publication <- Yes
                (3) $60 - $119          Member-Status <- Member
                                        Premium <- Umbrella
                                        Publication <- Yes
                (4) > $119              Member-Status <- Studio-Club
                                        Premium <- Picture
                                        Publication <- Yes
        end-case
    else {Age-Class = S/R}
        case Contribution-Amount of
                (1) < $24               Member-Status <- Nonmember
                                        Premium <- None
                                        Publication <- No
                (2) $25 - $39           Member-Status <- Member
                                        Premium <- None
                                        Publication <- Yes
                (3) $40 - $59           Member-Status <- Member
                                        Premium <- Mug
                                        Publication <- Yes
                (4) $60 - $119          Member-Status <- Member
                                        Premium <- Umbrella
                                        Publication <- Yes
                (5) > $119              Member-Status <- Studio-Club
                                        Premium <- Picture
                                        Publication <- Yes
        end-case
    end-if
    if Member-Status = Member then add Member-Info to Member-List
        else if Member-Status = Studio-Club
                then add Member-Info to Studio-Club-Member-List
    if Premium < > None then add Member-Info to Premium-List
    if Publication = Yes then add Member-Info to Publication-List
end while
```

**Figure 2.10 Pseudocode Representation of the Specification
for the Determine-Membership-Characteristics Activity**

it is possible to inadvertently skip some input conditions. However, decision tables are only useful for those basic activities in the data-flow diagrams that involve somewhat complex decisions. Many activities do not, and an alternate technique must be used to describe these activities. Therefore, pseudocode has the additional advantage that it can be used consistently throughout the activity specifications. In addition, empirical studies that have compared pseudocode and decision tables have found that pseudocode is produced faster than decision tables and that it is faster to create source code from pseudocode than from decision tables (Vessey and Weber, 1986). A final advantage of pseudocode over decision tables is that pseudocode can be created and edited on a word processor much more easily than decision tables.

2.5   Nonfunctional Requirements

The model of the proposed system described by the data-flow diagrams, activity specifications, and data dictionary describes the *functional requirements* for the proposed system. Functional requirements are those that relate directly to the functioning or operations of the system. They describe how the system should behave given certain input. *Nonfunctional requirements* are requirements or restrictions posed by the sponsor or the problem that do not relate directly to the functions or operations to be performed by the system. In other words, any important information about the system that cannot conveniently be represented in the model of the system is stated as a nonfunctional requirement. This information includes desired features or characteristics, quality guidelines, and any restrictions that may apply to the system. For example, speed of operation may be an important characteristic to the sponsor. To another sponsor, reliability might be a more important characteristic, and still another may wish to specify that the system be user friendly. Constraints, such as the number of data items a system should be able to handle, or the type of hardware the system will work with, are also nonfunctional requirements that need to be noted and passed on to the designers of the system. Error handling and the handling of extreme or unusual situations should also be covered by the nonfunctional requirements. A list of the kinds of issues to be covered by nonfunctional requirements is given in Figure 2.11.

An important thing to keep in mind when writing the nonfunctional requirements is that they should be written so that they can be empirically verified after the system is created. In other words, the developers must be able to demonstrate that the final version of the system in fact meets or exceeds the sponsor's nonfunctional requirements. For example, the sponsor may include a requirement that the system process each transaction "quickly." When the system is installed, the sponsor may complain that the system does *not* respond quickly and that the developers have not fulfilled their contract. The developers can just as easily argue that the response *is* quick. To avoid arguments and name calling, it makes sense to specify exactly what the sponsor means when he or she says "quickly." Does it mean that responses should be received in less than an hour, or does it mean in 10 seconds or less? If a response time value is written down in the requirements, tests can be run to ascertain if the system meets the requirement. Even more nebulous qualities,

User Interface and Human Factors
- What type of user will be actually using the system?
- Will more than one type of user be using the system?
- What sort of training will be required for each type of user?
- Is it particularly important that the system be easy to learn?
- Is it particularly important that users be protected from making errors?
- What sort of input/output devices for human interface are available, and what are their characteristics?

Documentation
- What sorts of documentation are required?
- What audience is to be addressed by each document?

Hardware Considerations
- What hardware is the proposed system to be used on?
- What are the characteristics of the target hardware, including memory size and auxiliary storage space?

Performance Characteristics
- Are there any speed, throughput, or response time constraints on the system?
- Are there size or capacity constraints on the data to be processed by the system?

Error Handling and Extreme Conditions
- How should the system respond to input errors?
- How should the system respond to extreme conditions?

System Interfacing
- Is input coming from systems outside the proposed system?
- Is output to go to systems outside the proposed system?
- Are there restrictions on the format or medium that must be used for input or output?

Quality Issues
- What are the requirements for reliability?
- Must the system trap faults?
- Is there a maximum acceptable time for restarting the system after a failure?
- What is the acceptable system downtime per 24-hour period?
- Is it important that the system be portable (able to move to different hardware or operating system environments)?

Figure 2.11 List of Nonfunctional Requirements to be Considered During the Creation of Requirements Specification

System Modifications
- What parts of the system are likely candidates for later modification?
- What sorts of modifications are expected?

Physical Environment
- Where is the target equipment to operate?
- Will the target equipment be in one or several locations?
- Will the environmental conditions in any way be out of the ordinary (for example, unusual temperatures, vibrations, magnetic influences, and so on)?

Security Issues
- Must access to any data or the system itself be controlled?
- How often will the system be backed up?
- Who will be responsible for back up?
- Is physical security an issue?

Resources and Management Issues
- What materials, personnel, computer time, and other resources will be required to build, install, and maintain the system?
- What skills or knowledge must the developers have to develop the system?
- What are the proposed intermediate and final deadlines for system development?
- What is the proposed budget for hardware, personnel, and other development costs?
- Who is responsible for system installation?
- Who will be responsible for system maintenance?

Figure 2.11 continued

I. User Interface and Human Factors Considerations
   a. Users will be novices and knowledgeable intermittent users.
   b. It is important that the system be easy to learn and easy to remember, as most usage will be intermittent.
   c. Users should be able to teach themselves to use the system, either with the aid of the user's manual, or by exploration.
   d. To enhance ease of use and increase user satisfaction, user errors should be minimized. Critical errors (e.g., destroying the text file being processed) should be blocked.
   e. A keyboard is the only input device for direct human input. A CRT and tones (beeps) are the available output media.

Figure 2.12 Some Nonfunctional Requirements for the Computerized Concordance System Shown in Figure 2.4

II. Hardware Considerations
    a. The system should be designed to run on an IBM/PC with two internal floppy disk drives, 256K of internal memory and using the DOS 3.1 operating system.
    b. The system software should fit on one 5 1/4 inch double-sided floppy disk capable of holding 400,000 bytes.
    c. The system should be capable of utilizing any standard printer supported by the DOS 3.1 operating system.
    d. The system will be designed for monochrome CRT displays.

III. Performance Characteristics
    a. The system must be able to handle at least 50,000 unique words.
    b. The system should be able to handle up to 35 references to each word.
    c. At least 250 words per minute should be processed by the system.
    d. The system should be capable of making a concordance for text files containing up to 100,000 bytes.

IV. Error Handling and Extreme Conditions
    a. The system should not fail if the capacity of 50,000 words is exceeded. Appropriate messages should be given to the user if this event occurs.
    b. If a word is referenced more than 35 times within a text file, an appropriate message should be given to the user. The first 35 references should be maintained, and the system should not fail.
    c. If the user asks the system to process a text file larger than the system's capacity, the system should provide an appropriate message, and should not fail.
    d. Whenever possible, user input should be checked for validity and appropriate messages should be provided, as well as a chance for the user to reenter the input.

V. System Modifications
    a. The number of words that can be processed and the size of the text file that can be processed are likely areas of later modification.
    b. Later enhancements might include mouse input and a direct manipulation interface.

Figure 2.12 continued

such as "user friendly," can be stated in testable ways. Rather than saying a system should be "easy to learn," the requirements should say something like the following: "The system shall be designed for ease of learning. Sales managers will be able to learn to use the system to produce sales reports with 5 hours or less of training. Clerks will be able to learn to use the system to update the inventory with 10 hours or less of training."

As an example of nonfunctional requirements, Figure 2.12 shows a list of some of the nonfunctional requirements for the computerized concordance system described earlier and shown in Figure 2.4. The requirements should be organized into categories such as user interface and human factors, hardware considerations, error handling and extreme conditions, and the like.

2.6 Feasibility

An important activity during the systems analysis stage is to determine the feasibility of the proposed system. Typically, the sponsor requires the software to run on a particular hardware configuration. Estimates should be made of the projected size of the system and any files to be used by the system. If the system uses much data, it is possible the data will simply not fit on the disks. If the proposed system is very complex, it is possible the software will not fit into the computer's memory. If throughput or response time is an important consideration, estimates based on the hardware's processing speed will have to be made. If hardware is to be purchased specifically to support the new system, these estimates will be necessary in order to determine what hardware should be purchased.

Other resources, such as time, money, and personnel, also have a direct influence on the feasibility of a system. A proposed system might be feasible if the developers were allowed five years and unlimited funds to work on it. However, such a timetable might be completely unacceptable to the sponsor. It might seem that having extra personnel to devote to the development of a system would allow a system to be developed faster, but this is simply not the case. As mentioned in Chapter 1, Brooks has dubbed this problem "the mythical man month." Brooks points out that if a software project was successfully completed in one year with three people involved full time and a total of 36 man-months of effort involved, it is definitely not true that the same project could have been done in six months by six people working full time. The compression of time and the addition of people cause the total required effort (and man-months) to go up dramatically.

Software developers are notoriously inaccurate in predicting system size and development effort. Invariably, they underestimate, usually by large factors. An entire area of software engineering is devoted to software size, effort, and cost estimation. That area is beyond the scope of this book. However, a good approach to use is to look at similar systems that have already been developed and base your estimates on them, taking into account considerations peculiar to the current situations. Then add a generous "fudge factor."

2.7 Requirements Specification Document

The models of the current and proposed systems represented in the data-flow diagrams, the data dictionary, and the activity specifications comprise the major part of the requirements specification document. However, there is important and necessary information that is not readily conveyed by the models. Other components are needed to complete the document. An outline of a typical requirements specification document is shown in Figure 2.13.

1.0 General Goals

2.0 Current System
    2.1 Data-Flow Diagrams of Current Physical System
    2.2 Data-Flow Diagrams of Current Logical System
    2.3 Data Dictionary for Current System
    2.4 Structure of Files in the Current System

3.0 Proposed System
    3.1 Data-Flow Diagrams of the Proposed Logical System
    3.2 Data-Flow Diagrams of the Proposed Physical System
    3.3 Activity Specifications
    3.4 Data Dictionary for the Proposed System
    3.5 Structure of Files in the Proposed System
    3.6 Nonfunctional Requirements
    3.7 Feasibility

4.0 Glossary

5.0 Sponsor Sign-off

Figure 2.13 Outline of the Requirements Specification Document

The first section, General Goals, provides a prose description of the problem to be solved and the proposed solution. It should be written at a general, introductory level so that someone not familiar with the problem can understand the goals of the project. For small systems, a page or two of prose might be sufficient. This section can evolve from the statement of system scope created during the initial stages of analysis.

In the second major section, the present system is modeled using data-flow diagrams of the current physical and logical systems, along with a data dictionary. Activity specifications may not be needed in describing the current system if sufficient detail can be obtained from the diagrams. A description of currently existing files should be included in this section. If the file is a physical one, describe how it is organized, what information is stored in it, and how it is accessed. Any data items that are stored in the file should already have been defined in the data dictionary. This is a good way to check the accuracy of the data-flow diagrams, by the way. Do the diagrams account for the creation of all items in the data file? If not, the diagrams are not complete. If the file is electronic, the composition of each record should be described using data dictionary notation. Record components that already have been defined in the data dictionary need not be defined again in the file structure section, but any new terms must be defined. The description should also indicate other characteristics of the file, such as its length, whether it is modifiable or read only, and any other relevant characteristics. Note that this entire section can be eliminated if there is no current system.

In the third major section, the proposed system is described. Models of the proposed physical and logical systems are presented in data-flow diagrams, along with a data dictionary and activity specifications. In addition, the nonfunctional requirements of the system are included in this section, along with a section exploring the feasibility of the proposed system.

The fourth major section of the requirements specification document is the glossary. A glossary is a dictionary of words and terms, along with their definitions. The glossary in a requirements specification document includes all words, phrases, and abbreviations used in the body of the document that might not be known to the readers of the document. Because the potential readers include people from both the sponsor's organization and the developer's organization, terms that might be unfamiliar to either audience should be defined.

Finally, the requirements specification should include a sponsor sign-off. The sponsor sign-off is the contract between the customer and the developers. In formal situations, the sponsor sign-off might be many pages long and require the advice of lawyers to create. In less formal situations, it is still a good idea to have a sponsor sign-off. The document should simply state that the sponsor certifies that the requirements as stated in the document are complete and final. The developers should agree to produce software that meets these requirements. And both parties should agree that no changes can be made in the requirements without the joint, written approval of both parties. Intermediate or final deadlines should be mutually agreed on. This document protects both parties, but is particularly important to the developer. Many sponsors ask for "minor" changes once a project is underway that, in fact, require a major redesign of the system to incorporate. Not being familiar with the technical aspects of software design and development, they cannot see why one suggested change may be easy to make and another may not be. It is best to make it clear "up front" that *any* change must be approved by both parties, that it may be impossible to make some changes, and that changes cause delays in meeting deadlines.

2.8   Evaluating the Requirements Specification

An extremely important activity during each stage in the software development life cycle is to critically evaluate the products being produced. Not only should the finished products be reviewed, but partially completed work should be evaluated as well. Evaluation serves multiple purposes. One important function it serves is as a means of assessing and measuring the progress that is being made. Is the project ahead of or behind schedule? Are there any indications that the project is easier or harder than initially thought? Another important function of the evaluation activity is to assess the quality of the work that has been carried out. Does the work at least meet or perhaps exceed the standards set down by the management? What additional work needs to be done to correct any flaws in the work being evaluated?

Evaluation is particularly important in the early stages of the software life cycle. As mentioned in Chapter 1, studies have shown that errors resulting from problems with the requirements specification occur frequently (Jones, 1978; Basili and Perrone, 1984; Yeh, 1984) and are the most expensive errors to correct in a completed system (Boehm, 1981). To keep the cost of software development down, errors in the requirements specification must be eliminated or reduced. In the early phases of the software development cycle, the primary technique available for evaluation is a *review*. A *review* is simply an evaluation of technical material by a group of people working together. The goal of a review is to obtain accurate information concerning the status and/or quality of the technical material. Reviews may be *formal* or *informal*. A review is *formal* if a written report of the findings is made and if the participants must take responsibility for the results. A review is *informal* if it simply involves a sharing of opinions among the participants. While informal reviews are helpful during the analysis stage, a formal review of the requirements specification document is bettter.

2.8.1 Conducting a Formal Review

A formal review is essentially a test. For any test to be successful, the testor must clearly understand what it is he or she is testing for, what the expected results are, and how the test will be conducted. Before discussing the criteria that should be used in evaluating the requirements specification, let us look at how to conduct formal reviews.

Two different formats are typically used in conducting a formal review: *structured walk-throughs* and *inspections*. In *structured walk-throughs,* the material being examined is presented by a reviewee to a team of reviewers (Freedman and Weinberg, 1982; Yourdon, 1978). The reviewee "walks" the reviewers through the material, and the reviewers make comments on issues of concern. The term structured means "organized" in this case and is used to indicate that the walk-through technique is being applied in a formal review process. Although structured walk-throughs were originally developed as a means of reviewing detailed designs, the format has proved effective at other stages in the development life cycle. The number of people involved in a walk-through varies and typically includes from three to six people. However many people are involved, the following roles need to be assumed:

- A moderator who presides over the session and keeps the session on track. The moderator should enforce the ground rules for the session, focus the direction of the session, and curtail any prolonged discussions or arguments.

- A secretary who keeps records of the comments and decisions. Brief notes are sufficient, as walk-throughs are intended only to point out areas that need work and are not intended to provide detailed solutions to problems.

- A reviewee, who presents the work to be reviewed.

- A person who reviews the work from the point of view of the maintainer/ modifier. Her or his concerns are for the future. How easy will it be to maintain or modify the product?
- A person who checks the work against the organization's standards. Does the work meet the quality standards, documentation standards, feasibility standards, and the like, of the organization?
- A person who takes the point of view of the potential user of the system.

A significant amount of work must be done before a walk-through is conducted. The participants must be selected, informed of their role or roles in the session, and informed of the time, date, and place. The participants must receive copies of the materials for review sufficiently far in advance to have time to review them. The choice of the appropriate amount of material for review is important. If there is too much material, the reviewers will have difficulty finding the time and the motivation to do a good job of reviewing. Furthermore, the review session itself will be long and unpleasant, as error after error is uncovered and the time goes on and on. Five to ten pages of written specifications are a suggested amount. The participants should be able to preview the material in approximately one hour, making notes as they go. When walk-throughs are used for code review, 50 to 100 lines of code are the suggested amount of material to be reviewed. One to three pages of material are suggested for design walk-throughs.

During the walk-through session, the major activity is the presentation of the material by the reviewee. The reviewee walks the participants through the material in a systematic way while the participants offer suggestions and criticisms. Minor errors, such as typing or spelling errors, should not be discussed, but should be handled by having the participants give the reviewee edited and annotated copies of the material. As errors are disclosed during the session, a note should be made, but no attempt should be made to solve the problem. It is the reviewee's job to correct the problem following the meeting and inform the reviewers later of actions taken. Note that the errors discussed in the session should have been discovered prior to the session by the reviewers. The purpose of the walk-through is not to discover errors, but to identify and record them.

Walk-through sessions should be held in an open, nondefensive atmosphere. To help maintain such an atmosphere, higher-level managers are typically not included in a walk-through. A walk-through should not be a vehicle for evaluating the employee who is the reviewee, but should focus on the materials being reviewed. It is important that the reviewers focus their comments on the materials, and not on the reviewee. It would be a poor idea to say "You made a mistake when you . . . ." A better approach would be to say "I think there may be a problem in . . . ." Each reviewer should remember that his or her turn may come soon and should treat the reviewee as he or she would like to be treated. Setting a time limit of no more than two hours for the session helps to define the scope of material to be covered and keeps members motivated.

The secretary of the session should make copies of the list of suggestions generated during the walk-through and distribute them to all participants. Each participant can check to make sure the list is complete. The reviewee should act on the suggestions, possibly after consultation with the reviewers or other colleagues. In some cases, a written report of the actions taken may be required. If the errors were sufficiently serious, a second walk-through of the revised material may be necessary. To create a better work atmosphere, it is a good idea to assign responsibility for any errors discovered following the walk-through to the entire review team rather than to the reviewee.

An *inspection* is another form of review (Fagan, 1979; 1986). The main difference between an inspection and a walk-through is that inspections follow a strict format and comprise a formal part of the evaluation of the software product. Walk-throughs, on the other hand, can vary in formality from a casual peer review to a formal milestone. Like structured walk-throughs, inspections require planning. One important aspect is to decide who should attend. In an industrial setting, participants might include members of the planning and analysis team, management representatives not directly involved in the project, a quality assurance representative, and one or more sponsor representatives. Depending on the size of the project, a total of three to four to ten or so people may be included. Some of the reviewers should be trained in review techniques. One person should be in charge of scheduling and setting up the review. A moderator for the review should be selected, as well as a secretary to record the decisions made and to produce a report of the review. The participants must be prepared for the inspection by being aware of the purpose and format of the review and having received and studied the necessary information. They should understand the criteria the work is to meet in order for the review to be completed. If possible, a checklist of inspection items is used. Such checklists are available commercially or can be developed in-house. The advantage of using a checklist is that it provides structure for the review, provides a means of recording the results, ensures systematic and thorough coverage, and provides historical perspective for future projects. An example of a such a checklist, developed by Hetzel (1988), is shown in Figure 2.14. The example is used to assess the quality assurance activities of an organization. The portion shown in the figure deals with requirements. The moderator should be in charge of organizing, conducting, and reporting on the inspection session. In follow-up, the moderator or possibly the entire inspection team assures that all fixes are effective and that no secondary defects have been introduced.

2.8.2 Criteria for Requirements Specification

Fairley (1985) lists eight properties that the requirements specification should possess. Requirements specifications should be:

- Correct
- Complete
- Consistent
- Unambiguous
- Functional

Quality Measurement Diagnostic Checklist - Requirements

Select a recently completed (or nearly completed) major project and grade each question as either a Yes, Mostly Yes, Mostly No, or No.

Definition	Y	MY	MN	N
1. Was a requirements document produced?	—	—	—	—
2. Was a definition of "success" included?	—	—	—	—
3. Was a definition of "failure" included?	—	—	—	—
4. Were the requirements at a high enough level?	—	—	—	—
5. Were the requirements at a low enough level?	—	—	—	—
6. Were the requirements clearly structured?	—	—	—	—
7. Was there an index?	—	—	—	—
8. Were quality requirements included?	—	—	—	—
9. Was feasibility clearly established?	—	—	—	—
10. Was an effective change mechanism set up?	—	—	—	—
11. Was the change mechanism effectively used?	—	—	—	—
Total	—	—	—	—

Completeness				
1. Were the requirements reviewed for completeness?	—	—	—	—
2. Were they reviewed by the right people?	—	—	—	—
3. Did they turn out to be complete?	—	—	—	—
Total	—	—	—	—

Simplicity and Understandability				
1. Were the requirements understandable?	—	—	—	—
2. Was the test included with the requirement?	—	—	—	—
3. Were the requirements reviewed for simplicity?	—	—	—	—
4. Was overcomplexity avoided?	—	—	—	—
5. Did the requirements overly specify the design?	—	—	—	—
Total	—	—	—	—
Grand Total	—	—	—	—

Figure 2.14 Example of a Checklist That Might Be Used in Evaluating Requirements (Adapted with permission from W. Hetzel, *The Complete Guide to Software Testing*. Wellesley, MA: QED Information Sciences, Inc., 1988.)

- Verifiable
- Traceable
- Easily changed

Let us look at these properties more closely.

Correctness and completeness. A correct, complete set of requirements is one that correctly and completely states the desires and needs of the sponsor. If the requirements are incorrect, the software may meet the requirements as stated, but will not do what the sponsor wants it to do. If the requirements are incomplete, the software may do only part of what the sponsor hoped it would do.

Consistent. Consistency is obtained if the requirements do not contradict each other. Inconsistency results when one requirement contradicts another.

Unambiguous. If a requirement is subject to more than one interpretation, it is ambiguous. Requirements should be stated simply and completely so that they are unambiguous.

Functional. Requirements should state what the sponsor desires — the functions and activities to be performed by the system. They should not state how the problem is to be solved or what techniques are to be used. Such decisions should be left to the system designers.

Verifiable. The requirements must be verifiable in two ways: do the requirements satisfy the sponsor's needs, and does the system satisfy the requirements? In the first case, the requirements must be compared to the sponsor's desires and needs. Do the requirements correctly and completely specify the sponsor's desires and needs? In the second case, once the system has been developed, it must be compared to the requirements. Does the system meet the requirements as they are stated?

Traceable and easily changed. The requirements should be organized and written in a segmented, top-down manner that allows for easy use (traceability) and easy modification. A numbering system is useful to label the paragraphs and parts of the manual for cross-referencing, indexing, and easy modification.

Assessing these qualities is not an easy task. Little progress has been made in the formalization and automation of the analysis process. This is not surprising, given the nature of the task. Prototyping is one approach that can be used to evaluate and reformulate requirements. Prototyping seems to be most useful in those situations where the requirements cannot be completely stated from the beginning. By creating a prototype, the sponsor can refine the requirements and zero in on the type of system desired. The best tool currently available for assessing requirements and specifications is the formal review, combined with rigorous, logical thinking on the part of the reviewers. Several techniques can be used to make the review process more productive. These techniques are based on the crucial guideline stated in Section 2.1 that requirements should be testable (verifiable). A reliable way to assure that the requirements are testable is to write the test cases along with the requirements. A *requirements validation matrix* can be used to organize the test cases and requirements. The matrix includes each requirement in one column, with its associated test cases in another column. A simple example based on the noncredit courses office example is shown in Figure 2.15. The matrix shows that test cases 18, 35, and 103 must be successfully completed before we can be assured that requirement 1 has been met. Notice that test cases 35 and 103 are also used to test other requirements. Contrary to what might be initially expected, it is not necessary to come up with a unique test for each requirement. Most test cases will test part of several requirements, although several different tests are usually needed to completely cover each requirement.

The use of a requirements validation matrix is an excellent way to ensure that the requirements specification meets the desired qualities of the system. It has a serious drawback, however, which makes it difficult to use in a college course on software development involving a project component. The drawback is that the developers must have the time and knowledge to create the test cases as soon as a draft of the requirements specification is available. Typically, the design of the project must be undertaken early in the term, and the topic of testing must be postponed. Testing is not covered in this book until Chapter 7. Nonetheless, using the criteria of testability when writing and reviewing the requirements is important.

Indexing and organizing the requirements is another technique that aids the testing of the requirements. When the requirements are organized by function, it is easier to check that all the functions have been included and if redundant or inconsistent functions exist. Organization may also bring out the structure of the problem and highlight new, simpler approaches or omissions. Decision tables are another good way to make the requirements more organized and testable. By carefully checking decision tables, completeness is also assessed.

REQUIREMENT	TEST CASES
1. Provide the capability to cancel only one class out of several a student is registered for	18, 35, 103
2. Provide a listing, by class, of the current enrollment	52-61, 103
3. Generate an invoice copy when a cancellation is processed	35, 83-87

Figure 2.15 Portion of a Requirements Validation Table That Might Be Used to Assess the Verifiability of Requirements

Boehm (1984) suggests the following techniques in addition to reviews and the use of checklists:

Reading. Having someone other than the author or authors read the specification. Another person often has a different point of view, and can pick up misconceptions or faulty logic that the authors may have missed.

Manual or automated cross referencing. Cross referencing is used to verify details of the specification. For example, cross referencing can make sure all data items in the specification are defined in the data dictionary, that all data that flow into or out of an activity specification at a high level also flow into or out of the lower-level activities, that all activities in the data-flow diagrams are defined in an activity specification, and so on. Automated cross referencing is discussed in more detail in Chapter 8.

Interviews. Discuss the specification with the sponsor.

Simple or detailed scenarios. Prototypes created on paper or machine are an effective means of evaluating specifications.

2.9 Case Study: Rev-Pro — A Management/Pricing Tool for Arts Administrators

In learning about any new technique or concept, it is easiest if you start with simple, small examples and progress to more complex examples. The principles that apply to these smaller examples apply equally well to larger examples, but a higher level of complexity is involved. In this text, the examples used in the body of the chapters to illustrate various ideas are typically small examples. However, it is useful to see the techniques applied to larger, more complex examples. With this idea in mind, each chapter will include a case study section. The case study that is discussed is an actual project carried out by a group of six students in a software engineering class. The processes that the students went through and examples from the documents they produced will be presented and briefly discussed. More extensive excerpts from some of the documents are presented in Appendix A.

As you progress through the case study sections in each chapter, compare the case study to the project you are working on. While the case study can serve as guide for your project, remember that each project has its own particular characteristics and problems to be solved. It is suggested that you review the section entitled "Checklist of Project Activities" for the chapter before or while reading the case study, as the case study discussion follows the progression given in the checklist.

2.9.1   The Problem

When you enjoy a concert or performance of some type, you probably do not stop to think about everything that goes into putting on that performance. For example, a great amount of organization and management is needed. In the majority of cases, an artistic performance is a business venture and requires business management as well as other sorts of management. It is the job of arts administrators to handle the business-management side of artistic performances.

The case study to be described here involved the development of a software package to aid an arts administrator in handling budget considerations related to concert series ticket sales. The underlying problem is the same one faced by every business concern and can be briefly stated as: "My costs are X-dollars. If I can generate Y-dollars in revenue by selling N widgets, then my profit will be Y-minus-X dollars." An important facet of this problem is that different pricing strategies can affect sales. For example, pricing the widgets too high might reduce sales and result in lower profits. On the other hand, setting the price too low may result in increased demand, but the revenues will not cover the costs. Ideally, the entrepreneur should set up various "what-if" scenarios and pick the right pricing strategy to make a reasonable profit.

The sponsor of the case study project worked in a university environment and was concerned that concert series be self-supporting, but not profit-making. Thus, the goal in this particular case was to obtain "breakeven"—an even balance between costs and revenues. The sponsor wanted a system to help him make informed guesses about how tickets should be priced and how many tickets needed to be sold to obtain breakeven. The user wanted to be able to enter different ticket-pricing strategies and different estimates of ticket sales and see how they worked together to produce breakeven.

Here is the problem restated in somewhat more detail. To calculate the breakeven point for a concert series, two primary pieces of information are needed: total costs and total estimated revenue. Calculating the total costs is straightforward and simply involves totaling a series of cost amounts. In the university setting, total estimated revenue comes from two sources: estimated revenue from the sales of tickets and income from other sources (nonticket revenues such as grants, subsidies, and donations). Calculating nonticket revenues simply involves totaling up the amounts from each of the various sources. Calculating the estimated revenue from the sales of tickets is more complex.

To calculate the estimated revenue from ticket sales, the administrator must first do what is called "scaling the hall." Scaling the hall involves dividing up the theater seats into different price categories and assigning single-ticket prices to these seats. For example, the front-row seats might be priced higher than the rear seats, and seats in the balcony might be the cheapest of all. Next, the administrator figures out the pricing for a series. In a series, a subscriber gets tickets for all the events in the series (a full subscription) or for a subset of the events in a series (a minisubscription). Different levels of discounts apply on the series tickets. For example, an adult full-series subscription might involve a discount of 20 percent off of the single ticket price, while a student full-series subscription might involve a discount of 50 percent. Lower discounts might apply for minisubscriptions. Putting the discount pricing levels together with the price categories produces "pricing grids." Pricing grids are two-dimensional tables that show the price of tickets at each discount level and for each price category. For example, the table could be used to find the price a student would pay for a full-series subscription with a seat in the balcony section, or the price an adult would pay for a full-series subscription with a seat in one of the front rows. A different pricing grid table would be used to find miniseries' prices.

In the next step, the administrator estimates the demand for each discount level and each pricing level. In other words, an estimate of the expected ticket sales is made for each cell of the pricing grids. By multiplying the estimates times the prices and totaling all of these products, the total estimated ticket revenues can be calculated. The total of estimated ticket revenues is added to the nonticket revenues to give the total estimated revenues from all sources. This figure is then compared to the costs to see if breakeven will be achieved.

At the time the project was initiated, the sponsor was making all of these calculations using paper and pencil, a general spreadsheet program on an Apple IIe computer, and a hand calculator. When new data became available or if a mistake was made, the calculations had to be redone. If various "what-if" alternatives were to be considered, each scenario had to be done by hand. The sponsor wanted a software system that collected and integrated all the necessary information, allowing him to quickly update or change some information and see the effects of these changes throughout the system. The target computer was an IBM-PC.

2.9.2 Analysis of the Rev-Pro System

Because the main purpose of the proposed system was to aid the user in making projections of revenue from ticket sales, the system was dubbed "Rev-Pro" — short for "revenue projections." The team of students assigned to the Rev-Pro project had a number of meetings with the sponsor as soon as the project was initiated. The sponsor was to be the user of the system, although the sponsor expected that other arts administrators would find the system useful. The sponsor was able to show the team actual examples of projections he had done before on paper and to explain to them the processes he had gone through. Copies of these documents were obtained and studied by the team and used in creating a statement of system scope. The statement of system scope formed a first draft for the General Goals section of the Requirements and Specification document (see Appendix A, Part 1). The sponsor knew what information belonged together and thus could identify tables of information that might eventually form a single display screen in the final system.

The group chose to use MacWrite and MacDraw or MacPaint as tools in creating their Requirements and Specification document. This choice was based on the availability of these software packages to the students, and the lack of other, possibly more appropriate, tools. The style guidelines for producing the data-flow diagrams, data dictionary, and activity specifications were given by the instructor. Pseudocode was chosen for use in writing the activity specifications.

A high-level model of the current physical system was created. The current physical system involved the administrator, tables and calculations done by hand, and tables and calculations done using a spreadsheet package on an Apple IIe computer. Because the current logical system was exactly what the sponsor wanted for the proposed logical system, only the proposed logical system model was created. Creating this model required a series of drafts. Earlier drafts were reviewed by the sponsor and changes made based on his remarks.

The highest level data-flow diagram for the system is shown in Figure 2.16. Notice that the system consists of five major activities. The TABULATE COSTS activity involves getting the list of cost items and their amounts from the user and calculating the total. The nonticket revenue sources and their amounts are gotten from the user in the TABULATE NONTICKET REVENUES activity, and a total for income is computed. In the SCALE THE HALL activity, the user indicates what price levels are to be used, the price of a single seat at each price level, and how many total seats there are at each price level. In the PRODUCE MASTER

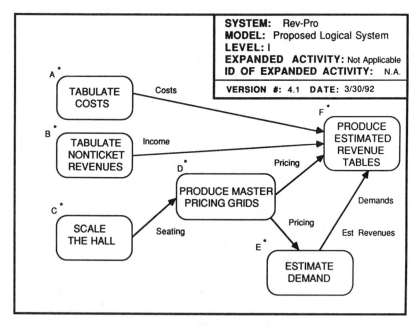

* Indicates additional detail is provided in later figures of the Rev-Pro Case
  Study Requirements and Specification Document excerpts.

**Figure 2.16 Highest Level Data-flow Diagram for the Proposed
Logical System of the Rev-Pro System Case Study**

PRICING GRIDS activity, the user indicates how many different types of series there will be, how many discount levels there will be, and the size of each discount for each level in each series type. Master pricing grids displaying the pricing grid for each type of series are then produced and displayed. The ESTIMATE DEMAND activity solicits and accepts the estimated ticket demand for each discount level at each price level for all series, calculates totals, and displays the estimated revenue for each price level. The last activity, PRODUCE ESTIMATED REVENUE TABLES, combines information obtained by earlier activities to calculate the grand total estimated revenue and the breakeven point.

Appendix A includes most of the data-flow diagrams and activity specifications needed to complete the model of the proposed logical system. In the interests of simplification, some activities are not expanded down to their lowest levels. This was done only when it was felt that the activity was self-evident (e.g., PRINT COST TABLE) or when a similar activity is explained in detail elsewhere. For example, the details of producing a master pricing grid for full-series subscriptions are provided. The details of producing pricing grids for miniseries and group rates are not provided. As you look at the model, you will notice that some of the activities from the highest level data-flow diagram (Figure 2.16) require no lower level diagrams (e.g., SCALE THE HALL) while others may require lower level diagrams (e.g., ESTIMATE DEMAND).

A portion of the data dictionary for the proposed logical system is shown in Figure 2.17. A more complete data dictionary is provided in Appendix A, Part I.

During meetings with the sponsor and while the models of the system were being created, a list of nonfunctional requirements was assembled. These are presented in Appendix A, Part I.

Once a model of the proposed logical system was created, feasibility was assessed. The system was judged to be feasible for a number of reasons. First, the system is basically a small, specialized spreadsheet-type application. There are many such systems already on the market, indicating feasibility. Second, the number of total activities shown across all levels of the data-flow diagrams is 29. Although the implementation of the system was expected to result in more program units (modules) than there are activities in the data-flow diagram, even three times the number (87) would not have been an excessively large number of program modules. Third, the system did not require file handling, so file capacity was not an issue. Finally, the data dictionary provided an estimate of the number of data values that would need to be stored during program execution (approximately 200). This number seemed within reasonable limits.

The requirements were assessed in part through the use of prototypes. Paper versions of the various tables to be displayed by the system were shown to the sponsor. The source of the items shown in the tables — whether direct input from the user or a calculated value — was verified through discussion and by reference to the Proposed Logical System Model. Additional assessment came from a formal review conducted by the entire class and from the instructor.

Data Dictionary

Part I: Data Stores

Income = {Unearned-Income-Category + Unearned-Income-Amount} $_0{}^5$ +

{Earned-Income-Category + Earned-Income-Amount} $_0{}^5$ + Tot-Unearned +

Tot-Earned + Income-Base

A data store that contains all income figures and information.

Costs = {Fixed-Cost-Category + Fixed-Cost-Amount} $_0{}^{10}$ + {Variable-Cost-Category +

Variable-Cost-Amount} $_0{}^{10}$ + Fixed-Costs + Variable-Costs + Total-Costs

A data store that contains all cost figures and information.

Seating = Tot-Seats + Num-Cats + {Num-Seats + Num-Comps + Net-Seats + Single-Price} $_1{}^7$

+ Tot-Num-Comps + Tot-Net-Seats

A data store that contains all seating information for each price category, all general

seating information and the price of single tickets for each price category.

Pricing = Num-Events-Full + Num-Disc-Full + {Disc-Full-Level + Disc-Full-Rate} $_0{}^5$ +

{Full-Single-Disc-Price} $_0{}^{35}$ + Tot-Pot-Rev(no disc) + Tot-Pot-Rev (no disc) +

Avg-Cost/Seat + Avg-Rev/Seat(no disc) + Avg-Rev/Seat(w. avg. disc)

A data store that contains all pricing information and figures.

Demand = {Full-Demand} $_0{}^{35}$ + Tot-Full-Demand

A data store that contains all demand information.

EstRevenue = {Tot-Est-Rev-Full} $_1{}^7$ + Gtot-Est-Rev-Full + Est-Series-Full-Rev

A data store that contains information on overall estimates of revenue based on demand.

**Figure 2.17 A Portion of the Data Dictionary for the Proposed
Logical System of the Rev-Pro Case Study**

Summary

Requirements analysis and specification involves understanding and specifying the problem to be solved and the limits within which it is to be solved. The results of the analysis stage are expressed in the requirements specification document. Because the requirements specification serves as a contract between the developers and the sponsor, it must be readily understandable, be mutually agreeable, precisely state all functions of the proposed system, state all constraints, provide testable criteria, state all desired qualities, and include error and default conditions.

One widely used approach to analysis is the structured analysis method. In this method, models of the current physical, current logical, proposed logical, and proposed physical system are created, as necessary. Each model consists of data-flow diagrams, a data dictionary, and activity specifications. Data-flow diagrams show both activities and the flow of information in the system being modeled. A data dictionary lists and defines all the data elements shown in the data-flow diagrams. Activity specifications are detailed descriptions of the activities in the data-flow diagrams. Activity specifications can be created using pseudocode and/or decision tables.

While the models of the system created using data-flow diagrams, a data dictionary, and activity specifications describe the functional requirements for the proposed system, it is necessary to describe nonfunctional requirements as well. Nonfunctional requirements include desired features or characteristics, quality guidelines, and any restrictions that may apply to the system.

The feasibility of creating the proposed system must be assessed during analysis to ensure that the system will meet hardware, cost, scheduling, and other resource constraints.

The requirements specification document must be formally reviewed before software development proceeds. Two approaches to formal reviews are walk-throughs and inspections. The requirements specification should be evaluated on a number of criteria, including correctness, completeness, consistency, lack of ambiguity, functionality, verifiability, traceability, and ease of change. Other methods of evaluation include reading, cross referencing, interviews, and scenarios.

Checklist of Project Activities

_____   Set up a schedule of analysis activities and assign personnel.

_____   Begin meeting with the sponsor of the project as soon as possible. It is best to have at least two people meet with the sponsor each time. Different people will think of different questions to ask, will take different perspectives on a problem, and will aid in verifying and recollecting what went on in the meetings. (But take notes anyway.)

_____   If possible, set up regular meeting times with the sponsor.

_____   A meeting with a sponsor *is* a meeting. Use the guidelines for a good meeting discussed in Chapter 1. In particular, have specific goals set up for each meeting, and come to each meeting prepared.

_____   Ask the sponsor the five W questions — and the H question. Write down the answers.

_____   Get copies of any forms, data, printouts, and the like that the sponsor uses in the current system.

_____   If the sponsor is not the user of the current system, interview or observe the activities and responsibilities of the people who are.

_____   If the sponsor will not be the user of the proposed system, interview the people who will be. Be sure to assess their knowledge and skill in using computers, and analyze their tasks and responsibilities in the system.

_____ Write down an initial description of the system in the form of a statement of system scope.

_____ Make a list of the objects in the system and identify their type.

_____ Make a list of the operations in the system, and associate each operation with an object.

_____ Decide on a tool or set of tools to be used in creating documentation.

_____ Agree on stylistic guidelines and standards for the data-flow diagrams, a data dictionary, and activity specifications.

_____ If there is a current physical system, create a model of it, including data-flow diagrams, a data dictionary, and activity specifications.

_____ If there is a current logical system, create a model of it.

_____ Verify the current physical and logical system models by having the sponsor and other people from the current system examine and comment on the models.

_____ Create several versions of the proposed logical system and the proposed physical system.

_____ Assess the proposed logical and physical systems by reviews and by seeking comments from the sponsor.

_____ Choose the best logical and physical system models from among those proposed.

_____ Solicit and list nonfunctional requirements. Ask the sponsor to rank order the nonfunctional requirements by desirability.

_____ Assess the nonfunctional requirements by determining if each is verifiable.

_____ Assess the feasibility of the proposed system.

_____ Assemble the requirements specification document.

_____ Assess the complete requirements specification document.

_____ Get the sponsor to sign off on the requirements specification, indicating a contractual agreement between the sponsor and the developers.

Terms and Concepts Introduced

requirements analysis	decision tables
specifications	functional requirements
analysis	nonfunctional requirements
systems analysts	activity specifications
data-flow diagram	abstraction
sequence	decomposition
decision	current physical system
iteration	current logical system
structured analysis	proposed physical system

data abstraction	proposed logical system
basic activities	feasibility
data dictionary	inspection
pseudocode	formal review
walk-through	

Exercises

1. Draw a data-flow diagram describing the activities involved in purchasing a soft drink from a vending machine. Make sure not to force a time sequence onto any of the activities when the sequencing is not strictly necessary.

2. Draw a high-level data-flow diagram of the current physical system of a typical self-service gas station (no repair work done).

3. For the Camp Runamucka system described next, create the following documents:

   (a) One data-flow diagram of the current *physical* system

   (b) Data-flow diagrams (as many as necessary) showing the different levels and parts of the current *logical* system.

   (Do not expect your first attempts to be perfect or neat. It will probably take several trys to get good diagrams.)

   Camp Runamucka is a summer camp for youths. Sessions are one week long, and are offered for eight weeks during the summer. Campers can participate in a variety of activities, such as archery, arts and crafts, boating, and swimming. The camp administrative staff consists of a director, a secretary, a nurse, and an activities coordinator.

   The camp is advertised in magazines. The secretary handles telephone inquiries, mail inquiries, and mails out applications. The applications contain the following information: the camper's name, address, and so on, some preliminary health information, the sessions the camper wishes to attend, and a list of activities the applicant is interested in participating in. Each application must be accompanied by a $50 deposit for each session. The secretary screens each application to make sure all necessary information has been included. If not, the application is returned with a note. The correctly filled out applications are passed on to the director, who creates a bill (in duplicate), files one copy in an invoice file, and has the secretary mail out the other copy. The director also creates sessions rosters. The director passes the applications to the nurse, who creates a file containing the preliminary health information for each camper. The nurse also mails a health form to each camper, to be filled out by the family physician and returned to the camp secretary, who passes them on to the nurse. The returned health forms are then filed along with the preliminary information. The nurse passes the applications to the activities coordinator. The activities coordinator creates lists of participants in each selected activity. In creating these lists, the coordinator refers to the session rosters created by the director and checks the health records of each camper to make sure they are physically able to participate. The activities coordinator passes the applications back to the secretary, who files them in a file of registered campers. When payments are received, the secretary sends a receipt to the camper and gives a copy of the receipt to the director. The director uses it to update the invoice file.

4. Make a decision table to indicate how to dress for the weather. Assume the conditions are that it may or may not be cloudy, and it may or may not be cold. If it is cloudy, the person should take an umbrella. If it is cold, the person should take a coat.

5. Make a decision table describing the algorithm used for determining salary for sales representatives. Some representatives work on a commission basis and others on a noncommission basis. If the sales rep makes sales totaling more than $10,000, he or she is entitled to a 10 percent bonus on the base salary. If the sales representative is on a commission basis, he or she receives a commission of 18 percent.

6. Make a decision table to describe the decisions made for a cooking activity, Cook-It. Cook-It cooks only fruits or vegetables. If it is a fruit, it should be baked. If it is a vegetable, it is boiled. If it is hard, chop it first. If it is not hard and it is yellow, peel it first. If it is hard, yellow, and a vegetable, add salt.

7. Make a decision table for the Toy-Test activity. Toy-Test is an activity designed to test toys in different ways. If the toy is made of plastic, it should be stepped on. If it is made of metal, hit it with a hammer. If it has stickers on it, try to peel them off. If it is metal and painted, scratch the paint with a nail. If it is metal, has wheels, and has stickers, then submerge it in water for one hour.

8. Make a decision table describing customer billing for gas consumption. If the customer is billed using a fixed rate, a minimum monthly charge is assessed for use of less than 100 cubic feet of gas. If consumption is greater than or equal to 100 cubic feet, the schedule A rates are applied. However, if the customer is billed using a variable rate, schedule A rates apply to consumption below 100 cubic feet, and additional consumption is billed using schedule B rates.

9. Create a decision table to assign risk categories and charges to applicants for car insurance. Use the following rules. If the applicant is under 21, apply a surcharge. If the applicant is male and under 26 and married, or male and over 26, assign him to risk category B. If the applicant is a single male under 26 or a female under 21, assign the applicant to risk category C. All other applicants are assigned to risk category A.

10. Write pseudocode descriptions for any or all of the decision activities described in Exercises 4 to 9.

11. Write a pseudocode description of the activities involved in purchasing a soft drink from a vending machine.

12. Write a pseudocode description of the activities involved in balancing a checkbook. Assume the activity starts with a known prior balance, a list of checks that have cleared (sorted by check number), a list of checks that have

been written (sorted by check number), the total amount of all deposits, and the total amount of all banking fees that have been deducted from the account. The goal is to find the current total amount in the account or the deficit amount.

13. Create a data dictionary describing the organization and contents of a personal check.

14. Create a data dictionary describing the organization and contents of the white pages of a telephone directory.

15. For each of the requirements and specification statements listed, indicate if the statement is satisfactory as is, needs some revision, or needs major revision. If the statement needs revision, explain why.

   a. For a computerized concordance system: "The system will process text files with a maximum size of 100 kilobytes."

   b. For a public television membership system: "Contribution amounts will be stored as real numbers."

   c. For a computerized checkbook system: "The user may print out the data on a printer or save the data to a disk file."

   d. For a computerized checkbook system: "It will be easy for the user to correct mistakes."

   e. For a computerized checkbook system: "The system will allow a user to sort checks by check number, by date, by amount, or by payee."

   f. For the television membership system: "The system must produce useful summary reports."

   g. For a computerized concordance system: "The file name will be typed in by the user using all capital letters."

3. Preliminary Design: Designing the User Interface

Any system designed for human use has the same two facets: functional capabilities and a *user interface*. The functional capabilities are the operations that the system is capable of carrying out. The user interface is the access the user has to those capabilities. An analog, wind-up watch, for example, is a system that has basically three functions: keeping time in hours, minutes and seconds, adjusting to a new time, and being wound to keep it running. The user interface for using the timekeeping function is the watch face. The user looks at the position of the hour, minute, and second hands relative to the numbers on the face of the watch. The watch can be wound by rotating the winding stem several times. To adjust the time, the user pulls the winding stem out and twists it until the hour and minute hands are in the correct configuration. The existence of electronic watches makes it clear that there are alternate ways to design systems to carry out these functions. Some electronic watches perform exactly the same functions and have exactly the same user interface as wind-up watches, with the exception of the need to wind the watch. Other electronic watches display the time using digits and use sequences of button presses to set the time. Clearly, both types of watches are successful at their primary function, keeping time. Which user interface is better? You decide after you have read this chapter.

3.1 Preliminary Design Begins with the Design of the User Interface

Once the requirements specification has been completed, the next major phase in the software development cycle is the design phase. The design phase consists of three major activities: the preliminary design of the user interface, the preliminary design of the software structure, and the detailed design.

The preliminary design of software systems involves designing both the user interface and the software structure. In systems that involve extensive interaction with human users, it is particularly important to design how the system will look and respond to the user first, before designing the software structure. While this is a somewhat less traditional approach to software design, it is finding increased favor among software developers. The development of *user interface management systems,* an automated approach to user interface design and implementation, is a direct outgrowth of this philosophy. (See Chapter 8 for a discussion of user interface management systems.) The goal is to make the user interface and the functional components of the final system as separate as possible, with minimal interfaces. In essence, the user interface and the functional components become separate systems.

The advantages of this approach are many. First, the best approach to solving any large problem is to break it down into subparts, each of which consists of easier problems to solve than the original problem. Separating the functional and user interface components of a system is often a logical breakdown of a software problem and leads to less complex solutions. Furthermore, the source code related to interfacing can be as much as 70 percent of the entire source code (Shneiderman, 1987). It makes sense to treat such a large part of the system as a separate design problem. Second, the breakdown of the system into its two major components makes maintenance and enhancements easier. In particular, changes in the user interface can be made with less effort if the functional portions of the system are not involved. Thus, events such as a switch to new hardware or a change in operational procedure that necessitate alterations in the user interface have minimal impact on maintenance efforts. Third, separate components support the concept of *reusability*. Reusability refers to the practice of taking portions of previously developed software and using them in new software, perhaps with some minor alterations. Experience has shown that considerable time, effort, and cost can be saved by the reuse of software components, particularly when the software was designed and implemented with the goal of reusability in mind (Jones, 1984; Standish, 1984; Prieto-Diaz and Freeman, 1987). The user interface can involve reusability in two ways: (1) by using portions of previously developed software, and (2) by being the potential source of reusable software in the future. Finally, by treating the user interface as a separate component of the system, the developers are better able to take advantage of software that supports the creation of user interfaces, such as screen generator packages.

3.2 Factors Affecting the Quality of Computer User Interfaces

In the early days of computing, the major goal of any software development project was to get the program to work. Computer programs then, as now, were intended to save large amounts of manual labor. Early computers and software (in the 1940s) were used primarily for scientific and military purposes where massive amounts of computations were needed. For example, computers were used in the calculation of navigational and ballistic tables and in weather prediction. In the 1950s, when cheaper, more powerful computers were introduced, the production of software shifted toward the processing of business data and away from strictly scientific and military applications.

In these days gone by, a program was considered successful if it ran. It was considered even more successful if it gave correct answers and if it executed quickly. Due to the high cost of computer hardware, the relative slowness of the hardware, and the lack of computer memory, a lot of a programmer's skills were related to packing the most efficient program into the smallest space. The programmer's role in an organization was special, as well. Programmers were viewed as artists. Few formal approaches to programming existed. Many learned to program mainly through trial and error. Managers tended to leave programmers pretty much to themselves. The hardware costs of computing were so much greater than the software and personnel side that the programmer and the software were often considered as afterthoughts.

Today, as we noted in Chapter 1, the picture is entirely different. Computer hardware is now hundreds of times more sophisticated and cheaper. Software and personnel costs far outweigh hardware costs. The number of different applications to which computing is applied has exploded. The style of computer interaction has changed from only batch computing to both batch and interactive computing. To emphasize how the picture has changed, it is interesting to note that in the early 1980s there were four times as many computers in use as there were programmers (Musa, 1985). This ratio is no doubt even higher today. The whole complexion of computing has changed. The two most important changes vis-à-vis software engineering are (1) the development of software engineering itself, and (2) the importance of the user in the computing picture.

The historical factors that led to the development of software engineering were discussed in Chapter 1. What is of relevance here are the factors that affected the role of the user. The changes in hardware design and cost had a profound impact on spreading the use of computers, but changes in software design were also a factor. Computers became more accessible to a wider audience in part because the way people interact with the computer was made easier. The introduction of interactive computing was important because it made computers a hands-on tool. Furthermore, computer use spread to nonprogrammers. Nonprogrammers require software that was easy to use. This is a trend that is continuing. Computer use is continuing to spread to a broader range of people, and more care and thought are being taken in designing the user interface to meet the needs of the new audiences.

Any software, whether it is an operating system, a programming language, or an applications program, is a system in the sense discussed previously. The user's satisfaction with a software system will have to do with the quality of the two basic facets of the system: its functionality and its user interface. The system must perform the desired tasks. If it does not, it does not matter how well the user interface is designed. Decisions concerning what functions to include in a system are made during the analysis and requirements stage. Excessive functionality can also be a problem. If the system is too complex, learning the system and using the system become more difficult. User satisfaction is also related to the quality of the user interface. Although there are many ways to judge the quality of a user interface, here are five general factors that are related to user interface quality:

1. **Ease of learning.** How long it takes the user to learn enough to begin using the system successfully.

2. **Speed of use.** How long it takes to carry out specified tasks.

3. **Frequency of user errors.** How frequently the user makes mistakes in carrying out specified tasks.

4. **User satisfaction.** The user's attitude toward a system. How well the user likes the system.

5. **Knowledge retention.** How easy it is to remember how to use the system after some interval.

The ideal system would succeed in all these categories, but that is often not possible. In one application, very low error rates may be required. However, low error rates might only be obtainable through reduced performance speed or longer learning times. In another case, speed may be all important, and some user satisfaction may have to be sacrificed. The designers of the system should know which of these factors are more important, and the rankings of the relative importance of these factors should be explicitly stated in the requirements and specifications.

3.3 Know the User Before Designing the Interface

As well as understanding what qualities are important in a system, it is important to gather information about the target users of the system before the user interface is designed. Users come in all shapes and sizes—from preschoolers using a computer graphics game to computer professionals writing a new compiler, from customers using an automatic bank teller to medical technicians using a CAT scan device. Differences in background, abilities, and motivation can be substantial. While there is truly no typical user, there does appear to be a three-way classification system that is a useful starting point (Shneiderman, 1987). The three categories are *novice, knowledgeable intermittent user,* and *frequent user.*

Novices are those who have rarely or never used a computer system. They may have little knowledge concerning the task to be performed, and they may even be very anxious about using a computer. Systems designed for such users should strive to keep the number of commands or actions needed to perform some activity to a bare minimum. Informative feedback should be provided at every step, the chance of error should be reduced as much as possible, and error messages should be constructive and specific.

Knowledgeable intermittent users are those who have used a variety of systems on an intermittent or sporadic basis. They are able to remember the underlying concepts of how different systems work, but they forget the detailed aspects of using the systems. Their effective use of systems is aided by using simple and consistent commands, menus, and terminology, and through the use of recognition (for example, menus) rather than recall (for example, commands). They should be protected from "dangerous" activities (for example, initializing a disk already containing files) to allow the user to feel free to explore the system. Help screens may be useful to such users.

Frequent users are "power" users. They are users who are completely familiar with the system and thoroughly understand its functions and commands. Such users typically want fast response times, limited feedback, and the availability of shortcuts. Because they use a system frequently, they are willing to sacrifice some ease of remembering for speed. The system should have the ability to accept strings of commands, allow shortcuts through menus, allow the use of abbreviations, and provide other accelerators.

These categories of users serve only as a broad classification. More specific facts should be gathered about the potential users of a proposed system.

When a system is targeted for only one of these types of users, it is much easier to design the interface than when the system must accommodate more than one type of user. If multiple user types must be accommodated, a typical strategy is to use a layered approach. In the layered approach, the system may be used with a minimal set of commands and actions to get started. As the user gains more familiarity and confidence with the system, a second layer of complexity can be introduced. The second layer can include more sophisticated commands. The layered approach must be supported not only by the design of the software, but by user manuals, help screens, and error messages.

3.4 Interaction Styles

Four different ways of interacting with a software system are in wide use today: *menu selection, form fill-in, command language,* and *direct manipulation.* With *menu selection,* the user is presented with a list or menu of items to choose from. For example, a list of function options might be presented. The user must then perform some action to indicate which of the presented options he or she wishes to select. Electronic bank machines often use menus to present options. For example, the user might choose from the options "withdraw from checking," "withdraw from savings," or "make a payment." Each option might have a number beside it, and the user selects his or her option by entering the number. Examples of two kinds of menus are shown in Figure 3.1. (See Section 3.6 for a discussion.) *Form fill-in* is often utilized when the user must enter multiple pieces of information. The user sees a screen that contains a series of titles identifying the fields where the needed information is to go, similar to what would be seen on a paper form. Typically, the user must move a cursor to the appropriate field and type in the required information. (See Figure 3.9 for a sample form fill-in screen.) With *command languages,* the user must initiate any interaction with the system by entering a command (a string of characters). It is up to the user to know what commands are available and how to enter them. (See Figure 3.2 for an example of some commands from a text-editing system.) A command language is called a language because it has a vocabulary (set of meaningful words) and a syntax (set of rules for relating the words), just as a spoken language or a programming language does. The operating systems on most mainframe computers and many microcomputers use command language user interfaces. In *direct manipulation,* the objects in the task environment are represented visually and manipulated to indicate the desired activities. The user must have some means of pointing to the desired object and moving it. The Macintosh operating system, with its use of icons to represent objects and a mouse for input, is a prime example of direct manipulation. Video games, display editors, and touch screens are other examples. (See Figures 3.1 and 3.3 for examples of direct manipulation interfaces.)

Each of these styles is more or less suitable for particular tasks. Each style has advantages and disadvantages for different types of users. And each style influences the ease of designing and building software. We will discuss each of these interaction styles in more detail later.

3.5   Golden Rules of Interface Design

Regardless of the experience of the user or the style of interface being used, certain principles hold for almost all interactive user interfaces. Shneiderman (1987) calls these guidelines the "Eight Golden Rules of Dialog Design:"

1. **Strive for consistency.** The user interface should be consistent in terms of syntax, terminology, actions, and layout. Actions required in one situation should be similar to those required in similar situations. Consistent terminology should be used throughout — in menus, prompts, system messages, and manuals. Display layout should be consistent. For example, all menus should follow the same format and all error messages should appear in the same location.

2. **Enable frequent users to use shortcuts.** Power users of a system are best served by having powerful shortcuts available to them. These shortcuts allow them to reduce the number of steps required to carry out an action, increase the pace of the interaction, and increase their productivity.

3. **Offer informative feedback.** *Every* action performed by the user should result in some sort of feedback from the system. The idea of feedback for unsuccessful actions, that is, error messages, is a familiar one. However, feedback for successful actions is just as important. Frequent and minor actions can elicit modest feedback, while infrequent and major actions should produce more substantial response. The feedback can be a simple audio

tone, a phrase or sentence, a change in the task object itself (for example, the altering of text in a word-processor system), or some change in the icon representing some task dimension.

4. **Design dialogs to yield closure.** Each sequence of actions should have a discernible beginning, a middle, and an end. The feedback at the end of the sequence gives the user a sense of completion and relief, signals the user that contingency plans and ideas concerning the sequence can be dropped, and indicates that the user can begin working on the next action sequence. For example, the actions required to fill in one page of a form fill-in screen should be designed as a sequence, with a clearly designated beginning, middle, and end.

5. **Offer simple error handling.** Whenever possible, make the system so that the user cannot make serious errors. Provide facilities that allow the user to readily undo operations. In cases where error messages are necessary, the error messages should be simple, pinpoint the exact source of the error, and offer information on how to correct the error. The user should be able to correct the error without having to retype the entire command.

6. **Permit easy reversal of actions.** Whenever possible, actions should be reversible. This greatly increases productivity, as the user does not have to go back to the beginning and retrace earlier actions. It also encourages the user to explore the system and become a more proficient user. The units of reversal may be a single action, a data entry operation, or a group of actions.

7. **Support user-centered interaction.** Users should perceive themselves as the initiators of action in a human–computer interaction, not as the responders. The computer is the tool, and the human is the user of that tool; the interface should reflect this relationship. A way to describe a well-designed interface that promotes user-centered interaction is to say that the system is *transparent* to the user. In a transparent system, the user is able to focus on the tasks she or he wishes to perform, and the computer becomes invisible. The user's energies can be focused on task goals, rather than on dealing with the computer interface.

8. **Reduce short-term memory load.** Humans are capable of keeping only a limited amount of information currently active in their short-term memories. Ideally, the information active in short-term memory should be task related, not computer related. Displays should be designed to reduce demands on short-term memory. For example, multipage displays that require the user to remember information from previous pages should be avoided. Menus should be used instead of command languages. On-line help should be provided for a quick memory refresh.

Keeping these golden rules in mind, let us now look at each interaction style in more detail.

3.6 Menu Selection

Menu selection systems are particularly attractive for use with novice and intermittent users, although they can be very appealing to frequent users as well. The advantage that menus have over other styles of interaction is that they can almost eliminate the need for training and the memorization of command sequences. Menus also provide a structure to the task sequencing that guides the novice and intermittent user effectively through the task. Menus must be well designed, however, to be effective. Design issues include the *semantic organization* of the interface, the structure of the menu system, and issues related to the operation and layout of the menus (Brown, 1986; Kiger, 1984; Landauer and Nachbar, 1985; McDonald, Stone, and Liebelt, 1983). These issues will be discussed next.

The *semantic organization* of an interface refers to the organization or relationship of the different functions, or groups of functions, of the system to each other. For example, a department store is a system for selling merchandise that has a semantic structure we are all familiar with. All the thousands of different items the store sells have been divided into different categories and are managed and sold by departments. Babies', children's, women's, and men's clothing, for example, are typically each handled in different departments. These divisions make more sense to us than, say, putting all shirts — babies', children's, men's, and women's — into the same department. It is easy to imagine how a computerized department store directory using menus might be organized. The user might first select the broad category he or she is interested in, for example, men's clothing. The next menu might ask for a category of men's clothing, for example, outerwear, suits, shirts, sports clothes, underwear, or shoes. Suppose the user picks shoes. The next screen might simply list all the brands and types of shoes the store carries and where they are to be found. The organization of the information into different, successive screens represents the semantic organization of the user interface.

A department store is an example of a *hierarchical* semantic organization. In a hierarchy, there is a one-to-many relationship among superordinate and subordinate elements in the structure. For example, the men's department, a single entity, contains many subcategories of items. Hierarchies are natural and understandable to most people and lend themselves readily to menu selection interfaces. Other semantic organizations might be *linear* or *networks*. In a *linear* organization, one series of options follows another series, always in the same order. A multiple-choice exam in which the user is not allowed to go back to earlier questions would be an example of a linear organization. In a *network,* some activities may be reached from many different origins. For example, many systems allow the user to print out the current screen at various times, no matter what prior sequence of commands was used to generate the screen. The function of printing, then, is linked to many other functions in such systems.

The designer of a menu selection interface should first determine which of the three underlying semantic structures the system has and match the menu system structure to it. Care must be taken in determining the categories for each menu.

Categories must be comprehensible and distinctive. Some guidelines for forming menu categories are:

1. **Logically similar items should be grouped together.** On a typical restaurant menu, for example, broad categories of items, such as appetizers or main dishes, are grouped together. Within these categories, other groupings might occur. For example, entrees might be grouped by their main ingredient: poultry, meat, or seafood.

2. **The groups formed must cover all possibilities.** For example, a menu concerning marital status should include the categories of single, married, divorced, and widowed to cover all possible respondents. It is possible some of the choices might produce exactly the same outcome; for example, singles and divorced might subsequently be treated the same by the system. Nonetheless, it makes it easier for a user to respond if the categories are all listed separately.

3. **Do not create overlapping items.** For example, a college advising system that offered a choice of information on either "A Liberal Arts Education" or "Majoring in the Arts" might be confusing.

4. **Use familiar but distinctive terms.** The categories single, married, divorced, and widowed are familiar and distinct. Unmarried, wedded, legally separated, missing partner, and so on, are less familiar and probably confusing terms. Choosing the right terminology can be a difficult task. It is a good idea to get feedback from potential users throughout the design and testing of the interface to guide the choice of terms.

3.6.1 Kinds of Menus

Several different kinds of menus have been devised. Probably the most common is the *single-screen* menu. In this design, all the choices available from the current menu appear on a single screen. Once the user makes his or her selection, the menu disappears. In a *multiple-screen menu,* the choices continue on to additional screens. The user must page through the multiple screens until the desired option is located. In most circumstances, it is probably best to make sure the number of options will fit on a single screen. However, multiple screens may be appropriate in some situations. For example, if the common options will fit onto the first screen, infrequent options can be placed on later screens. Novice or infrequent users will rarely need to go to the later screens and will not be hindered by the wide choice of options. Frequent users will appreciate the speedier response time afforded by the extended options.

Permanent menus are options that are displayed constantly and are constantly available to the user. For example, the user of a word processor might have several options permanently displayed on the bottom line of the screen, such as "Open New File," "Save File," "Quit," or "Print." The user may choose one of these options by pressing a function key or some other special key sequence.

Pull-down or *pop-up* menus are another kind of menu that can be used. With pull-down menus the tital of the menu is permanently displayed. The user may activate the menu by moving a cursor to the title and selecting the menu. A small box then appears on the screen presenting the entire menu. The user chooses an option (for example, by moving the cursor onto the chosen option). The menu box disappears once the cursor moves off the menu box. Claris's MacPaint for the Apple Macintosh (Version 1) uses a combination of permanent and pull-down menus. A sample screen is shown in Figure 3.1. The permanent menu is the choice of drawing tools shown on the left side of the screen. (The drawing tools are represented as *icons. Icons* are pictures that symbolize or stand for some function or entity in the system.) The user chooses a drawing tool by using a mouse to move a cursor onto the icon of choice and pressing a button on the mouse to indicate that a choice has been made. The available pull-down menus are indicated by the titles across the top of the screen (that is, File, Edit, Goodies, and so on). To activate a pull-down menu, the user uses the mouse to move the cursor onto the menu title of choice. While the user holds down the button on the mouse, the menu is superimposed on the screen. To select a menu option, the user moves the cursor onto the option and releases the mouse button. In Figure 3.1, the **Style** menu has been pulled down, and the user has just selected the **Outline** option. The option is highlighted to indicate it has been selected. Notice the keystroke symbols next to the options in the **Style** menu, for example, ⌘B next to the **Bold** option. These symbols indicate that the option may be selected through the use of the indicated keystrokes as well as through menu selection. A frequent user might find keystrokes faster to use than menu selection.

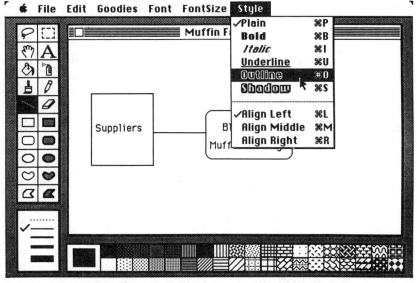

Figure 3.1 Sample Screen from MacPaint Illustrating the Use of Permanent and Pull-down Menus in a User Interface

Pop-up menus are activated by moving the cursor (using a mouse) onto some object in the task environment and then holding down a button on the mouse. The relevant menu pops onto the screen near the task object. The user can select options from the pop-up menu in a manner similar to pull-down menus.

3.6.2   Other Menu Design Considerations

Users like to know where they are within the semantic structure of a system (Billingsley, 1982). They also prefer to have some ability to go back and/or to exit if they change their mind about what they want to do or realize they have made a mistake. Feedback should be given to users to show them where they are in the system and what options they have concerning exiting or going back. A common solution is to have titles for each menu. The title should be the phrase that was used as the option (choice) in the previous menu. Using our department store directory example, the initial menu might have included the option Women's Clothing. If the user selects this option, the next menu should have the title Women's Clothing. It would be confusing to the user if the next menu were titled Ladies' Apparel, even though the two phrases are synonymous. As well as the title of the current menu, the screen should include the ability to go back to the previous screen and/or to exit the system.

A second design decision is how the menu option is selected. One approach is to use a mouse to move a cursor and a button-press to indicate selection, as in the MacPaint example just described. Other menu selection techniques include touch screens, light pens, and keyboard input. When keyboard input is used, the typical scheme is to associate numbers or letters with the menu options and have the user indicate her or his choice by entering the desired number or letter. The choice of numbers or letters depends on the particular situation being designed (Perlman, 1984). With letters, single key presses can be used to select up to 26 different items. However, letters can be confusing if the letter used as a selector conflicts with the command or option being chosen. With numbers, only nine (ten if zero is used) single-keypress selectors are available. Numbers also have the disadvantage of being harder to type, often requiring the user to look at the keyboard. In some cases, the first letter of an option makes a suitable selector. If the choices are Yes or No, for example, the use of the letters Y and N would be appropriate and probably easier for the user to understand than numbers or letters, such as "A" and "B."

Another important consideration in menu design is consistency (Teitelbaum and Granda, 1983). Phrasing should be consistent throughout the system. It is confusing to the user if the terms exit, quit, stop, and end, for example, are used interchangeably. Pick one phrase and use it consistently. The choice of selector mechanism should also be consistent. If numbers are used as selectors on one menu, they should be used on all menus. The location of titles and permanent menus on the display should be consistent from menu to menu. Likewise, the format of the options, whether indented or left justified, should be consistent from menu to menu. (Other screen formating guidelines are discussed in Section 3.9.)

Table 3.1 Summary of Guidelines for Designing Menu Selection User Interfaces

---

1. The menu structure should follow the semantic organization of the task: linear, hierarchical or network.

2. Menu categories should be comprehensive and distinctive:
   Logically similar items should be grouped together.
   The groups formed must cover all possibilities.
   The menu items should not overlap.
   The terms used should be familiar but distinctive.

3. Within a menu, items should be logically organized. If no other organization applies, order the selections alphabetically.

4. The selection method should be well thought out. Keyboard characters, cursors, light pens, and touch screens are all possible selection mechanisms.

5. Allow the user to move to previous menus and the main menu from each lower-level menu, if possible.

6. Include information on each screen that tells users what options they have to go back, exit, or go forward.

7. Include information on each screen that tells users where they are within the system. The most common technique is to include a title for each menu.

8. Consistent layout and terminology from screen to screen are important.

9. To aid the frequent user, allow shortcuts.

A summary of the guidelines presented here for designing a menu selection interface is presented in Table 3.1.

3.7   Form Fill-in Interface

In tasks where a significant amount of data entry is necessary, a form fill-in interface may be the best choice of interface style (Ogden and Boyle, 1982). In this style of interface, a number of field titles appear on the screen with blank space or underlines next to them indicating where and what information is to be entered. The user fills in the form by moving a cursor to a field and typing in the required data. Because the screen forms are similar to paper and pencil forms, users feel comfortable with the mode. However, some amount of training is usually needed to familiarize the user with the format of the entries, with keyboard usage, and with the meaning of the field labels. Form fill-in is more appropriate for knowlegeable intermittent users or frequent users than for novice users. Very little empirical work has been done on form fill-in interfaces; however, a number of design guidelines have been proposed by practitioners (Brown, 1986; Smith and Mosier, 1986).

The first step in designing a form fill-in interface is to determine which information is to appear on each screen. As much as possible, put all related material together on one screen along with a meaningful title for the screen. If the user is forced to remember information entered on an earlier screen, errors and inconvenience result. The appearance and layout of the form on the screen are important facets of the interface design. The screen should not be so crowded that reading becomes difficult. Spreading the items out on the screen and neatly aligning them provides readability and a sense of orderliness. Logically related fields can be grouped together and blank space used to separate groups of fields. Logical sequencing of the fields is important, as well. For example, city, state, and zip code fields should follow the standard order. Familiar terms should be used for field labels. Terminology or abbreviations should be used consistently.

There are guidelines for designing the data entry field, as well. When possible, use underscores or other marks to indicate the number of characters required or spaces available for the entry. Sometimes fixed characters in the entry field can guide data entry. For example, a field for a telephone number could be formated as (___)___-____, with clearly marked spaces for the area code, prefix, and number portions. If a series of numbers is to be entered that can be of variable length (for example, a dollar and cents amount), it is convenient if the first digit entered appears in the rightmost position of the field and then migrates left as additional digits are entered. If a field is optional, it should be marked as such. When feasible, a message explaining the field and its contents can appear in a window (for example, at the bottom of the screen) whenever the cursor is positioned on the field. (See Section 3.11 for a discussion of error message design.)

Cursor movement should be made as convenient as possible. Cursor movement arrow keys are easy to use. Tab keys, return keys, and mouse-directed cursors are other possibilities for easy use. The use of obscure combinations of control, option, or shift keys with other key presses to move the cursor should be avoided. However, such combination key presses can be used as alternative selection methods in order to provide the frequent user with powerful commands or shortcuts. Error correction should be allowed within fields (at the character level) and among entire fields. Provide helpful error messages when unacceptable values are entered into a data field. A message such as "Invalid entry. Reenter value." is not a helpful message. A message such as "Social security numbers should have 9 digits." is more helpful. Finally, make it clear to the user what is to be done when all necessary fields have been filled. The user should be allowed to check and change any entries before confirming and going on.

A summary of the guidelines for designing form fill-in interfaces is given in Table 3.2.

3.8 Command Languages

Command languages are formal languages, just as programming languages are. The main difference between programming languages and command languages is the immediacy of the effect. In using a programming language, a series of commands is created, saved, and later executed as a group. In using a command language, each command is typically interpreted and executed immediately. Many

Table 3.2 Summary of Guidelines for Designing Form Fill-in User Interfaces

1. The fields on each screen should be logically grouped and sequenced.

2. If possible, all related material should appear on one screen.

3. The format of the screen should aid readability and give a sense of orderliness. Consistent layout among similar screens or screen components is important.

4. The field labels should be familiar. If abbreviations are used, they should be readily understood and used consistently.

5. Entry fields should be visually delineated by underscores, boxes, or some other means. When appropriate, visual templates can be used, for example, with telephone numbers or social security numbers.

6. When space permits, a message explaining the field and its contents should appear at a standard position on the screen whenever a field is active.

7. Cursor movement should be convenient, and the cursor should be easily visible.

8. Error correction should be allowed both at the character level and the field level throughout the time the screen is active for input or update.

9. Helpful error messages should be provided when invalid entries are made.

10. It should be made clear to the user what is to be done when all the necessary fields have been filled.

operating systems, text editors and adventure games use command language interfaces. Command languages have a vocabulary, a syntax (rules of grammar), and semantics (meaning), just as programming languages do. To use a command language, therefore, a user must learn both the vocabulary and syntax of the language, while mastering the semantics (meaning) of the commands. This requires substantial training and memorization, making command languages suitable mainly for frequent users (Ogden and Boyle, 1982). Another disadvantage of the command language interface style is that it is difficult to provide good error handling and help facilities. The major advantage of command language interfaces is that they provide the user with a great deal of flexibility and creativity in using the system.

The syntax of a command language can range from the simple to the extremely complex. In a simple language, each command produces a single action. In other words, each unique command has a single unique action associated with it. If the total number of commands is kept small, such an approach can produce a system that is simple to use and simple to learn. When the number of choices is large, the system can become very difficult to learn (Jorgensen, 1987). The word processor, WordStar, and the text editor vi offered on UNIX systems are examples of systems that offer large vocabularies of simple commands. However, because of the large vocabularies and because the designers have attempted to keep the number of keystrokes necessary to invoke these commands to a minimum, the commands are often nonmnemonic and involve the use of control keys and/or other awkward contrivances. For example, consider how much practice it might take to learn to

Positioning within file

^F	forward screenfull
^B	backward screenfull
^D	scroll down half screen
^U	scroll up half screen
G	goto line (end default)
/pat	next line matching pat
?pat	prev line matching pat
n	repeat last / or ?
N	reverse last / or ?
/pat/ + n	n'th line after pat
?pat? – n	n'th line before pat
]]	next section/function
[[	previous section/function
%	find matching ( ) or { }

Note: ^ refers to the control key.

Figure 3.2 Commands from the Text Editor vi for Positioning the Cursor Within the File Being Edited

use just the vi commands to position the cursor within a file as shown in Figure 3.2. Note that the commands shown in Figure 3.2 are only part of the approximately 150 basic commands of vi.

More complex command languages involve the use of commands combined with arguments or with options and arguments. In some cases, one or more arguments may be required. For example, the *copy* command on IBM PC/DOS requires one argument: the name of the source disk file. There are many options with this command that allow the user to specify an optional alternate file name for the file copy, indicate the source and target disk drives, and so on. Other commands can be used in a simple form, for example, the PC/DOS *dir* to show the contents of the disk in the current default disk drive, or with options, for example, *dir b:* to show the contents of a specified disk.

3.8.1 Guidelines for Designing Command Languages

A major design flaw in many command languages is simply that they contain too many commands and allow the user too many alternate ways of accomplishing a task (Rosson, 1983). This makes the command language difficult to remember. Furthermore, errors become easy to make. The designer of a command language should give careful consideration to limiting the number of commands. An added advantage of limiting the commands is that it reduces the complexity of the underlying system.

Meaningful and distinctive names should be chosen for the commands (Landauer, Calotti, and Hartwell, 1983). If abbreviations are to be used, they should be carefully chosen (Schneider, 1984). In particular, the abbreviation strategy should be consistent throughout the command language. Simple truncation (using the first letter or first several letters of a command) is often effective. Dropping the vowels from a command to form an abbreviation is another approach. If abbreviations are to be used, it is a good idea to allow the full command to be functional as well. New users of a command system often prefer to type out commands in full until they become comfortable with the system.

The structure of the command syntax should be consistent (Green and Payne, 1984). The various components of the command, that is, command, objects, arguments, and options, should consistently appear in the same position across commands. Prompting can be offered for intermittent users. For example, Digital Equipment Corporation's VMS operating system allows the user to type in a command such as "copy" and then press the return key. The system then prompts the user with the message "From:". After the user enters the source file name, the system prompts with "To:". The user then enters the name of the destination file. For greater speed, the "copy" command can also be entered as a single line of text containing the command, the source file name, and the destination file name.

Command menus offer possibilities for making a system easier to learn and also making it much more appealing to intermittent users. The word processor, WordStar, for example, makes extensive use of command menus. A menu containing frequently used commands is constantly displayed at the top of the screen. Lower-level menus concerning less frequently used commands can be called up by the user. The lower-level menus are also automatically displayed if the user begins to type in a command sequence and pauses for more than a certain number of seconds (the delay time can be adjusted by the user). An option that removes some or all of the menus is available. This allows power users to utilize more of the screen space for the document being edited.

A summary of some guidelines for designing command language user interfaces is given in Table 3.3.

Table 3.3 Summary of Guidelines for Designing Command Language User Interfaces

1. Limit the number of commands. Is it really necessary to have several alternative means of accomplishing the same task?
2. Meaningful and distinctive names should be chosen for the commands.
3. If abbreviations are used, the abbreviation strategy should be consistent throughout the command language.
4. If abbreviations are used, the full command should be functional as well.
5. The structure of the command syntax should be consistent.
6. Prompting should be offered as an aid to intermittent users.
7. Command menus may be appropriate in some designs as an aid to intermittent users. The menus should be optional to allow frequent users to turn off the command menu and thus utilize the entire screen.

3.9   Direct-Manipulation Interfaces

In a direct-manipulation interface, the task world is visually represented to the user and the user directly manipulates the objects in the world to achieve his or her goals. In well-designed systems of this sort, the user's tasks are often greatly simplified compared to other forms of user interface, and the user may have strong feelings of mastery and competence (Roberts, 1980). The effects of forgetting are minimized, and users often feel confident and willing to explore more powerful aspects of the system (Hutchins, Hollan, and Norman, 1986). There is some evidence that systems using direct manipulation are somewhat harder for novices to learn than command and menu systems; however, the most important factor is probably the care with which the interface is designed and built, rather than the style of interface chosen (Potosnak, 1988). Examples of systems that use direct manipulation include display editors, video games, touch screens, the Lisa and Macintosh operating systems, and other software that utilizes a mouse or joystick in obtaining input.

The components of a direct-manipulation interface are the visual interface and a selection or pointing device. The visual interface represents the task space, and the selection or pointing device is used to input commands. Display editors are a common example of direct manipulation. WordStar, Word, EMACS, vi, and MacWrite are all display editors. In display editors the text to be edited is displayed on the screen. The screen represents a single page or portion of a page containing text. A cursor is used to indicate the point in the text where alterations or additions can currently be made. To add text, the user simply types in characters, which then appear at the cursor position. To alter the position of the cursor, the user can press arrow keys or use a mouse or joystick. The main advantage of display editors compared to line editors is the visibility of the interactions. The cursor provides a clear indication of the focus of action in the text. Because the screen represents a page of text, "what you see is what you get" (otherwise known as "wysiwyg"). The user knows that the form of the document on the screen is the form that it will appear in when it is printed. Each user action immediately results in an action in the text, so the user receives immediate feedback.

Many video games are examples of pure direct-manipulation interfaces. As a simple example, consider the game known variously as Brickles or Brick-Out, as shown in Figure 3.3. (Brickles is shareware for the Macintosh, available from K. Winograd, 2039 Country Club Dr., Manchester, NH 03102.) In this game, the user sees a wall made of bricks on the screen. The bricks are knocked out (erased) when struck by a bouncing ball. The user can control the direction the ball bounces by hitting the ball with a paddle. The paddle is represented on the bottom of the screen as a rectangle. The paddle can be moved only horizontally across the bottom of the screen, usually through the use of a joystick or mouse. This simple game highlights the essential characteristics and positive aspects of direct-manipulation interfaces. First, the rules of the game and how to operate the game are easy to learn. Thus users can immediately begin using the system to perform the task it

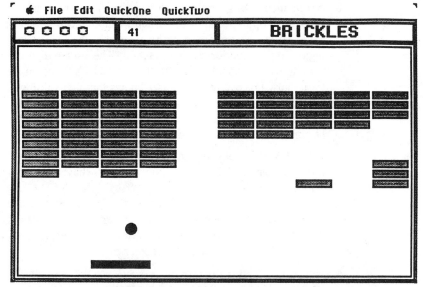

Figure 3.3 Sample Screen from the Video Game Brickles, Illustrating a Direct Manipulation Interface (Brickles is shareware from Ken Winograd, 2039 Country Club Dr., Manchester, NH 03102.)

was designed to perform. Second, there are no such things as syntax errors or error messages. Basically, users cannot make a mistake. Of course, they may come up with a very low score on the game, but it will not be because they made a mistake in their input. Third, once introduced to the game, users have very little to recall when using the system again after a period of time. Finally, many people find using the system fun.

Other systems use a combination of direct manipulation and other sorts of user interface. For example, many display editors (for example, WordStar, Word, MacWrite) and electronic spreadsheets (for example, Multiplan, Lotus 1-2-3, CalcStar) combine menu selection with direct manipulation of the text or numeric entries.

Although direct-manipulation interfaces are fairly new, there are some guidelines for their design (Potosnak, 1988).

1. **The icon should be easy to understand.** The meaning of an icon should be as obvious as possible. Nonetheless, what is obvious to one person may not be obvious to another. Consider some of the international signs that have been developed. Silhouettes of a person in a skirt or a person in pants are used to designate women's and men's restrooms. A smoking cigarette covered by a red circle with a red slash across the cigarette signals a nonsmoking area. A poorly chosen icon would not convey its message as well.

2. **Avoid misleading analogies.** Once the meaning of an icon is understood, users develop expectations of what operations can be performed on or with the icon. For example, the trash can used in the Macintosh Finder is an analogical representation of file deletion. The user will draw inferences concerning what can and cannot be done with files based on their knowledge of trash cans. For example, the user knows that items thrown into a real-world trash can can be retrieved, at least until trash collection takes place. Is it correct to assume that files placed in the trash can icon can be retrieved? (It is, but only before the "trash can" has been "emptied.")

3. **Do not violate population stereotypes.** Different user populations may have different expectations of how an icon behaves. For example, in Canada a blinking green on a stop light signals that left turns are allowed and oncoming traffic has a red light. In the United States, a left turn arrow is used in the same context. In the computer context, populations such as children and novice users might have different interpretations of icons than older people or more experienced computer users.

4. **Use icons for appropriate purposes.** Icons may not always be faster or easier to use than a command or other method. The effort involved in selecting and/or moving an icon may be more than the effort of typing or pointing. For example, using a mouse to perform arithmetic operations on a calculator icon will take longer than using a keypad or keyboard. The designer must take into account the fact that moving the hand from the keyboard to the mouse or joystick, and vice versa, takes time. A skilled typist might be slowed by being forced to use direct manipulation based on mouse or joystick input. One solution is to provide a set of keystrokes to perform the same commands that can be done through direct manipulation. By doing this, those who prefer direct manipulation can be satisfied, as well as those who prefer keyboard commands.

5. **Carefully design the iconic interaction.** The way icons are used as part of the overall interface is more important than the meaning of each separate icon. The semantics of the interface design, consistency, layout, ease of learning, and so on, are all important facets of the interface. The choice of style is to a certain extent only cosmetic.

3.10   Designing Screen Displays

Screen layout and design are an important component of most interactive systems. Although a number of practitioners have suggested guidelines for designing screens (Smith and Mosier, 1986; Pakin and Wray, 1982), there are no standard guidelines to follow in designing all screens. Tasks to be performed by systems vary widely, as do the characteristics of the user population. For example, a screen that is easy to read for an adult intermittent user might be too complex for an elementary school student and too sparse for an expert user.

The interface designer should begin designing the output without any concern for screen size, available fonts, or device characteristics. The designer should think in terms of what the optimal logical order of output is for the task at hand. Once the optimal output has been designed, it can be mapped onto the physical system. Pages or groups of items can be created, each of which is presented on one screen. Within one screen, groups of items can be visually related by the use of blank lines and spaces, boxes, highlighting, reverse video, color, or special fonts. Left and right justification and centering can be used for organization. In multiscreen interfaces, consistency between screens is important. The location, structure, and terminology of related components should be consistent as the user moves from screen to screen.

One of the best techniques to use in designing screen layout is to prototype a variety of layouts and let potential users of the system provide feedback. As an example of the value of experimentation, consider the poorly formatted information shown in Figure 3.4. Suppose we were designing a system for radio station disc jockeys and librarians that displays information concerning one compact disc, long-playing record, or tape on a screen. The information is to include the artist or group, the type of medium (long-playing record album, compact disc, or audio tape), the title of the album, compact disc, or tape, a list of the selections on the medium, and the time (in minutes and seconds) for each selection. Although the information is all present in Figure 3.4, it is fairly difficult to read. In Figure 3.5a, blanks have been added to separate the fields. Even this simple addition aids readability. In Figure 3.5b, the selection titles and times have been organized into two left-justified columns. Notice that the colons in the selection times are not lined up. In Figure 3.5c, the colons are lined up, thus giving the reader a quick visual clue as to whether the selection is under or over ten minutes long. Infrequent users of the system might not be familiar with the order of the information in the display. Labels could be added as an aid to understanding. Figure 3.5d shows the information with labels added and the selections sorted and grouped by album side. In Figure 3.5d, the labels are in capitals and lowercase, and the information

```
MICHAEL HEDGEROW/LP/BREAKFAST ON THE GRASS
WINDY HILL PRODUCTIONS, INC.
1.LAYOVER 2:30
1.THE HAPPY COUPLE 3:18
1.ELEVEN SMALL ROACHES 11:01
1.THE FUNKY AVOCADO 2:03
1.BABY TOES 12:05
2.BREAKFAST ON THE GRASS 2:21
2.TWO DAYS OLD 4:43
2.PEG LEG SPEED KING :19
2.THE UNEXPECTED VISITOR 2:45
2.QUIET ANTICIPATIONS 3:19
2.LA NONO 3:57
```

Figure 3.4 Example of a Poorly Designed Screen Display

MICHAEL HEDGEROW   LP   BREAKFAST ON THE GRASS
WINDY HILL PRODUCTIONS, INC.

1. LAYOVER   2:30
1. THE HAPPY COUPLE   3:18
1. ELEVEN SMALL ROACHES   11:01
1. THE FUNKY AVOCADO   2:03
1. BABY TOES   12:05

2. BREAKFAST ON THE GRASS   2:21
2. TWO DAYS OLD   4:43
2. PEG LEG SPEED KING   :19
2. THE UNEXPECTED VISITOR   2:45
2. QUIET ANTICIPATIONS   3:19
2. LANONO   3:57

Figure 3.5(a) Example from Figure 3.4 with Blanks Inserted to Aid Readability

MICHAEL HEDGEROW   LP   BREAKFAST ON THE GRASS
WINDY HILL PRODUCTIONS, INC.

1. LAYOVER   2:30
1. THE HAPPY COUPLE   3:18
1. ELEVEN SMALL ROACHES   11:01
1. THE FUNKY AVOCADO   2:03
1. BABY TOES   12:05

2. BREAKFAST ON THE GRASS   2:21
2. TWO DAYS OLD   4:43
2. PEG LEG SPEED KING   :19
2. THE UNEXPECTED VISITOR   2:45
2. QUIET ANTICIPATIONS   3:19
2. LANONO   3:57

Figure 3.5(b) Example from Figure 3.5(a) with Title and Time Columns Added

is in capitals only. Figure 3.5e shows the reverse strategy: the labels are capitalized and the information is written in capitals and lowercase. Research has shown that capitals and lowercase letters are easier for people to read (Shneiderman, 1987). Thus the version in Figure 3.5e is preferable to the version in Figure 3.5d.

This example illustrates that even small changes in layout can produce a great difference in readability. It also suggests that experimentation with paper and pencil mockups and on-screen examples is very important in designing screen layouts.

Table 3.4 presents a summary of guidelines for designing screen displays.

MICHAEL HEDGEROW   LP   BREAKFAST ON THE GRASS
WINDY HILL PRODUCTIONS, INC.

1. LAYOVER	2:30
1. THE HAPPY COUPLE	3:18
1. ELEVEN SMALL ROACHES	11:01
1. THE FUNKY AVOCADO	2:03
1. BABY TOES	12:05
2. BREAKFAST ON THE GRASS	2:21
2. TWO DAYS OLD	4:43
2. PEG LEG SPEED KING	:19
2. THE UNEXPECTED VISITOR	2:45
2. QUIET ANTICIPATIONS	3:19
2. LANONO	3:57

Figure 3.5(c) Example from Figure 3.5(b) with the Colons in the Times Lined Up

Artist: MICHAEL HEDGEROW
Title: BREAKFAST ON THE GRASS
Type: LP
Company: WINDY HILL PRODUCTIONS, INC.

Side	Selection	Time
1	LAYOVER	2:30
1	THE HAPPY COUPLE	3:18
1	ELEVEN SMALL ROACHES	11:01
1	THE FUNKY AVOCADO	2:03
1	BABY TOES	12:05
2	BREAKFAST ON THE GRASS	2:21
2	TWO DAYS OLD	4:43
2	PEG LEG SPEED KING	:19
2	THE UNEXPECTED VISITOR	2:45
2	QUIET ANTICIPATIONS	3:19
2	LANONO	3:57

Figure 3.5(d) Example from Figure 3.5(c) with Labels Added

Table 3.4 Summary of Guidelines for Designing Screen Displays

1. Keep the characteristics of the user in mind while designing the screen display. Different designs are appropriate for different sorts of users.

2. Group logically related items together visually through the use of blank lines and spaces, boxes, highlighting, reverse video, color, or text style variations.

3. Use left, center, and right justification or other forms of alignment to organize information.

4. In multiscreen interfaces, consistency among screens is important.

5. Experiment with different layouts. Paper is cheap.

ARTIST: Michael Hedgerow
TITLE: Breakfast on the Grass
TYPE: LP
COMPANY: Windy Hill Productions, Inc.

SIDE	SELECTION	TIME
1	Layover	2:30
1	The Happy Couple	3:18
1	Eleven Small Roaches	11:01
1	The Funky Avocado	2:03
1	Baby Toes	12:05
2	Breakfast on the Grass	2:21
2	Two Days Old	4:43
2	Peg Leg Speed King	:19
2	The Unexpected Visitor	2:45
2	Quiet Anticipations	3:19
2	Lanono	3:57

Figure 3.5(e) Display in Figure 3.5(d) with the Entries in Capital and Lowercase Letters

3.11 System Messages Design

System messages include prompts, feedback, and error messages presented to the user during an interaction or on the printed output of a system. The quality and style of these messages are an important determinant of how well users like a system and how productive and successful they are in using the system (Shneiderman, 1982; Mosteller, 1981). In this section, considerations common to all system messages will be considered first, followed by a discussion of error messages. Most of the guidelines presented here have been proposed by practitioners (Shneiderman, 1987; Dwyer, 1981). Little empirical research has been done on the design of system messages.

Probably the most important consideration in designing system messages is style. The style of the messages used by a system and by its error messages conveys who is in control of the interaction. As much as possible, the design of the system should give the initiative in controlling the system to the user. The interface should then convey this control to the user. Using user-centered phrasing helps in this respect. In user-centered phrasing, the messages suggest that it is up to the user to initiate actions. For example, the messages "Ready for next command" or simply "Ready" are user centered, while "Enter command" is not. The presence on the screen of a message that tells the user how to cancel a command or undo the effects of an incorrect command also aids in providing a user-centered atmosphere.

An additional style consideration is the use of anthropomorphic messages. In this style of interaction, the designer attempts to make the computer "talk" as if it were a person. For example, an automated bank teller used by the author displays a message saying "Hello, Barbee. What transaction would you like to choose today?" once the sign-in procedures have been completed. Such chatty and informal "conversation" from an inanimate and supposedly efficient machine is at the least inappropriate and at the worst offensive (Spiliotopoulos and Shackel, 1981). The motivation of designers that use anthropomorphized interfaces is to be commended: they are no doubt striving to make the computer seem more familiar and accessible to the user. Unfortunately, however, suggesting that a computer has humanlike capacities only misleads the user. While humans can readily think, know, understand, and respond to emotions, computers cannot. Once the user discovers that a system with an anthropomorphic interface is not, in fact, very much like a human, they may feel deceived and "taken in." Second, a computer is a tool and, as a tool, should be subservient to the user's needs. Computers are intended to be under the control of the human user. Our relationships to other people are not typically of this sort. When confronted with an anthropomorphic interface, a user may attempt to treat the computer as another individual and thus be diverted from their goal of using the computer as a tool.

Anthropomorphic feedback is probably also best avoided. For example, an experimental study has shown that giving children value judgments with positive feedback (for example, "Excellent," "You're doing great") did not improve learning or satisfaction in a drill and practice program. However, the presence of a simple count of number correct and incorrect did improve learning (Shneiderman, 1987).

3.11.1   Error Messages

Anyone who has used a computer for any time at all has had the experience of getting a poorly designed system or error message. A poorly designed error message is one that does not clearly convey to the user the source of the error, does not suggest what can or should be done about the error, is hard to find on the display or printout, and/or conveys a negative or condemning attitude toward the user. While the experienced computer user has probably learned to take such insulting and worthless error messages more or less in stride, a novice user can find them extremely frustrating and anxiety producing. For users at all levels, poorly designed error messages reduce productivity (Mosteller, 1981; Shneiderman, 1982).

As an aid in understanding the design of error messages, consider what sorts of things error messages do or might do for the user of a system. First, the occurrence of an error message is, in itself, a signal that an error has occurred. In other words, an error message, at the minimum, alerts the user to the fact that an error has occurred. Second, an error message may inform the user of the source or cause of the error. Finally, an error message can inform the user what can be done to correct or recover from the error, or direct the user to an alternative source of information on how to correct the error. Error messages differ in the degree to which they meet these three functions. A system that responds only with a beep to invalid input or that simply fails to respond to invalid input is using error messages that provide only the first function; they simply tell the user an error has occurred. An error message such as "Syntax error" or "Invalid input" provides the first two functions; it tells the user that an error has occurred and indicates the cause of the error. Error messages such as "Missing left parenthesis in Line 25" or "Enter an amount of $500 or less" provide all three functions. These two messages each signal an error, indicate the cause of the error, and suggest (by implication) what can be done to correct the error.

Except in special cases, an error message should be designed to be complete, that is, provide all three functions described. Additional guidelines for designing error messages are that they should be specific, provide constructive guidance, use a positive tone, and have a good physical format. These guidelines are discussed next.

3.11.2 Guidelines for Error Message Design

Specificity. Error messages should specify as completely and closely as possible the exact source of the error and what can be done to correct it. Compiler messages, for example, should specify not only the kind of error (for example, missing parameter in procedure call), but the exact line in the source code in which the error was discovered. Additional information, such as the name of the procedure being called, could be added to reinforce the line number information and make locating the error in the source code easier. Execution time error messages should also provide the user with specific information about the source of the error. Knowing that division by zero caused the program execution to terminate is only part of the information needed to correct the error. The line number in the source code that contains the offending statement is useful information, possibly along with the name of the variables involved in the computation. As a complement to the specificity of the error messages, it is also appropriate that the user be able to correct the error by altering only the portion of the input containing the error. For example, to force a user to reenter all the fields in a form fill-in interface because one field is found to contain invalid data would be inefficient and annoying to the user. Many command languages have exactly this drawback. Although the error messages may be specific, the user is forced to type in the entire command again. For example, suppose a user has entered a command to rename a file. The command includes the command word, *rename,* the name of the file to be renamed, and the new name for the file. An error in entering the file name for the source file might result in the error message "Invalid file name for source file," and the user is required to reenter the entire command. As an alternative, the system could ask the user to reenter only the file name or enter a carriage return to cancel the command.

Constructive Guidance and Positive Tone. Perhaps you have been the lucky recipient of a message such as "Fatal error. Job aborted." Such messages are used on too many systems. The tone of this message and others similar to it is unnecessarily hostile and violent. They can easily be rewritten in more neutral terms and in a way that includes more information on what has happened and what can be done to correct the problem. Other negative words, such as "illegal," "invalid," "error," or "bad," should also be excluded from error messages. The message should simply state the problem and state, or imply, its solution. Consider, for example, how the following error message from a popular Pascal compiler for microcomputers could be rewritten. The error message is currently: "Invalid string length." While this is not a bad error message, a better message with a more positive tone and one that provides more information would be "The length of a string must be in the range 1...255 characters."

A question of some debate among interface designers is whether or not to use tones and beeps to signal errors or warnings to users. On one hand, a sound is almost certain to be noticed by the user, whereas a visual message might be overlooked. On the other hand, a user might be caused embarrassment when a sound signals to others nearby that the user has just made an error. If sounds are used as signals, it should be possible for the user to adjust the volume of the sound and possibly to turn off the sound entirely, substituting some visual signal.

Good Physical Format. The guidelines for displaying error messages include those for any display, as were discussed in Section 3.10. In particular, error messages should be presented in a consistent location on the screen or printout. The error messages should be visually isolated from the rest of the display through the use of spaces, boxes, highlighting, reverse video, color, or special fonts. Visual clues as to the source of the error can be used along with an error message. For example, an invalid data item could be highlighted or printed in inverse characters.

3.11.3 An Ounce of Prevention

A discussion of error messages is not complete without a discussion of error prevention. The best way to approach the design of a user interface is not to make elaborate plans for handling errors, but instead to aim for the avoidance of errors (Norman, 1983). That is, an interface should be designed so that, as much as possible, the user is prevented from making errors in the first place. When errors do occur, the system should provide intelligent and time-saving responses to those errors.

While preventing errors may seem difficult, it is actually a realistic goal for many systems. A careful application of the techniques and guidelines that have been presented earlier in this chapter will go a long way toward reducing errors. Broadly, these techniques include understanding the user and designing the system to match the user as well as the functions being implemented. Shneiderman (1987) and Norman (1983) discuss additional techniques for error prevention. These include *correct matching pairs, complete sequences,* and *correct commands.* Each of these will be discussed next.

There are many situations where a matching pair of symbols is needed in input to a system. For example, matching left and right parentheses or brackets are frequently used in programming languages, spreadsheet formulas, and bibliographic search systems. A common error is to forget the matching right symbol. This omission can be prevented by using the technique of *correct matching pairs.* In this approach, the editor automatically adds the closing parenthesis when the opening parenthesis is entered and places the cursor in between so that the contents can be entered.

In the *complete sequences* technique, the designer recognizes that certain actions may consistently require a series of steps to complete and combines these steps into a single action. For example, many users like to keep backup copies of text files. For these users, completing the editing of a text file involves three actions: saving the edited file, leaving the editor, and making a backup copy of the file. On some systems, these three actions are combined into one command. Another situation that frequently requires complete sequences is in writing source code in a programming language. For example, a *while* statement in Pascal typically requires four keywords: *while, do, begin,* and *end,* in that order. Some context-sensitive editors provide a feature that provides the complete template for a *while* structure as soon as the keyword *while* is typed or when the user somehow indicates that a *while* structure is desired. The user then fills in the remaining components of the structure with less chance for syntax errors. Other examples of complete sequences include systems that execute the series of actions needed to log on or boot up and automatically display the contents of the directory and/or system or mail messages.

The final technique is *correct commands*. In this technique, incorrect actions are blocked or the chance for incorrect choices is substantially reduced. Many mechanical devices are designed to block incorrect actions. Lawn mowers shut off when the operator lets go of the handle, cameras prohibit double exposures, cars cannot be put into reverse while traveling at fast forward speeds, and so on. Similar approaches can be used in software design. For example, users can be blocked from choosing menu options that do not exist or menu options that are not appropriate at a particular stage in an action sequence; they can be prevented from asking for files that do not exist or from destroying files that should not be destroyed; and they can be prevented from entering invalid characters as part of a data entry operation. The use of menu systems and direct manipulation are important approaches for reducing errors. In command language interfaces, a well-designed language and the use of automatic command completion can help reduce errors.

3.12   User Training and Aid:
Printed Manuals

No matter how well designed the user interface of a system is, all users will require some amount of training to learn to use the system. For some users, exploration of the system on their own will be sufficient. Other users will learn from another person. The remainder will require some type of training materials. Training materials can be paper documents of various sorts, or they may be computer based. This section will discuss printed manuals. A more complete discussion of how to write a user's manual is given in Appendix B. On-line materials will be discussed in Section 3.13.

The primary form of printed training and aid material is the traditional user manual. User manuals are documents that describe the various features of the system. Different forms and features of user manuals have evolved. These include quick reference cards with brief presentations of the syntax and vocabulary of the system, "dictionaries" or alphabetical listings of the vocabulary of the system along with definitions or descriptions, and novice user tutorials. Each of these forms and features in user manuals has evolved to meet the varied requirements posed by different users.

In writing a user manual, just as in designing the interface, the first step is to know the user. The writer must understand the characteristics of the user and must know how the user will be using the manual. Will the users be novice, intermittent, or expert users, or some combination of these types? What reading level will the users have? Will the manual be mainly used for training, for reference, or for both? What sort of tasks will the users be performing on the system? How do these tasks relate to the users' job or personal goals? Will most users be using the system in similar ways, to perform similar tasks, or will there be great variability in what the users expect from the system? The writer must thoroughly understand the system as well. It is impossible to teach someone else about something if you do not understand it yourself.

To understand the difficulties involved in writing manuals, consider the problem from a somewhat abstract point of view, as presented in Figure 3.6. In the figure, the head represents the user's world. The user comes into a learning situation knowing what sort of task goals he or she needs to accomplish and the steps that are involved in carrying out these tasks without the aid of a computer. Presumably, the user also has the idea that the computer should be able to help in some way in achieving the goals. On the other side of the figure is the computer world. The computer world is divided into two related domains. First, the computer

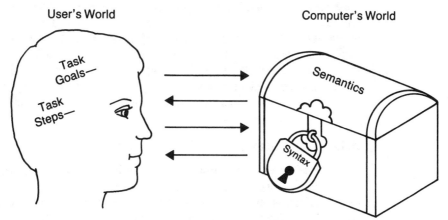

Figure 3.6 Abstract Representation of the Problems Involved in Writing User Manuals

world contains semantics. That is, the computer system has a set of functions that it is capable of executing. Second, the computer world has a set of syntactic rules and procedural rules (embodied in the user interface) that gives the user access to the functional capacities of the system. Therefore, the user has three kinds of knowledge to learn when confronted with a new system.

1. What are the functional capabilities of the system? What sort of tasks is the system capable of carrying out?

2. How do the functional capabilities of the system map onto the user's task goals? Which steps of the user's task can be carried out by the computer system being used and which cannot?

3. How does the user tap into the functional capabilities of the system to perform these tasks? What are the syntactic and procedural rules for activating these capabilities?

Different users may approach a system with none of these three sorts of knowledge, or they may already possess a certain amount of knowledge. Each of these types of users will require different things from a user manual. For example, consider writing a training manual for a word processor. One user — let us call her or him the No Background user — may know how to type, but has no knowledge of computer text editing. Such a user would need instruction on all three types of knowledge. A task-oriented training manual would be most appropriate for a No Background user. A second user — the Some Background user — might know how to type and be familiar with computer text editing, but know nothing about the current word-processing system. For such users, training in the semantics and syntax of the system is all that is necessary. The users can figure out for themselves how to map the semantics onto their task domain. A command dictionary might be all that these users would need. Finally, the Experienced user might be somewhat familiar with the word processor at hand, but needs to be reminded of how to do some task or wants to explore advanced features of the system. These users need only syntactic/procedural information. A quick reference card is useful in these cases.

While a more detailed guide to writing user manuals is provided in the Appendix, some general guidelines will be discussed. These guidelines are divided according to three aspects of manuals: content, organization and format, and writing style.

3.12.1 Content

Each of the three types of users requires different contents in a user manual. The No Background user requires a training manual. Experience and a certain number of empirical studies have suggested that manuals targeted for these users should strive to be *minimal* manuals (Foss, Smith-Kerker, and Rosson, 1987). In such manuals, the minimum amount of information necessary for the user to perform some meaningful task is presented. The user is guided step by step through the task. Minimal prose is included and error recovery can be dealt with. Ideally, the training manual should be accompanied by training software that mimics the actual software in many aspects, but prevents the user from making distracting errors. Diagrams and organizers presented prior to training can be a useful way to convey semantic information. For example, if a system involves different modes (for example, a send mode and a receive mode in an electronic mail system), a diagram that shows the different modes and their relationships to each other can be an effective training tool.

Some Background users require information about both the semantics and syntax of the system. Overviews and diagrams of the higher levels of a system can be useful to introduce them to the structure and capabilities of the system. Sample sessions of typical tasks (as opposed to training sessions) can also give quick insights into the system. The command dictionary should be well organized and formatted (see Section 3.12.2) and should probably include task terms from the user's domain, along with guidance to the syntax of the computer's domain. For example, a Some Background user may know that a document must be saved after editing with a word processor. The manual might include entries on "Saving Documents," "Closing Files," and "Saving Files." These entries should all point to the correct instruction in the manual for performing this activity (for example, "Exiting the System").

The Experienced user is probably best served by a quick reference card or on-line help that briefly reviews the vocabulary and syntax of the system. However, the command dictionary may also be used by the Experienced user to help gain advanced skills.

Manuals should also include a table of contents, an index, a glossary, and a list of error messages.

3.12.2 Organization and Format

It has already been suggested that training manuals should be task oriented. This implies such manuals are organized around the tasks they describe. To aid the mapping of the user's task world to the computer system world, the task as seen in the user's world is described first. Then the relationship of the task to the computer environment can be described. In other words, the task should be described from the outside in — from the semantics to the syntax. The concepts presented should be logically organized, preferably in increasing order of difficulty. Within each section the same organization should be followed. That is, begin with the motivation for the concept, describe how the concept relates to the task domain, introduce the computer-related semantic concept, and, finally, introduce the syntactic knowledge needed. Each section should have approximately the same amount of material.

Consistency is another important characteristic of well-written manuals. The organization of the manual and the organization within each section should be consistent. The reader should be able to find the same type of information in the same place in each section. This organization can be highlighted by the use of format. Blank spaces, different fonts, colors, boxes, and so on, can be used to visually signal the reader as to what type of information is being presented: task domain, high-level semantic, low-level semantic, or command syntax. Furthermore, main points and essential information can be visually emphasized, while explanatory and supporting material can be played down.

It is helpful if command references and quick reference cards are organized and formatted so that information is easy to find and easy to understand. Commands might be grouped by logical category, if the groupings are obvious. For example, a command reference for a word processor might group together file-handling commands, cursor control commands, formatting commands, and the like. Within each category, an organization based on frequency of use could be utilized, or an alphabetical ordering could be used. When a nonalphabetical organization is used, it is particularly important that the index and table of contents be complete and well written. Again, text layout and formatting play an important role in making the information easy to find and easy to understand.

3.12.3 Writing Style

Probably the best guideline the writer of a user manual can follow is KISS (Keep It Simple, Stupid!). Using simple declarative sentences forces the author to express only one idea in each sentence. Compound and complex sentences can be broken up into simple sentences. The use of negatives is often confusing and should be avoided.

Just as in designing the system messages, the manual should present the interactions with the computer as user centered. Avoid anthropomorphizing the computer. Consider the following examples, which tell the user how to display the next screen in a series of screen displays:

1. *Poor:* CutesyComputer will let you see the next screen when the F1 key is pressed.

2. *Poor:* The computer will show you the next screen when the F1 key is pressed.

3. *Better:* You can see the next screen by pressing F1.

4. *Better:* To see the next screen, press F1.

Notice that the first example makes it appear that the computer is a being, CutesyComputer, and that this being might just let you see the next screen if you can figure out how to press the F1 key. The second example is better, but still suggests that the computer is in charge, not the user. The last two examples are more user centered. They imply that the choice of what to do is up to the user. Example 3 uses the pronoun "you." This style is probably more appropriate for No Background readers. The terser style of example 4 is appropriate for Some Background and Experienced users.

It is also helpful to word instructions in a task-oriented way as well as in a user-centered way. Consider the following examples:

1. *Poor:* The computer must have a backup disk in Drive 2 to make backups.

2. *Better:* Put a backup disk in Drive 2 before making backups of files.

3. *Best:* To save a backup copy of a document, first put the disk labeled Backup Disk into Drive 2.

In example 1, the computer is clearly in charge. Example 2 is better because the user is the subject of the sentence. However, the task — backing up files — is described only in computer terminology. In example 3, the task is described in the user's terminology, and the user is the initiator of the action.

3.13   User Training and Aid:
On-line Facilities

To date, research suggests that on-line help facilities are not as effective as paper manuals (Magers, 1983; Cohill and Williges, 1982). Nonetheless, on-line facilities are of great help compared to no manual at all, a circumstance that frequently occurs. On-line help facilities also have, or could have, the following advantages:

- The information can be rapidly and inexpensively updated.
- All users are ensured of getting the latest material.
- Specific information can be located rapidly in a well-designed facility.
- There is a potential for graphics and animation that could be used in explaining or illustrating a concept.
- Successively more detailed explanations are rapidly and easily available.
- Quick cross referencing of terms is available.
- Lists of currently valid command choices based on the current state of the system can be made available.
- The user of on-line help avoids cluttering her or his workspace with a manual.

On-line help does have some drawbacks, however. Some of these drawbacks are related to the current state of display hardware. Specifically, studies have shown that screens are simply not as readable as printed materials (Muter and others, 1982; Gould and Grischkowsky, 1983). Furthermore, screens convey substantially less information than a manual and are slower to use. Another drawback to on-line help is that users are unfamiliar with on-line help and find the extra effort needed to learn to use the on-line help an interference to learning. Finally, if the screen is being used for the task, the on-line help blocks some or all of the screen, forcing the user to rely on short-term memory.

In spite of these drawbacks, on-line help should be seriously considered in designing the documentation for a system. Experienced users, in particular, find it useful. Furthermore, as display hardware improves and users, in general, become more sophisticated, on-line help will become a more widely accepted and useful form of user aid. In particular, the recent developments in the area of hypertext offer intriguing possibilities for on-line aid and training. A *hypertext* is a software system that embodies a hierarchical database. Unlike more traditional database systems, however, hypertext systems allow the nodes of information stored in the hierarchy to be of different types. For example, text, graphics, and executable code can all be accessed. A help system based on hypertext might offer the user seeking information on some topic a graphical depiction of the concept, a scrolling window of prose describing the concept, and the chance to try out the concept interactively, all on the same screen.

3.14   User Interface Design Development and Implementation

Up to this point, the present chapter has looked at different interface styles and offered guidelines for their design. Several questions still remain. How does one approach the development of the user interface design? What are the mechanics of design development? How is the design documented? How is the design evaluated? The rest of this chapter will be devoted to these topics, beginning with the development of the design.

Design is basically a creative process. The creative aspect of design is both a positive and a negative feature. It is positive because it makes design a challenging, interesting, and rewarding process. It is negative because it means that there is no algorithm that can be followed to produce a design. In fact, the process of design is very often not even linearly progressive. That is, the process of designing does not just start at the beginning, work through a series of predetermined steps, and emerge at the end with a good design. Often, design is transformational. Partial and interim solutions may be abandoned or evolve into completely new solutions. Design is basically a dynamic process, and a designer must be able to think dynamically and make the design evolve. However, the dynamic nature of design does not preclude discipline. Just as an artist or musician must have skill in using the tools and techniques of their art and an understanding of the foundations of their art, so must the designer of software interfaces have knowledge of interface design and skills in using the techniques of the trade.

By having read and studied the earlier sections of this chapter, you should have some understanding of the options available to the interface designer and how best to use those options. As an experienced user of software, you also have a fund of personal experiences to guide you in the design process. All that remains is to apply this knowledge to the design task.

The user interface can be seen as having a life cycle of its own. The phases in the cycle include:

1. Obtaining background information
2. Defining the semantics of the user interface
3. Defining the syntax and format of the interface
4. Choosing the physical devices
5. Developing the software
6. Integrating and installing the system
7. Providing on-site and product support

Although user interface design encompasses only the first four stages in the cycle, each of these phases will be discussed.

3.14.1   Obtaining Background Information

The user interface designer must be familiar with the content of the requirements specification document. He or she must thoroughly understand both the current situation and the proposed system. In particular, the designer must focus on the eventual users of the system. Probably the best approach to this task is to encourage both management and user participation at this stage and at all stages of the design process. At this stage, interviews and questionnaires can be used. Detailed task analyses and task frequency analyses are also useful. If possible, gather information from the designers and users of similar systems.

3.14.2   Defining the Semantics of the User Interface

At the early stages in the design of the user interface, the designer should consider the tasks to be performed by the system in the abstract. No decisions concerning style of interface, screen format, and the like, should be made at this time. The tasks should be broadly organized into categories. For each category, consider various task flow sequencing alternatives. Create and describe the different task and computer objects in the system world. Evaluate the semantic design by obtaining management, sponsor, and user feedback.

As a brief example, consider the noncredit courses office example from Chapter 2. In this example, the broad categories of tasks include registrations, cancellations, inquiries, and payments. Higher-level tasks related to registration (from the user's point of view) might include entering student information, checking for the presence of a student in the student file, retrieving a student file, updating a student file, entering requested-course information, retrieving course information, checking the course files, and mailing an invoice and confirmation to the student. The designer should decide which of these tasks may be done in any order and which must be sequenced. Of the tasks that must be sequenced, consider what the possible orderings are and which of these orderings seem the most natural and logical from the user's standpoint. For example, in registering a student, the first task must be checking for a student in the student file. The last task is mailing the invoice and confirmation. Various sequences of the other activities are possible. These sequences should be listed and evaluated. Another consideration at this point would be the amount of flexibility to be given to the user in the ordering of the tasks. A system could be designed so that the user must step through the tasks in a strict order. An alternate design might allow the user to perform the various registration tasks in (almost) any order and include a check to make sure all tasks had been done before leaving the registration task environment.

Task objects in the registration task environment that the designer might consider as possibilities include old-student information, new-student information, requested-course information, course information, and invoice/confirmation notices. Task objects in the computer environment might include student files, course files, invoice files, and invoice/confirmation forms.

3.14.3 Defining the Syntax and Format of the Interface

At this stage the designer decides on the style or styles of interaction to be used in the interface. Alternative display formats are considered and evaluated. Informative feedback for each operation is designed. The syntax for actions and responses to errors must be determined. Error messages are designed. Plans should be drawn up for any tutorials and/or help facilities, and the user manual should be written. Throughout this stage, mock-ups of the displays should be used. Paper mock-ups are fine in the initial stages. On-line mock-ups or *prototypes* are better as the design takes shape. Prototyping is a design evaluation technique that is being increasingly used. A *prototype* of a user interface is a model or imitation of the proposed user interface implemented on a computer. Prototypes can and should look and, to a great extent, operate just as the proposed interface will. For example, the prototype of a form fill-in interface might display the form, allow the user to fill in the fields, and allow the user to correct errors. However, the automatic error checking might not be implemented. A menu interface prototype might allow the user to make a selection and then display a fixed, dummy screen showing the supposed results of having made that choice. A number of prototyping tools are available, including hypertext systems, Prototyper (Smethers Barnes), MSWindows (Microsoft), and user interface management systems. Evaluation of the prototype and the user manual should be made by management, the sponsor, and users. Evaluation should include reviews, pilot tests, and field studies.

3.14.4 Choosing the Physical Devices

The physical devices needed to interface with the user must be chosen. Many sorts of input and output devices are available today, and more varieties of devices are appearing every day. Even among the standard devices — display screens, printers, keyboards, and mice — there are many possibilities. While it is beyond the scope of this book to discuss these in detail, designers should be aware of what is available and use these devices in creative ways. The work environment should be considered in making the selections, as well as design constraints.

3.14.5 Developing the Software

Once the design of the interface is completed, the software to support the interface and to provide the functional capabilities of the system should be designed and implemented using the software engineering principles discussed in the next four chapters of this book. Having designed the user interface gives the system designer a good headstart on the design of the system. In particular, the designer will know how the computer's task world must map onto the user's task world. It should be pointed out, however, that the system designer and the interface designer should have as a goal the creation of separate components of the final system, with well-defined, but minimal, communication links established between the two components. This design guideline has emerged recently as a natural outgrowth of the application of software engineering principles to design. The goal is to create a system that is easy to maintain and modify. The more the user interface is independent of the functional components of the system, the easier it is to modify. Thus changes in interface hardware, the work environment, and the skill level of users or changes due to user requests are more easily accommodated.

3.14.6 Integrating and Installing the System

As the system is developed and integrated, evaluation of the user interface should be continued. The evaluation should extend to user manuals, on-line help, and tutorials. A training subsystem or on-line tutorial might be developed. Once the system is installed, training and consultation for users should be provided.

3.14.7 Providing On-line and Product Support

Support for the product should continue after the system has been installed. On-line support can be provided in the form of consultants, suggestion boxes, evaluation forms, newsletters, and bulletin boards. Continued evaluation is important. The results of the evaluations and users' suggestions can be used to make improvements in the system.

3.15 Documenting the User Interface Design

To document the user interface design, two different types of documents are suggested. The first document results from the second step in the interface life cycle, defining the semantics of the user interface. In the semantic design document, prose, tables, diagrams, and lists can be used to present the semantic structure of the proposed interface. The categories of tasks are described along with a rationale for the categories chosen. Within each category, the tasks and the proposed sequences of tasks are described, again with rationales. The task and computer objects are listed and defined. In many cases, terms from the data dictionary can be used. The items in the design document should be cross referenced with the requirements and specifications document to ensure that all the requirements and specifications relevant to the user interface have been covered. In particular, the designers must ensure that every function the system is to be capable of performing is accessible from the user interface.

The second document, the interface prototype, results from the third step in the interface life cycle, defining the syntax and format of the interface. Part of this "document" could consist of software implementing the interface prototype. If software prototyping is not used, a set of illustrations of the proposed screen formats can be presented. On some systems, a word processor can be used to create screens, and then the "print-the-screen" key or keystroke sequence can be used to print a replica of the screen. If screen printing is not available, graph paper is a good medium, so that the precise layout of the information on the screen can be conveyed. Similarly, the format of printed output can be simulated with a word processor or using graph paper. Prose should accompany these illustrations to explain which of the actions described in the semantic design document are being handled by the illustrated interface. Proposed error-prevention techniques must be explained. Types of errors and proposed error messages must also be included.

Ideally, a draft of the user manual is created as part of the interface design. In a class project, however, this task may have to be postponed. Work on the user manual can begin after the preliminary system design, when the design of the interface has been more fully evaluated.

3.16   Evaluating the User Interface Design

Formal evaluation of the user interface semantics should take place as soon as the semantics are defined. Evaluation is intended to assure that all the requirements for the system are handled by the proposed semantics. Furthermore, the sponsor and users should evaluate the semantics to assess the degree to which the proposed system semantics match the user's task semantics.

Evaluation of the interface syntax and format is facilitated by a software prototype. However, the design can also be evaluated by having a human "play computer" with a user and by using paper "screens". Users must verbalize what actions they are performing (for example, which menu option they choose), and the human shows the correct "screens" and printouts as the user works her or his way through a session. Thinking aloud and comments should be encouraged during these sessions to maximize feedback. More formal evaluations by management, sponsors, and users are also needed. Again, the interface must be cross-checked with the requirements and specifications to assure that all required functions are readily accessible from the interface.

Checklists can be developed as an aid in evaluation. Shneiderman (1987) includes a long form and a short form of a user evaluation instrument in his book. Smith and Mosier (1986) have authored an extensive design evaluation checklist for user interface software, which is in the public domain (not copyrighted) and available from NTIS (see the bibliography at the end of this book). Each of the 679 items in the checklist includes a reference to a section in a guidebook on designing interface software. Their guidebook and evaluation form cover the following facets of interface design: data entry, data display, sequence control (interaction style), user guidance (feedback), data transmission, and data protection. Within each area are multiple subareas of evaluation. Figure 3.7 shows the portion of the checklist that deals with general considerations in data display. Figure 3.8 shows a portion of the checklist for user guidance. The portion shown deals specifically with error feedback. The authors suggest that each item in the checklist be given a weighting based on design criteria prior to evaluation. During evaluation, each item is to be

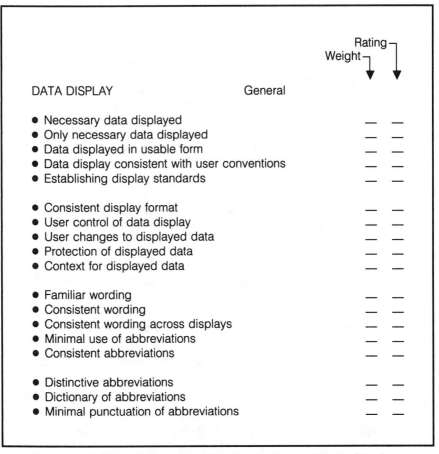

Figure 3.7 Items Related to the Evaluation of Data Displays from Smith and Mosier's Interface Evaluation Checklist (Smith and Mosier, 1986)

Rating
Weight

USER GUIDANCE   Error Feedback

- Informative error messages
- Specific error messages
- Task-oriented error messages
- Advisory error messages
- Brief error messages

- Neutral wording for error messages
- Multilevel error messages
- Multiple error messages
- Indicating repeated errors
- Nondisruptive error messages

- Appropriate response time for error messages
- Documenting error messages
- Cursor placement following error
- User editing of entry errors
- Cautionary messages

- User confirmation of destructive entries
- Alarm coding

Figure 3.8 Items Related to the Evaluation of Error Feedback from Smith and Mosier's Interface Evaluation Checklist (Smith and Mosier, 1986)

rated on a predetermined scale, for example, a scale of 0 to 7. Comments can also be noted on the evaluation forms.

By the way, what do you think about the user interface of analog versus digital watches now that you have read this chapter? Consider the ease of obtaining information from the device as it relates to the format of the display, the ease of use, the ease of learning to read the device, and the ease of learning to operate the device.

3.17 Case Study: Designing the User Interface for the Rev-Pro System

The design of the interface of the Rev-Pro system was crucial to the success of the system. The Rev-Pro system was to be created to replace a current manual system. The manual system involved the use of a spreadsheet package on an Apple IIe computer, a calculator, and paper and pencil. The sponsor wanted a system that would be easier to use than the manual methods. Because the system would be used on an intermittent basis, it was important that it be easy to remember how to use it as well.

The Rev-Pro team appointed two members to be in charge of the design of the user interface. They were familiar with the manual methods used by the sponsor and the limitations these had. They noted that the spreadsheet package was probably closest to the sort of approach the final system would involve. The spreadsheet package allowed the entry of data in organized rows and columns, and the calculation and recalculation of summary data. However, the sponsor wanted a more personalized system than the spreadsheet package could offer, with the ability to move back and forth among the various tables and categories of information.

The semantics of the proposed system were defined using the model of the Proposed Logical System described in the Requirements and Specification document and through interaction with the sponsor. A description of the proposed task flow was created and revised. A portion of the final version of the semantic design is shown in Table 3.5. (The complete semantic design is presented in Appendix A, Part II.) The table is organized into broad categories of tasks and subtasks within these broad categories. Although there is no necessary logical order among the three tasks — Scaling-the-Hall, Tabulate-Costs and Tabulate-Nonticket-Revenues — the sponsor felt that doing the tasks in the order stated here was more natural. This order, then, was proposed for the system. However, the system was required to allow the user to go back and forth among these activities. Thus, a user could skip ahead to, for example, Tabulate-Nonticket-Revenues, and then return to Scaling-the-Hall later. The subsequent activities — Produce-Master-Pricing-Grids, Estimate-Demand, and Produce-Estimated-Revenue-Tables — are all logically dependent on information from previous stages in the system and thus must follow the stated order to produce meaningful output. However, it was decided that, for the sake of consistency, the user would be allowed to move back and forth among these activities as well. The Semantic Design document was reviewed by the entire Rev-Pro project team, the sponsor, and the instructor.

Because the Rev-Pro system requires the user to enter a large number of data items and involves the display of many tables, the designers of the user interface felt that a spreadsheet-style of interface was probably the most effective style to use for most of the activities of the system. The spreadsheet style combines a form fill-in interface with menus. The user uses arrow keys or the return key to bounce a cursor among the fields of the form to be filled in, and uses special key sequences (e.g., function keys) to select an option from the menu or menus constantly displayed on the screen.

The prototype for the Scale-the-Hall screen is shown in Figure 3.9. When the user begins the scaling activity, all fields in the form (table) are empty. An empty field is indicated by a series of underline characters in the field. One underline is included for each potential character in the field. For example, the last row (Level 4) of Figure 3.9 has not yet been filled in by the user. As indicated by the number of underline characters, the number of seats can range from 0 to 99999, the number of complimentary tickets can range from 0 to 9999, single ticket prices

Table 3.5 A Portion of the Semantic Design of the User Interface of the Rev-Pro System Case Study

---

The Semantic Design of the User Interface for the Rev-Pro System

Overall: The major tasks for the user of the Rev-Pro system are listed below. The order in which the tasks are listed indicates the order the user will be required to follow. Although tasks B, C and D do not strictly have to go in the given order, the sponsor requested the order shown. Within each task, the subtasks are listed in sequential order.

A. Starting the system

 Description: Activities related to starting up the system
 1. Enter: start-up command

B. Scaling-the-Hall

 Description: Activities related to scaling the hall. The hall (theater) must be divided into different sections. Each section has a different price category associated with it. The user must indicate how many categories there are, the number of seats in each category, the price of a single ticket at each price category and the number of complimentary seats that will be given away in each category. Once all the data has been entered, the user may ask the computer to calculate the total of all complimentary seats and all gate seats. The user will be given the option of changing any entries and recalculating. The user may print out the entered and calculated information.

 Task Sequencing:
 1. Enter: total seats in the house
 2. Enter: number of price categories
 3. Observe: running total of number of seats left to assign
 4. Enter: number of seats for each price category (up to 7 different entries)
 5. Enter: number of complimentary seats for each price category (up to 7 different entries)
 6. Enter: the price of a single ticket for each price category (up to 7 different entries)
 7. Options: make any changes desired in entered data, (re)calculate totals
 8. Observe: all information entered, total of all complimentary tickets and total of all gate seats
 9. Option: print information
 10. Options: quit, go to next task

 Task Objects: See "Seating" in the Data Dictionary

---

can range from $0.00 to $999.99, and so on. The user must fill in the three fields at the top of the screen before proceeding to fill in the seating information. In particular, the system must know the number of price levels so that the correct number of price levels will be included on the table. When the user comes to the Scale-the-Hall screen, the cursor will be in the "Total Number of Seats" field. Entering a value and pressing the carriage return will cause a number to be entered and the cursor to move on to the next field. Entering a carriage return only will cause the cursor to move to the next field without changing the contents of the

```
                            SCALE THE HALL

    Total Number of Seats: _ 100        Total Number of Price Levels:   4

                    Number of Events Per Series:  _ 6


   LEV | # OF SEATS | # OF COMPS | SGL TICKET PRICE | # GATE SEATS | TOT REVENUE


   1  |   --400    |   --20     |   $ _15.00       |              |
   2  |   --300    |   --10     |   $ _13.50       |              |
   3  |   --200    |   ---0     |   $ _11.00       |              |
   4  |   -----    |   ----     |   $ ---.--       |              |



                            TOTAL POT. REVENUE: $

   F7:  Calculate      F8:  Print Screen      F9:  <---      F10: --->
```

Figure 3.9 Prototype Screen for the Scale-the-Hall Activity from the Rev-Pro Case Study

field. Notice that the columns headed "# GATE SEATS" and "TOT REVENUE," and the value "TOTAL POTENTIAL REVENUE" are all empty in Figure 3.9. These values will be filled in automatically when the user selects the "Calculate" option from the menu of command options displayed on the bottom row of the screen. The menu options use the IBM/PC command function keys. Pressing the command function key F7 will cause the system to calculate the number of gate seats and the total revenue for each price level, as well as total potential revenue. Pressing the function key F8 will cause the system to print the screen. Pressing F9 will cause the system to go back to the prior activity, and pressing F10 will cause the system to go forward to the next activity. Abbreviations were used on the screen design because of limited space. The abbreviations were chosen in consultation with the user to be sure they were meaningful. Additional screen prototypes for the Rev-Pro system are shown in Appendix B, Part II.

An alternative interface style that was considered for the Rev-Pro system involved a modified version of form fill-in where the user would be queried for input in a specified order. Once all the queries were answered, a table showing the entered values and the calculated values would be presented. If the user wished to change any entries, the entire sequence would be repeated. While this approach had the advantage of being easy to program, it had several disadvantages for the user. Probably the greatest disadvantage was that the user must reenter all the data, even if he only wished to change one data item. A second major disadvantage was that the user would not be able to see all of the previously entered data as he was entering later data. This alternative interface was rejected.

The user interface prototypes were evaluated using walkthroughs with the entire class, sponsor review, and instructor review.

The group decided that a user's manual that included a sample session with the system was needed. The manual also needed to include information on starting up the system and maintaining backups. One person was assigned to design and create the user's manual.

Summary

The user interface is the user's gateway to the capabilities of a software system. A widely used approach to software system design is from the outside to the inside, starting with the user interface. First the user interface is designed and then the functional parts of the system are designed to support or enable the user interface. Factors that influence the quality of an interface include ease of learning, speed of use, frequency of user errors, user satisfaction, and knowledge retention.

It is important to know the user before designing the interface. Different sorts of interfaces are appropriate for different sorts of users. A useful categorization of users is by computer experience and frequency of use: novices, intermittent users, and frequent users. The different interaction styles widely in use today include menu selection, form fill-in, command language, and direct manipulation. No matter which style is used, the interface should be consistent, offer shortcuts for frequent users, provide informative feedback, provide closure for each task, offer simple error handling, permit easy reversal of actions, support user-centered action, and reduce short-term memory load.

Menu selection interfaces are particularly appropriate for novices and intermittent users. The semantic organization and structure of menus is an important design issue. The organization and structure of the menus should structure the task in a logical way for the user. A variety of menu styles is available, including multi- and single-screen menus, permanent menus, and pull-down or pop-up menus.

Form fill-in interfaces are appropriate where a significant amount of data entry is necessary and work best with intermittent and frequent users. The forms should be laid out so that all information on the screen is logically related. The forms should provide meaningful labels for the fields and include information on the format of the data to be entered. Error correction should be easy, and information on task completion and exiting should be provided.

Command languages are powerful but difficult for novices and intermittent users to use. Command languages should consist of a limited vocabulary and a carefully constructed syntax. Both abbreviations and full commands should be allowed, and on-line help should be provided.

Direct-manipulation interfaces present the task world to the user in the form of icons that can be directly manipulated using a mouse or other pointing device. Direct manipulation is probably most suitable for novice and intermittent users. However, combined with other styles of user interface, it is appropriate for frequent users as well. The icons used in direct-manipulation interfaces must be well chosen.

Screen layout should make the information being presented clear and well organized. Although a number of display guidelines are available, it is important to experiment with various layouts for the application being designed.

Whenever possible, software should be designed to prevent errors from occurring. If used, error messages should be specific in describing the error, offer constructive guidance on how to overcome the error, have a positive tone, and be well formatted.

In writing user manuals, the author must know the audience and address the manual to that audience. Manuals may include training information, information on the semantics and syntax of the system, and quick reference materials. (Appendix B is a complete guide to writing user manuals.) An alternate or secondary source of user aid is on-line facilities. Although on-line facilities are typically not as effective as manuals, they are an important facet of user support.

The creation of a user interface involves a development cycle similar to the development of a software system. The phases of the cycle include obtaining background information, defining the semantics of the interface, defining the syntax and format, choosing the physical devices, developing the interface software, integrating the interface and the rest of the software system, installing the system, and providing on-site and product support. The best way to evaluate a user interface design is through prototyping.

Checklist of Project Activities

_____   Schedule user interface design activities and assign personnel.

_____   Assess the current physical and proposed physical system from the standpoint of user interface. What aspects of the current system's interface are good or poor? What aspects of the proposed system's interface are good or poor?

_____   Obtain information about the potential users of the system. Will they be novice, intermittent, or frequent users, or possibly a mixture? Will they be adults or children? If children, what age?

_____   If possible, observe the potential users using the current system. How do they approach their tasks? Interview them concerning the pros and cons of the current system.

_____   Try out software systems similar to the proposed system and assess the user interfaces.

_____   Define the semantics of the proposed system. Begin by organizing the tasks into categories. Consider various task flow sequencing alternatives for each. Make a distinction between objects in the task environment and actions in the task.

_____ Create a Semantic Design document for the semantics of the proposed system. Use prose, tables, diagrams, and/or lists. Cross reference this document with the requirements and specification to ensure that all requirements are met by the proposed system.

_____ Evaluate the Semantic Design document using reviews. Involve the sponsor and the potential users in the review process.

_____ Decide on the style or combinations of interface styles to be used. Consider alternative styles before deciding. Make prototypes to help in reaching a decision.

_____ Refine the prototype for the chosen interface style.

_____ Create a User Interface Design document based on the refined prototype.

_____ Evaluate the prototype and the User Interface Design document using reviews, pilot tests, and field studies. Include the sponsor and potential users in the review process.

_____ Revise the User Interface Design based on the reviews.

_____ Decide what other user aids might be needed, such as on-line help, tutorial systems, or off-line tutorials. Begin planning their design and implementation.

_____ Read "How to Write a User's Manual" (Appendix B).

_____ If possible, write a draft of the user manual based on the User Interface Design.

_____ If budget allows, choose the physical devices for the interface.

Terms and Concepts Introduced

user interface	direct manipulation
novice	transparency
knowledgeable intermittent user	semantic organization
frequent user	icon
menu selection	hypertext
form fill-in	prototype
command language	

Exercises

1. What are the pros and cons of the traditional wristwatch interface with a dial and winding stem compared to the interface provided by digital watches? Consider the various criteria used to judge computer interfaces, including ease of learning, speed of use, ease of remembering, frequency of errors, and user satisfaction.

2. Many device interfaces can be implemented in one of two styles: analog or digital. The speedometer of a car, for instance, is traditionally an analog interface, where the distance the pointer moves around the dial face indicates the magnitude of the speed. On the other hand, odometers (mileage indicators) are traditionally digital. The number of miles traveled is given in digits. Input devices can be analog or digital, as well. A steering wheel is analog. You turn it a little to the right to turn slightly right, and you turn it more to the right to make a sharper turn. A car radio that allows you to select channels by pushing a numbered button (which recalls a preselected channel) would be a digital device. For the following devices, decide whether an analog or digital interface would be better. Defend your decision.

speedometer	radio volume control
steering wheel	motor heat gauge
gas gauge	odometer
window opener	heater settings

3. Design a direct-manipulation interface for a computer version of Mr. Potato-Head. (Mr. PotatoHead is a trademark of the PlaySkool Corporation). Mr. PotatoHead is a toy for kids that allows them to construct different versions of heads by putting various parts onto a basic blank head. For example, eyes, mouths, hair, clothing, beards, and so on, can be placed on the head. Include a way for the user to vary the "style" of the part that is added (for example, eyes can be round, narrowed, or crossed).

4. Suppose you were designing part of the interface for an automated appointment calendar for knowledgeable intermittent users. The user can either make entries into the calendar or can refer to the calendar to see what appointments there are for a particular day. The input data consist of the date, the hour of the appointment (optional), and any message or notes the user cares to enter concerning the appointment. Each entry (there may be several for any one day) should be considered a separate entity. The user should be able to refer to the entries for any day, alter entries, delete single entries, or delete entries for an entire day. The user should be able to exit the system at will (updated information will be automatically saved). Do not concern yourself with the design of the interface for the editing of message entries (when they are initially created or altered). Likewise, do not consider error messages.

   Design a user interface for this system. Consider the interface style or styles to be used to access each function of the system. Include sample screens to show format and interface style across the system.

5. If you designed the interface in Exercise 4 to use a direct-manipulation interface, design it again assuming keyboard data entry only. (You may assume there are arrow keys to move a cursor around on the screen.) If you designed the interface in Exercise 4 based on keyboard data entry, redesign it based on direct-manipulation interfacing.

6. Suppose you were designing the interface for a checkbook balancing program for personal use (as opposed to business use). Assume the program is to be used by novice or knowledgeable intermittent adult users. The input to the program is to consist of:

   (1) Information concerning checks written (check number, date, amount, and payee)

   (2) Check status (outstanding, cleared, bounced, or voided)

   (3) Information concerning automatic deductions, such as banking fees and automatic payments (including date, reason, and amount)

   (4) Deposits (date, amount, and source)

   Output (to a screen or to a printer) is to consist of:

   (1) List of all input data, sorted by check number

   (2) Summary data, including current balance, total deposits, and total withdrawals

   Assume the system will work on a month by month basis and that checks that have not cleared the previous month will automatically be entered into the current month. Do not consider the interface for editing the entries or deleting old or unwanted information. Do not consider the design of error messages.

   (a) For each category of input listed, decide what sort of interface style would be best. Make a separate decision for each category. Defend your decision.

   (b) For each output category listed, decide what format would be most appropriate.

   (c) Now consider the interface of the system as a whole, including system start-up, movement among the functions of the system (including the various sorts of input and output), and exiting the system. What style or styles of interface are appropriate for each function, keeping in mind that consistency is an important quality of a good interface? Draw up a series of screens that show a rough outline of your proposed design of the user interface.

7. If you designed the interface in Exercise 6 to use a direct-manipulation interface, design it again assuming keyboard data entry only. (You may assume there are arrow keys to move a cursor around on the screen.) If you designed the interface in Exercise 6 based on keyboard data entry, redesign it based on direct-manipulation interfacing.

8. Color monitors and computers that support color graphics are becoming more readily available and cheaper every year. Very little research has been done on the effectiveness of color in user interfaces. Considering each of the different styles of user interface separately, how do you think color could be effectively used in the style? Is it possible that some styles would not be enhanced by the use of color? In what situations or for what sorts of users do you think

color might be irrelevant or even a distraction? Can you think of particular computer applications for which color might be of great value? Of some value? Of no value?

9. Icons are used in many parts of our culture and daily lives. List five different noncomputer icons. Which of these icons seems the most effective and why? Which of these icons seems the least effective and why?

10. Obtain a user manual for a piece of applications software. (Alternatively, obtain a manual for a piece of complex equipment, such as a camera, microwave oven, or VCR.) Evaluate the manual by considering the following:

    (a) What type of user/reader is the manual intended for?

    (b) Does the manual make clear what audience it is intended for?

    (c) Are the goals/purpose of the manual clearly stated?

    (d) Is the manual a tutorial or a reference manual or both? Are these facets clearly separated and labeled?

    (e) How is the manual organized?

    (f) What is the level of the writing style?

    (g) What is the quality of the writing style?

    (h) What types of nontext materials (for example, tables, graphs, or pictures) are included?

    (i) Is there a table of contents? An index? Are they well written and complete?

    (j) Are there useful supplementary materials such as quick-reference cards, lists of commands, or demonstration disks?

    (k) Is there a list of error messages and/or a troubleshooting guide? Are they complete and well written?

11. Describe and evaluate the user interface for a video game you are familiar with. Include a description and evaluation of the physical input/output devices and their configuration. Consider visual, auditory, and kinetic (movement) aspects of the interface. Describe and evaluate the role of color in the interface.

12. Name and describe three situations where voice input might be appropriate. Do not be concerned with feasibility. Consider user characteristics, environment, and the nature of the application. Compare it to other, more traditional types of input for each situation.

13. The classic movie *2001: A Space Odyssey* depicts two astronauts traveling on a spaceship. The ship is largely computer controlled. The astronauts interact with the computer mostly through natural language. The computer can understand spoken language and provides verbal natural language output. Do you think it would be easy and efficient to use natural language in such a situation? Would natural language in fact be an effective way to run all the activities of a spaceship? Under what situations would natural language be limiting or awkward?

14. Obtain a list of the error messages (related to either syntax errors or run-time errors) that can be produced by a compiler you have used. Take ten of these messages and rewrite them to make them better. (Do not be concerned with whether it is possible to write compilers or operating systems to produce the better messages.)

15. For each of the four interface styles discussed in the book, list at least three applications that might be best implemented using each style.

16. Describe ten examples of error-prevention and/or error-recovery techniques that you have encountered in using software.

17. List some of the errors a user might be likely to make in using the calendar program described in Exercise 4 or the checkbook program described in Exercise 6. Based on your interface design for these systems, would it be possible to prevent some of these errors? Could your interface be redesigned to prevent some or all of these errors? What features could you add to make error recovery easier?

18. Look at some computer-related periodicals and find advertisements and articles for new and/or unusual input and output devices. Describe what these devices do. What applications are suggested for each device? Describe at least one other application where the device would be useful.

19. Design the format of a form-driven interface (display) that would allow a user to enter all the necessary information that appears on the front of your driver's license or student identity card. Assume the display screen is 80 columns (characters) wide and 24 lines deep. Include a title at the top of the screen and a function menu with at least four primary options (for example, Save, Delete, Edit, Exit) somewhere on the screen.

20. Design a menu interface that allows the user to find out information about all the restaurants in a city. The information about each restaurant should include its ethnic type or specialty (for example, seafood, steaks, Chinese, home-cooking), its style (elegant, casual, fast-food), its cost (inexpensive, moderate, or expensive), its part of town (central, north, south, east, or west), and other specific information such as name, address, telephone number, hours, reservations required, and dress code.

21. Design a command language to operate a television set, including commands to select a particular channel, control the volume, turn the television on and off, adjust the lightness/darkness setting, adjust the horizontal hold, and adjust the vertical hold.

4. Preliminary Design: Designing the Software Structure and Data Structures

Once the important decisions concerning how the system will look to the user have been made, the next steps are to design the internal structure of the software and to design the data structures. The software must be designed both to carry out the functions specified in the requirements and specifications document and to support the user interface as it was designed during the user interface design process. Designing the software structure is the most critical step in creating a good, working software system. The software structure is the framework or skeletal structure of the software system. In designing the software structure, the modules that are to comprise the system are designated, and the interrelations among all the modules in the system are specified. If the software structure is not well designed, the system will be difficult to build, test, and maintain.

Unfortunately, there is no algorithm for producing a good design. Design is basically a creative process. However, the need for creativity does not exclude the use of disciplined approaches and systematic notations. Musicians, choreographers, artists, and writers have all developed standard forms to guide the creative process. For example, a symphony is a standard musical composition form, a pas de deux is a standard ballet form, a portrait is a standard art form, and an essay is a standard prose form. Similarly, standard notations exist for recording designs, such as musical and dance notations. Artists use sketching as a design notation and writers often use outlines. Analogous design guidelines and tools have been derived for software development. It should not be expected that the adoption of a particular design method will ensure the development of a good design. However, it is true that the careful use of a design method will improve software design.

Although a large number of design methodologies have been developed, most of these methods can be classified as one of three types: *top-down functional design*, *object-oriented design*, or *data-driven design*. In top-down functional design, the system is viewed in terms of its functions. Starting at a high-level

143

view, each level is refined into successively more detailed levels of functions. Structured design (Yourdon and Constantine, 1979) and step-wise refinement (Wirth, 1971) are examples of top-down functional design methods. Object-oriented design is based on the use of data and procedural abstraction. Each data or procedural abstraction constitutes an object, and the system is composed of a collection of objects. Object-oriented design is based on the ideas of Parnas (1972) and has been elaborated on by Liskov and Guttag (1986), Booch (1987), and Cox (1986). In data-driven design, the structure of the data processed by the system is used to derive the structure of the software. The Jackson design method (Jackson, 1975) and Warnier's logical construction of programs method (Warnier, 1977, 1981) are examples of data-driven methods.

While different methodologies are more suited for different types of systems, what is most important is that one methodology is chosen and used to direct and discipline the design process. The design method that will be described in this chapter is the structured design method (Yourdon and Constantine, 1979), which builds on the structured analysis technique described in Chapter 2. This method was selected for detailed consideration because structured design and related methods are the most widely used methods for both small- and large-scale systems and are used in a diverse number of application areas. Object- and data-oriented design methods are discussed in Chapter 8. Before beginning a discussion of structured design, however, there are some basic concepts related to the design process that you should be familiar with. These include *modularity, cohesion, coupling,* the concept of a *black box,* and the *top-down design* approach.

4.1 The Concept of Modularity

Modules are the basic building block of the software structure. What is a module? Unfortunately, communication in software engineering is hindered by a lack of consistent terminology. The term module is probably the most inconsistently used term in the area. One source of the inconsistency is related to the level of abstraction or detail one wishes to discuss. You may have heard the procedures, functions, or subroutines of a coded program referred to as modules. However, in discussing the design of a system or in looking at complex systems containing many separate programs, the term module can have different meanings. The term is sometimes applied to functionally related groups of procedures, functions, or subroutines, and it can also be applied to data abstractions (sometimes also known as *clusters*) and concurrent processes. The common theme to all these uses of the term module is that modules are used to describe a functional decomposition of the system. For our purposes, a *module* is a unit containing executable instructions, data structures, and/or other modules; it has a name; it can (often) be separately compiled; and it can be used in a program or it can use other modules. Thus an entire program could be considered a module, as could a library function to compute sines, a set of graphics routines, a data abstraction, a related set of data abstractions, or an Ada package. To understand what the term is referring to, it is necessary to take into account the context in which it is used. When the term module is used in this text, it should be assumed that it is referring to modules in general, across the entire range of abstraction, unless otherwise stated.

In most programming classes today, students are taught to create programs that contain several procedures, subroutines, or functions (that is, modules). Programs that are one continuous list of statements are discouraged. In high-level, block-structured languages such as Pascal, Modula-2, or Ada, modules are natural outgrowths of using the languages effectively. It is natural to use procedures, subroutines, and functions when writing programs in these languages. In fact, these languages were designed to encourage the programmer to create modular programs. When programming in a lower-level language such as assembly language or C, or in a language that is not block-structured, such as BASIC or COBOL, it is up to the designer and programmer to impose modularity. The most important criteria that should be used in creating modules are design criteria, including cohesion and coupling (see below). The design of the program or system should determine what goes into a module. However, another important design guideline is to make modules "the right size". Each unit should be small enough to be easily understood by itself. There is some disagreement about what is meant by "small enough." Weinberg's studies (1971) suggested that modules of more than 30 lines are difficult to understand. IBM advises that a module should not exceed 50 lines of code, thus enabling the code to fit onto one page of a source listing or onto a screen (Baker, 1972). The idea behind this second guideline seems reasonable. It makes sense to be able to view a module as a whole. However, documentation can play an important role in understanding. The lines of documentation should enter into IBM's line estimate, as well as programming statements. Martin and McClure (1985) suggest that modules of less than 10 lines can break the program into too many pieces and affect program efficiency. Another disadvantage of extremely short modules is that the overhead associated with the design, testing, and documentation of the modules is just as great as for longer modules, making the ratio of effort to functional payoff disproportionate for such modules. In some cases, other considerations may override the disadvantages of short modules. For example, if a program is implementing an abstract data type, such as a stack or queue, it makes sense to implement each of the standard operations associated with the type as a separate module. Although some of these modules might be quite short, it is important to maintain the spirit and power of the abstract data type.

One immediate advantage of limiting modules to 30 to 50 lines is that such modules will easily fit entirely onto a monitor screen or one page of a computer printout when the source code is being examined or edited. There is no need to scroll back and forth through the source code to seek out the pertinent section or to flip through pages of printout. Another advantage of short modules relates to the capabilities of human memory. While humans are capable of holding huge quantities of information on a long-term basis, there is a limit to how much information can be currently active in what is called short-term memory (Miller, 1956). When working on a problem, the facts and ideas that you are currently thinking about are stored in short-term memory. Such ideas and facts readily fade out of short-term memory (are forgotten) as soon as they are no longer needed for the task at hand. Furthermore, because the capacity of short-term memory is limited, some ideas and facts can be pushed out of your short-term memory by the entrance of new ones. In other words, there is only so much space available for juggling information, and the information that enters goes in on a first-in, first-out basis. When a programmer is trying to solve a problem, such as finding a bug in a module, short-term memory is used to hold the information and ideas he or she needs to know to find the bug. For example, the programmer might be thinking about the likely causes of the bug, the errors that were produced by the bug, what the module is supposed to be doing, and/or the algorithm used in the module. If the module being debugged is complex, the amount of information needed to solve the problem will exceed the capacity of short-term memory. The programmer will have to juggle parts of the problem into and out of short-term memory and probably use memory aids such as notes made with paper and pencil to solve the problem. On the other hand, if the module is short enough, all the necessary information for solving the debugging problem will fit into short-term memory, and a solution can be more efficiently and readily attained.

The idea of having programs broken up into modules is similar to the idea behind using paragraphs in written text. Paragraphs should be short enough to fit on one page or less. And the ideas expressed in each paragraph should be simple enough to be grasped as a whole. Even in text dealing with difficult subject matter, each paragraph should be "bite-sized." The reader should be able to read the paragraph, extract the major ideas, and put the ideas into short-term memory. Once there, the ideas can be contemplated or "chewed on" until they are understood and the reader is ready to go on to the next paragraph.

Modules, in the sense of subroutines, procedures, and functions, are an essential part of good programming practice. However, when designing a complex system, thinking only in terms of modules defined at this level is limiting. As a parallel example, consider an author trying to write a book. Certainly the author would not just start writing, but would think about what should be included in the book and in what order. In other words, the book would first be designed before it was written. If the author began the design process at the level of paragraphs, the book would probably never get written. The more logical approach is to begin the design process at a more abstract level — the level of chapters, for example. Once the order of and general content of each chapter have been tentatively decided on, each chapter can be reviewed individually and a list of subtopics generated. Each subtopic would be further refined before actual writing began. The process just described is *decomposition* — a problem-solving approach discussed in Section 2.2.2. Software design methodologies follow the same approach as our hypothetical author and likewise use decomposition. The system is first sketched out at a broad or high level and broken down into modules appropriate to the level of abstraction. Each of these modules is then refined into lower-level modules until each module represents a problem whose solution is known or is trivial. The design method being used determines exactly what is included in a module at each level of abstraction during the design process, but all design methods incorporate modularity in the sense discussed here.

4.1.1 Modules Should Be Cohesive

Chapters and paragraphs serve as good analogies to modules in another way. As you were no doubt taught, a paragraph should have a central idea. The central idea is expressed in a topic sentence, and the rest of the sentences in the paragraph relate to this central idea. Likewise, chapters should be built around a central, but somewhat broader, idea. Modules should be designed with this same principle in mind: each module should have a central idea or purpose. The components that make up the module should then all be related to carrying out this one central purpose. This concept is called *cohesion*. Cohesion refers to the degree to which the internal elements of a module are bound to or related to each other.

The goal in designing modules is to have highly cohesive modules. Ideally, each module in a system performs one, and only one, clearly defined function within the system. There is no "quick and dirty" formula that can be given for designing cohesive modules. But there are two guidelines that designers can use in deciding whether a proposed module has cohesion. To apply the first guideline, try coming up with a complete, one-sentence description of what function or functions the module is supposed to perform. In other words, try to create a "topic sentence" for your proposed "paragraph." Now, look at the sentence. Is it a simple sentence with one subject and one verb? If so, your proposed module will probably be cohesive. Or is it a compound or complex sentence, possibly with several subjects or several verbs? If so, your proposed module is trying to do too many things. The second guideline is closely related to the first: try to come up with a name for the module that is as descriptive as possible of the function or functions performed by the module. If it is very difficult to come up with a short, descriptive name, the proposed module is not cohesive. If it is easy to name the module and if the name is honestly descriptive, it is probably cohesive.

Consider some examples of module designs for a generic system that creates reports based on data saved in a file and on data the user enters into the system during an interactive session. Suppose one of the requirements the sponsor specified is that the system produce a final report and that all the information in that report should be saved in a file for possible use at a later session. A designer might propose a module called FinishUp, which is described as follows: "FinishUp prints the final report and saves the final calculations out to the disk." The "and" in the middle of the descriptive sentence signals that this module should probably be redesigned. Even though printing the final report and saving the data are activities that are both performed at the end of a user session, they are nonetheless two separate sorts of functions. One function is related to producing printed output, and the other to saving information for a later session. Two separate modules should be used here. The name FinishUp sounds like it might be the name of a cohesive module because it is short. But the name was not chosen according to the guideline stated previously. The name is supposed to describe the *function* performed by the module, not when or how or why a module is used. FinishUp describes *when* the module was going to be used. A fairer name, one that would have shown that the module as originally designed was not cohesive, would have been PrintReportandSaveCalcs. In the new design, there should be two cohesive modules, one called PrintFinalReport and another called SaveCalculations.

As a second example, suppose the designers realize that although the user will be making entries in a variety of different tables, in all cases the entries will consist of a short line of typed (character) input followed by a carriage return. After each entry is made, the system needs to check the input to make sure it is valid. Rather than having the input validated within the module that creates each table, they wisely decide to centralize the error handling and have one module called from different parts of the system to validate any input. They decide to create a module called ValidateInput whose description is "Validates a single entry from the keyboard." Further exploration of what needs to be done by the module reveals, however, that in some cases the characters entered are to be interpreted as real numbers, in some cases as integers, and in some cases as literal characters. A truer description of the module would be "Validates real, integer, and character entries from the keyboard." The new description includes multiple activities, so the module is no longer cohesive. It is time to redesign the original module into three separate modules, each of which is cohesive: one for reals, one for integers, and one for character input. These could be named ValidateRealInput, ValidateIntegerInput, and ValidateCharacterInput.

4.1.2 Modules Should Be Loosely Coupled

The third criteria for evaluating the design of modules is *coupling*. Coupling refers to the degree of interconnectedness between modules (Yourdon and Constantine, 1979). The more one module has to interact with one or more other modules, the more coupled that module is. The goal in designing modules is to reduce the degree of coupling—to produce loosely coupled modules. Coupling, or interaction with other modules, is created in a variety of ways. For example, passing parameters, using global data, using any input or output device, returning from a subroutine to some point other than the calling point, and using multiple entry points or multiple return points all create coupling. Obviously, a certain amount of coupling is inevitable. Even the best designed modules may need to perform input or output operations and will certainly need to pass parameters. The object is to reduce such coupling to the minimum. For example, one module should typically *not* be involved with doing both input and output or input from two different devices. Likewise, a designer should keep an eye on the number of parameters being passed to a module. If the number seems large (greater than four or five), the module is becoming highly coupled. The large number of parameters may signal that the module is no longer cohesive. Check to see if all (or a majority) of the parameters will be used each time the module is called. If not, the module may be performing too many functions. Possibly the module is trying to be all things to all other modules. If so, the module should be redesigned to be more specialized, and other modules may need to be created to handle some of the other functions. The other causes of coupling (using global data, returning to a subroutine from some point other than the calling point, and using multiple entry or return points) are all programming techniques that should be avoided. In fact, aside from global data, these techniques are simply not allowed in most high-level languages.

One major reason coupling is avoided is because it creates connections or paths among modules that allow bugs to travel around through the system. If a module is very loosely coupled, then any errors that occur within that module are most likely due to the processing done within that module. However, once a module communicates with another module in any way, an error that appears to be located in that module may actually originate as a result of the communication with the other module. This makes it much more difficult to trace down and correct the error. Furthermore, the more the connections, the harder it is to determine which connection is related to the bug. Errors that occur as a result of the interfacing of modules are the most common and most costly types of errors to fix in software. Errors isolated within modules are rarer and cheaper to fix. Therefore, it makes sense to lessen the coupling among modules as much as possible to reduce the opportunities for errors to occur and to reduce the overall cost of developing the software.

4.1.3 Modules Should Be Black Boxes

The final guideline in designing modules is to attempt to make each module a black box. A *black box* is a system with known input and predictable output, but whose inner workings are unknown or irrelevant to the user. The user's goal is to be able to perform some function with the black box, without having to understand how the box operates. This concept is also known as *information hiding* (Parnas, 1971), the idea being that each module hides the internal details of processing and communicates only through simple interfaces. Cars, washing machines, and video recorders are all examples of systems we may use regularly in a black-box fashion. To use a washing machine, for example, we know that you put the dirty clothes into the tub along with some detergent (input), push a couple of buttons to select the type of cycle we want (more input), and then wait for the washer to do its thing, producing clean clothes (output). When we use a washing machine in this fashion, we typically do not know (and do not wish to know) exactly how the washer transforms dirty clothes into clean clothes. The operations the machine goes through to produce the clean clothes are hidden from us, as though hidden inside a black or opaque box. Even though we do not understand the internal workings of the device, it is quite easy to explain to someone how to use the machine. It is easy to describe the different sorts of input the system is capable of handling and the expected output.

The modules in a software system should have the same sort of black-box qualities associated with them that the washing machine has. Ideally, it should be possible to describe what a particular module does in a simple and definitive way. It should be easy to describe exactly what input or parameters must be passed to the module and what the exact output will be. "Black-box-ness" is clearly related to the degree of cohesion and coupling that a module has. If a module is cohesive, it has a single, clearly defined function, and therefore it will be easy to describe when and how it is to be used. If a module is loosely coupled, it will have a limited set of input or output parameters or perform a limited set of input or output operations. This also makes it easy to describe and use as a black box.

When a module functions as a black box, it does not necessarily mean that what goes on inside the module is simple. The module may contain several procedures, subroutines, functions, and/or data structures. The actual algorithm used in a procedural module might be very complex. Nonetheless, when a designer is creating a software structure, it is helpful to view each module as a black box and not worry about the details of how each module performs its function. In the preliminary design phase, it is important to look at the overall picture and not worry too much about the details. The details can be filled in later, during later stages of the preliminary design and during the detailed design phase. Thus modules that can be treated as black boxes help to reduce the complexity of the design problem.

A further advantage of designing modules that function as black boxes is that such modules are more likely to be *reusable modules* (Jones, 1984). Experience has shown that some activities are needed in a variety of different software. Sorting, for example, is needed in many different applications. Rather than having to write a completely new sorting routine every time a new software system is created that requires sorting, it makes sense to write a general-purpose sorting module and then just copy it from one software system to another. In other words, a module written for one particular application might be reused in other applications. If a module is carefully designed to handle a range of uses, has good black-box characteristics, and is well documented, it is a good candidate for being reused. Sorting is a simple example. Collections of related procedures, subroutines, functions, and their accompanying data structures can also be viewed as modules and can be reused as a unit. Sometimes reusable modules are called *off-the-shelf modules*. This name evokes an image of a whole library of reusable modules. Modules can be selected from the library and put together in various ways when building different applications and thus save the developers innumerable hours of design, coding, and testing time and effort.

4.2 Designing the Software Structure

Once the user interface has been designed, the next major step in the preliminary design process is to design the software structure, keeping in mind the guidelines for good module design discussed previously. The software structure represents all the modules in the system and their relationships to each other. Furthermore, the functions to be performed by each module are specified at this time. The structured design method developed by Constantine and Yourdon (1979) will be used here.

This method takes the data-flow diagrams created during the analysis stage and provides guidelines for producing a software structure based on the data-flow diagrams.

4.2.1   Structure Charts Are Used to Represent the Software Structure

In the structured design method, the software structure is represented in the form of a *structure chart*. A structure chart is a hierarchical, tree-shaped diagram in which all the modules in a system are represented as rectangular boxes, and the calling relationships among the modules are represented as arrows connecting the boxes. In addition, data flow is represented in a structure chart by labeling the arrows with the names of the data items being passed from one module to another.

Figure 4.1 shows the standard and optional notation that is used in structure charts. Figure 4.2 is a simple, abstract structure chart illustrating how the notation is used. Notice that the structure chart in Figure 4.2 is shaped like an upside-down tree. There is only one module at the top or root, and the other modules branch out and down from this module. This topmost module, labeled MAIN, represents the main or controlling module for the system. MAIN can directly call or activate three other modules, labeled A, B, and C in the figure. The small diamond at the top of the lines connecting MAIN to B and C represents a decision that must be made by the MAIN module. On any one cycle through the system, MAIN may call B *or* C, but not both. That is, MAIN must make a decision as to whether to call B or C. At the next level down, the structure chart shows that A can call modules W and X and that C can call modules Y and Z. The lines connecting C to Y and Z have a curved arrow surrounding them. The curved arrow represents *iteration*. (Iteration means repetition.) In this example, modules Y and Z are to be called repeatedly by module C as the system cycles through a series of cases. Finally, notice the short arrows lying next to the arrows connecting the modules. The short arrows with open circles represent the flow of data between modules and the direction of the flow. The lowercase letters on the short arrows represent the actual data items moving between the modules. In the figure, data item a is created in module X (probably through input) and is passed up to module A, which in turn passes it up to the MAIN module. The MAIN module passes only data item b to module B, but both data items c and d to module C. Module C then passes c to module Y and also passes data item d to module Z. Short arrows with filled circles represent the flow of a control signal or flag. In Figure 4.2, a flag, f, is created in the module W and passed back to module A.

To make structure charts easier to draw, the short arrows may be omitted if the following convention is used. Any data items flowing down to a module (being passed as input to a module) should be indicated on the left side of the line connecting the two modules. Data items flowing up from a module (being passed as output from a module) should be indicated on the right side of the line connecting the two modules. As a further aid, lowercase letters might be used to indicate the data items in the structure chart, and then the actual, full names of the data items

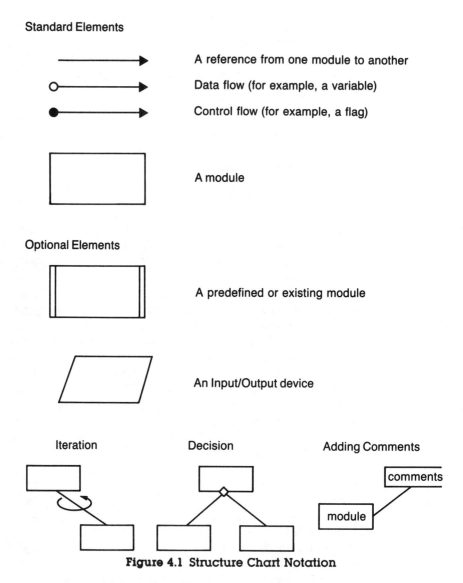

Figure 4.1 Structure Chart Notation

can be given in a key in one corner of the page containing the structure chart. Figure 4.3 shows an abstract structure chart drawn using these modified conventions.

4.2.2 Structured Design Uses the Top-down Approach

The structured design method is based on the decomposition problem-solving approach as discussed in Section 2.2.2. However, decomposition is often called the *top-down approach* or *stepwise refinement* when the structured design method

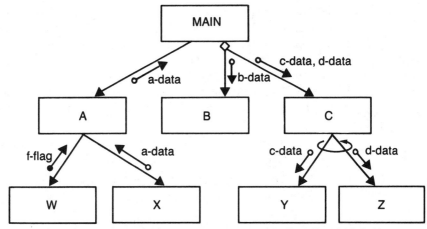

Figure 4.2 Abstract Structure Chart Using Standard Notation

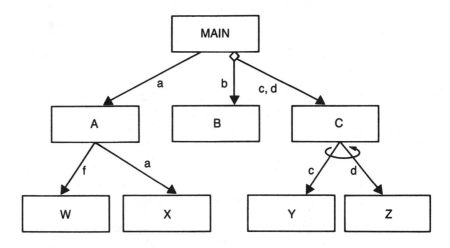

Key

a   a-data-item
b   b-data-item
c   c-data-item
d   d-data-item
f   f-flag

Figure 4.3 Abstract Structure Chart Using Modified Notation

is discussed. The idea is to begin by looking at the problem to be solved as a whole and trying to restate that problem as a small set of subproblems. Each of these subproblems is then approached as a separate problem and is defined in terms of *its* elemental subproblems. The process continues downward until the subproblems are seen to be trivial or easy to solve. The top-down approach is sometimes referred to as *stepwise refinement* because at each stage in the process a single higher-level step is refined into several smaller steps or tasks. At each level of refinement, the number of subtasks should be fairly small, and each task should be independent of the other tasks.

As a not too serious example of the top-down approach, consider the way Dear Liza helps Dear Henry get the hole in his bucket fixed in the folk song shown in Figure 4.4. The topmost or central problem is to fix the hole in the bucket. Along

---

There's a hole in my bucket, dear Liza, dear Liza.
There's a hole in my bucket, dear Liza, a hole.

Then mend it, dear Henry, dear Henry, dear Henry.
Then mend it, dear Henry, dear Henry, mend it.

With what shall I mend it, dear Liza, dear Liza?
With what shall I mend it, dear Liza, with what?

With straw, dear Henry, dear Henry, dear Henry.
With straw, dear Henry, dear Henry, with straw.

But the straw is too long, dear Liza, dear Liza.
The straw is too long, dear Liza, too long.

Then cut it, dear Henry, dear Henry, dear Henry.
Then cut it, dear Henry, dear Henry, cut it.

With what shall I cut it, dear Liza, dear Liza?
With what shall I cut it, dear Liza, with what?

With a knife, dear Henry, dear Henry, dear Henry.
With a knife, dear Henry, dear Henry, a knife.

But the knife is too dull, dear Liza, dear Liza.
The knife is too dull, dear Liza, too dull.

Then sharpen it, dear Henry, dear Henry, dear Henry.
Then sharpen it, dear Henry, dear Henry, then sharpen it.

With what shall I sharpen it, dear Liza, dear Liza?
With what shall I sharpen it, dear Liza, with what?

With a stone, dear Henry, dear Henry, dear Henry.
With a stone, dear Henry, dear Henry, a stone.

Figure 4.4 Folk Song Illustrating the Top-down Problem-solving Strategy

But the stone is too dry, dear Liza, dear Liza.
The stone is too dry, dear Liza, too dry.

Then wet it, dear Henry, dear Henry, dear Henry.
Then wet it, dear Henry, dear Henry, then wet it.

With what shall I wet it, dear Liza, dear Liza?
With what shall I wet it, dear Liza, with what?

With water, dear Henry, dear Henry, dear Henry.
With water, dear Henry, dear Henry, with water.

With what shall I fetch it, dear Liza, dear Liza?
With what shall I fetch it, dear Liza, with what?

With a bucket, dear Henry, dear Henry, dear Henry.
With a bucket, dear Henry, dear Henry, a bucket.

But there's a hole in my bucket, dear Liza, dear Liza!
There's a hole in my bucket, dear Liza, a hole!

Figure 4.4 (continued)

the way to getting the hole fixed, however, there are a series of subproblems to be solved. Notice that each of these subproblems is encountered *along the way,* on the path to the solution. These subproblems are not immediately obvious when first looking at the problem. The top-down approach, then, helps to guide us through the steps needed to reach the final solution (or a dead-end) without bogging us down in details at the early stages of the problem-solving process.

The product of each solution step in the top-down approach is a set of modules that comprises one part of the system. Each module handles one step or process necessary to solving the total problem. The first modules to be designed are those at the top of the structure chart. They represent the big decisions that have to be made to organize the operation of the system. Each of these higher-level modules is then refined into lower-level modules. The refinement process continues at lower and lower levels until the modules being defined handle the basic subproblems — the nitty-gritty details.

Consider a more serious, but still simple, application of the top-down approach to problem solving. Assume the problem is a burned-out light bulb in a ceiling light fixture. At the highest level, the problem solution is "Fix-the-burned-out-bulb." What do we need to do to "Fix-the-burned-out-bulb"? The answer, moving only to the next level of abstraction, is to "Get-a-new-bulb" and "Change-the-bulbs." We have now refined the initial, overall problem into two subproblems: getting a new bulb and changing the bulbs. To follow along in the top-down approach, we now refine each of these subproblems. Turning first to "Get-a-new-

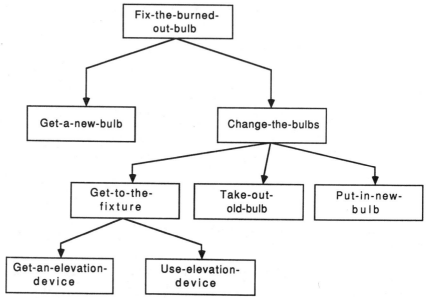

Figure 4.5 Structure Chart Showing a Solution to the Problem of Fixing a Burned-out Light Bulb in a Ceiling Fixture

bulb", we may decide that that problem is trivial because we know exactly where to go to get a new bulb. We need not consider the "Get-a-new-bulb" problem any further or do any refinements of the problem. However, the "Change-the-bulbs" problem needs more refinement. To change the bulbs, we might decide, will require three subprocesses: "Get-to-the-fixture," "Take-out-old-bulb," and "Put-in-new-bulb." The "Take-out-old-bulb" and "Put-in-new-bulb" processes are completely understood and need not be refined further. However, the "Get-to-the-fixture" problem is not yet solved. To get to the fixture, we will need to obtain some object to stand on or in some other way elevate us up to a level where we can reach the light fixture. Then we must actually climb or use our means of elevation. We now have two more refinements: "Get-an-elevation-device" and "Use-elevation-device." Assuming we have a chair, ladder, stool, or a strong, obliging friend available, these subproblems are solved, and the entire problem can be considered solved. Figure 4.5 shows a structure chart for the solution to the "Fix-the-burned-out-bulb" problem.

4.3   Using Transform Analysis to Create the Software Structure

Structured design techniques include two different, but closely related methods for going from the data-flow diagram description of the proposed system to the software structure for the system: *transform analysis* and *transaction analysis*. Transform analysis is the more basic of the two methods and will be discussed first. Transaction analysis will be discussed in Section 4.4.

Transform analysis is based on the idea that most systems and subsystems are centered around an activity or set of activities where incoming data are collected for processing or transformation into a new form, ready for output. The activity or set of activities that is concerned with carrying out the transformation of the data is called the *transform center.* Information flow and activities that have to do with collecting the data and readying them for the major transformation process are termed *afferent flow.* (Afferent means "coming in.") Data flow and activities that have to do with taking the results of the major transformation process and readying them for output are termed *efferent flow.* (Efferent means "going out.")

Figure 4.6 shows a simple data-flow diagram that has been marked to indicate the afferent flow, the efferent flow, and the transform center. The data-flow diagram in Figure 4.6 represents some of the activities that might occur within a magazine subscription system when a current subscriber renews her or his subscription. Notice that the three activities in the afferent flow area of the diagram are all related to collecting input data and editing or rearranging that information. The values collected during input have not been changed; only the format of the input has been altered. In the central transform, a calculation is made using the two pieces of input data. Thus, in the central transform, the input data are actually being changed or transformed from their original form into some new form. Finally, the newly calculated expiration date is added to the subscriber's record, and the record is written out. These activities involve output of the transformed data, or efferent flow.

In using transform analysis, the idea is to partition the data-flow diagram into its major afferent, efferent, and transform portions. Then each of these portions is partitioned into afferent, efferent, and transform portions. In turn, these portions are subsequently partitioned, and so on, in a recursive manner, until the ultimate input and output sources have been reached. Each of these passes over the partitions is called a *factoring* of the system and results in roughly one level or generation of modules being added to the structure chart representing the software structure of the system.

To begin, it is assumed that there will be one main or controlling module at the top of the system. This main or controlling module is not one of the activities in the data-flow diagram, but represents the control center for the entire system. It will be the entry and exit from the entire system. It is represented as the topmost, root module in the structure chart of the system. The first-level factoring is then performed. In first-level factoring, the complete data-flow diagram is divided into afferent, efferent, and transform portions. First-level factoring, and all subsequent levels of factoring, follow the steps given next.

4.3.1 Steps Involved in First-Level Factoring during Transform Analysis

There are two major steps involved in first-level factoring, as follows.

1. *Identify the afferent and efferent data elements and activities, thus isolating the transform center.* To identify the afferent flow, begin at those activities where

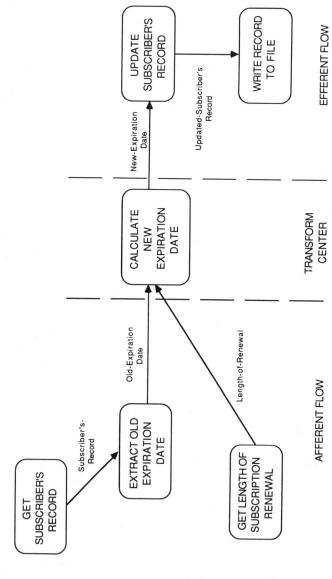

Figure 4.6 Simple Data-flow Diagram Divided into Afferent Flow, a Transform Center, and Efferent Flow

158

physical input to the system takes place. Then follow inward from the input point until the activities affecting the data flow are no longer just editing or readying the data, but are actually transforming it in some way or are performing calculations on the data.

To identify efferent flow, begin at the point of physical output and move backward into the system until the activities are no longer involved with formatting the data for output, but appear to be transform activities.

The remaining activities, which do not form part of the afferent or efferent flow, comprise the transform center.

2. *Create one or more of each of the following kinds of modules: an afferent processing controller, a transform control center, and an efferent processing controller.* These modules are controlled directly by the main or system module. The purpose of the *afferent control* module is to coordinate the receipt of all incoming data and ready it for the transformations that will be applied. The incoming data, in their final form, are passed by the afferent processing control module to the system module, which passes them on to the transform control center. The *transform control center* oversees the main processing or transformations of the data and then passes the raw results back to the system module. The system module hands the raw results over to the *efferent processing control* module, which coordinates all activities associated with producing the final form of the output.

As a simple example, let us apply first-level factoring to the data-flow diagram in Figure 4.6. The two leftmost activities, GET SUBSCRIBER'S RECORD and GET LENGTH OF SUBSCRIPTION RENEWAL, involve physical input, so they are clearly afferent activities. Following inward from these activities, EXTRACT OLD EXPIRATION DATA is encountered. Here data are still being collected that are needed for the processing to be done, so this activity is part of the afferent flow. Moving farther inward, CALCULATE NEW EXPIRATION DATE is next. The key word here is "calculate," which indicates that transformation of the data is taking place. Therefore, the boundary between the afferent and transform parts of the system has been reached. Approaching the data-flow diagram from the point where physical output emerges, WRITE RECORD TO FILE is encountered first. This represents physical output and is clearly efferent. Moving inward, UPDATE EXPIRATION DATE is next. As this activity involves readying the record for output, it is part of the efferent flow. The activity already labeled as a transform is next on the inward path, so the boundary between efferent flow and the transform center has been reached.

In step 2 of first-level factoring, afferent, efferent and transform control center modules are created. Figure 4.7 shows the structure chart for the first-level factoring of the data-flow diagram in Figure 4.6. A module called GET RENEWAL INFORMATION has been created to handle the collection of the input data needed for the central transform, the module labeled CALCULATE NEW EXPIRATION DATE. The module labeled SAVE UPDATED RECORD coordinates the activities associated with output of the transformed data. Notice that the names of the modules represented in the structure chart may or may not match the activities named in the nodes of the data-flow diagram. Furthermore, because the object of

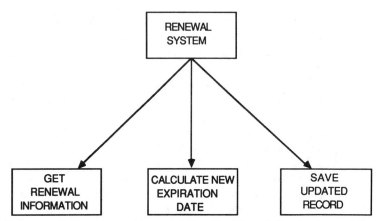

Figure 4.7 Structure Chart of the First-level Factoring of the Subscription Renewal Data Flow Diagram in Figure 4.6

factoring is to create controller modules, there may be *more* modules in a structure chart than there are activities in the data-flow diagram.

4.3.2   Steps Involved in Lower-level Factoring during Transform Analysis

Once first-level factoring has been done, second-level factoring is done, and then third-, fourth-, and so on, until the structure chart encompasses all the activities represented in the data-flow diagrams. Second- and lower-level factoring is done by expanding each of the modules produced in the preceding level of factoring into lower-level afferent, efferent, and transform control modules. To perform the second- and lower-level factoring, the following steps are carried out at each level of factoring:

1. *To factor modules from afferent portions of the system, identify the main activity or transformation needed to obtain the data in its desired form at this level. Then specify the afferent portion of that transformation.* That is, specify what form or sort of input is needed at the module being factored and what transformations must be carried out on the data coming from lower levels to put them into that form.

2. *To factor modules from efferent portions of the system, identify the main activity or transformation needed to bring the data one step closer to their final form. Then specify the efferent portion of that transformation.*

3. *To factor modules in the central transform portion of the system, the flow as represented in the data-flow diagram will typically serve as a guide.*

Figure 4.8 shows a complete factoring of the data-flow diagram in Figure 4.6. The complete factoring was obtained by working from the first-level factoring shown in Figure 4.7. In general, it is easiest to do a complete factoring of each component of the data-flow diagram — the afferent, efferent, and transform por-

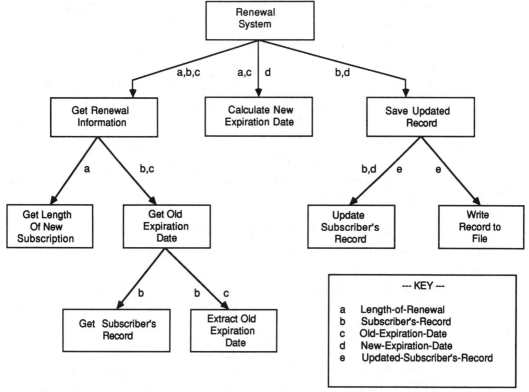

Figure 4.8 Structure Chart of the Complete Factoring of the Subscription System in Figure 4.6

tions, in turn—down to their respective lowest levels. (An alternate approach would be to create all second-level modules across the afferent, efferent, and control parts of the system, then all level 3 modules, and so on. Such a level-by-level approach is *not* suggested.) Using the suggested approach, the GET RENEWAL INFORMATION module is factored into its lower-level modules first. Following the guidelines given, we ask what information this module needs and in what form. Examining the data-flow diagram, we see that this module needs Old-Expiration-Date and Length-of-New-Subscription. Further examination of the data-flow diagram shows us that getting Length-of-New-Subscription is trivial, because this activity takes place at the level of physical input. We can add a module below the GET RENEWAL INFORMATION module called GET LENGTH OF NEW SUB-SCRIPTION. This module is a terminal module, and we need not factor it or consider it any further. Getting Old-Expiration-Date is slightly more complex and will require a transformation before it can be obtained. Specifically, the transformation module GET OLD EXPIRATION DATE is added below the GET RENEWAL INFORMATION module. GET OLD EXPIRATION DATE is then factored into two terminal modules, the afferent module, GET SUBSCRIBER'S RECORD, and the transform module, EXTRACT OLD EXPIRATION DATE. The afferent portion of the system has now been completely factored.

Turning to the efferent portion of the system, the first-level factoring produced the SAVE UPDATED RECORD module. What activities must be performed on the raw data as they come from the central transform to save an updated record? The data-flow diagram indicates the data must first be transformed from their raw state into a field on a record (inserted into the subscriber's record), and then the record must be written out. A transform module, UPDATE SUBSCRIBER'S RECORD, and an efferent module, WRITE RECORD TO FILE, are added. Because no subactivities are involved in updating the record or writing it out, the two new modules are terminal modules and need not be considered further.

The transform part of the system as shown in Figure 4.7 needs no further factoring, as only one activity, CALCULATE NEW EXPIRATION DATE, is involved.

4.3.3 Some Characteristics of Structure Charts Using Transform Analysis

As pointed out earlier, we can think of an entire structure chart as a *tree*, consisting of *nodes* (the modules) and *branches* (the lines connecting the modules). The topmost node is the beginning of the tree and is referred to as the *root* node. Nodes that have no branches coming out of them are *terminal* nodes. A *subtree* (for present purposes) is any node at one level, plus all the nodes in the next lower level directly attached by branches. Notice that within each subtree of a structure chart the modules should be organized in a left-to-right order starting with afferent-, followed by transform-, followed by efferent-type activities. It is possible that some subtrees may not contain one or more of the three types of activities. In other words, one activity may be factored so that its lower-level modules include one or more afferent modules and one or more transform modules, but no efferent modules. In another case, factoring might produce only efferent modules. This is perfectly acceptable and is even expected to happen. In factoring the afferent portion of the system, few of the subtrees will include efferent activities. In factoring the efferent portion of a system there will be few, if any, afferent activities. Notice also that each type of portion (afferent, efferent, and control), if included, may consist of more than one activity. For example, there may be two or more afferent activities in a subtree or two or more transform activities.

4.3.4 Transform Analysis Applied to the Concordance System Example

The subscription system example just covered was a simple one. Another system, starting with a more complex data-flow diagram, provides a more realistic example. Consider the data-flow diagram shown in Figure 4.9. It is the same data-flow diagram shown in Figure 2.4 and describes the data flow in a concordance program. If you recall, a concordance is an alphabetical listing of all the words that occur in a text, along with information concerning where the words appeared and how

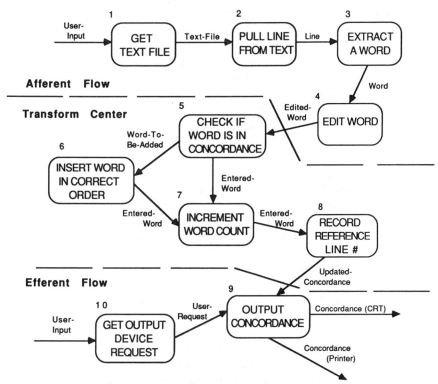

Figure 4.9 Data-flow Diagram of the Computerized Concordance System with Afferent Flow, Efferent Flow, and Transform Center Indicated

many times each word appeared. In this example, it is assumed that the input to the system is a text file containing text broken up into a series of numbered lines. As the concordance is built, words will be pulled from each line and edited. For example, a word that has an initial capital letter because it is at the beginning of a sentence will be edited to make the first letter lowercase. Likewise, words that are hyphenated because they occur at the end of a line will have the hyphen removed. Each edited word will then be checked against those already in the concordance. If the word does not match a previous entry, it will be inserted alphabetically in the concordance, its frequency count will be set to one, and the line number where it was found will be recorded. After the entire text has been processed, the program will ask the user whether he or she wishes the output to be sent to a printer or to appear on the monitor. The concordance entries will then be formatted correctly and output.

To design the software structure for this system, the initial step is to perform a first-level factoring. The data-flow diagram must first be marked off into afferent, efferent, and transform portions. Starting with the physical input from the user, we work inward until transformation activities are encountered. In Figure 4.9, the activities numbered 1 to 4 are all concerned in one way or another with getting and editing a single word, while activity 5 (CHECK IF WORD IS IN CONCORDANCE) involves working with the concordance. Activity 5, then, appears to be a transformation, and the boundary between afferent and transform flow is between activities 4 and 5. Working from the output inward, activity 9 (OUTPUT CONCORDANCE) clearly is an efferent activity. But what about activity 10? Here is an input activity (GET OUTPUT DEVICE REQUEST) that feeds into an efferent activity. By strict rules, activity 10 should become part of the afferent flow. The function of activity 10, though, is to make a simple determination concerning the ultimate destination of the output. Because its function is so closely tied to the output activities, it is best to include the activity in the efferent portion of the system. By so doing, the modular integrity of the system will be maintained. All activities directly related to output will be grouped together. Continuing inward, we come to activity 8. Activity 8 is concerned with building the concordance and is part of the transformation flow. The boundary between transformation and efferent flow is between activities 8 and 9.

To continue first-level factoring, control modules for the afferent, efferent, and transform activities are created and added to the system module in the structure chart. Naming the modules is an important step in their design. The name of the module should clearly and concisely express its function. Sometimes a good idea for the name of a module can come from looking at the name of the data element that flows to or from the module. For example, at the boundary between activities 4 and 5, the data element being passed is Edited-Word. All the activities prior to activity 4 were presumably related to obtaining Edited-Word. A reasonable name for the first-level afferent control module is thus GET EDITED WORD. Similarly, the data element flowing between the last transform activity and the first efferent activity is Updated-Concordance. The efferent control module can reasonably be named OUTPUT CONCORDANCE. All the activities in the transform portion have to do with creating the concordance, so the transform control module is named BUILD CONCORDANCE. The structure chart as it would look following first-level factoring is shown in Figure 4.10. Notice that the two branches from the system module to GET EDITED WORD and BUILD CONCORDANCE have been enclosed in a curved arrow to indicate that these two activities will be performed repeatedly.

Second-level factoring is then performed on the afferent portion of the system. Beginning with the GET EDITED WORD module, and remembering the lesson taught by Dear Liza, we ask "What needs to be done to get an edited word?" The answer: get a word and then edit it. What needs to be done to get a word? Pull a word out of a line of text. Where does the line of text come from? From a text file named by the user. Using this sort of reasoning, the modules shown in the afferent part of the structure chart in Figure 4.11 are designed.

Finally, second-level factoring is applied to the efferent and transform portions of the data-flow diagram. Figure 4.11 shows one possible design that might result.

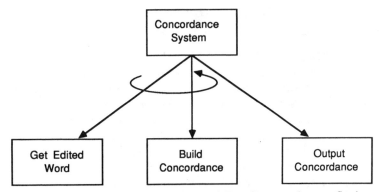

Figure 4.10 First-level Factoring of the Concordance System Shown in the Data-flow Diagram in Figure 4.9

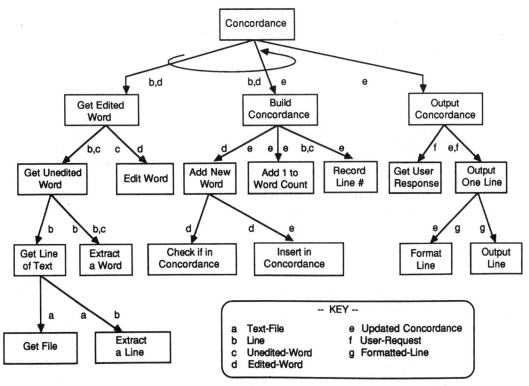

Figure 4.11 Complete Factoring of the Data-flow Diagram for the Concordance System

4.3.5 Reviewing the Structure Chart Created during Transform Analysis

Once the entire structure chart has been created, it is a good idea to review the structure. Are there some modules that might be combined? Are there modules that are not cohesive and should be broken up? The shape of the structure is important, too. The ideal shape for a structure chart is onion shaped, starting with a small sprout at the top (the system module), spreading out into a nice, fat body in the middle (the middle level controlling modules), and then tapering in toward the bottom. The shape should be, like Goldilock's chair, not too wide, not too tall, but just right. In other words, the designer should avoid having too many modules being called from a single module, causing the structure to spread out. This is called *fan-out*. In this case, one module is possibly in charge of too many other modules. The responsibilities should be divided among several controlling modules. Some fan-out is desirable, particularly in the middle levels of the structure. However, the lower levels of the structure should exhibit *fan-in* as the utilitarian modules of the system are reached. Fan-in occurs when several middle-level modules call on one lower-level module and when the factoring of portions of the structure reach their natural termination (have no subactivities). The designer should also avoid creating a long string of modules, one below the other. If this occurs, each higher-level module has too little responsibility; it is only controlling one lower-level module. The modules should be consolidated and restructured into a shorter, wider design.

As a final note, do not worry about going into too much detail in the structure chart. It is better to have too much detail, rather than too little. Some of the modules can be combined during the detailed design stage, if necessary. Meanwhile, having the extra modules in the structure chart highlights the fact that the indicated functions must be carried out. Furthermore, many functions that appear to be trivial initially turn out to be substantial functions when the detailed design is created.

4.4 Using Transaction Analysis to Derive a Structure Chart

Although transform analysis is the most frequently used structured design technique, transaction analysis is an important technique to understand. Transaction analysis is used when a single activity in a data-flow diagram results in multiple data streams flowing out of that activity. The term *transaction* is typically used in business-oriented data processing to mean a single piece of business. In structured design, its meaning is broadened to include any datum that triggers one of a selection of actions or activities. An example will probably make the concept clearer. Figure 4.12 shows part of a data-flow diagram for an automated teller machine for a bank. To use an automated teller, a customer must first insert a plastic card into the machine and type in a user code number. The machine reads identifying information from a magnetic strip on the card and verifies the user code number. The

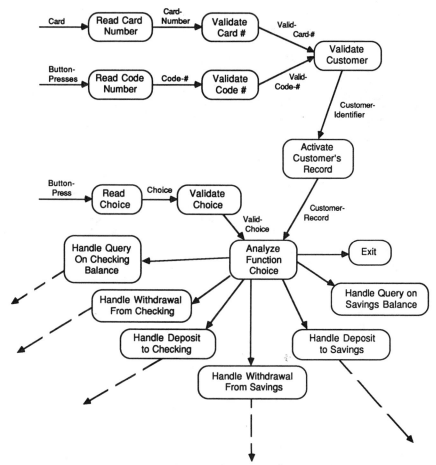

Figure 4.12 Data-flow Diagram of an Automated Teller Machine System

customer may then choose from a menu of banking operations, such as withdrawing money from his or her checking or savings account, depositing money to checking or savings, and paying bills. In this system, the customers' choice of which operation they wish to use is the transaction. In the data-flow diagram in Figure 4.12, the fanning out of activities from the ANALYZE FUNCTION CHOICE activity illustrates the characteristics of a typical transaction-centered system.

Due to the transaction center, the structure chart for a transaction-centered system may take on a different shape than the typical transform-centered system. Figure 4.13 shows what the upper levels of a structure chart for the automatic bank teller system might look like. A transaction-centered system still has afferent flow and efferent flow along with a transaction center, similar to transform-centered systems. However, the concept of efferent activities must be broadened to encompass all the various activities that might be triggered by a transaction. These might

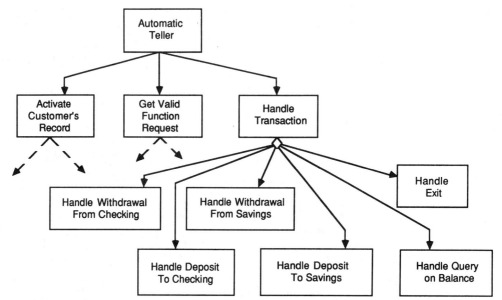

Figure 4.13 Upper Levels of a Structure Chart for the Automated Teller Machine System

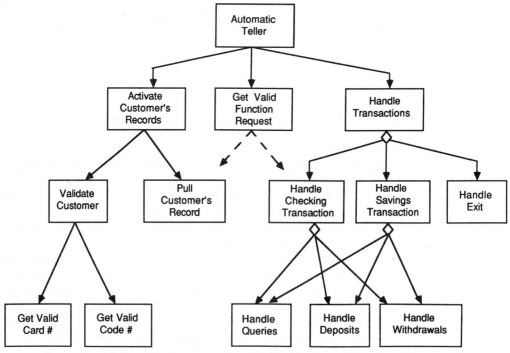

Figure 4.14 Alternate Version of the Structure Chart Shown in Figure 4.13

include afferent, efferent, or transform types of activities, or possibly even further transactions. Furthermore, it is important to realize that transaction centers can be embedded in either the afferent, efferent, or transform portions of an otherwise transform-oriented data-flow diagram. For example, the modules that might come below the HANDLE WITHDRAWAL FROM CHECKING module could include GET WITHDRAWAL AMOUNT, CALCULATE NEW BALANCE, and UP-DATE CUSTOMER RECORD. These are typical afferent, transform, and efferent modules, respectively. Any factoring of these modules would follow the guidelines given previously for transform analysis.

When factoring a transaction center, watch for potential cases where modules can be combined. Combining modules will help to keep the structure from becoming too wide. For example, in the automated teller system the functions of depositing from savings, withdrawing from savings, and displaying the current balance might be combined under a common control module, HANDLE SAVINGS TRANSACTIONS. This configuration is shown in Figure 4.14. The resulting combined module should be checked for cohesion. If the combination results in a module with low cohesion, the module should be redesigned.

4.5   Designing the Data Structures

Data abstraction is an important new approach to program design and development that has emerged in the last ten years (Liskov and Guttag, 1986). The central principle of data abstraction is that a system is defined primarily in terms of the data objects in the system. More specifically, data abstraction means that permissible operations on the data objects within a system are emphasized, while the implementation details of the data objects are suppressed. The purpose of using data abstraction is to provide more sophisticated means of building data objects, to provide easier information hiding, and to provide a more formalized approach to the specification of modules. Formal notations have the advantage of being concise and unambiguous, they allow formal reasoning, and they provide a basis for formal verification of the software produced from the specifications. To the extent that the processes become more formal, they also become candidates for automation. Automating the software development process is a goal being actively sought today. To understand the data abstraction approach to software development, abstraction and the different kinds of abstractions will be discussed first. How to specify these different abstractions using informal notation will be discussed next. The use of informal notation in these examples helps to explain abstraction by specification. You may not choose to use this notation in your design documents, but the ideas can be applied during design to make the design better. Furthermore, the objects and operations identified during system analysis form a natural basis for building abstract data types.

Abstraction is the application of a many-to-one mapping that reduces the complexity of a problem by hiding details. High-level programming languages are an excellent example of the use of abstraction in software development. In a high-level language, the programmer deals with constructs available in the language rather than the complex series of machine instructions into which the constructs must be translated. However, as the software being developed becomes more complex, there is increasing demand for even higher levels of abstraction. One approach to this problem is to invent very high level languages which contain some sets of general data structures and a powerful set of primitives to manipulate them. The flaw in this approach, however, is the choice of abstractions and the number of abstractions that might be needed. The alternative fostered by the proponents of data abstraction is to design into a language mechanisms that allow programmers to construct their own abstractions as needed. The use of procedures and functions is one way (and a very important way) to achieve programmer-defined abstractions. The second way is the use of *abstraction by specification*.

In abstraction by specification, the meaning of a procedure or a data object is based on its specification. (Note that the term specification is being used here in the sense of a module description, not strictly in the sense of a requirements specification.) If we have the specifications, we do not need to examine the details of the procedure or data object to understand how to use it. The specifications *are* the abstraction of the procedure or data object they specify. Thus the behavior or what can be done is relevant, while the method of implementing that behavior is irrelevant. For example, in viewing a sort procedure in the abstract, the fact that an array is sorted is relevant, while the sorting algorithm used in implementing the procedure is irrelevant. For our purposes, there are two basic kinds of abstractions: *procedural abstractions* and *data abstractions*. Procedural abstractions are abstracts of a single event or task that involves operations. Data abstractions (or *abstract data types*) consist of a set of objects and a set of operations characterizing the behavior of the objects.

4.5.1 Specification of Procedural Abstractions

It is important that abstractions be given precise definitions; otherwise, they become less valuable in building the software. The specification of a procedure consists of a header and a semantic part. Figure 4.15 shows the template for the specification of a procedural abstraction. The header gives the name of the procedure and includes the number, order, and types of its input and output parameters. No global parameters are allowed. The input parameters and their types are listed between parentheses next to the keyword **proc**, and the output parameters and their types are listed between parentheses following the keyword **returns**. The semantic part of the specification defines the meaning of the procedure — what the

procedurename = **proc** (input parameters) **returns** (output parameters)
    requires Clause stating any constraints on use of the procedure
    modifies Clause identifying all modified inputs
    effects Clause defining the behavior of the procedure

Figure 4.15 Template for Specifying Procedural Abstractions

procedure or function does. It consists of three parts, the **requires**, **modifies**, and **effects** clauses. The **requires** and **modifies** clauses are optional. The **requires** clause states any constraints under which the abstraction is defined. For example, if a procedure to search an array assumes the array is in sorted order, this information would be included in the **requires** section. The **modifies** clause lists the names of any input parameters that are modified by the procedure. The **effects** clause describes the behavior of the procedure for all input parameters not excluded by the **requires** clause. The specifications are informally written in English.

Figure 4.16 shows two procedural abstraction specifications. Notice that the *reverse* procedure modifies its input parameter and has no output parameters. In addition, *reverse* does not have a **requires** section, as it will behave correctly on any valid input. The *search* procedure does have a **requires** section, because its behavior is constrained to sorted arrays. *search* has one output parameter, i. Neither of its input parameters is modified, so no **modifies** clause is required.

4.5.2 Specification of Data Abstractions

Every software developer must overcome the limitations imposed by the programming language in which the software is to be developed. Procedural abstractions allow the software developer to extend the target language with new operations. Data abstractions allow the developer to add new data types to those already built into the language. And both sorts of abstraction free the system designer from any consideration of the target language. This is an important advantage to the data abstraction approach. Data abstraction allows the designer to defer decisions about the actual data structures to be used until the uses of the data are completely understood. Rather than deciding on the data structure to be used up front, the abstract data type, with its objects and operations, is introduced. Design can proceed based on the use of the abstract data type, and implementation decisions can be deferred until the detailed design stage.

The specification of a data abstraction consists mainly of a list of the operations defined for the data type and explanations of these operations. A template for specifying a data abstraction is shown in Figure 4.17. It consists of a header, an **Overview** section and an **Operations** section. The header contains the name of the data type and a list of its operations. The **Overview** section gives an overall

```
reverse = proc (s: string)
        modifies  s
        effects On return s contains the string originally in s, but in its reverse
            order. For example, if s = 'xyz' before the call, then on return
            s = 'zyx'.

search = proc (a: array [integer], x: integer) returns (i: integer);
        requires The array a is sorted in ascending order.
        effects If the target x is in the array a, returns i such that a[i] = x;
            else i is -1.
```

Figure 4.16 Two Sample Procedural Abstraction Specifications

datatypename = **data type is** list of operations
Overview
    a descriptive overview of the data abstractions
Operations
    a set of procedural specifications defining the allowable operations

Figure 4.17 Template for Specifying Data Abstractions

description of the data type. The **Operations** section contains a specification for each operation. Each operation is specified with a procedural abstraction, as described previously.

One simple example of a specification of an abstract data type is shown in Figure 4.18. In this example, a data type called *clocktime* that can represent clock times is defined. In this case, the clock time includes hours, minutes, and seconds. The operations defined allow the user to create an instance of a *clocktime,* set the hour, minute, and seconds integers, and get (read) the current values of the hour, minute, and seconds integers.

A slightly more complex example is given in Figure 4.19. In this example, a file of invoice records is defined. The structure of the invoice records has previously been defined in another data abstraction specification. Each invoice record contains, among other items, an invoice identification number, also previously defined to be part of each invoice record. The abstraction defined here specifies five different operations. Others are possible. Notice, for example, that there is no operation that allows us to read an invoice record without removing it from the file using *pull-invoice*. To read an invoice record and leave the file unchanged, we would need to use the operations *find-invoice, pull-invoice,* and *add-invoice,* in order.

clocktime = **data type is** createclock, setclock, gethour, getminutes,
    getseconds
Overview
    clocktime is a collection of three ordered integers. The first integer
    represents hours, the second represents minutes, and the third
    represents seconds.
Operations
    createclock = **proc** ( ) returns (clocktime)
        effects Returns three zeros representing hours, minutes, and
        seconds, respectively.
    setclock = **proc** (h, m, s: integer)
        effects Sets the three clocktime integers to the values of h, m,
        and s, respectively.
    gethour = **proc** ( ) **returns** (h)
        effects Returns the value of the hour integer in h.
    getminutes = **proc** ( ) **returns** (m)
        effects Returns the value of the minutes integer in m.
    getseconds = **proc** ( ) **returns** (s)
        effects Returns the value of the seconds integer in s.

Figure 4.18 Specifications for an Abstract Data Type to Represent Clock Times

invoicefile = **data type is** create, empty-file, add-invoice,
      find-invoice, pull-invoice

Overview
    invoicefile is a sequence of invoicerecords (defined elsewhere).
    Each invoicerecord contains a unique invoiceid# (defined
    elsewhere).

Operations
    create = **proc ( ) returns** (invoicefile)
        effects Returns a new, empty invoicefile
    empty-file = **proc** (ifile: invoicefile) **returns** (boolean)
        effects Returns a true if ifile is empty.
    add-invoice = **proc** (ifile: invoice, i: invoicerecord)
        modifies ifile
        effects Adds i to the sequence of records in ifile
    find-invoice = **proc** (ifile: invoicefile, id: invoiceid#) **returns**
      (boolean)
        requires empty-file (ifile) is false.
        effects Returns a true if ifile contains an invoicerecord
           with an invoiceid# = id; else returns false.
    pull-invoice = **proc** (ifile: invoicefile, id: invoiceid#) **returns**
      (i: invoicerecord)
        requires find-invoice (ifile, id) is true.
        modifies ifile
        effects Copies the invoicerecord with invoiceid# id
           into i and removes it from the invoicefile, ifile.

Figure 4.19 Specifications of an Abstract Data Type Defining an Invoice File

4.5.3   Advantages of Using Abstraction by Specification

One major advantage of using abstract data types and procedural abstractions is that the way the specification is implemented is irrelevant to the preliminary design process. A specification basically represents an agreement between the suppliers and users of an abstraction. (User here means a designer or a programmer, not an end user.) The supplier agrees to create a module that meets the specification. The user agrees not to ask anything about the implementation of the module and agrees to assume only what is given in the specification. This means that the implementation can be changed to another without affecting any of the programs that use the abstraction. For example, a sort abstraction could be implemented using a heap sort algorithm, a merge sort algorithm, or whatever. Although there might be changes in efficiency among the different implementations, to the user of the abstraction the only important feature is that sorting is achieved.

The independence of each abstraction means that, to write a program using an abstraction, the programmer need only understand the behavior (specification) of an abstraction and need not understand its implementation. Systems based on abstractions are easier to build, as each abstraction can be worked on separately. Abstractions also make a system easier to understand because the system can be looked at from one of many levels of abstraction. At each level, one sees only the abstractions at that level and lower-level abstractions are hidden.

Systems based on abstractions are easier to modify and maintain because one or several abstractions can be changed without changing anything else in the system. The amount of work required for modifications can be reduced by identifying potential modifications during the design of the program and designing the data abstractions so that the effect of the modifications will be limited to a small number of abstractions. The efficiency of a system can be fine-tuned by working on isolated portions of the system. Finally, the use of abstractions allows the designers of a system to design and even implement modules that use abstract data types before the actual data structures to be used have been determined. Thus, critical decisions about the data structures can be made later in the design of the system when more knowledge of the system has been gained.

4.5.4 Some Criteria for Writing Good Specifications

A major goal of writing abstract specifications is to allow the implementer of the system a wide latitude in how the abstraction is implemented. However, a good specification should be restrictive enough to rule out any implementation that is unacceptable to the users of the abstraction. Common mistakes include failing to state needed requirements in the **requires** clause (for example, ruling out undesired side effects of a procedure call), failing to identify when certain exceptions (for example, unacceptable values) should be signaled, and failing to specify behavior at boundary cases (empty strings, zeros, and the like).

Second, a good specification should be general enough to ensure that few, if any, acceptable implementations are precluded. In general, specifications that avoid suggesting or specifying the details of operations are best. For example, there would probably be no reason to specify that a search of an unordered array must be done from low to high. The implementer should be free to choose the order.

Finally, a good specification should be clear and easy to read. The specification is intended to facilitate communication among people. Care should be taken to make sure the specification is not only complete and unambiguous, but understandable to readers. The use of short, precise sentences is recommended. The inclusion of simple examples is often helpful.

4.5.5 Role of Abstraction by Specification in Software Design

If a language that directly supports abstract data types such as Ada, Clu, or C++ is being used to implement the system, or if an object-oriented programming language such as Smalltalk is used to implement the system, the transition from analysis to specifications to implementation is quite natural and smooth (see Chapter 8 for a discussion of object-oriented programming). However, even if none of these languages is used, the concepts of data abstraction provide important lessons that can be learned and applied to the design of data structures and procedural abstractions. In particular, the approach emphasizes a point made earlier: designers should put aside concerns about implementation details and look at the proposed system in the abstract. The objects and operations identified during analysis can be viewed and defined as data abstractions and procedural abstractions. Each activity in a data-flow diagram can be viewed as a set of objects and a set of operations characterizing the behavior of the objects. By keeping the tenets of abstract specification in mind while defining functions in data-flow diagrams, the benefits of increased modularity and data encapsulation can be more easily derived during the design phase.

4.5.6 Pragmatic Concerns in Designing Data Structures

In the initial stages of preliminary design, the system components are viewed in the abstract. However, once the abstract data types and their associated procedures have been defined, decisions must be made concerning how to implement the data abstractions. A choice must be made concerning what type of structures are to be used (for example, arrays, stacks, linked lists, or files) and the exact composition of the selected data structures. If files are to be used or created by the system, the exact nature of the files must be decided on. Will the file be a sequential or a random access file? The makeup of each record should be spelled out. The design must describe each field in the record, telling the type of data that it will contain and the number of bytes or characters the field will occupy. Then calculate the amount of space it will take to store each record. Estimate the maximum amount of space that will be occupied by the file by multiplying the number of bytes per record times the maximum number of records that the system will be designed to handle. Specify where the file is to be stored (for example, floppy disk, hard disk, or tape). Find out the exact amount of storage available on the device where the file is to be stored. Remember that the total storage physically available on the device might not be the same as is available for file storage. On disk systems, for example, space is allocated for the operating system's needs. Furthermore, space on disks is sometimes allocated to users in fixed-sized units, and the entire disk might not be available to your system. Next, compare the maximum expected size of the file to the storage available. Will the file fit onto the storage device, or will provisions have to be made to break the proposed file up into several files? For example, if a large file keyed on last names is to be utilized by a system, it may be necessary to break up the file into two: one for last names starting with the letters A to M and another for last names starting with the letters N to Z.

Similar calculations should be made concerning large data structures that are to be stored in primary memory during program execution. If you are considering using a large array of records, for example, compute the number of bytes that will be used to hold each record and the total space necessary to store the entire array. Use the technical manuals for the target language and target computer to obtain the information needed to make these calculations. Such manuals should also tell you how much space may be used for data storage during program execution, or possibly how to adjust the amount of space available. Compare the amount available to the amount you expect to use. Remember when you make this comparison that the proposed amount is very probably an underestimate. Also remember that all the other variables and constants used in your system will be vying for the same memory. To be safe, add a generous "fudge factor" of 50 percent or more to the estimated storage requirements. Will the data structure actually fit into the available storage, or will it be necessary to use either temporary or permanent files? If the system does not actually use the maximum allocated space initially, so much the better. When modifications are made to the system at a later time, the extra space will allow room for expansions with less effort.

Speed of access should be kept in mind when designing the data structures. Arrays and linked lists, for example, are kept in main memory during the entire program execution. Files are stored on secondary storage devices. Access from secondary storage is hundreds of times slower than access from main memory. If the system is designed so that records are accessed as needed during program execution, the system will be slow. However, it may be possible to open the necessary file or files when the system is started up and load their entire contents into main memory. The program will then be able to access the data at high speed. When the system is shut down, the data can be stored back out to the file or files.

4.6   Creating the Preliminary Design Document

The work involved in the preliminary design is embodied in a preliminary design document. The preliminary design document should contain the following sections:

- Cover page
- Table of contents
- Design description
- Module designs
- Major data structures design

The cover page should include the project title, the name of the document (for example, Preliminary Design Document), the date, and the names of the authors.

A table of contents follows the cover page. It is often useful in reviewing and using a design document. It should list the major sections and the contents of each of the sections. Page numbers should be included. However, it is probably a good idea to number the pages of each section independently, using a section prefix such as a capital letter or Roman numeral. For example, the pages in the Design Description section might be numbered consecutively from D-1 to D-n or from III-1 to III-n.

The remaining sections of the preliminary design document are described next.

4.6.1 Contents of the Design Description Section

The design description section of the preliminary design document is composed of two subsections: a section containing the software structure charts and a data dictionary. The software structure charts show the design of the module structure for the entire system. If the structure chart for the entire system will not fit easily on one page (and that is very often the case), then break down the system into subsections. The first structure chart should show the highest-level modules. Subsequent structure charts should show the lower-level sections of the system for each of the modules shown in the first structure chart. If needed, each of these subsections can be further expanded with lower-level structure charts. (Note that here, unlike data-flow diagrams, each separate page represents simply one part of the entire structure chart. In data-flow diagrams, each page represents an expanded view or blow-up of the details involved in an activity shown in a higher-level data-flow diagram. New, smaller-grained activities not shown in the higher-level data-flow diagrams are shown in the lower-level diagrams.)

Following the guidelines given earlier for creating structure charts, each module in the charts should be named or labeled. Ideally, the name used for the module in the structure chart will be the name that will be used in the source code when the module is coded. Unfortunately, some languages, such as older versions of BASIC, do not name their subroutines or functions. The name of the module must then be added as a comment in the source code. Other languages may place a limit on the length of the module names. If this limit is too restricting, it is difficult to come up with good, descriptive names for the modules. In this case, it may be necessary to have a descriptive name for the module as it appears in the structure chart and a shorter, source code name for the module as well.

Each module in the structure chart should have an identification number and/or letter assigned to it, hereinafter called the *module ID*. The module ID will be used throughout the subsequent stages of the development process to identify the module and to tie it back to the design document. Some thought should be put into assigning module IDs so that the ID number relates to the module's location in the structure chart. For example, the afferent control, transform control, and efferent control modules (the first-level modules) for some systems might be labeled A, B, and C, respectively. The second-level modules controlled by A might then be labeled A1, A2, . . . , An. The third-level modules controlled by A1 are labeled A1.1, A1.2, . . . , A1.5, and so on, while the third-level modules controlled by A3 are labeled A3.1, A3.2, . . . , A3.n. A similar scheme is used to label the modules below the B and C control modules.

The flow of data throughout the system should be shown on the structure charts. As it is often difficult to fit a descriptive name for the data items onto the lines in a structure chart, a lowercase letter might be used next to the lines to represent each data item. A key relating the letters to the data elements they represent can be provided on each chart.

Finally, it is extremely useful to have a one-page representation of the entire structure of the system. Typically, there is no way that all the components of a structure chart for an entire system — the module names, the module IDs, and the data flow — can be fitted onto one page. To obtain a one-page representation, the modules can be drawn as small boxes containing only the module ID. The lines showing the calling relations are also included. On a separate page or possibly as a key on the same page, the module IDs can be associated with the module names. The one-page structure chart should be the first diagram in the design description section. It provides a map or overview of the entire system structure. The shape of the software structure can be assessed by looking at this diagram, and it can be used when reviewing the rest of the design document as a guide to the relationships among the modules.

Ideally, structure charts should be produced using a computer. Some software is available specifically for drawing structure charts (see Section 8.4). As an alternative, the MacDraw or MacPaint software for use on Macintosh computers are easy-to-use software packages that can readily be used to produce structure charts. A less preferred choice would be to use a text editor to print the module names in their correct locations and then draw boxes around the modules and add connecting lines using a pen or pencil. In some cases, drawing the structure charts using a horizontal orientation simplifies the process of drawing the charts. By drawing the diagram horizontally, it can be easier to fit the structure on the page, and it is easier to use a word processor to enter just the module names. Figure 4.20 shows the same structure chart shown in Figure 4.8 drawn horizontally. Notice that short

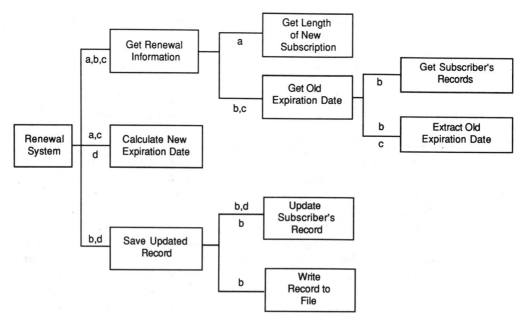

Figure 4.20 Horizontally Oriented Version of the Structure Chart in Figure 4.8

arrows are not used to represent data elements. Instead, a convention is observed in which data items that appear above the horizontal connecting lines are those being passed out of the associated module, and items below the line are being passed into the module.

The second subsection of the design description section is a data dictionary identifying and defining the data elements shown on the structure charts. The names of the data elements should be designed at this time. In other words, the names of the data elements as they appear on the structure charts should be the actual identifier names that will be used when the source code is written. The most important guideline in creating data element names is to use meaningful names. The names should be meaningful and relate to the use of the data element in the system. Examples of meaningful names in the Concordance System example are "Entered-Word", "Edited-Word" and "Line". Examples of poorly named data elements for any system would be "X" or "Integer Array" or "DataFile". (See Chapter 6, Section 6.9 for further discussion of identifier naming.)

To design the identifier names, the designers must know what the target source language will be, and any restrictions imposed on the syntax of the identifiers in that language must be known. How many characters long can an identifier name be? Are numbers and punctuation marks allowed in identifiers? It is a good idea to come up with some guidelines or conventions for naming identifiers, particularly if the target language imposes restrictions. The guidelines might be simply syntactic (for example, all identifiers will begin with a capital letter and subsequent letters will be lowercase) or they might be broader. For example, a system to be written in FORTRAN, where identifiers are limited to six characters or fewer, might impose the following guidelines: "All module names will be six characters long, all global data items will have five-character names, any nonglobal data elements passed as parameters will have four-character names, and local identifiers will have two-character names." The idea behind such a scheme is that the designers, coders, testers, and those doing maintenence on the system will immediately be able to tell the nature of an identifier by simply looking at its length.

For each entry in the data dictionary, the identifier should be listed along with a definition similar to that given in the data dictionary of the requirements and specification document.

4.6.2 Contents of the Module Designs Section

The module designs section of the preliminary design document contains the preliminary design for every module in the system. During the preliminary design, the purpose and role of each module in the system should be described. However, the details concerning exactly how the module will perform its function need not be considered. *Module headers* are used to represent the preliminary design of the modules. A module header is a collection of comments that accompanies a module in a source code listing of a program. The exact contents of a module header will be described later. The advantage of using a module header in preliminary design is that it saves time and effort in the later stages of software development. During the preliminary design phase, as much information as possible about the module is put into the module header. In the detailed design stage, more information about the module is added to the header. For example, information such as the algorithm to be used in the module and the name of the programmer are added during detailed design. During the coding stage, the actual source code statements for the module are written and inserted into the framework already created by the module headers. If the module headers have been carefully designed and written, the coder will not need to write many additional comments during the coding process.

The information to be included in each module header is described next. A sample module header is shown in Figure 4.21.

Title. The module's name as given in the system structure charts. The module name may or may not become part of the source code. If a separate source-code name will have to be used, it should be listed as well.

Module ID. The identifying number/letter assigned to the module when the structure charts were designed. It will be used to reference the module design to the structure charts and to provide a shorthand way of referring to the module throughout development and maintenance.

Purpose. This is the heart of the preliminary design for each module. The purpose section should describe the module's purpose or objective. What does the module do? What function does it perform? The purpose should be given using several well-written English sentences. It should be stated clearly and completely enough that it can be used during the review process to judge the cohesion of the module.

```
{***************************************************************
- TITLE:    SortItemSizes
- MODULE ID:    A4.3
- PURPOSE:  This module sorts a list of sizes, in ounces, that a
-   particular grocery item is available in into ascending order.
- METHOD:
-
- USAGE:  GetItemSizes
- EXTERNAL REFERENCES:   none
- CALLING SEQUENCE:
-     Sizes - (I/O)  An integer array of sizes to be sorted.
-     Count - (I)  An integer indicating the number of items
-        in Sizes.  Count must be >0 and <= 25.
- INPUT ASSERTION:   The input array must contain 1 to 25 integer
-   values, in any order.
- OUTPUT ASSERTION:   The items in the array will be ordered such
-   that item1 <= item2 ... <= itemN.
- VARIABLES:
-
- AUTHOR(S):
- REMARKS:  Because only 25 or fewer items are to be sorted each
-   time the procedure is called, a QuickSort is not needed.  An
-   n-squared sort can be used.
***************************************************************}
```

Figure 4.21 Example of a Module Header Created during Preliminary Design

Method. The method section is filled in during the detailed design phase. Eventually, it will contain a description of how the module carries out its purpose. A step-by-step breakdown of the algorithm to be used in the module is provided.

Usage. The usage section contains a list, by name, of all modules that may use (call) the module being described. This information can be obtained by looking at the structure charts, but it is a good idea to include it in the module header anyway. The coder is thus reminded of which modules might be using the module and can take into account possible problems that might be caused by the interfacing of the modules. Furthermore, the information can be useful during maintenance if the structure charts are somehow not available.

External references. A list of all modules, routines, or programs called from or activated by the module being described is given in the external references section. Once again, the idea is to keep the coder aware of possible sources of interfacing problems and provide system structure information.

Calling sequence. The calling sequence lists and describes the arguments being passed to the module and those returned from the module. Each argument is listed in the order it appears syntactically in the definition of the procedure. For each argument, give its name and describe if the argument is used to pass a value in (import), pass a value out (export), or both. In addition, briefly describe the argument, and indicate any limits on the range and type of value permitted. The calling sequence can be evaluated during review in assessing the coupling of the module.

Input assertion. The input assertion states any assumptions that are made by the module. The input assertion(s) must be true for the module to execute correctly. For example, if a module assumes that a string passed in as a parameter contains only digit characters, this should be stated as an input assertion.

Output assertion. The output assertion states what the results of the action performed by the module will be. It should be accurately and precisely stated. Note that the output assertion does not state how the results are achieved, but only what the results are to be. For example, a module to convert a digit character string into an integer might include the output assertion that the output parameter variable named ValidInteger will contain a positive integer between 0 and 65,536.

Variables. Any variables used in the module that are not part of the calling sequence are noted in the variables section. These might include global variables used in the module and/or local variables. For each variable, indicate its type and how it is used within the module.

Author or authors. Gives the name or names of the programmers responsible for the initial coding of the module. If any portion of the code is to be borrowed from some other source (for example, a book or previous program), the original source should be acknowledged. This information might not be available until the detailed design or coding stage, but the heading can be put into the module header, and the actual name or names filled in later.

Remarks. Additional comments or remarks that might help a reader understand the module or its history should be included in the remarks section. For example, many software developers keep a careful record of modifications made to a module, including the date and nature of the modification. During preliminary design, ideas concerning the algorithm to be used might be noted in the remarks section.

It is a good idea to create the module headers on a computer using the editor that will eventually be used in creating the source code. In this way, the module headers will automatically become part of the source code of the system, and the coders will not need to take the time to type in the headers themselves. The module headers can be printed out on a line printer for inclusion in the preliminary design document. Use of a standard format makes the module headers easier to read. To facilitate the creation of the module headers, a module header template can be created. The copy and paste functions of the editor, if any, can then be used to copy the template and make a fill-in form for each header.

4.7 Evaluating the Preliminary Design

A major goal of the design process is to find the best solution that fulfills the requirements stated by the sponsor. Just as there are many different house plans that might meet a family's requirements (four bedrooms, two baths, family room, and so on), there are typically many different alternative designs that will meet the majority of the sponsor's requirements. However, only a few of the designs will be good ones. The trick is to determine which designs are good.

The formal review is the predominant method of design evaluation. (The procedures to be used in conducting formal reviews are discussed in Section 2.8.1.) Reviews should be conducted at several points in the design process. This allows the designers to measure their progress and get feedback on the proposed designs. At each review, two basic questions should be kept in mind:

1. Does the design fulfill the requirements?
2. Is the design the best possible one—the simplest, most efficient, and most effective solution?

The first question is easier to answer than the second question. To determine if the design fulfills the requirements, the reviewers can go through the requirements one by one and assure that the proposed design meets each requirement. In fact, it is a good idea to cross reference each requirement with its corresponding module and/or data structure. Both functional and nonfunctional requirements should be reviewed vis-à-vis the preliminary design. The effectiveness of this process depends on the quality of the requirements. To the extent that requirements are unclear, missing, or wrong, the quality of the design will be affected. It is common to discover flawed or missing requirements during the design process, and any errors should be remedied before the preliminary design is completed.

Answering the second question is more difficult. Hetzel (1988) suggests two different techniques for assessing the goodness of a design. The first technique is evaluation through *alternative analysis*. In this approach, designers present several design alternatives, and the advantages and disadvantages of each are discussed at one review session. After the session is adjourned, each reviewer must come up with at least one alternative design that has not yet been considered. At a second meeting, the alternative designs are considered along with the original designs, and a design decision is reached. The second technique is to use *competitive designs*. In this case, the early design is not undertaken by just one team, but by several individuals or teams in parallel. The entire design task is then awarded to the winning individual or team. (A monetary reward can make this approach even more effective!) Although this technique sounds as though time would be wasted on the extra designs, Hetzel cites one case study in which two *years* of development effort were saved because a better and simpler design was selected through the competitive design process. Clearly, the extra effort involved in the competitive design approach paid off in this instance.

Prototyping is another approach that can be used to evaluate designs or certain aspects of designs (Agresti, 1986). Prototyping was discussed in Chapters 1 and 3. The basic idea when prototyping a preliminary design is to build a simplified representation or model of the critical design features and then use the prototype to test or explore the design features. Prototypes can be used to test the proposed design of database configurations, transaction sequences, response times, or security features. As an example of automation in the prototyping process, prototyping systems have been created that can estimate response times for database designs. The system accepts basic information concerning the nature of the database and the accesses that each transaction requires. Using known input and output times, the system can then project response times for different transactions under various hypothetical database structures. Prototyping should begin early in the preliminary design phase.

4.8   Case Study: Preliminary Design of the Rev-Pro System

For the preliminary design, the Rev-Pro project team decided to use the traditional approach to design. A couple of the team members were assigned to work on the initial draft of the design, with other team members providing feedback and aid in the documentation chores. The team used MacDraw to document the structure charts, following the conventions of Figure 4.6. The Turbo Pascal editor was used to create the module headers. Although deciding which programming language to use is often done after the preliminary design is completed (see Chapter 5), in this case the team had already decided that Turbo Pascal was the best alternative for them. This decision was made on the basis of the languages available for the target machine (an IBM/PC), features of the Turbo Pascal language and compiler, and the team members' familiarity with Pascal.

To design the structure of the system, the designers took into account the model of the Proposed Logical System as shown in Figure 2.16 (see also Part I of Appendix A) and the User Interface Design (see Table 3.5, Figure 3.9, and Part II of Appendix A). Although the highest level data-flow diagram of the system (Figure 2.16) suggests that the system is transform-centered, the semantic design of the user interface makes the system appear and act transaction-centered. In the semantic design, the user will begin with the Scale-the-Hall activity. From that activity, the user can go forward to the next activity, even if he or she has not completely filled in the Scale-the-Hall data fields. Once in the next activity, the user can complete that activity, or at any time exit to the previous activity, or exit to the next activity. Subsequent activities also provide the options of going forward or backward. This ability to progress forward or backward through the activities is what makes the system transaction centered.

Figure 4.22 shows the first-level factoring of the system. Notice that the six major activities are all defined as modules directly below the main module, reflecting the transaction-centered nature of the system. Each of the high-level modules were then examined and factored separately. For each of these factorings, the user interface design and the Proposed Logical System model were considered. Consider the Tabulate-Costs activity, for example. In the working, final version of the system, this activity will involve displaying the Costs screen to the user with none of the spaces filled in, allowing the user to fill in the spaces with appropriate data, and providing the user with the options of calculating the remaining table values, printing the screen, going back to the previous activity, or going forward to the next activity. These subactivities were apportioned among four modules defined below the Tabulate-Costs module: Initialize-Costs, Get-Fixed-Costs-

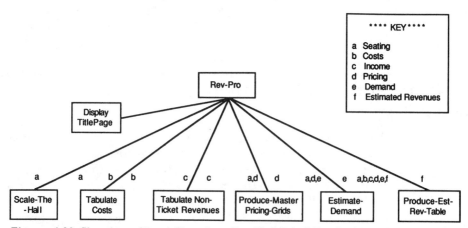

Figure 4.22 Structure Chart Showing the First-level Factoring of the Rev-Pro System

Info, Get-Variable-Costs-Info, and Print-Costs. The Initialize-Costs module was designed to display the initialized (no values) cost screen. The Get-Fixed-Costs and Get-Variable-Costs modules were designed to control the collection of cost information, and the Print-Costs module would print the Costs display screen. The Get-Fixed-Costs module was further factored into two different modules, Read-Real and Read-String. Read-Real was designed to read in real values entered by the user for a specified field on the form (e.g., dollar amounts) and to make the conversion from characters to real. Read-Real also provides error-trapping and error-correction by blocking the entry of all nonnumeric characters. Read-String was designed to read in string values of a specified length for a specified field on the form (e.g., a fixed-cost category name).

Figure 4.23 shows the complete factoring of the Rev-Pro system. (*Note:* Parts of the system related to minisubscriptions and group rates were not included. These parts duplicate the functions of other parts of the system with only minor changes, and were left out here and in subsequent illustrations for simplification of the presentation.) Notice how the factoring of most of the other high-level activities in the system mirrors the factoring of Tabulate-Costs. Most involve similar "Initialize," "Get . . . Info," and "Print" modules. Notice also that the modules

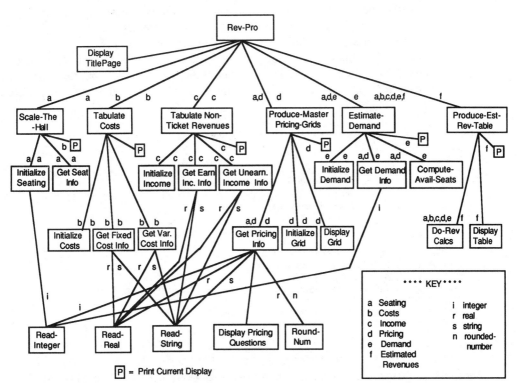

Figure 4.23 Structure Chart Showing the Complete Preliminary Design of the Rev-Pro System Case Study

Read-Real, Read-String, and Read-Integer become utility modules used by higher level modules throughout the system. In evaluating the shape of the structure chart, there is clearly a great amount of fan-out from the main module, Rev-Pro. This fan-out is caused by the transaction-oriented nature of the system, and could not be avoided without changing the semantic design of the user interface. Under each of the transaction-type modules, however, there is only moderate fan-out. Most second-level modules have a fan-out of four. Fan-in is provided by the use of Read-Real, Read-String, and Read-Integer as utility modules. Thus the shape of the system structure seems reasonably balanced—not too wide and not too deep.

In designing the major data structures for the system, the designers referred primarily to the data dictionary and structure chart. The system utilizes six major data stores: Seating, Costs, Income, Pricing, Demand, and Estimated Revenue. Typically, a module that needs at least one piece of information from a particular data store will use many pieces of information from that data store. To aid in data encapsulation, the designers decided to create one separate large record for each of the major data stores. The fields in the records were to be the various data items related to that particular data store. For example, the Costs record would have one field consisting of the data structure representing the fixed-costs categories and fixed-costs amounts, a second field consisting of the data structure representing the variable costs categories and amounts, a third field containing the total of the fixed-costs (Fixed-Costs), a fourth field containing the total of the variable costs (Variable-Costs), and a fifth field containing the total costs (Total-Costs).

Next, the memory space requirements for the major data structures were calculated. It was assumed, based on the architecture of the target machine, that each integer and real value would require four bytes of memory and each string would

```
{ ****************************************************************
- TITLE:  Initialize-Costs
- MODULE ID:  C.1
- PURPOSE:  Set up and display the current values of the Costs
-  table.  If the user has not yet entered any cost data, the
-  table will be empty.  If the user has previously entered cost
-  data, the table will contain these data.
- METHOD:
-
-
- USAGE:  Tabulate-Costs
- EXTERNAL REFERENCES:  none
- CALLING SEQUENCE:
-      Costs (I/O):  a record containing the cost variables
- INPUT ASSERTION:
- OUTPUT ASSERTION:
- VARIABLES:
- AUTHOR(S):
- REMARKS:
******************************************************************}
```

Figure 4.24 Sample Module Header from the Rev-Pro Case Study Preliminary Design Document Showing the Preliminary Design of the Initialize-Costs Activity

```
{ * * * * * * * * * * * * * * * * * * * * * * * * * * * * * * * * * * * * * * * * * * * * * * * * * * * * * * * * * * * * * *
- TITLE:  Get-Fixed-Costs
- MODULE ID:  C.2
- PURPOSE:  Accept fixed-costs information entered by the user
-  and update the display screen as appropriate.  Includes error
-  checking features.
- METHOD:
-
-
- USAGE:  Tabulate-Costs
- EXTERNAL REFERENCES:
-      ReadReal
-      ReadString
- CALLING SEQUENCE:
-      Costs (I/O):   a record containing the cost variables
- INPUT ASSERTION:
- OUTPUT ASSERTION:
- VARIABLES:
- AUTHOR(S):
- REMARKS:
* * * * * * * * * * * * * * * * * * * * * * * * * * * * * * * * * * * * * * * * * * * * * * * * * * * * * * * * * * * * * * }
```

Figure 4.25 Sample Module Header from the Rev-Pro Case Study Preliminary Design Document Showing the Preliminary Design of the Get-Fixed-Costs Activity

require one byte per allowable character. The maximum allowable sizes were used in making the calculations. The total estimated was less than two kilobytes of memory. The target machine had a 256K memory. Therefore, the memory space requirements for the chosen data structures were judged to be a minor consideration.

Following informal review of the design by the project group and formal review by the instructor, the group began finalizing the preliminary design and creating the module headers. Sample module headers are shown in Figures 4.24 and 4.25. The final version of the Preliminary Design document was evaluated by the instructor.

Summary

Although a complete and thorough understanding of the sponsor's requirements are essential for the successful development of a software system, probably the most critical and creative aspect of development is the design. The user interface design determines how the system will look to the user from the outside, while the preliminary design determines how the system will provide the desired functions to the user.

Modularity is a central concept in design. Modules form the building blocks of a design. Modules are important because they provide abstractions for the designer to work with. Each module represents one idea or function in the system. Using the top-down approach, modules at the higher levels of the system represent broad functions, while modules at lower levels of the system represent detailed functions. Good modules are cohesive (encompass only one central function) and loosely coupled (do not have many interactions with other modules) and act as black boxes (provide well-defined abstractions).

In the structured design method, the primary representation of the preliminary design is a structure chart. A structure chart is a hierarchical diagram in which the modules of a system and the relationships of the modules to each other are represented. Data-flow diagrams created during the requirements analysis stage are used as a basis for creating the preliminary design. Transform and/or transaction analysis are applied to the data-flow diagrams to create the design. Transform analysis is based on the idea that most systems or subsystems are centered around one or more activities where incoming data are transformed into a processed form, ready for output. Activities that have to do with collecting and readying the data for the central transform are called afferent flow, while activities related to the formatting and output of data are called efferent flow. In transform analysis, the data flow is partitioned into afferent, efferent, and transform portions, recursively, using factoring. As each factoring of the system is made, one level of the system structure hierarchy is created. Transaction analysis is used when a single activity in a data-flow diagram triggers one of a selection of activities. In transaction analysis, the concept of efferent activities is broadened to include all the various types of activities that may be triggered by a transaction center.

Another central facet of design is the design of the major data structures of the system. The ideas of data abstraction and abstract specification are important new influences in software design. In data abstraction the operations on the data objects within a system are emphasized, while the implementation details of the data objects are suppressed. The meaning of a data object or a procedural abstraction is based on its specification. The designer or programmer can use the specification as an advanced feature of a programming language and not be concerned with the method of implementation. Feasibility and speed are important pragmatic factors to consider in designing data structures.

The preliminary design is represented in the preliminary design document. The major components of the document are the design description, the module designs, and a description of the major data structures. The design description consists of the structure chart for the proposed system and a data dictionary. The module designs are documented in module headers, which describe the major purpose of each module in the system and how it relates to other modules in the system.

During review, the preliminary design should be evaluated for how well it meets the system requirements and how good the design is. A good design is one that is simple, efficient, and effective.

Checklist of Project Activities

_____ Decide which person is in charge of the preliminary design activities.

_____ Plan a schedule of preliminary design activities and set deadlines.

_____ Assign personnel to be responsible for the different activities.

_____ Determine the strategy to be used during the design process: the traditional approach, evaluation through alternative analysis, competitive design, or prototyping, and plan the progression of preliminary design activities accordingly.

_____ Decide on a set of conventions for drawing structure charts.

_____ Determine the medium to be used in creating the structure charts.

_____ Based on the data-flow diagrams created during analysis, design the software structure, documenting the design as a structure chart. Use transform and transaction analysis as appropriate. Be sure to allow a lot of time for the design process, and expect to throw away several versions before finding a workable design.

_____ Evaluate the structure chart for shape. Does it have too much fan-out or fan-in? Is the structure too shallow or too deep? Redesign as necessary.

_____ Evaluate the modules for cohesion and coupling.

_____ Design the major data structures for the system.

_____ Calculate the primary and/or secondary memory space required for the storage of the proposed data structures. Compare the calculated space to the actual space that will be available to check the feasibility of the design. Redesign as necessary.

_____ Conduct a formal or informal review of the preliminary design before the design is finalized.

_____ Update and edit the data dictionary from the requirements and specification document to reflect the preliminary design. Decide on the actual source code names for the data elements.

_____ Decide on a format for the module headers.

_____ Decide on a medium for documenting the module headers.

_____ Create the module headers for each module in the structure chart.

_____ Assemble the preliminary design document.

_____ Formally review the preliminary design document.

Terms and Concepts Introduced

top-down functional design methods

top-down design

object-oriented design methods

stepwise refinement

data-driven design methods

transform analysis

structured design method

transaction analysis

module

transform center

cohesion

afferent flow

coupling

efferent flow

black box

factoring a system

information hiding

fan-out, fan-in

reusable modules

module ID

software structure

module header

structure chart

data abstraction

procedural abstraction

prototyping

abstraction by specification

Exercises

1. For each of the following modules, decide if the module is cohesive. If it is not, explain why not.

    (a) SignOn: SignOn accepts and verifies the user's password and activates the SnapShot file.

    (b) ProduceSummaries: ProduceSummaries produces NewSubscriber, Renewals, or ExpiredSubscriptions summary reports.

    (c) MenuDisplay: Displays the main menu.

    (d) ProcessWithdrawal: Processes data on withdrawal form. Removes student from class roster and updates bursar file.

    (e) FormatDayReport: Formats DaySummary data for output.

2. In the following (nonsensical) Pascal procedure, pinpoint each occurrence of coupling.

```
procedure Coupled (var A, B, C, D, E, F, G: integer; Ch1, Ch2: char);
begin
      case Ch1 of
            'a': write ( Newfile, 'It is the first letter.');
            'b': readln (Oldfile, Ch2);
            'c': C := Convert(D, E);   {Convert is a user-defined function}
            'd': GlobalVar := A + B;
            'e': D := ord (Ch2)         {ord is a system-defined function}
      end {case};
end {procedure Coupled};
```

3. Name some devices or systems that you use as black boxes. Under what conditions does the system being a black box become a hindrance to its use?

4. Draw a structure chart based on the data-flow diagram created for Exercise 11 in Chapter 2 (the soft drink purchasing system).

5. Draw a structure chart based on the data-flow diagram for the current logical system created for Exercise 3 in Chapter 2 (the Camp Runamucka system).

6. Draw a high-level design (structure chart) for each system described next. Decide whether each system is basically transform centered or transaction centered.

    (a) A ticket distribution outlet system. The system handles reservations and ticket sales for multiple events.

    (b) A system to calculate and print out mortgage payment schedules. The system takes as input the amount of the mortgage loan, the interest rate, the years, and the payment schedule (weekly, biweekly, or monthly) and displays or prints the payments, the remaining balance owed, the interest paid, the principal, and the total interest paid to date.

(c) A fast-food restaurant control system. Takes customer orders and relays them to the kitchen, calculates the total bill and makes change, maintains sales statistics, and maintains inventory control.

(d) A system to calculate the heating efficiency of a house. The user enters various statistics concerning the size, insulation, geographic location, and so on, about the house. The system calculates the number of thermal heat units needed to maintain a certain temperature in the house.

7. Create a specification for an abstract data type, CourseFile, that might be used in the noncredit courses system. A CourseFile contains a series of course listings. Each course listing consists of a unique course number and other information that need not be considered for this exercise. What would be the minimal operations needed for this data type? Describe the data type using the format shown in Figure 4.18.

8. Create a specification for an abstract data type, PersonalCheck, that might be used in designing a personal checkbook system. Use the data dictionary definition of a check from Exercise 12 in Chapter 2 as a starting point. Include the operations create, set-payee, set-date, set-amount-in-words, set-amount-in-numbers, set-checknumber, get-payee, get-date, get-amount-in-words, get-amount-in-numbers, and get-checknumber.

9. Discuss the advantages and disadvantages of using alternative analysis and competitive designs as techniques for evaluating designs.

5. Detailed Design and Choosing a Programming Language

In the detailed design phase, the actual contents of each module in the proposed system are designed. A decision is made concerning the algorithm to be used in each module, and the design of the data structures is refined. The decisions made during the detailed design phase are expressed in the detailed design document. Just as blueprints are used by builders in constructing a house, the detailed design document is used by programmers to guide the creation of the software during the coding and integration phase of software development.

The skills needed in the detailed design phase are those taught to most programmers. Designing each module is much like writing a short program. The designer must first make sure that he or she understands the problem to be solved. What is the input? What processing is required? What output should be produced? Input and output may be in the form of parameters passed into and out of the module, or they may be raw input or final output to some peripheral device. Next, the designer must decide what algorithm is most appropriate for the task or function the module is to perform and sketch out how the algorithm will be implemented. The designer must understand the data structures to be used and must also make decisions concerning the design of local data structures, constants, and variables.

Although detailed design is often named as one of the stages in the software development cycle, it is important to note that detailed design is typically done in parallel with the later stages of the preliminary design and not as a separate stage. Once detailed design begins, design flaws in the preliminary design are often discovered. This results in a reiteration through the preliminary design and detailed design of the flawed part of the system. In this chapter the issues of algorithm selection, program efficiency, and methods of documenting detailed design will be covered.

A very important issue in building a software system is deciding what programming language will be used. Often the very success or failure of the system can hinge on the choice of language. There are a number of issues to be considered in choosing a language. One issue is pragmatic concerns and is related to sponsor requirements, programmer's training and knowledge, language support availability, and so on. Another issue is from the software engineering standpoint. The language chosen should support the goals of software engineering and should thus aid in the development of efficient, reliable, and maintainable systems. These issues will be discussed in the last half of the chapter.

5.1   Selecting an Algorithm

During the detailed design the designer is working on one module at a time from the entire system. Her or his task is to choose an algorithm to implement each module. If the preliminary design was well done, each module should present a neat, cohesive problem for the designer. There should be a minimum of coupling for the designer to be concerned with, and the purpose or task of the module should be clearly spelled out. Furthermore, the designer should have a relatively free hand in deciding how to implement the module if the module was designed as a black box, using the principles of abstraction and information hiding. Nonetheless, the detailed designer has quality guidelines to be followed in choosing an algorithm. The three major guidelines for selecting an algorithm are *correctness, efficiency,* and *appropriateness*. Each of these will be discussed separately.

5.1.1   Choosing a Correct Algorithm

Correctness is essential in choosing an algorithm. The algorithm chosen should process the supplied data correctly and/or perform the required operations correctly. Although this might seem like an obvious guideline, it nonetheless bears some discussion. In particular, it is easy to overlook certain conditions where a chosen algorithm might fail. Negative numbers, zeros, and boundary conditions (for example, the last value in an array) are just some of the many conditions that can cause an algorithm to fail. A knowledge of testing strategies can help to make the detail designer better at choosing correct algorithms. These strategies will be discussed in Chapter 7.

When students are taught to program, they are expected to develop some algorithms on their own as part of the learning process. The copying of algorithms from other sources is typically discouraged. This trend, however, is completely reversed in the development of software in industry. The copying of algorithms is, as it should be, encouraged. Building systems or parts of systems based on reusable modules has already been mentioned. Rather than starting from scratch, the builder has coded, tested, and maintained modules to work from. A great deal of time and effort can be saved by incorporating reusable modules. If such modules are not available, the next best choice is to copy an algorithm from some other source. There are books containing collections of algorithms (for example, Knuth, 1973 a, b; *Collected Algorithms from ACM*), and periodicals such as *Communications of the ACM* that regularly publish algorithms. All these sources are readily available. The idea here is to avoid reinventing the wheel. Why spend hours struggling to come up with a correct, clever, and efficient algorithm when someone else has probably already done it — and tested it better than you have, as well? Although it might be a fun exercise for you, managers see time as money and do not care to pay for the time you spend developing an algorithm that has already been developed.

5.1.2   Choosing an Efficient Algorithm

The *efficiency* of a computer algorithm refers to the amount of computer resources expended by the algorithm. The computer resources that can be expended include primary and secondary memory and central processing unit (CPU) time. Due to the great technological advances in computer storage, time is typically the more important resource to be considered. To avoid slight inconsistencies due to different machines, programming languages, translators, and the like, time efficiency is typically calculated in terms of the number of abstract processing steps required to carry out an algorithm. Consider, for example, the algorithm shown in pseudocode in Figure 5.1a for computing the sum of the series of positive integers from 1 to N, where N is an input parameter. The basic operations include initializing the sum to zero and adding the value of the variable, Counter, to the sum. For any input value of N, the first basic operation is performed exactly once. The second basic operation, however, is performed N times during execution of the algorithm. This means that if N = 3 there would be a total of 1 + 3 = 4 basic operations performed. If N = 25, there would be 26 basic operations performed, and if N = 50,000, there would be 50,001 such basic operations. Thus, the function that describes the relationship between N and the number of basic operations required to process N is a linear function. We say that the *order* of this algorithm is linear or order N. (Note that constants in the function describing the efficiency of an algorithm are dropped when computing the order of the algorithm.)

Now examine the algorithm in Figure 5.1b. This algorithm also finds the sum of a series of positive integers from 1 to N. However, it uses Gauss's formula

a. Iterative Algorithm

```
SeriesSum = 0
for Counter = 1 to N do
        SeriesSum = SeriesSum + Counter
write "The sum of the integers from 1 to N is", SeriesSum
```

b. Algorithm Based on Gauss's Formula

```
SeriesSum = (1.0 + N) * (N/2.0)
write "The sum of the integers from 1 to N is", SeriesSum
```

Figure 5.1 Pseudocode for Two Algorithms for Finding the Sum of a Series of Integers from 1 to N

rather than iteration. The basic operation for this algorithm is the computation of the formula. If $N = 3$, one basic operation would be performed. If $N = 25$, one basic operation would be performed. And if $N = 50,000$, there would still be just one basic operation performed. The function that describes this relationship is a constant function, and the order of the Gauss algorithm is order 1. Clearly, using Gauss's algorithm is a much more efficient method of computing the sum of a series than the iterative method.

This same method of tabulating basic operations can be used to order the efficiency of any algorithm. Table 5.1 presents a list of standard orders and some sample algorithms for each order. Table 5.2 shows the relationship of different values of N to the various efficiency functions given in Table 5.1. Table 5.2 is

Table 5.1 Standard Orders of Efficiency and Sample Algorithms

Order	Name	Sample algorithms
1	Constant	Gauss algorithm for sum of a series
log N	Logarithmic	Binary search of ordered array; search of a binary search tree
N	Linear	Search of an unordered list; sum of elements in array or linked list; copying a file
N log N	N log N	Quick Sort; Merge Sort
N^2	Quadratic	Bubble Sort; Selection Sort; Insertion Sort
N^3	Cubic	Matrix multiplication
2^n	Exponential	Brute-force code breaking; brute-force search of game-move options (for example, chess)

Table 5.2 Relationship of Different Values of N to the Efficiency Functions in Table 5.1.

Order	1	10	100	1,000	10,000
			Values of N		
Constant	1	1	1	1	1
Logarithmic	1	4	7	10	14
Linear	1	10	100	1000	10,000
N log N	1	40	700	10,000	140,000
Quadratic	1	100	10,000	1,000,000	100,000,000
Cubic	1	1000	1,000,000	1,000,000,000	10^{12}
Exponential	2	1024	1.27×10^{30}	1.07×10^{301}	1.99×10^{3010}

Entries in the table represent the total number of basic operations required.

presented to highlight the real importance of selecting an efficient algorithm. The greatest gains in improving the efficiency of an algorithm come from finding an algorithm with a lower order of efficiency. Notice, for example, the spectacular reduction in the total number of basic operations required to process 10,000 items if an algorithm of order N log N (for example, Quick Sort) is used rather than one of order N^2 (for example, Selection Sort). Clearly, there is a great payoff in working to reduce the order of an algorithm.

Possibly you noticed the horrendous number of basic operations required by exponential algorithms. In fact, exponential algorithms are generally considered impractical for implementation. To solve problems that are based on exponential algorithms, an approach to programming called *heuristic programming* is used. In heuristic programming, guidelines or rules of thumb are used to take shortcuts to solving the problem. In a heuristic program, unlike an algorithmic program, there is no guarantee that any solution will be found to the problem. (Algorithms, on the other hand, are guaranteed to find a solution for any proper input.) However, the heuristic program can be executed in a feasible amount of time. Thus there is a trade-off in heuristic programs between efficiency and the likelihood of finding a problem solution. Many problems in the area of artificial intelligence require heuristic programming.

Once an algorithm of the lowest possible order has been selected, there may be ways to further improve the efficiency by fine-tuning the algorithm or by selecting among several algorithms with the same order of efficiency. For example, the efficiency of Quick Sort can be improved by using an order N^2 sort to sort the subsets of elements containing ten or fewer elements created during the partitioning of the array. If certain restrictions apply to the data such that certain cases will never occur (for example, empty arrays, negative values or data already in sorted order), the algorithm can take advantage of these restrictions. If hash tables are being used, the hashing functions can be fine-tuned to produce fewer clashes.

Efficiency of both time and space can be gained by a wise choice of data structures. Perhaps the algorithm can be written to use a sparse matrix rather than a full two-dimensional array. Perhaps a queue can be implemented in an array rather than as a linked list. The wise designer considers the pros and cons of various possibilities.

5.1.3   Choosing an Appropriate Algorithm

A final consideration in the selection of an algorithm is its appropriateness for the particular hardware and software of the target system. To pick an extreme example, it would be foolish to design a system based on random access files if the target system implements only sequential files. In another case, the speed and characteristics of the system input/output devices might influence the choice of an external sorting algorithm. Details concerning how the system and the target translator handle dynamic allocation of memory could influence the choice of data structures and algorithms as well. These are only a few examples, but they highlight the kinds of concerns the designer should keep in mind.

5.2   When Efficiency Is Particularly Important

So far the discussion has focused on efficiency within a module. In some cases, however, the overall efficiency of the entire system is a primary concern to the sponsor. The sponsor may require fast throughput or rapid response time. Experience has shown that the best approach to obtaining system efficiency is to first design and code the system using the design principles discussed so far, including the use of the most efficient algorithms possible. Once the system or a significant part of the system has been implemented, its performance can be measured. One way to assess performance is to count the number of times each statement in a program is executed when the program is run. A more sophisticated measurement might assign weights to the different kinds of statements. For example, a simple assignment statement would be weighted less than a statement that involved the calculation of an expression. These measurements can be made using special software designed for this purpose (Knuth, 1971). Another way to assess performance is through time measurements made using the system clock. Such measurements may be even more useful than line counts in some cases, because they assess the actual elapsed time required for code execution. The bottlenecks in the system can be pinpointed using these methods and the bottlenecks corrected by reconfiguring the system, using a new algorithm for the problem section or possibly rewriting the critical sections directly in machine language. One approach to reconfiguring the system that can result in increased efficiency is to combine two or more of the modules that are part of the bottleneck. This increases efficiency by eliminating the overhead associated with linkage and passing parameters.

It should be emphasized again that efficiency tuning is done only *after* the system has been implemented based on the initial design. Why should you wait until after the system has been implemented to work on its efficiency? This approach to optimization is based on the observation that typically 80 percent or more of the execution time of a program is spent on 20 percent or less of the code (Knuth, 1971). While this may seem like a surprising fact, it is true. Furthermore, it is not usually possible to predict where this 20 percent of the code will be until the program is actually implemented and monitored. Thus, it makes no sense to spend a lot of time fine-tuning parts of the program, while possibly reducing its readability and maintainability, when the parts being fine-tuned are not sources of inefficiency.

5.3   Documenting the Algorithm Design

A primary product of the detailed design phase is the design of the algorithm. The design must be represented in some form for the purposes of review and to be passed on to the coders. There are several popular ways of diagramming algorithms. *Flowcharts* are one of the oldest and most widely known methods.

Nassi–Shneiderman charts and *pseudocode* are two other well-known techniques. Pseudocode was defined and described in Chapter 2. Nassi–Shneiderman charts will be discussed next. Flowcharts will not be discussed for several reasons. One reason is that, while flowcharts are easy for people to follow, they have some weaknesses as a design tool (Brooke and Duncan, 1980; Shneiderman, et al., 1977; Shneiderman, 1982). The goal of the detailed design is to produce a good design. A good design is a structured design. Unfortunately, flowcharts do not guide the designer toward a structured design the way Nassi–Shneiderman charts or pseudocode do. The designer using flowcharts is perfectly free to design what is unaffectionately called "spaghetti code." In structured code, the flow of control is always top to bottom. Backward branches are not allowed. In spaghetti code, following the flow of control is like trying to follow the path of one piece of spaghetti in an entire plate of spaghetti; branches may occur from any place to any place else in the code. Other reasons for not covering flowcharts is that they are not generally used in the industry today, they are difficult to draw and difficult to update, and they have been shown empirically to be less effective as a detailed design tool.

5.3.1 Representing Detailed Design with Nassi–Shneiderman Charts

Nassi–Shneiderman charts were developed as a way to represent structured programs (Nassi and Shneiderman, 1973). They are founded on the fact, shown by Bohm and Jacopini (1966), that any process that is algorithmic can be represented as a combination of exactly three basic constructs: sequence, selection, and iteration. Sequence is represented in Nassi–Shneiderman charts as horizontal rectangular boxes. For example, in Figure 5.2a, step A of some algorithm is represented as a rectangle, and action B is represented as a rectangle just below the action A rectangle. This indicates that step A should be done first, and then step B, a sequence of steps. Selection occurs when a choice must be made among two or more alternative steps. An *if-then-else* situation is represented as shown in Figure 5.2b. The condition that is to be tested is indicated in a rectangle containing slanted lines that divide up the space below the rectangle into two areas. One area represents the action to be taken if the condition is true; the other area represents the action to be taken if the tested condition is *false*. In Figure 5.2b, step A is to be performed if condition X is *true*; step B is to be performed if X is *false*. In some situations, a certain action is to be performed if condition X is *true*, but nothing is to be done if X is *false*, an *if-then* condition. Figure 5.2c illustrates how an *if-then* situation can be diagrammed. In other situations, selector X might take on any of several values, each of which has different actions associated with it. Such an idea is embodied in the *case* statement available in some high-level languages. Figure 5.2d shows how a *case*-type condition is represented for an example with five different conditions.

The third basic construct represented in Nassi–Shneiderman charts is iteration (repetition). In iteration, some action or set of actions is repeated based on the outcome

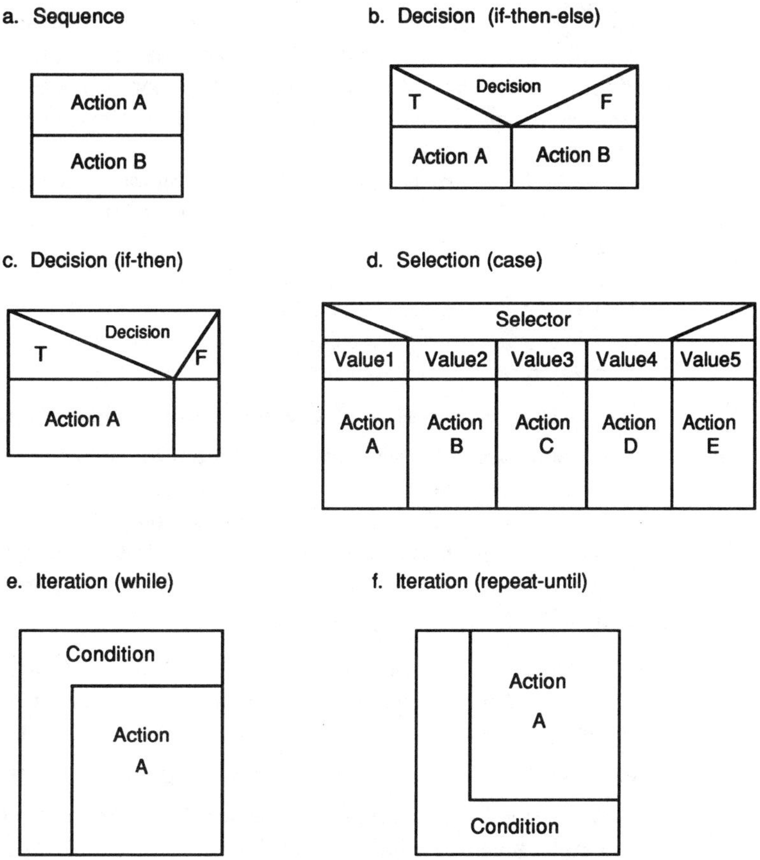

a. Sequence

b. Decision (if-then-else)

c. Decision (if-then)

d. Selection (case)

e. Iteration (while)

f. Iteration (repeat-until)

Figure 5.2 Components Utilized in Drawing Nassi-Shneiderman Charts

of a particular condition. In certain cases, the condition is tested before the action segment is done. These cases are categorized as *while*-type iterations and are represented as shown in Figure 5.2e. The condition is placed in the top, L-shaped form, and the action part is shown as the rectangle enclosed within the L-shaped condition. The diagram is read from top to bottom. The condition is tested first. If it is *true,* the action segment enclosed within the L-shaped condition form is executed once from top to bottom. Then flow of control returns to the top of the construct and the condition is tested again. If it is true, the action segment is executed again. But if the condition is *false,* the action segment is *not* executed, and the flow of control drops out of the *while* construct, down to whatever construct is below it.

Another form of iteration is the *repeat-until* construct (see Figure 5.2f). As with the *while* construct, there is an action part and a condition part, but the order of the two parts is reversed. In the *repeat-until* construct, the condition part is represented as an L-shaped form below and surrounding the action part. In these segments, the action part is executed first, and then the condition is tested. If the condition is *true,* flow of control returns to the top of the structure and the action is executed again. If the condition is *false,* flow of control passes to whatever construct is below the *repeat-until* segment.

These three constructs represent the basic building blocks for drawing Nassi–Shneiderman charts. There are also a few rules for reading or creating Nassi–Shneiderman charts:

1. **The charts are always rectangular.** The width of the rectangles is not significant. They may be as wide or narrow as necessary to legibly and accurately represent the algorithm.

2. **The flow of control in a Nassi–Shneiderman chart always starts at the top.**

3. **Flow of control always moves from top to bottom, except when iteration is involved.** When the end of a *while* segment is reached, control passes back to the top of the construct (the condition part). When the end of a *repeat-until* segment is reached, the condition is tested and control may pass back to the top of the construct (the action part) or on down to the next segment.

4. **Vertical lines may never be crossed.**

5. **A rectangle may be exited in a downward direction only.** If a decision is involved, the rectangle must be exited directly under the appropriate decision outcome.

6. **A rectangle may be empty, representing a null or empty action.**

7. **A rectangle may represent another Nassi-Shneiderman chart (for example, a call to another procedure.)**

An example of a Nassi–Shneiderman chart using structured English prose is shown in Figure 5.3. In this example, part of a system for processing correspondence regarding magazine subscriptions is represented. Notice that the chart includes calls to other procedures or subroutines, which would be represented in separate Nassi–Shneiderman charts. Nassi–Shneiderman charts can also be written using phrases that are much closer to actual source code. Figure 5.4 shows a Nassi–Shneiderman chart in which variable names and operators are used. The algorithm in the chart takes a string array of nonblank characters, InString, and converts them into a valid unsigned integer in the variable IntegerValue. It assumes that no plus or minus signs are involved. Notice that the chart includes a call to a Boolean function, CheckIfNumber, which checks to see if the character passed to it is a numeric character. CheckIfNumber would have to be designed with a separate Nassi–Shneiderman chart. The point of presenting the two examples is to show that Nassi–Shneiderman charts can be written with different levels of detail, just as pseudocode can. Thus, Nassi–Shneiderman charts can be used to document preliminary design as well as detailed design. The choice of the level of detail in the chart depends on the goals of the designer. For detailed design, it is

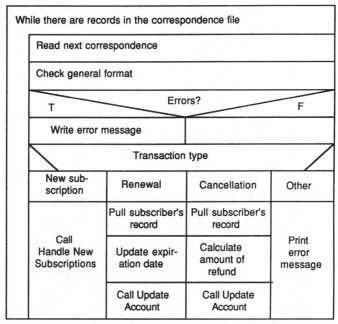

While there are records in the correspondence file			
Read next correspondence			
Check general format			
Errors? T / F			
Write error message			
Transaction type			
New sub-scription	Renewal	Cancellation	Other
Call Handle New Subscriptions	Pull subscriber's record	Pull subscriber's record	Print error message
	Update expiration date	Calculate amount of refund	
	Call Update Account	Call Update Account	

Figure 5.3 Nassi-Shneiderman Chart Showing Processing of Correspondence Records in a Magazine Subscription System

probably best to aim for the level of detail such that each phrase in the chart results in no more than ten lines of programming language source code (Shneiderman, 1982). If the Nassi–Shneiderman chart is written at too high a level, the programmer might not implement the module as the designer intended. On the other

IntegerValue = 0	
Position = 1	
While ErrorStatus = OK and Position <= InputStringLength	
NumberCh = Instring (Position)	
Call CheckIfNumber (NumberCh)	
NumberCh is a number T / F	
DigitValue = integer form of NumberCh	ErrorStatus = BadCharacter
IntegerValue = (IntegerValue * 10) + DigitValue	
Position = Position + 1	

Figure 5.4 Nassi-Shneiderman Chart for an Algorithm to Convert an Array of Characters into an Unsigned Integer Value

hand, if too much detail is given, the coder will hardly have anything to do. The designer has probably wasted time that should have been spent on designing other modules. The example in Figure 5.3 is closer to the level that should be aimed for.

Many advantages are associated with Nassi–Shneiderman charts:

- Easy to learn
- Easy to read
- Easy to convert to source code
- Good at encouraging structured design
- Flexible in the level of detail shown
- Standarized

The greatest disadvantages of Nassi–Shneiderman charts are the difficulty in drawing them and the difficulty in modifying them when a design change is made. Typically, the designer must draw up the entire chart by hand and then try to enter the information into a computer. A word processor will produce very nice looking Nassi–Shneiderman charts. The underscore character can be used to produce horizontal lines and the vertical bar character (|) can be used for vertical lines. The tab functions aid in the spacing of the different components. After the chart is printed out, slanted lines can be added with pen or pencil. Software for drawing (for example, MacDraw or MacPaint) can also be used, and specialized software for drawing and editing Nassi-Shneiderman charts is also available.

Even if Nassi–Shneiderman charts are not used, learning how to construct them and seeing several algorithms drawn up in Nassi–Shneiderman form give new insights into the structure of programs and modules that should not be missed. They present a more abstract view of the structure that cannot easily be seen by viewing pseudocode or even source code. The complexity or simplicity of a module is readily apparent from viewing a Nassi–Shneiderman chart, just as the complexity of a building is evident from its steel girders or wooden framework.

5.3.2 Representing Detailed Design Using Pseudocode

An alternative detailed design representation is structured pseudocode. Pseudocode has the great advantage that it is composed solely of text and can be readily produced on a word processor or text editor. Furthermore, most people trained as programmers find it very easy to use pseudocode for design. Pseudocode has already been discussed in Section 2.4.1 as a tool for writing activity specifications in the requirements and specifications. When pseudocode is used for detailed design, the level of the pseudocode is typically lower and more fine grained than would be seen in an activity specification. Activity specifications spell out the general purpose and functions of an activity in the system. A detailed design spells out the steps in a particular algorithm to be used in the module being designed. Each line of pseudocode should expand into no more than ten lines of source code.

Because there are many possible styles of pseudocode, it is a good idea to set up some standards for the pseudocode to be used in the detailed designs. These standards should include the set of structures to be allowed, the set of operators (for example, arithmetic and logical operators), the syntax, and some guidelines for formatting and layout (for example, indenting). Examples of the level of detail desired could be provided, as well, so that the designers agree on the amount of detail that should be incorporated into their designs.

5.4 Data Structure Design Revisited

As the overall design of the system becomes more refined, the data structures will also be refined. As this work progresses, it is a good idea to keep in mind the goals of information hiding and data abstraction. Information hiding, discussed in Section 4.1.3, refers to the principle that each program unit should only be allowed access to data or procedures that are required for the unit to perform its function. The unit should specifically be denied access to any other objects and should not be allowed to affect objects other than the necessary ones. Furthermore, the information hidden in the unit should not be open to corruption from any other unit that is not supposed to use that information.

A good preliminary design will incorporate information hiding. However, several techniques and approaches are available for implementing information hiding that can be applied at the level of detailed design as well. The language Modula-2 includes the concepts of definition and implementation modules and Ada includes the concept of a *package* to directly support information hiding. An Ada package consists of the definition of an object and its associated operations. The actual code implementing the object may be separate from the package definition (specification). For example, an object such as a queue of integers and its associated operations can be implemented in an Ada package. The package header would describe the types of operations allowed on the queue (for example, Add, Remove, CheckIfEmpty) and would define the allowable access to the queue from outside the package. The package body would include implementations of the operations Add, Remove, and CheckIfEmpty. A package is essentially a template for a queue. An instance or several instances of a queue would be created as needed in the program.

Other programming languages, such as FORTRAN, Pascal, and COBOL do not have constructs that directly support information hiding. In such languages, the careful use of modularity and language features can simulate information hiding. For example, a data structure for the integer queue described above might be defined in Pascal as:

```
type IntegerQueue = record
        Qarray: array [1..500] of integer;
        Head: 0..500;
        Tail: 0..500
    end;
```

The procedures AddToQueue, RemoveFromQueue, and CheckIfQEmpty could each be implemented as separate procedures or functions. Although direct access to instances of IntegerQueue that are declared either globally or locally is not prohibited by the language, the code should be designed and written so that any access is through the defined procedures only. The use of such techniques simulates the information hiding of Ada or Modula-2. One major advantage of the information hiding approach is that changes in the details of the data structure require minimal changes throughout the rest of the code.

While information hiding goes hand in hand with data abstraction, *user-defined types, subtypes,* and *derived types* are good techniques for introducing data abstraction and data security as well. In user-defined types, the programmer defines an ordered set of elements that can be used as indexes. For example,

> type Ages = (Infant, Toddler, Preschool, Child, Preteen, Teen, Adult);

A variable of type Ages, for example, NextAge, could then be used as a loop control variable and could take on the successive values Infant to Adult. The values could also serve as indexes to an array.

Subtypes utilize a limited range of built-in or user-defined type. For example,

> type Youngsters = (Infant..Preschool);

would define the subrange of Ages from Infant to Preschool. While

> type Units = (0..9);

would define the set of integers from 0 to 9 to be a subrange of integers.

Derived types declare a new type to be equal to an existing type. For example,

> type DollarAmount is new integer;
> type Total is new integer;

The two types are logically distinct, but the same operations (for example, addition and subtraction) can be performed on them.

In languages with no mechanism for user-defined types and limited built-in types, entities in the problem domain must be mapped onto objects of built-in types. For example, the integers 0 to 6 might be used to stand for the ordered age categories in the preceding example. The programmer must then remember this correspondence while coding. Range restrictions must be explicitly tested in the program. Unfortunately, it is easy to forget to check ranges.

5.5 Detailed Design Document

The heading for this section is somewhat misleading. Typically, no separate new document is produced that contains just the detailed designs. Instead, the module headers produced during the preliminary design phase are expanded to include the

```
{*************************************************************
- TITLE:    SortItemSizes
- MODULE ID:    A4.3
- PURPOSE:  This module sorts a list of sizes, in ounces, that
-   a particular grocery item is available in into ascending
-   order.
- METHOD:    Selection Sort
-
-   i = 1
-   while i < NumberOfItems  do
-       find the smallest item in the currently active
-           portion of the array
-       swap the smallest item with the item in the i th position
-       increment i, making the currently active portion
-           of the array smaller
-   end-while
-
- USAGE: GetItemSizes
- EXTERNAL REFERENCES:   none
- CALLING SEQUENCE:
-       Sizes - (I/O)  An integer array of sizes to be sorted.
-       Count - (I)  An integer indicating the number of items in
-           Sizes.  Count must be >0 and < = 25.
- INPUT ASSERTION:   The input array must contain 1 to 25 integer
-   values, in any order.
- OUTPUT ASSERTION:  The items in the array will be ordered
-   such that item1 <= item2 ... <= itemN.
- VARIABLES:
-       i - an integer used to index the array, Sizes
- AUTHOR(S):
- REMARKS:  Because only 25 or fewer items are to be sorted each
-   time the procedure is called, a QuickSort is not needed.  An
-   n-squared sort can be used.
*************************************************************}
```

Figure 5.5 Portion of a Detailed Design Document

documentation for the detailed design. If pseudocode is used and if the preliminary design was produced using the editor for the target language, the detailed designs can be inserted into the system shell using the editor. An example of this approach is shown in Figure 5.5. Notice that the pseudocode for the algorithm has been inserted into the method section of the module header that was created during the preliminary design and shown in Figure 4.16. Preliminary designs created and printed using other methods must be collated with their module headers and kept in some orderly fashion. A notebook of module designs can be created, or separate unit folders can be kept for each module or set of related modules.

5.6   Evaluating the Detailed Design

One major purpose in carrying out the detailed design of a system is to evaluate the preliminary design. As detailed design progresses, flaws in the system structure and data structures designs will become evident. The effort involved in correcting these flaws will be less than if coding were done directly from the preliminary design. Evaluating the detailed design thus has two positive outcomes: it provides a further check of the preliminary design, and it provides a check of the detailed designs themselves. Both walk-throughs and formal reviews (see Section 2.9) are appropriate methods of evaluating detailed design.

The evaluation should focus on each module individually, with consideration given to the interfacing of modules as well. Some of the factors to be considered in evaluation are as follows:

- Does the proposed design fulfill the specifications for the module and provide the desired function?
- Is the specified design logically correct?
- Is the design well structured?
- Is the module's interface consistent with the structural design of the system?
- Is the complexity of the design reasonable?
- Have appropriate error-handling and/or input-editing features been included?
- Is the design appropriate for the target programming language?
- Is the module documentation complete?
- Does the design meet the input assertions?
- Does the design satisfy the output assertions?
- Are all input parameters used somewhere in the module?
- Are all output parameters assigned a value somewhere in the module?
- Are all input/output parameters modified somewhere in the module?
- Does the design include any hardware-dependent or system-dependent features?
- Are the designs of any local data structures appropriate?

5.7 Choosing a Programming Language: Pragmatic Concerns

The choice of which programming language to use in developing a nontrivial software system is crucial. The use of an appropriate language is essential for avoiding difficulties in the later stages of the system's life cycle. Coding and testing are facilitated by a suitable language, and maintenance is eased. Ease of maintenance is particularly important, as the cost of owning and maintaining the software may be twice the initial development cost. Two sorts of factors relate to the choice of a programming language. These include pragmatic concerns and factors related to the programming language itself. Pragmatic concerns include the following:

1. **Sponsor requirements.** In some instances the sponsor may specify that a particular programming language is to be used. Possibly a list of permissible

languages may be supplied by the sponsor. Sponsor specification of the target language is often done when the sponsor will be responsible for maintenance of the system. This is common practice in contracts for software systems from U.S. government agencies, such as the Department of Defense.

2. **Knowledge of the coders.** When other factors do not argue against it, it is most cost effective to choose a language the coders are already familiar with. Although learning a new programming language is typically not difficult for programmers, they will require a certain amount of practice in coding in a new language. They must learn to use the features provided by the language effectively and to understand the limitations of the language.

3. **Languages used in previous and/or concurrent projects.** This factor is related to the knowledge of the coders. Languages used on previous projects are already known by the coders who worked on the earlier projects. Another consideration is that programmers often have multiple ongoing projects. They may be maintaining one system while working on the development of another. When different languages are in concurrent use, errors due to confusion between the languages are inevitable.

4. **Availability and quality of the language compiler.** The compiler for the chosen language must be available for the target hardware and operating system configuration. Furthermore, the compiler must be of reasonable quality and, if the compiler must be purchased, of reasonable cost. The quality of the compiler relates to the efficiency of the object code the compiler produces, its reliability, and the quantity and quality of its error messages.

5. **Availability of supporting software development tools.** The availability of editors, debuggers, linkers, and other software development tools such as cross-referencers and execution flow summarizers is important. Such tools make the system easier to develop and test. (See Section 8.4 for further discussion of software development tools.)

6. **Portability.** If the system being developed is intended to operate on a variety of different machines and/or under a variety of different operating systems, it is important to select a language that enhances portability.

5.8 Choosing a Programming Language: Programming-in-the-Small Concerns

Aside from pragmatic concerns, characteristics of individual programming languages should be considered when choosing a target language. Although there are many ways to classify programming languages, the discussion here will focus on those characteristics and features that software should have from the viewpoint of software engineering. That is, we will examine features a language can possess that can facilitate the development of efficient, reliable, and maintainable software.

Broadly, the software engineer can view the features of a language from two different aspects (Bell, Morrey, and Pugh, 1987). One viewpoint is to examine those features that support what can be called *programming in the small*. Programming in the small refers to the coding of individual modules and small programs by one individual. Features such as the simplicity, clarity, and orthogonality of the language, the syntax of the language, and the number and type of control and data abstractions are all related to programming in the small. The second viewpoint is *programming in the large*. Programming in the large refers to the development of a system through the coordinated effort of a group of people, where each person is responsible for different components of the system. Features of languages that relate to the interfacing of modules, the support of functional and data abstraction, and separate compilation of program modules are all of concern for programming in the large. Each of these features will be discussed later.

5.8.1 Power and Suitability

The power of a language refers to its ability to carry out desired programming tasks simply and with little programming effort. Power is directly related to the features and data structures supported by the language, and is therefore to a certain extent a composite of the additional features discussed later. Power is also relative to the programming problem being solved. For example, COBOL would not be considered a powerful language when used to do systems programming. It has virtually none of the special sorts of operations and commands a systems programmer needs, such as support of exception handling and concurrency. Likewise, C would not be a powerful language for business applications. C does not support those features, such as output formatting, widely used by business applications programmers.

Different languages were designed for different purposes, and have different strengths. COBOL, as mentioned above, was designed for business applications, and emphasizes file manipulation and report-production. Pascal was initially designed as a teaching language, but has the advantage of supporting complex data structures. C and Modula-2 are appropriate for systems programming. Ada and FORTH were designed to support real-time applications where speed and efficiency are important, and can handle exceptions. Ada, Modula-2 and concurrent Pascal handle concurrency. Special languages also exist for artificial intelligence programming (for example, LISP), and for other specialized computer applications. By choosing a suitable language, the software engineer can put power into the hands of the designers and programmers.

5.8.2 Simplicity, Clarity, and Orthogonality

The *simplicity* of a programming language refers to the size of its vocabulary. The fewer the number of operators, operands, and reserved words in a language, the simpler the language. Simplicity is desirable because it allows a programmer to become completely familiar with the entire language. If a language has a large vocabulary, some features may be rarely used and therefore may not be completely understood. Simplicity is also important because the vocabulary must be understood not only as separate units, but in terms of the interactions created by relating the terms. Thus the more complex the vocabulary is the more complex the interactions.

Examples of complex languages include PL/1, COBOL, and Ada. COBOL based on the ANSI 74 standard contains approximately 300 reserved words. The new ANSI 85 standard of COBOL includes all the old words and adds approximately 47 new reserved words. In contrast, Pascal contains 74 reserved words and standard identifiers, Modula-2 contains 64 reserved words and standard identifiers, and FORTRAN contains 48 basic statement types. As evidence for the complexity of Ada, consider that the reference manual to describe the features of standard Ada contains 300 pages (Department of Defense, 1982).

The *clarity* of a programming language refers to the degree to which a language is natural, meaningful, and unambiguous to the programmer. Early programming languages typically reflect the architecture of the computers they were designed to run on. Furthermore, the early language constructs reflect concerns with run-time efficiency. These influences produced languages that are efficient and easy to translate into machine code, but which sometimes lack readability and clarity. Consider, for example, the FORTRAN arithmetic *if,* which has the following format:

if(arithmetic-expression)LineNumber1,LineNumber2,LineNumber3

In this statement, the arithmetic expression is first evaluated, and then branching occurs to LineNumber1 if the result is positive, to LineNumber2 if the result is zero, and to LineNumber3 if negative. Not so coincidentally, early IBM machines had a machine instruction that compared a value in memory to a value in a register and branched based on the sign of the result.

Orthogonality is another desirable feature for a programming language. *Orthogonality* refers to the degree to which the programmer is free to combine language features. For example, if a language has programmer-defined functions, can the value returned by the function call be any of the built-in types? If any of the built-in types are excluded (for example, reals), then that feature is not completely orthogonal. Although Pascal is more orthogonal than many languages, it does lack orthogonality in the feature just mentioned, function types, and in other areas. For example, while most scalar types can be read and written in standard Pascal, Booleans can be written but not read, and enumerated types cannot be read or written. Lack of orthogonality places constraints on programmers, requires them to remember many exceptions and special cases, and results in the writing of extra, sometimes awkward, code to handle the exceptions.

No language in existence today completely meets the goals of simplicity, clarity, and orthogonality while still being a powerful, useful language. Nonetheless, as software engineers have shown the importance of readable, clear, maintainable code, language designers are more and more recognizing that these characteristics — simplicity, clarity, and orthogonality — are important.

5.8.3 Language Syntax

The *syntax* of a programming language is the set of rules that describe how the tokens from the vocabulary of the language can be combined to form meaningful instructions. Ideally, these rules should be simple and consistent and promote the clarity of the source code. Quirks and flaws in the syntax of a language can cause considerable inconvenience and result in both minor and serious errors.

A syntactic flaw common to several languages is the use of a pair of tokens such as *begin . . . end* or bracketing conventions to group statements together. A very common programming error is to omit the closing token. The use of explicit keywords such as *endIf* or *endWhile* reduces the number of errors and results in clearer source code. For example, consider the amount of editing needed to add a second statement to the Pascal code

```
if TotalSales > BonusLevel then
      Bonus := Commission + (BonusPercent * TotalSales);
```

To add a second statement requires creating a compound statement with a *begin* and *end:*

```
if TotalSales > BonusLevel then
      begin
            Bonus := Commission + (BonusPercent * TotalSales);
            BonusMonths := BonusMonths + 1
      end
```

Contrast this with the explicit keyword approach taken by Ada. The original statement would be

```
if TotalSales > BonusLevel then
      Bonus := Commission + (BonusPercent * TotalSales)
endIf
```

and the modified form would be

```
if TotalSales > BonusLevel then
      Bonus := Commission + (BonusPercent * TotalSales);
      BonusMonths := BonusMonths + 1
endIf
```

Notice that the modification in Ada requires only the insertion of the new statement.

Explicit keywords have the added advantage of eliminating the renowned "dangling *else*" problem that occurs in many languages. As an illustration of the problem, consider the following pseudocode. Is the dangling *else* associated with the first, outer *if* or the second, inner *if?*

```
if conditionA then
       if conditionB then
              action1
  else
       action2
```

In Pascal and Modula-2, the rule is that an *else* is associated with the most recent unterminated *if* lacking an *else*. Thus, in this example, the *else* would be associated with conditionB, the inner *if*. If we wished the *else* to be associated with conditionA, there are two possible Pascal solutions. The first uses a null statement to match the inner *if:*

```
if conditionA then
       if conditionB then
              action1
       else   {null statement}
  else
       action2
```

The second solution surrounds the inner *if* with *begin* and *end:*

```
if conditionA then
       begin
          if conditionB then
              action1
       end
  else
       action2
```

A much more elegant solution is obtained by using explicit keywords:

```
if conditionA then
       if conditionB then
              action1
       endIf
  else
       action2
  endIf
```

Another important syntactic issue concerns the format of the source code statements. It is important for the readability and clarity of the code that the programmer have control over the format of the code. Older languages such as FORTRAN and COBOL impose a strict formatting style on the programmer. For example, FORTRAN requires that columns 1 to 5 be used for statement labels (numbers) and columns 7 through 72 be used for programming statements. These requirements stem from the early method of source code input, the punched card, which was 80 columns wide. With free formatting, the programmer can use indentation and blank lines to convey the structure of the code and enhance its readability.

The understandability of a program can also be improved through the use of meaningful identifiers. Restrictions on the length of identifiers, such as those imposed by FORTRAN or earlier forms of BASIC, force the programmer to use cryptic, often meaningless identifiers. In languages without such restrictions, the programmer can add documentation to the program simply by choosing meaningful identifiers. In addition, the language should prohibit the use of programming language vocabulary as identifiers. An array named True or a variable named Else could cause great confusion to a reader of source code containing these identifiers. (The topics of formatting and identifiers are discussed in more detail in Section 6.9.)

5.8.4   Control Structures

In the late 1960s and the 1970s, there was substantial debate concerning structured programming and what control structures are necessary to describe the flow of control in a program. Following the structured programming guidelines, it is now generally accepted that a few basic control structures should be used. The three categories of control structures are *decision structures, loop control structures,* and *exception handling.*

Decision constructs include one-way, two-way and multiway decisions. The *if . . then* and the *if . . then . . else* statements are well-established means of embodying one-way and two-way decisions, respectively. There are no particular problems with these statements, given the problem of the dangling *else* is resolved as discussed previously. A *case* statement is typically used to embody multiway decisions. *Case* statements consist of a *case* selector and a series of *case* alternatives, each identified by a *case* label. The power and reliability of the *case* statement are related to the design of the statement. In particular, the following factors are important:

The type of the *case* selector should be as unrestricted as possible. In AlgolW and Algol68, the *case* selector must be an integer. This requirement is quite restrictive. In Pascal and Ada, the selector can be an expression that evaluates to any scalar type except real.

It should be possible to specify multiple alternatives in the *case* label. For example, the *case* label might consist of the three values −1 or 0 or 1, or a range of values, for example, 1 . . . 100.

Potential errors are avoided if the programmer is forced to specify actions for all possible values of the *case* selector. Pascal does not define what happens if the *case* selector fails to match any of the *case* labels. Ada was designed to correct this oversight and requires that actions be specified for all outcomes. This can be done by including all possible values of the *case* selector in the set of *case* labels, by specifying a range of values, or by use of the *others* statement to cover unnamed cases. In the following example, the first *case* label specifies two values, Newborn or Infant; the second *case* label specifies a range of values; and the third label covers all other values.

```
type Ages is (Newborn, Infant, Toddler, Preschool, Child, Teenager,
        Adult);
case Person of
    when Newborn | Infant => Infant_Seat;
    when Toddler..Child => Lap_Belt;
    when Others => Shoulder_and_Lap_Belt;
end case;
```

Loop control structures are usually of two types: (1) structures that allow for a predetermined number of iterations, and (2) those that use the evaluation of some condition to control the number of iterations. The *for* statement, *repeat-until,* and *while-do* are the most common repetition constructs.

A statement to implement a predetermined number of repetitions typically takes a form similar to

```
for loop-counter-variable := initial-expression step increment to
    final-expression
```

How each component of the statement is implemented affects the usefulness and reliability of the statement. These issues include:

The type of the loop-counter variable should not be restricted to integers. Any ordinal type should be allowed, including user-defined types. The use of reals as loop-counter variables should not be allowed, as the unit of increment is not clear.

Neither the loop-counter variable, initial expression, increment, nor final expression should be modifiable within the loop body. If statements within the body can modify any of these loop components, such as is allowed by Algol60, it may be difficult to determine how many loops will be executed. Furthermore, it is possible to create *for*-loops that never terminate.

The scope of the loop-counter variable should be limited to the *for* statement. When the loop terminates, the loop-counter variable should be undefined. Pascal implements *for* loops in this way. However, because Pascal requires that the loop counter be declared in the same manner as other variables, programmers are led into thinking the variable maintains a value after loop termination. It is not clear what the value of the loop counter should be or will be upon termination, and errors can result from using the loop-counter variable outside the scope of the loop.

The *repeat-until* and *while-do* statements do not have some of the potential problems associated with the design of *for* loops because loop termination is under the control of the programmer, rather than the language translator. The *repeat-until* loop places the test for loop termination at the end of the loop body, and the *while* loop places the test at the beginning. Thus it is possible that the statements in the body of a *while* loop may not be executed even once. In the *repeat-until* loop, the body of the loop will always execute at least once.

For the majority of cases where conditional repetition is needed, the *while-do* and *repeat-until* statements are sufficient. However, there are situations, such as the recognition of some exception condition, where it is appropriate to exit from within the body of the loop. Consider, for example, the processing of a stream of data of unknown length, where the end of the data will be signalled by a special datum. More specifically, consider the processing of a stream of characters where the end of the stream will be signaled by a carriage return. A first draft, intuitive implementation of this process might be

```
repeat
        ReadACharacter;
        ProcessTheCharacter
until Character = CarriageReturn
```

Obviously this is incorrect, because the carriage return will be processed by ProcessTheCharacter. A correct version can readily be created, as shown next, but only by adding a Boolean and markedly increasing the length and complexity of the program segment.

```
Done <= false;
repeat
        ReadACharacter;
        if Character = CarriageReturn then
                Done <= true
        else
                ProcessTheCharacter
until Done
```

A neater solution is provided by Ada, which allows for an exit from the loop to the statement immediately following the loop through the use of the *exit* statement. For example, the character reading example above could be coded as

```
loop
        ReadACharacter;
        exit when Character = CarriageReturn;
        ProcessTheCharacter;
end loop;
```

Ada also allows for the exiting from within nested loops through the use of loop names, using the following format:

```
OuterLoop:
        loop
                action(s);
                loop
                        action(s);
                        exit OuterLoop when exit-condition;
                        action(s)
                end loop;
        end loop OuterLoop;
```

The third control structure is *exception handling*. *Exceptions* are unexpected events or errors that occur during the execution of a program. The source of the exception can be from a hardware source or from software errors that may or may not have been anticipated by the programmer. For those cases where the programmer has anticipated the error, code must exist for handling the exception and resuming normal execution. Typically, hardware exceptions are handled by the operating system. If an exception occurs that was not anticipated by the programmer, the operating system attempts to handle the problem. Serious exceptions result in program termination.

Programming languages such as COBOL, FORTRAN, Modula-2, and Pascal do not provide special features for exception handling. If an error occurs that affects the processing only within the procedure where the error is detected, the error can be handled locally, and the absence of such features does not have much effect. However, when the effects of an error spread across several modules, the programmer must resort to some awkward contrivances. For example, flags (for example, Boolean variables) can be created that must be passed as parameters to every potentially affected procedure, function, or subroutine; or global variables (which should be avoided) can be used. Within the potentially affected procedures, a series of tests of the flags must be made. Possibly, further tests must be made when control returns from a call to a procedure, function, or subroutine.

When program size or speed is particularly critical, these methods of exception handling are not acceptable. *Real-time systems,* where the computer is interacting with an actual, physical environment and responding to events under time constraints, and *embedded systems,* where data processing is embedded in a complex of data-gathering and analysis equipment, are prime examples of systems where program size and speed are critical. Reliability is another crucial factor for these systems. Errors must not cause the system to fail. Efficient exception-handling capabilities are important in creating such systems. Ada was designed specifically for creating real-time and embedded systems and has powerful constructs for exception handling.

Ada includes built-in exceptions and user-defined exceptions. Each exception has a name. Built-in exceptions have assigned names, and user-defined exceptions are named and declared like other identifiers. Utilizing or drawing attention to a user-defined exception is called *raising an exception*. Executing the sequence of instructions when an exception is raised is termed *handling the exception*. The block of code that is executed when handling the exception is part of the *exception handler,* a collection of actions to be taken when any of the one or more defined exceptions occur.

Any program unit in Ada may have an associated exception handler. It must appear at the end of the unit. The exception handler is defined by the reserved word *exception* and takes a form similar to a *case* statement. The body of the exception handler consists of a series of one or more *when* statements, each followed by one or more statements to be executed if the exception occurs. The statement can be a procedure call. An *others* clause can be included to handle all exceptions not named in the handler. Thus the format for an exception handler is

```
exception
      when exception-identifier => { statement(s) };
      when exception-identifier => { statement(s) };
            . . .
      when others => { statement(s) };
```

An exception can also be raised at a given block and not be handled locally. In this case the exception will propagate to the level of the containing unit(s) until it is handled. The ultimate containing unit is the operating system.

When an exception is raised and the appropriate exception handler has concluded its processing, control does not return to the point where the exception was raised, but to the end of the unit in which the exception was handled. This feature, combined with the propagation of raised exceptions through containing units, makes the exception control construct particularly useful for handling nonhardware errors encountered during processing. The propagation of such errors would normally have to be handled explicitly by the programmer through the use of flags and parameters.

The following example in Ada illustrates the use of the exception features. Note that the statements in the exception body are procedure calls.

```
declare
      Insufficient_Funds: exception;
      Check_Amount: real;
begin
      Get (Input_File, Check_Amount);
      if Current_Balance - Check_Amount <= 0.0 then
            raise (Insufficient_Funds)
      else Current_Balance := Current_Balance - Check_Amount;
exception
      when Insufficient_Funds => Handle_Overdraft;
      when Numeric_Error => Bad_Input;
      when others => Log_Unknown_Error;
end;
```

In this example, the exception Insufficient_Funds is declared within the program unit. The raising of the Insufficient_Funds exception would cause the flow of control to pass to the program unit named Handle_Overdraft. The program unit, Bad-Input, which is the exception handler for the built-in exception condition Numeric_Error, is also declared within the unit. The use of the *others* statement is illustrated also. If any exception other than Insufficient_Funds or Numeric_Error were to occur during execution, the exception handler Log_Unknown_Error would be called.

5.8.5 Data Types and Strong Versus Weak Typing

As Nicklaus Wirth, the designer of Pascal and Modula-2, has so succinctly stated: Algorithms + Data Structures = Programs (Wirth, 1976). Control structures, as discussed previously, are used to express algorithms. Data structures are represented through data types. It is important that a programming language provide facilities that allow the representation of a wide variety of data structures. Recently, concern has focused on providing methods for data abstraction. These methods focus on *data types, strongly typed languages,* and features that support *abstract data types.* The issue of abstract data types is related to programming in the large and will be covered in Section 5.9.1.

A *data type* is a set of objects and a set of operations that can be applied to any object of that type. Almost all languages use data types to some extent. Typically, the programmer is required to declare the type of all objects (for example, real, integer, or Boolean) to be used in the program. For each type, the programming language then defines what operations can be applied to the objects (for example, mathematical operations or logical comparisons). A language having these features is said to be *typed.* Thus FORTRAN, COBOL, Algol, C, Modula-2, Ada, and Pascal are all typed languages. For a language to be considered *strongly typed,* the compiler must be able to check to see that each operation performed on an object is one of the set of defined operations for that data object type. Of the languages just mentioned, only Ada, Modula-2, and Pascal are strongly typed. Such languages place some restrictions on what sorts of things a programmer can do with data objects, but provide greater clarity in the source code and increased reliability. Languages such as Lisp and APL allow *dynamic typing.* That is, a variable can change its type at run time. In this case, type checking cannot occur at compile time, but must take place at run time. Dynamic typing provides additional flexibility, which is quite useful in some applications (for example, artificial intelligence programs), but requires particular caution in its use on the part of the programmer.

Categories of data type facilities provided by programming languages include *simple data types, structured data types,* and *constants.* Each of these facilities will be discussed next.

5.8.6 Simple Data Types

Simple data types are the basic or primitive data types provided by a programming language. These typically include reals, integers, Booleans and characters, along with their associated operations (arithmetic, relational, and so on). Ada, C, Modula-2 and Pascal include the pointer data type, as well. Pointers allow a data object to be referred to indirectly by referring to the pointer that points to or references the data object. Pointers are of greatest use in situations where the amount of data to be structured is not known in advance, or where the form of the data structure may vary during program execution. However, source code using pointers must be carefully designed and written to avoid obtuse and error-prone code.

The ability to declare user-defined types is a definite enhancement to a language. By using user-defined types, the programmer can extend the simple types and provide greater abstraction, readability, and reliability. For example, consider how age ranges might be modeled in Pascal using a user-defined type, Ages:

```
type Ages = (Infant, Toddler, Preschool, Child, Teenager, Adult);
var Person: Ages;
```

The data object Person may then only take on the literal values in the range Infant to Adult. Incorrect assignments such as

Person := Retiree;   or   Person := 16;

will be caught by the compiler. In the absence of user-defined types, the programmer would be forced to create an alternate representation for the age categories, possibly based on integers or characters. For example, the programmer might define a constant such that Infant = 0, so that the assignment

Person : = Infant

would be valid. However, the statements

Person : = −35   or in FORTRAN   Person =5.82

where the real value 5.82 would be converted into a (rounded) integer, would also be considered valid. These examples point out the value of a strongly typed language as well as the value of user-defined types.

It is also useful to be able to define subranges of types. Subranges include a subset of the values from some other type, but include all the allowable operations. For example:

type Youth = Infant .. Teenager;
     SingleDigit = 0 .. 9;

In this example, Youth is a subrange that includes the range of values from Infant to Teenager from the Ages type declared above. SingleDigit is a subrange from zero to nine of the built-in simple type, integers. Any operations allowable for objects of type Ages is valid for objects of type Youth. Likewise, any integer operation is allowable for objects of type SingleDigit, as long as the result is an integer of type SingleDigit. In a strongly typed language, the compiler can generate code to carry out run-time checks to make sure the value being assigned to a subrange type is valid (within the range). This takes the responsibility for such checking off of the programmer and provides more reliable code.

5.8.7 Structured Data Types

Structured data types include arrays and records. Arrays are sequentially organized aggregates of like-typed data elements, where each element is indexed by its relative position in the structure. Arrays can differ on the type of composite data element, the number of dimensions, and the size of each dimension. Ideally, there should be no restriction placed on the type of the composite data element. Similarly, there should be no restriction on the index type other than that it be a subrange of any ordinal type. An important issue in the implementation of arrays is the time at which the size of the array must be known. In some languages, such as FORTRAN, Pascal and Modula-2, the size of the array must be known at compile time. Such arrays are known as static arrays. Static arrays simplify type checking and the creation of run-time code to check for out-of-range indices, but they reduce flexibility. A programmer working with static arrays must change the declarations and recompile every time the program is run with data using arrays of different sizes, or (more likely) create a static array at least as large as the maximum that will be needed. This is often not an easy estimate to make, and it often results in wasted space. Furthermore, no general purpose routines can be written to handle an array of arbitrary size, because such languages require that the array parameters of procedures must specify their size statically. This often results in inefficiency and extra code. Ada, in contrast to static-array languages, allows the declaration of array types in which the array bounds are unspecified. Subtypes of that type are then created which set up specific array bounds. Consider, for example, a data structure to represent a variety of crossword puzzles. A two-dimensional array type might be declared as:

```
type Puzzle is array (integer range <>, integer range <>) of
    character;
subtype SundayPuzzle is Puzzle (1..50, 1..50);
```

This creates a data type, Puzzle, which is a two-dimensional array of unspecified size that will contain characters and be indexed by integers. A procedure that has a formal parameter of type Puzzle will accept any actual parameter that is a two-dimensional array of characters with integer subscripts, such as SundayPuzzle. Furthermore, the bounds of any array of type Puzzle only need to be available when the array declaration is encountered during run time. The bounds themselves can be expressions. For example, assuming the integer variables Width and Height have been defined, the following declaration will be legitimate:

```
DailyPuzzle: Puzzle (1..Width, 1..Height);
```

and DailyPuzzle can be passed as an actual parameter to a formal parameter of type Puzzle.

Records are the second structured data type. Records are data structures that are collections of heterogeneous data objects where each element (field) may be of a different type and where individual components (fields) are referred to by their field name, rather than by their position in the structure. For example, consider the following Pascal record declaration, which might be used to hold information on a subscriber to a magazine or newspaper:

```
type SubscriberType =
    record
        Name:   array[1..50] of char;
        IDNumber: 10000..99999;
        IssuesSent: 0..104;
        IssuesRemaining: 0..104;
        SubscriptionType:  (New, Renewal, Free, Lifetime)
    end;
```

Each component of a record can be a simple or a structured data type (for example, Name is an array). Likewise, records can form components of a structured data type, such as an array or another record.

Fields of records are referred to by appending their name to the name of the record variable. For example, if Subscriber were a record variable of type SubscriberType, the following statement would set the IDNumber to 87654:

```
Subscriber.IDNumber := 87654;
```

Preceding the field name with the record variable name is probably better than the COBOL approach, which gives the field name first:

```
IDNumber of Subscriber
```

To avoid tedious repetition of the record variable name, it can be dropped in Modula-2 or Pascal when the field names are used within a *with* statement. For example,

```
with Subscriber do
        begin
              IDNumber := 87654;
              IssuesSent :=0;
              SubscriptionType := New
        end;
```

COBOL allows the record variable to be omitted if there is no ambiguity in the field name alone. This is not a good practice, as it encourages programmers to use unique names for similar data objects simply to facilitate shorthand referencing. Furthermore, it may not be clear from the text which record variable is being referenced.

5.8.8 Constants

Constants are data objects whose value does not change throughout the execution of the program. In Pascal and Modula-2, constants are explicitly declared through the use of a *const* statement. Unfortunately, these languages permit only constants of built-in simple data types (that is, real, integer, character, or Boolean), although Modula-2 does allow expressions and sets to be used in a constant declaration. No constants can be created for user-defined types or structured types. Furthermore, these languages require that the value be assigned to the constant at compile time (the constant is statically defined). Ada, on the other hand, allows user-defined typed constants and also includes the dynamic assignment of values to constants. Examples of constants in Ada are

```
Legal_Age:  constant Age := Adult;
Largest_Digit: constant := 9;
Max_Area: constant := Max_Height * Max_Width;
```

Constants can also be structured types in Ada; for example,

Null_Tree: *constant* Tree;

5.8.9 Procedural Abstraction

As discussed in Section 2.2.2, the use of abstractions is an important technique that allows the designer of a program or system to focus on *what* the program or system is to do before focusing on the details of *how* it is to be done. The design of the program evolves as levels of abstraction. Each lower level specifies the system in greater detail than the level above it. There are two primary ways that a program designer can achieve abstraction: abstraction by specification (data abstraction) and procedural abstraction. Abstraction by specification is used to describe the data structures of a system and their associated operations. Procedural abstraction is used to describe operations or activities. Through the use of procedural abstractions such as functions and procedures, the program becomes modular, and its modular structure reflects the levels of abstraction designed into the program.

As a tool for abstraction, procedures can be thought of as creating new programming statements in the source language, while functions can be seen as creating new operators. A call to a procedure appears as a statement in the source code and includes the procedure name and a list of actual parameters. Ideally, procedures have their effect by modifying only parameters passed to them. Functions, on the other hand, return only a single value and must be embedded within an expression. Functions should accept but not return values through their parameters. Unfortunately, most programming languages do not prevent the programmer from accessing and/or modifying data objects defined outside the environment of the function or procedure and producing side effects.

Parameters passed to a function or procedure can be of three types: input, output, or input/output. Input parameters are read-only values. A procedure or function can read and use the value of the parameter, but cannot modify the value of the actual parameter. Output parameters are write-only values. An output parameter is used to hold and return the value of the result of some computation. It should not be read from. An input/output parameter is a read/write value. The parameter can be read from and can be modified by the procedure.

Of the three sorts of parameters, functions should be allowed to have only input parameters. However, most programming languages, including Pascal, Modula-2, and FORTRAN, do not necessarily enforce this restriction. Ada allows only input parameters to functions, but still allows the modification of nonlocal variables. Thus, in most cases the programmer must be responsible for avoiding side effects when using functions.

Three common techniques are used to implement parameter passing. These include *call by reference, call by value,* and *call by value result.* In *call by reference,* the location of the actual parameter is passed or bound to the formal parameter. Thus any modifications made to the parameter during execution of the procedure are permanent. This method is appropriate to implement input/output and output-type parameters. It is particularly useful for passing large data structures because no copying of the data structure is required. FORTRAN uses only call by reference.

Call by value is a suitable technique for implementing input parameters. In call by value, a copy of the value of an actual parameter is passed to the formal parameter. The formal parameter thus acts like a local parameter. Modifications made to the parameter during execution of the procedure or function have no effect on the actual parameter. Call by value allows expressions to be passed as parameters. The value of the expression is computed and passed as to the formal parameter at the time the procedure or function is called.

Call by value result is a mix of the call by reference and call by value schemes. In call by value result, the actual parameter is initially copied into the formal value, as in call by value. Intermediate modifications of the formal parameter made during the execution of the procedure have no effect on the actual parameter. However, upon exiting the procedure, the final value (result) of the formal parameter is copied back into the actual parameter.

The specifications for Ada include three types of parameters, *in, out,* and *in out,* which are defined similar to the input, output, and input/output parameters just described. However, the specifications do not state how these parameters should be implemented. This leaves some ambiguity as to when the use of expressions is appropriate and when the name of the formal parameter is referring to a value or to the actual parameter.

5.8.10 Scoping and Information Hiding

Scoping refers to the region of a program in which a particular identifier may be referenced. The scoping rules of a language determine the scope of an identifier. BASIC and COBOL are languages that have *global scoping*. In these two languages, all identifiers are known anywhere in the program. This severely limits the usefulness of these languages for the development of large programs. In FORTRAN, scope is limited to the program unit in which the identifier is declared. Because the nesting of subroutines and functions is not allowed, identifiers declared in a subroutine or function are known only in that unit. The use of common blocks does allow the sharing of data among program units, however, and effectively creates global names.

Algol60 was the first *block-structured language*. Pascal, Modula-2, and Ada, direct descendants of Algol, are also block structured. In a block-structured language, program units can be nested within other units. Identifiers declared in an outer block are available for use in any inner block that does not declare a new identifier with an identical name. Consider, for example, the Ada program skeleton shown in Figure 5.6a. In this example, the procedure Inside is defined within procedure Outside. The integer variables C and D defined within Outside are therefore known to Inside. Likewise, the global variable B, defined in the Main procedure, is also known to Inside. The global variable A is not known to Inside, because Inside has declared a local variable with the name A. The declaration of the local variable A suppresses references to the global A. A complete list of the

```
procedure Main is
    A, B: integer;
    procedure Outside is
        C, D: real;
        procedure Inside is
            A, E: char;
        begin
            - - - body of Inside
        end Inside;
    begin
        - - - body of Outside
    end Outside;
begin
    - - - body of Main
end Main;
```

(a)

MAIN	OUTSIDE	INSIDE
the integer A	the (global) integer A	the integer B
the integer B	the (global) integer B	the real C
the procedure Outside	the procedure Inside	the real D
	the procedure Outside	the procedure Inside
	the real C	the character A
	the real D	the character E

(b)

Figure 5.6 (a) Example of the Rules of Scoping in Ada; (b) List of the Identifiers Known by Each Ada Program Unit of the Example in Figure 5.6(a)

identifiers known by each unit of the example in Figure 5.6a is given in Figure 5.6b. Ada also allows the accessing of entities declared in outer units by nested units through the use of prefixes and dot notation. The prefix names the unit where the entity was declared. For example, the procedure Inside in Figure 5.6a could refer to the integer A declared in Main as Main.A.

Scoping provides some information hiding facilities to the software engineer. The developer of one section of a program or system need not be concerned with the reuse of names. More importantly, locally used data objects and procedural abstractions can be hidden from other parts of the system. The nesting of a procedure, for example, indicates that the nested procedure is needed only by the program unit it is nested in. The scoping rules of the language enforce the declaration.

5.9   Choosing a Programming Language: Programming-in-the-Large Concerns

As discussed in Chapter 1, the study of software engineering was largely developed in response to the problems encountered in developing large software systems. When a system consists of tens of thousands or even hundreds of thousands of lines of code, different approaches are needed than when a smaller system is being developed. Such approaches are the focus of this book. The programming language used in implementing the system is only one facet of system development. Clearly, tools and techniques beyond the particular programming language used are needed to facilitate the development of large systems. Recently, the trend has been to integrate such tools with a particular language to create what is called a *computer-aided software engineering environment*. The nature and purpose of these environments will be discussed in Chapter 8. The remaining sections of this chapter will look at the features of programming languages that relate to programming in the large: programming as a group project.

5.9.1   Procedural and Data Abstraction

Two important concepts that have already been discussed that aid an individual programmer in solving problems are procedural abstraction and data abstraction. The most prevalent programming language mechanisms for aiding procedural abstraction for programming in the small are procedures and functions. Programming in the large, however, requires a higher level of abstraction than that provided by procedures. Furthermore, programming in the large requires sophisticated means of supporting data abstraction. In particular, a programming language should include the following features:

- Mechanisms for the high-level encapsulation of both procedural and data abstractions

- A clear distinction between the specification (description) of an abstraction and the implementation of the abstraction

- Mechanisms to protect outside access to encapsulated information

- Simple methods for importing modules from other sources (that is, making use of reusable modules)

As a constructive comparison, consider the support provided by Pascal and Ada for the features just listed. (Note that Modula-2 lies somewhere in between these two languages.)

Pascal provides only procedures and functions to support procedural abstractions. There are no standard mechanisms for encapsulating collections of procedures. The lack of a mechanism for encapsulating procedures or functions also makes the encapsulation of data abstractions impossible. This is because a data abstraction consists of data objects and their associated operations. The operations are implemented as procedures or functions. Thus, Pascal does not make a clear distinction between the specification of an abstraction and its implementation, nor does it provide encapsulation. This does not mean that a programmer cannot follow the spirit of abstraction in designing and implementing a data abstraction. Consider, for example, the implementation of an abstract data type, a stack of data objects (for example, single characters). The specifications might include the operations Push, Pop, StackIsEmpty, and CreateStack. A design that supported data abstraction would implement each operation as a separate procedure or function. As much as possible, the user of these procedures should not be required to know anything about how the stack is implemented. For example, the user should not need to know whether an array or a linked list or a whatever is used to implement the stack. The Pascal code shown in Figure 5.7 illustrates this idea. The code uses the stack to print a series of up to 100 characters in reverse order of input. A reader cannot tell from examining this code whether an array or a linked list is to be used as the primary data structure. In fact, either could be used. Figure 5.8 shows an implementation based on an array.

Figures 5.7 and 5.8 point out another weakness of Pascal's data abstraction features. This weakness is the lack of protection afforded to the data abstraction. Because the data structure (the stack) must be declared globally, the programmer is free to

```
procedure ReverseInput;
{Procedure which takes a series of characters entered by the
user and displays them in the reverse order of entry. A period
is used to signal the end of input.}

const Period = '.';

begin
    {Present instructions to the user.}
    writeln ('Enter the series of characters you wished to see
        displayed in reverse order.');
    writeln ('Enter a period to terminate the series.');

    {Read the characters and push them on the stack.}
    read (NextChar);
    while NextChar <> Period do
        begin
            if not (StackIsFull) then Push (NextChar);
            read (NextChar)
        end;

    {Pop characters from the stack and display them}
    while not  (StackIsEmpty) do
        begin
            Pop (NextChar);
            write (NextChar)
        end
end { procedure ReversInput };
```

Figure 5.7 Pascal Code Showing the Use of a Stack to Print a Series of Input Characters in Reverse Order

```
const StackMax = 100;

type  StackType = array [ 1..StackMax] of char;

var Stack : StackType;
    Top:  0 .. StackSize;


procedure CreateStack;
   begin
       Top := 0
   end;

procedure Push (NextChar:  char);
   begin
       Top := Top + 1;
       Stack [Top] :=' NextChar
   end;

procedure Pop (var NextChar:  char);
   begin
       NextChar := Stack[Top];
       Top := Top - 1
   end;

function StackIsEmpty: boolean;
   begin
       StackIsEmpty := (Top = 0)
   end;

function  StackIsFull:  boolean;
   begin
       StackIsFull := (Top = StackMax)
   end;
```

Figure 5.8 Pascal Code Showing the Implementation of a Stack Based on an Array

access it in other ways than through the specified stack operations (Push, Pop, and so on). Although this violates the spirit of data abstraction, there is nothing to prohibit it. For example, the programmer could blank out all cells of the stack array. While this might cause no particular problems initially, it certainly would if the data type were to be later reimplemented as a linked list.

Ada provides more features that support abstraction than does Pascal. Encapsulation units supported by Ada include *program units, subprograms, packages, tasks,* and *generic units,* most of which may be separately compiled. *Program units* may consist of any of the other sorts of encapsulation units. A *subprogram* is either a procedure or function and expresses a sequential action. A *task* defines an action that is logically executed in parallel with other tasks and is used to implement parallel programming systems. *Packages* are collections of data types, data objects, subprograms, tasks, or even other packages. A *generic unit* is a template for subprograms and packages and is particularly useful in building reusable software. Generics are discussed in Section 5.9.2. All programming units generally consist of two parts, a *specification* and a *body.* The *specification* provides information to the user on how to use the unit and what components of the unit are visible to the user. The *body* contains the implementation details and can be logically hidden from the user. The specification and the body can be separately compiled. Thus, Ada provides for a separation of abstractions and their implementation and provides a variety of means of encapsulation.

As an example of the use of an Ada package to promote abstraction, consider the implementation of an abstract data type, DollarsCents. For simplicity, the operations required for this type will include:

BuildDollarsCents: an operation that creates a dollar and cents value based on the provided dollar amount and cents amount

Dollars: returns the Dollars amount only of a DollarsCents value

Cents: returns the Cents amount only of a DollarsCents value

AddDollarsCents: returns the sum of two given DollarsCents values

Figure 5.9 shows the specification part of the package for the abstraction, DollarsCents. The specification is used by the programmer to describe to users of

```
package DollarsCents is
type
      amount is private;
      function BuildDollarsCents (DollarPart, CentsPart: in integer)
      return amount;
      -- given a dollar value in integer and a cents value in integer,
      -- BuildDollarsCents returns a DollarsCents number

      function Dollars (ValueIn: in amount) return integer;
      --  given a DollarsCents number, Dollars returns the
      --  dollar component of the number

      function Cents (ValueIn: in amount) return integer;
      -- given a DollarsCents number, Cents returns the
      -- cents component of the number

      function AddDollarsCents (Value1, Value2: in amount) return amount;
      -- given two dollar values in Value1 and Value2, returns
      -- an amount equal to their sum

      private
         type amount is
            record
                  DollarAmount: integer;
                  CentsAmount: integer;
            end record;

      end DollarsCents;
```
Figure 5.9 Ada Specification for a DollarsCents Data Type

the package how the package can be used and what operations are available. Only the operations specified, the name of the package, and the name of the type may be referenced by users. All other details are hidden. Logically, this would imply that the details of the representation of the abstract type would also be hidden. However, to enable separate compilation of the specification and body parts of a package, the specification must contain a declaration of the representation. This is shown in the bottom portion of Figure 5.9. DollarsCents will be represented by a record containing DollarAmount and CentsAmount fields. Although the declaration information is contained in the specification part of the package, the user of the package is not allowed to directly reference the representation of the type. Figure 5.10 shows the body of the package for the DollarsCents abstraction. In the

```
package body DollarsCents is

        function
            BuildDollarsCents (DollarPart, CentsPart: in integer)
                return amount is
            begin
                return (Dollars, Cents)
        end BuildDollarsCents;

        function
            Dollars (Valueln: in amount) return integer is
            begin
                return Valueln.DollarAmount
        end Dollars;

        function
            Cents (Valueln: in amount) return integer is
            begin
                return Valueln.CentsAmount
        end Cents;

        function
            AddDollarsCents (Value1,Value2: in amount) return amount is
            begin
                if Value1.CentsAmount + Value2.CentsAmount > 99 then
                    return (Value1.DollarAmount + Value2.DollarAmount + 1,
                        Value1.CentsAmount +
                        Value2.CentsAmount - 100)
                else
                    return (Value1.DollarAmount + Value2.DollarAmount,
                        Value1.CentsAmount + Value2.CentsAmount)
        end AddDollarsCents;
end DollarsCents;
```

Figure 5.10 Body of an Ada Package Implementing the DollarsCents Abstract Data Type

body the operations of the type are defined. The programmer should be able to alter the representation and the operations without affecting those parts of the program that use the package. Thus, packages promote abstraction and information hiding.

5.9.2 Generics

Although the strong typing provided by Ada, Modula-2, and Pascal provides many advantages, one disadvantage of strong typing can be a lack of flexibility in the use of data types. For example, suppose a stack-of-characters abstract data type had been defined with the usual stack operations of Push, Pop, and so on. If another stack type is needed, but one in which the elements are integers instead, the specifications and implementation would be identical to the first, with only slight changes. In Pascal and Modula-2 the only solution would be to write another set of procedures or functions to implement Push, Pop, and so on, with integers. To provide somewhat greater flexibility, Ada provides for the use of generics. *Generics* allow the programmer to define templates for program units. These templates can be used with parameters to create different instances of the generic package or procedure. For example, a generic stack package could be created using the following specification outline:

```
generic
        type StackItem is private;
        package Stack is
                procedure Push (Element: in StackItem);
                function Pop return StackItem;

                .
                .
                .

        end Stack;
```

To declare two instantiations of the stack package, one with characters and one with integer elements, the following declarations could be used:

```
package CharStack is new Stack (character);
package IntegerStack is new Stack (integer);
```

5.9.3 Separate Compilation

One of the most important features a programming language should have to make it suitable for use in large programming projects is facilities for separate compilation. *Separate compilation* means that independent program units may be independently compiled and subsequently integrated to form a complete program. The integration process is performed by a program called a *linkage editor* or *linker*. Separate compilation is important in software engineering because it allows individual programmers to work independently on units of the system. At the same time, each programmer can access units written by other programmers. If each programmer had to edit and recompile the entire system each time a new unit was added, an excessive amount of time would be used, and program development would be slowed considerably. Separate compilation also facilitates the use of library routines and reusable modules.

The continued popularity of FORTRAN is in large part due to the large library of scientific and engineering subroutines available in FORTRAN. FORTRAN supports separate compilation of subroutines and provides easy access to library routines. However, FORTRAN does not check the interfacing of external routines. No check is made for a match of the number or type of actual parameters to the formal parameters of the external routine or for the alignment of variables in *common* blocks. It is the responsibility of the programmer to ensure correct interfacing.

There is no support for separate compilation in standard Pascal. In standard Pascal, all modules must be placed into a single program for compilation. This limitation on Pascal is in part an outgrowth of the block-structured nature of the language. In a block-structured language, identifiers used within a block need not be defined within that block; they may be defined in outer blocks. However, when a procedure is being compiled, the compiler must have available the definitions of all identifiers used within the block. Thus, procedures that refer to global identifiers cannot be independently compiled. Most implementations of Pascal include facilities that allow separate compilation through the use of units, importing, and exporting. In some versions global identifiers are forbidden in the external modules. Other nonstandard extensions allow the inclusion of library routines and the integration of assembly language routines. The disadvantage of using nonstandard extensions to the language is that programs written using the extensions are less portable than those written in standard Pascal.

The designers of Ada recognized the need for separate compilation. In Ada, both subprograms and packages may be compiled as separate units. Strong type checking across modules is carried out to ensure that the modules are used according to their specifications. A feature of Ada that makes it especially suitable for programming in the large is that the specification and implementation of a unit may be compiled in separate parts. This feature facilitates the parallel development of independent units. Once the specification of a unit has been compiled, it is available for use by other compilation units. Obviously, execution is not possible until the implementation units have been compiled, but units using the specified unit may be successfully compiled. When the implementation units are added, the type checking that is carried out during compilation ensures that the implementations meet the specifications.

5.10 Case Study: Detailed Design and Language Choice for the Rev-Pro System

As the preliminary design of the Rev-Pro system began to take shape, team members started working on the detailed design of some of the modules. They began by working on some of the middle-level modules. Because there is a certain amount of similarity in the tasks performed by these middle-level modules, the members knew that the work they put into designing these chosen modules would help them in designing the other modules. Furthermore, as the detailed design progressed, they discovered the need for other modules to be added to the structure chart (e.g., Read-Real and Read-String), thus validating the preliminary design.

The detailed design was documented by adding a pseudocode description of the modules to the Method section of the module headers created during preliminary design. Examples of module headers with the added pseudocode are shown in Figures 5.11 and 5.12. Figure 5.11 shows the module header for the Initialize-Costs module, and Figure 5.12 shows the module header for the Get-Fixed-Costs module.

```
{*************************************************************
- TITLE:  Initialize-Costs
- MODULE ID:  C.1
- PURPOSE:  Set up and display the current values of the Costs
- table.  If the user has not yet entered any cost data, the
- table will be empty.  If the user has previously entered
- cost data, the table will contain these data.
- METHOD:
- display titles
- for i = 1 to 10 do
-     if Fixed-Costs-Category has been initialized then
-         display Fixed-Cost-Category
-     else display blanks
-     if Fixed-Costs-Amount has been intitalized then
-         display Fixed-Cost-Amount
-     else display '$' and blanks
- end-for
- for i = 1 to 10 do
-     if Variable-Costs-Category has been initialized then
-         display Variable-Costs-Category
-     else display blanks
-     if Variable-Costs-Amount has been intitalized then
-         display Varaible-Costs-Amount
-     else display '$' and blanks
- end-for
- if totals have been calculated before then
-     display Fixed-Costs, Variable-Costs and Total-Costs
-     else display field labels and blanks
- USAGE:  Tabulate-Costs
- EXTERNAL REFERENCES:  none
- CALLING SEQUENCE:
-     Costs (I/O):  a record containing the cost variables
- INPUT ASSERTION: Costs may contain zero or more user-entered
- values.
- OUTPUT ASSERTION:  A table of the current values of fixed and
- variable costs categories, amounts and totals will be
- displayed.
- VARIABLES:
- AUTHOR(S):
- REMARKS:
*************************************************************}
```

**Figure 5.11 Sample Module Header from the Rev-Pro Case
Study Including Detailed Design of the Initialize-Costs Module**

```
{***********************************************************************
- TITLE:  Get-Fixed-Costs-Info
- MODULE ID:  C.2
- PURPOSE:  Accept fixed-costs information entered by the user
-   and update the display screen as appropriate.  Includes
-   error checking features.
- METHOD:
-      repeat
-         ReadString (Fixed-Costs-Category)
-         ReadReal   (Fixed-Costs)
-         if (user presses a function key) or (user entered only
-            a carriage return)then user wishes to exit
-         else if category entered but no cost then
-            signal error
-            ReadReal (Fixed-Costs)
-         else if cost entered but no category then
-            signal error
-            ReadString (Fixed-Costs-Category)
-         else if all fixed-costs are full then
-            get ready to read first variable-cost category
-         else get ready to read next fixed-cost category
-      until (user wishes to exit) or (all fields are full)
- USAGE:  Tabulate-Costs
- EXTERNAL REFERENCES:
-      ReadReal
-      ReadString
- CALLING SEQUENCE:
-      Costs (I/O):  a record containing the cost variables
- INPUT ASSERTION: The Costs record contains zero or more
-   user-entered fixed-costs values.
- OUTPUT ASSERTION: The Costs record contains zero or more
-   user-entered fixed-costs categories and fixed-costs amounts.
- VARIABLES:
- AUTHOR(S):
- REMARKS:
***********************************************************************}
```

Figure 5.12 Sample Module Header from the Rev-Pro Case Study Showing Detailed Design of the Get-Fixed-Costs-Info Module

As mentioned in the Case Study section of Chapter 4 (Section 4.8), the Rev-Pro team had made the decision to use Turbo Pascal as the implementation language for the system early on in the project. Their decision was based on a number of software engineering factors. Pragmatic concerns included the knowledge of the coders, languages used in previous projects, and availability and quality of the language compiler. All of the Rev-Pro team members were familiar with the Pascal language, although none of them had used Turbo Pascal. The other languages known by most or all team members included IBM Assembler, COBOL, C, Snobol, and APL. None of these other languages was appropriate for the project (see below). In speaking with other students and staff who had worked on projects on IBM/PCs, the team heard that Turbo Pascal was well-suited for such projects. Turbo Pascal has built-in functions for strings, screen handling, file handling, and using the function keys. It handles the external compiling and linking of procedures. Furthermore, Turbo Pascal is a compiler rather than an interpreter and thus produces fast-running programs.

Pascal was deemed a suitable language for the project for a number of reasons. Pascal is a general-purpose language, unlike the other languages the team members knew. Assembler language and C are most appropriate for systems programming and for real-time programming. COBOL is appropriate for business applications and might have been appropriate for this project. However, a COBOL compiler was not available. Snobol is a language designed specifically for string handling and was not general enough for the project. Likewise APL, a language designed primarily for mathematical programming, was not general enough. Although standard Pascal does not support separate compilation, Turbo Pascal does. This gave the team the ability to split up the project into separate pieces to be worked on by individuals. Some other weaknesses of standard Pascal, including the lack of string types and the use of sequential file types only, are remedied in Turbo Pascal. The major weakness of Pascal vis-a-vis programming in the large is its failure to support higher levels of data and procedural abstraction. This cannot be easily remedied without completely redesigning the language. (Modula-2 is just such a redesign of Pascal; see Wirth, 1985).

Summary

Detailed design involves designing the contents of each module from the system structure chart. An algorithm is selected and an outline of the algorithm is inserted into the module header for the module, thus creating the detailed design document.

The algorithm chosen should be correct, efficient, and appropriate for the system hardware and software environment. When efficiency is particularly important, the system's performance should be monitored after the system is created to determine which portion or portions of the system are the most active. These portions can then be fine-tuned to obtain the desired efficiency. Flowcharts, Nassi–Shneiderman charts, and pseudocode are common ways of documenting algorithmic design. However, flowcharts do not support structured design and Nassi–Shneiderman charts are difficult to edit. Pseudocode is the suggested detailed design method.

During detailed design, the design of the data structures will become more refined. Keeping in mind the goals of information hiding and data abstraction can improve the quality of the design.

Evaluation of the detailed design provides another important check on the quality of the system design before coding begins. Walk-throughs or formal reviews can be used to evaluate the detailed design.

The choice of the programming language to be used in building a system is crucial. Both the creation and maintenance of a system can be greatly affected by the target language. Pragmatic concerns include sponsor requirements, knowledge of the coders, languages used in previous or concurrent projects, the availability and quality of a language compiler, availability of development tools, and portability. Other concerns focus on characteristics the language should have from a software engineering point of view. These concerns relate both to the code within individual modules or small programs (programming in the small) and to the coding of large systems requiring group efforts (programming in the large).

Programming in the small concerns include the simplicity, clarity, and orthogonality of a language. The syntax of a language should be simple and consistent and support the writing of clear, readable code. The language should provide a number of carefully designed basic control structures and handle exceptions. In general, strong data typing is preferred, and a variety of data types, including simple, structured, and constant data types, should be defined in the language. Procedural abstraction is an important facility for a language to have. It allows the programmer to create essentially new programming statements in the language through the use of procedures. The procedures provide abstractions of the activities they perform, allowing the programmer to focus on a higher level of the problem being solved. Three common techniques are used for passing parameters to procedures. These include call by reference, call by value, and call by value result. Scoping can provide some valuable information-hiding facilities to a programmer and is a good feature for a language to have.

A number of language features can facilitate programming in the large. In particular, features that support higher levels of data and procedural abstraction are important. Additional features that can be important include a distinction between the specification of an abstraction and its implementation, mechanisms to protect outside access to encapsulated information, and simple techniques for importing (using) modules from other sources. A generics capability allows the inflexibility of strong typing to be overcome, while separate compilation allows individual programmers to work independently on separate parts of the system.

Checklist of Project Activities

_____ Decide on a detailed design notation. Pseudocode or Nassi–Shneiderman charts are suggested alternatives.

_____ Set up standardization guidelines for the chosen design notation. For example, if pseudocode is used, determine the exact format of the different sorts of statements.

_____ Determine the medium on which the designs are to be created (for example, the text editor to be used with the target programming language, a word processor, or typewriter). In general, the medium used for the preliminary designs is the one used for the detailed design. The detailed design is inserted into the module headers created during preliminary design.

_____ For each module being designed, choose the best algorithm. The algorithm should be correct, efficient, and appropriate. When possible, find and plan to use existing modules. If a reusable module is not available, try to find a published algorithm to use. As a last resort, design your own algorithm.

_____ If efficiency is a special concern, make especially sure that the algorithm being designed is of the most efficient order possible. Do not attempt to fine-tune the efficiency of the module or program during design. Remember that the choice of an efficient algorithm is much more important than using a few extra-efficient program statements. Efficiency can be added after the system has begun to take shape and when empirical tests can be run on the system to determine the sources of inefficiency.

_____ Design the data structures to be used within each module. Keep in mind the advantages of data abstraction and information hiding.

_____ Choose a programming language for the project. Take into account both pragmatic concerns and software engineering concerns.

_____ Evaluate the detailed designs by holding a number of walk-throughs and/or formal reviews at various stages in the detailed design process. Use the list of questions in Section 5.6 as a guideline in doing the reviews.

_____ Following each evaluation session, make the appropriate changes to the designs and update the design document.

Terms and Concepts Introduced

algorithm efficiency	data types
order of algorithms	strongly typed languages
heuristic programming	abstract data types
Nassi–Shneiderman charts	dynamic typing
pseudocode	simple data types
user-defined data types	constants
subtypes	structured data types
derived data types	call by reference
simplicity (of a programming language)	call by value
clarity (of a programming language)	call by value result
orthogonality (of a programming language)	scoping
exceptions	block-structured language
control structures	generics
loop control structures	separate compilation
decision structures	

Exercises

1. Write a detailed design using pseudocode for a module based on the following module header. Fill in the METHOD section and VARIABLES section as appropriate.

```
TITLE: MakeChange
MODULE ID: C5.3.2
PURPOSE: Takes the amount owed and the amount tendered by the
    customer and computes and displays the number of pieces of change
    of each denomination (dollars, quarters, dimes, nickels, pennies) owed
    to the customer.
METHOD:
USAGE: HandleSale
EXTERNAL REFERENCES: none
CALLING SEQUENCE:
    AmtOwed - (I)  A real number indicating the amount owed by the
        customer
    AmtTendered - (I)  A real number indicating the amount tendered by the
        customer.
INPUT ASSERTION: The amount tendered must be >= the amount owed.
OUTPUT ASSERTION: The amount owed + (the sum of the value of each
    piece of change given * the number of pieces of that type) = the amount
    tendered
VARIABLES:
AUTHOR(S):
REMARKS:
```

2. Rewrite the detailed design created in Exercise 1 using a Nassi–Shneiderman chart.

3. Evaluate the detailed design created in Exercise 1 or 2 using the criteria given in Section 5.6.

4. Evaluate a language you are familiar with (besides Pascal) for clarity and orthogonality. Come up with at least one example each of lack of clarity and nonorthogonality.

5. Contrast two languages in terms of their programming in the small features. Specifically, compare:

   - Number, type, and quality of the decision structures
   - Number, type, and quality of the loop structures
   - Number, type, and quality of the exception-handling constructs
   - Whether they involve strong or weak data typing
   - Number, type, and quality of simple data structures
   - Type and quality of constants
   - Number, type, and quality of the structured data types
   - Support for procedural abstraction
   - Scoping and information-hiding abilities

6. Contrast two languages in terms of their programming in the large features. Specifically, compare:

   • Support for procedural and data abstraction

   • Use of generics

   • Support of separate compilation

7. Using a programming language you are familiar with, create an abstract data type for a queue of integers. Now write a segment of code that uses the queue to enqueue and deque. If you implemented the queue using an array, implement it again using a linked list (if the language supports pointers). How well does the language you used support abstraction and information hiding? How much of the code for using the queue did you have to change when the underlying data structure was changed? The less the code that had to be changed, the more abstract is the data type you created.

8. Create an Ada specification and the body of an Ada package for a WeatherReport data type. A WeatherReport consists of a temperature, a barometric pressure, and a wind speed. The operations should include:

   MakeAReport: creates a new WeatherReport

   TempIs: returns the temperature from a WeatherReport

   BarPressureIs: returns the barometric pressure from a WeatherReport

   WindSpeedIs: returns the wind speed reading from a WeatherReport

   TempIsGoingUp: compares two WeatherReport temperatures and indicates if the second is higher than the first

Use the examples in Figures 5.9 and 5.10 as a guide, or find a reference book on Ada.

9. For each of the following systems, indicate what language might be most appropriate to implement the system. Consider both programming in the small and programming in the large concerns. Do not consider hardware or other pragmatic concerns. Defend your choice.

   (a) A system to compute various investment scenarios for individuals or couples. The system is input/output intensive. Several form fill-in screens obtaining information from the user are needed, as well as menu-driven input. A variety of reports must be displayed and/or printed. Although a number of numerical computations are done, they are not complex. Most computations involve some table look-up from tables stored as files.

   (b) A system to tutor students on the functions of the kidneys. Includes graphic displays, multiple-choice questions, fill-in-the-blank questions, and modest record-keeping facilities (for example, the number of questions attempted and the number each student gets right).

   (c) A real-time system to record the activities of a rat in a Skinner box. The Skinner box contains a lever that the rat can depress. If the rat depresses the bar so many times, it receives a reward (for example, a drop of water or a food pellet). The system must record the number and timing of all bar presses (that is, when they occurred relative to each other and relative to clock time). The system must also control the dispensing of the reward by counting how many bar presses have occurred or how much time has elapsed since the last reward and then dispense the reward at the correct time.

(d) A pretty printer for a block-structured language such as Pascal or Modula-2. The pretty printer accepts a text file containing a syntactically valid program or module in any format and reformats it into a standard format. The reformatted program is saved into a new file. The pretty printer is invoked by a single command from the user.

(e) A system to calculate the movement of moons around a planet. The calculations involve analyzing a large body of data and performing complex calculations. The calculations must be accurate to many places.

6. Coding and Integration

Once the detailed design phase is complete, the coding and integration stage begins. During this phase of the software development cycle, the source code for each module is written and documented, using the detailed design as a blueprint. As each module is written, it is checked out to remove any obvious errors. The modules are then assembled together or *integrated* to form the system. As the modules are integrated, the system is tested. When integration has been completed, the entire system is given further testing.

It is important to consider ahead of time in what order the modules are to be coded and what strategy will be used in building the system. The approach used in coding the modules and assembling the system is called an *integration strategy*. There are several alternative methods, each of which has its pros and cons. These alternative integration strategies will be discussed in this chapter. To produce a quality system, it is also important that the code be well written. Good coding practices will also be covered herein.

6.1 Coding and Testing Are Carried on in Parallel

As soon as the coding of the module begins, formal testing begins. Throughout the integration phase, coding and testing are closely interwoven. The approach chosen to guide integration affects both the progression of the coding and the scheduling of testing activities. A detailed discussion of testing methods will be postponed until Chapter 7, but an introduction to the three different levels of testing is necessary in order to understand the integration process. The levels include *unit testing, integration testing,* and *acceptance testing.* In *unit testing,* individual modules (units) are tested to determine if they meet their specifications and if they are correctly coded. Each module is tested in isolation when it is unit tested. In *integration testing,* groups of integrated modules, and eventually the entire system, are tested. One facet of integration testing is to test sets of module interfaces and confirm that the modules have been linked together properly. Another facet of integration testing is to determine if the system or subsystem meets the requirements and functions correctly. *Acceptance testing* is carried out by the sponsor to evaluate the finished product.

No matter which integration strategy is used, each module should be unit tested before it is integrated with other modules. A detailed discussion of unit testing methods is given in Chapter 7. Integration testing is carried out as the modules are integrated. The integration testing techniques discussed in Chapter 7 can be used with any of the various integration strategies.

6.2   Some Alternative Orders of Module Integration

Among all the modules that comprise the system, which modules should be selected for coding and integration first? There are two major approaches. One approach, called the *Big-Bang method,* is nonincremental. In the Big-Bang method, every module in the system is coded separately. Next all the modules are integrated at once, causing the disastrous effect for which the method is named: a big bang. Often, unit testing is skipped. This is the traditional method used by beginning programming students and by masochistic programmers.

Other integration methods are incremental. In *incremental development* methods, some portions of the system are coded, unit-tested and integrated before other portions of the system. Thus the entire system is created in incremental steps, rather than in one monumental effort. There are many alternative approaches to incremental integration. Here are three major ones:

Top down. The command-level modules are coded and unit tested first in the top-down approach. Command-level modules are those at the top of the system structure chart. Then modules from a lower level down (selected using a depth-first or breadth-first approach) are unit tested and added on. Progressively lower levels of modules are tested and added on until the entire system has been coded.

Bottom up. In the bottom-up method, the lowest-level modules in the system structure chart are coded and unit tested first. Next, higher level modules are added to create subsystems. Bigger and bigger subsystems are then created by adding the higher-level modules onto the subsystems one level at a time, until the main module is reached.

Threads. A minimal set of modules that performs some specific, primary function is coded first in the threads approach. Peripheral functions can then be coded and added to the primary function. Other functions from the system are then coded and integrated, until the entire system is complete.

Other variations and combinations of these methods are possible. Choosing the best order for a particular project depends on several factors. These factors include the amount of test harness or throwaway code that must be written to support the testing activities, the location of critical parts of the system, the availability of hardware, and scheduling concerns. Each integration method listed will be evaluated next in light of these factors.

6.2.1   Big-Bang Integration Method

The Big-Bang method has almost nothing to recommend it. Anyone who has programmed anything other than a trivial system has discovered the difficulty of trying to find a bug that may have originated in any one of the many modules in the system. Debugging is made many times harder if the entire system is coded first, before any testing is done. Wise programming students soon learn that the time spent up front in building and testing a system piece by piece is time well spent. In the strategy of adding components one at a time to a system, called *incremental development,* each module is unit tested before it is added to the system and the system is tested as a whole after each module is added. When errors are discovered during incremental development, it is likely that they are related to the most recently added module. They may be caused by a coding or logic error in the newly added module or by an interface error. It is much easier to find a bug when the likely location is known than when the entire system is suspect. Furthermore, interfacing errors are more difficult and expensive errors to fix than coding errors. The Big-Bang method makes the task of locating interface errors more difficult than any of the other integration methods.

If the Big-Bang method is being used and each module is unit tested before it is integrated, an excessive amount of *test harness* software must be written. A *test harness* is software that is written exclusively for the purpose of testing other software. It is discarded after testing is completed. A *driver* is test harness software that simulates a calling module and calls or activates the module being tested. If necessary, it passes parameters to the module and monitors the return from the module. It should print out the results of the test and appropriate messages. For example, suppose a module called ReadScores was being tested. ReadScores is designed to read a sequence of scores from a disk file and store it in an array called Scores. The driver would have to be designed to pass the empty array to ReadScores and call ReadScores. When flow of control returns from ReadScores to the driver, it might print a message that control had returned and then print out the contents of the array Scores to indicate successful operation of ReadScores.

A *stub* is test harness software that simulates the activities of a module that is called from the module being tested. For example, suppose the ReadScores module included a call to another module, ValidateScore, which is designed to check each score as it is read in from the disk to see if it is syntactically valid and within a certain range. To test ReadScores, a stub version of ValidateScore might be created that actually does nothing at all but print a message saying "ValidateScore called" and then return back to ReadScores. In other situations, a stub might randomly generate a number or value, return some constant value, execute a timing loop that consumes a specified amount of time, or ask the tester to input some value through the keyboard.

If the Big-Bang integration method is used along with unit testing, each unit must have at least a driver written to carry out the unit tests and possibly one or more stubs. There is a greater amount of effort involved in writing test harnesses for this method than for any of the others. Such efforts slow down progress on the project, and the test harnesses themselves will contain errors. Because the test harnesses are destined to be thrown away, they are often written in an ad hoc manner and contain more than the usual percentage of errors. It is sometimes difficult to tell if the errors uncovered during testing are due to the software being tested or to the test harness. It makes sense, therefore, to minimize the amount of test harness that must be written.

The Big-Bang method also makes no distinctions between critical or central parts of the system and peripheral parts of the system. Critical components are those that provide several central functions (meet several requirements) of the system, have a high level of control over other functions of the system, are complex or which have critical performance requirements. There are several reasons why it is often a good idea to code and integrate a particular part of a system first. One reason may be that the design of a part of the system may be suspect. Perhaps the system is very complex and attempts to do something not attempted before. If the questionable part of the system can be coded and integrated first, testing can commence on that subsystem. If the tests are successful, the rest of the implementation can proceed, knowing that there is a good chance for overall success. If the tests are not successful, the critical part of the system can be redesigned and recoded with a minimal loss of effort. Another reason one part of a system may be considered more critical has to do with reliability. Whichever part of the system is created first receives the greatest amount of testing. The core of the system is tested and retested as more components are added to it. Where reliability is particularly important (for example, in real-time systems), the components to be integrated first should be those that comprise the essential activities of the system. Another advantage to implementing a critical part first is that this often allows the sponsor to see part of the system in operation. This reassures the sponsor that progress is being made on the system and allows the sponsor to give the developers important feedback before the rest of the system is coded.

The Big-Bang method does not provide flexibility in scheduling. Integration testing cannot begin until all modules are coded and unit tested. If the personnel involved in integration testing are not the coders, they must sit idle until coding is complete. Progress on the system is hard to measure. Although the number of modules that have been coded and unit tested can be measured, nothing operational can be tested to see if the design of the system is truly feasible. When the modules are finally integrated, it may become obvious that major redesigning and recoding are needed. Suddenly the project is no longer on schedule. While Big Bang does reduce flexibility in scheduling, it does make the scheduling process itself easier. There is no need to figure out the progression of coding, unit-testing and integration testing, because everybody begins coding all at once and keeps going until all units are coded.

A final criticism of the Big-Bang method is that it requires concentrated use of the hardware in a short period of time. This may not be a problem if hardware resources have been dedicated to the project. With shared resources, however, progress might not be as rapid as desired. The alternative integration methods all allow some flexibility in hardware use because different activities are taking place in parallel, some of which require the use of hardware and some of which do not.

6.2.3 Top-down Integration Method

In the top-down integration method, the modules at the top of the structure are coded and integrated first, then modules from successively lower levels are added on. Because of the incremental nature of top-down integration, hardware use is spread out, and errors are easier to isolate. Due to the integration of higher-level modules first, the hierarchical structure of the system and the critical high-level interfaces can be tested early. It is often possible, with the use of stubs, to allow the sponsor to assess the system early. Although stubs must be written to test the system, they are typically easier to write than drivers. Programmer morale is often better when the top-down approach is used because there is clear evidence of a "working" system, and the sponsor is reassured to see visible progress being made. The difficulties of the top-down method stem from the fact that the lowest-level modules often are the ones which perform input and output activities. Because they are not coded until the last, writing the test cases for the upper level modules can be difficult. Furthermore, critical lower-level modules, if any, do not receive extensive testing.

6.2.4 Bottom-up Integration Method

In bottom-up integration, the lowest-level modules are coded, unit tested and integrated first. Then modules from the next higher level are added on, forming subsystems. The creation of one such subsystem is called a *build*. Successive builds are made until the entire system has been integrated. The bottom-up method eliminates the need for stubs, but driver modules must be written. Because of the incremental nature of the bottom-up method, it is easier to isolate errors than in the Big-Bang method, and hardware usage is more spread out. The lower-level modules will receive more testing than the higher-level modules. If the lower-level modules happen to be the critical modules, the bottom-up approach can be useful. The main disadvantage of the bottom-up method is that no operational skeleton of the system is available during the early stages. Thus the hierarchical structure of the system cannot be assessed until late, any critical interfaces at the higher levels of the system will not be tested until late, and the sponsor has no opportunity to assess the operation of the system.

6.2.5 Integration Using Threads

In general, the best approach to integration is to begin by selecting a minimal set of modules that perform some processing capability or function, called a *thread*. This set will probably include some means of input and/or output, along with some processing. The modules selected will usually come from different levels in the structure chart, and a diagram of them will look like a small tree. A good choice for the first thread to be built is one of the critical or typical functions of the system. Once the thread has been built in its initial form, other modules can be added on to complete the thread. An advantage of this approach is that other threads from the system can be integrated in parallel and separately from the initial thread. The separately developed threads can then be integrated to build the entire system.

A natural outgrowth of the threads approach is that early, skeletal versions of the system are available early. This allows the sponsor to provide feedback, and early evaluation of the system design can be made as well. In fact, some large systems, such as an airline reservation system, have actually been delivered to the sponsor in successively more complex versions (Gifford and Spector, 1984). The earliest version included only the most central function, for example, ticket reservations. Later versions added on less central functions, such as baggage handling and seat assignment capabilities. The method improves programmer morale, as well. Different parts of the system can be assigned to different programmers or groups of programmers, and each programmer or group sees progress being made on a functioning portion of the system.

6.2.6 Example Using the Threads Approach

As an example of how the functional modules approach might be used in building a system, consider the concordance system design from Chapter 4. The structure chart from Figure 4.10 is reproduced in Figure 6.1.

According to the threads approach, the first modules to be coded and integrated should be the minimal set of modules that together perform some central processing function. By scanning the second level of the structure chart, we see that three major operations are performed by the system: getting edited words, building the concordance, and outputting the concordance. Of these three functions, the one most central to the overall purpose of the system is building the concordance. It seems reasonable to focus our first efforts in this part of the system. This central function requires input (edited words). But it should not be too difficult to write a stub that reads edited words from a file, for example, and feeds them to the central function.

Looking at the modules that comprise the central function, we see that the next level of detail involves three activities: ADD NEW WORD, ADD 1 TO WORD COUNT, and RECORD LINE NUMBER. Of these, ADD NEW WORD is the most basic activity and is a good candidate for early coding and integration. Below ADD NEW WORD, there are two modules, CHECK IF IN CONCORDANCE and INSERT IN CONCORDANCE. We should be able to stub in CHECK IF IN CONCORDANCE in such a way that it always says the word is not yet in the concordance. The module that actually inserts the word, INSERT IN CONCORDANCE, should be coded as part of the first set of functional modules.

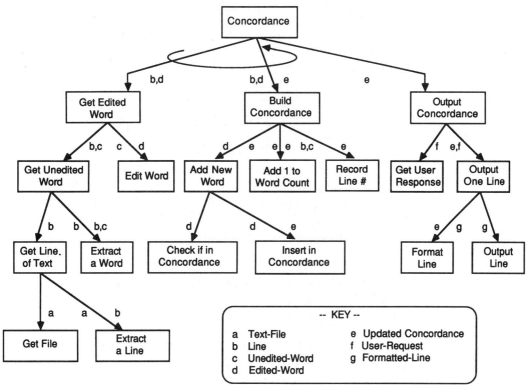

Figure 6.1 Structure Chart for the Concordance System

To complete the first integration stage, we will need some means of outputting the concordance. The entire set of functions under the OUTPUT CONCORDANCE module does not need to be included. These functions are mostly concerned with formatting the output and sending it to the output device of the user's choice. In the first stage, the OUTPUT CONCORDANCE module can be stubbed in with a module that simply lists all the words placed in the concordance by the completely coded modules from the central portion of the system.

Figure 6.2 shows a structure chart of the proposed first stage of the integration plan. Notice that only three modules, BUILD CONCORDANCE, ADD NEW WORDS, and INSERT IN CONCORDANCE, will be coded completely in this initial stage. They are indicated in the figure by boxes with heavy lines. Stub and driver modules are indicated by boxes with lighter lines. The system module, CONCORDANCE, can be coded as a driver. It should contain a loop that repeatedly calls, in turn, the stub GET EDITED WORD and the actual module BUILD CONCORDANCE. After the loop has been exited, the CONCORDANCE driver should call the stub OUTPUT CONCORDANCE. When flow of control returns from OUTPUT CONCORDANCE, the system should be exited. The two modules called by BUILD CONCORDANCE that are not to be coded yet, ADD 1 TO WORD COUNT and RECORD LINE NUMBER, should be stubbed in. Likewise, CHECK IF IN CONCORDANCE should also be stubbed in.

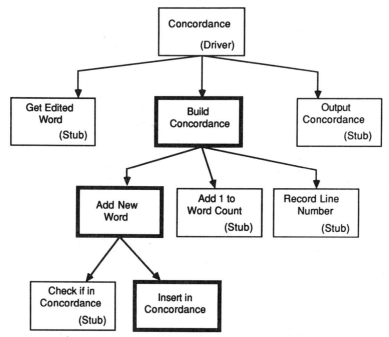

Figure 6.2 Structure Chart Representing the First Stage of Integration for the Concordance System

In the second stage of integration, the remaining three modules in the central part of the structure diagram could be coded and integrated. A logical order might be to add CHECK IF IN CONCORDANCE first, because there would be no need to alter the GET EDITED WORD stub when it is added. ADD 1 TO WORD COUNT and RECORD LINE NUMBER might be added next. When they are added, GET EDITED WORD must be modified to pass both edited words and appropriate values for the line variable.

The input part of the concordance system appears to be more complex than the output portion; therefore, it should be integrated next. Examining the activities performed in this portion and considering what would be needed in the way of drivers and/or stubs, it appears that a top-down integration strategy would be appropriate for this part of the system. GET EDITED WORD, GET UNEDITED WORD, and EDIT WORD would be coded and integrated first. GET LINE OF TEXT can be stubbed in so that it reads prepared lines of text from a file and passes them back to GET UNEDITED WORD. EXTRACT A WORD can be stubbed in so that it reads appropriate words from a file and passes them back. Once this core of input modules is functioning correctly, GET LINE OF TEXT and EXTRACT A WORD can be coded and integrated. GET FILE and EXTRACT A LINE would be stubbed in at this point. Finally, GET FILE and EXTRACT A LINE would be coded and integrated. (See Figure 6.3.)

In the output part of the system, both GET USER RESPONSE and FORMAT LINE would be fairly easy modules to stub in, so the remaining modules OUTPUT CONCORDANCE, OUTPUT ONE LINE, and OUTPUT LINE should be coded first. The coding and integration of GET USER RESPONSE and FORMAT LINE would complete the integration of the entire system.

6.3 Producing and Documenting the Integration Plan

Once the high-level design has been completed, an integration plan can be developed. Based on the high-level design, decisions can be made concerning the integration strategy to be used, as in the previous concordance example. A schedule can be determined for coding, unit testing, integration, and integration testing. Personnel can be assigned to the different activities.

All the decisions made at this juncture need to be recorded and documented for later reference. One approach that can be used to illustrate the integration strategy

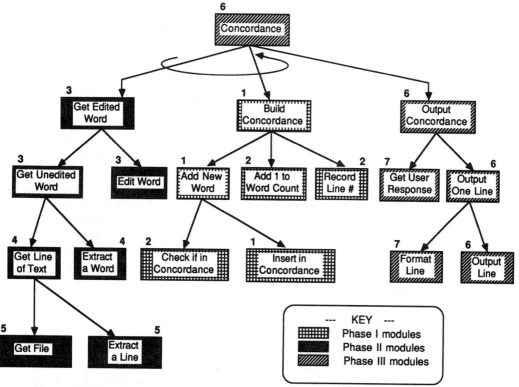

Figure 6.3 Structure Chart Showing the Stages of Integration for the Concordance System

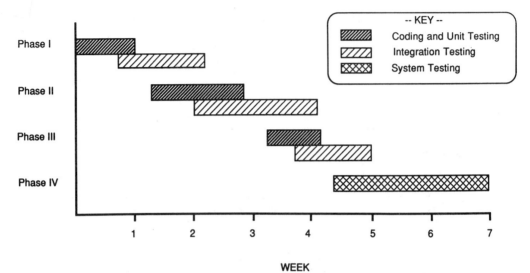

Figure 6.4 Gantt Chart Representing the Scheduling of Coding and Integration for the Concordance System

is to draw up a modified structure chart or set of structure charts. For example, the major stages in the integration can be indicated by color coding the modules in the chart or by using some other visual means of identifying the modules. Within each major stage, the modules can be numbered to indicate the substages of development. Figure 6.3 shows a structure chart for the concordance system modified to indicate the order in which the modules are to be integrated. A verbal description should accompany the chart and include a defense of the integration approach taken.

A *Gantt chart* is a compact way of presenting the proposed schedule for development. A Gantt chart is basically a horizontal bar graph. The horizontal axis represents units of time, such as weeks or months. The vertical axis represents different components of the project. A horizontal bar is added to show the starting time and duration of each component of the project. An example of a hypothetical Gantt chart for the coding and integration of the concordance system is presented in Figure 6.4. A more detailed verbal description should accompany the graph. The document should also indicate how personnel are to be assigned.

The integration plan should be evaluated before it is implemented. The feasibility of the plan as well as the approach taken should be assessed.

6.4 Factors That Affect the Quality of the Source Code

Although it has been pointed out several times within these pages that coding takes only a small portion of the overall software development effort, the source code is nonetheless the end product or physical manifestation of all the effort. As such, the same care and pride of work should go into producing the source code as go into the design and testing. Poor coding techniques can ruin an otherwise well-designed system. (On the other hand, good coding can probably not do much to save a poorly designed system!) Quality is an important goal during coding. The source code and internal documentation should be written so that the conformance of the code to its specifications can be easily verified and so that debugging, testing, and modification efforts are enhanced.

Several factors contribute to the quality of the source code:

- Use of structured coding techniques
- Good coding style
- Well-chosen local data structures
- Well-written internal comments
- Readable, consistent source code format and identifier naming

Each of these will be discussed in turn in the following sections. It is not the intent of these sections to teach programming, but to show how software engineering principles carry over into coding activities.

6.5 Structured Coding Techniques

There is no strict agreement on exactly what is meant by structured coding. However, structured coding is basically an approach to programming that involves three standards for program structure. These include avoidance (some say the absolute avoidance) of the unconditional *goto*, the use of top-down flow of control only, and the production of *single-entry, single-exit* constructs.

The idea of structured programming is closely tied to the Bohm and Jacopini (1966) theorem introduced in Chapter 2 concerning the three sufficient programming language constructs: sequence, selection (for example, *if-then-else*) and iteration (for example, *while*). Bohm and Jacopini demonstrated that these three constructs form a sufficient set of constructs for describing the flow of control of every conceivable algorithm. Each of these constructs is *single entry, single exit*. That is, control always enters at one point (and one point only) and leaves at one point (and one point only). Even if the constructs are nested, the single-entry, single-exit structure can be maintained. Furthermore, the unconditional transfer of control, or *goto*, is not a necessary construct. If an algorithm is implemented using only the sufficient constructs, the code will be *top down*. This implies that whenever a (noniterative) branch occurs in the code the flow of control will be downward in the code.

Most modern programming languages implement several structured constructs, including *if-then, if-then-else, case, while, for,* and *repeat-until.* Use of these constructs makes top-down programming convenient. However, structured programs can be obtained by using nonstructured constructs. The general guideline to follow is to make each required action follow each decision as closely as possible. Macros, functions, procedures, or subroutines can sometimes be used to implement a structured construct. Some organizations have guidelines for producing structured code using nonstructured languages. A number of textbooks are also available that introduce structured programming styles for nonstructured languages.

Assuming that a structured style of programming is to be followed, there is still the issue of whether or not to allow the use of *gotos*. Certainly *gotos* must be used in languages or versions of languages lacking high-level control structures (for example, COBOL, FORTRAN, BASIC) to emulate high-level control structures. The question is whether *gotos* should be used in languages having high-level control structures and in nonstructured ways. The answer is a qualified yes. In certain situations the use of *gotos* can produce clearer, simpler code than does strict adherence to structure. They are particularly useful for handling exceptions, to transfer control to local error-handling code, or to terminate execution of the procedure. *Gotos* used in this way should transfer control to the statement immediatley after the compound construct they are embedded in. An example of a segment of FORTRAN code containing error handling is shown in Figure 6.5. Notice that the error conditions cause transfer of control to statements immediately following the *do* loop, to help maintain the top-down structure of the code. Notice also that *gotos* used in this way cause the single-exit rule to be violated. This is unavoidable in this situation.

In other cases the use of *gotos* can produce more natural and even more efficient code. Consider the two pseudocode segments in Figure 6.6 for searching a table for a target item. Version A of the search algorithm uses standard structured

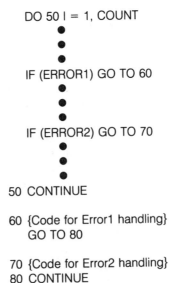

```
DO 50 I = 1, COUNT
        •
        •
        •
IF (ERROR1) GO TO 60
        •
        •
        •
IF (ERROR2) GO TO 70
        •
        •
        •
50 CONTINUE

60 {Code for Error1 handling}
   GO TO 80

70 {Code for Error2 handling}
80 CONTINUE
```

Figure 6.5 Example of FORTRAN Code Containing Error Handling Based on the Use of GOTOs and Multiple Exits

Version A

```
I = 1
while I <= TableSize and Table(I) <> Target do
    I = I + 1

if I > TableSize then
    {code for Target not found}

else    {code for Target found}
```

Version B

```
for I = 1 to TableSize do
    if Table (I) = Target then goto Found

NotFound:    {code for Target not found}

Found:   {code for Target found}
```

Figure 6.6 Two Pseudocode Segments for Searching a Table for a Target Value; Version A Uses Structured Code; Version B Uses Nonstructured Code

constructs. Version B uses a *goto* and statement labels. Version A requires a total of three (Boolean) tests, while version B requires only two. Furthermore, version B takes fewer steps. Arguably, Version B is more natural and readable than version A, as well.

These examples are not meant to suggest that you should begin using *gotos* willy-nilly in your programming. The point is that strict adherence to structured programming rules may not always produce the clearest, most efficient code. The rules of structured programming can be broken at times as long as the resulting code is actually clearer than code performing the same actions that adheres strictly to the rules. When in doubt, however, it is probably best to stick to the structured style.

6.6 Coding Style

Style is a consistent way or pattern of carrying out some activity, chosen from among alternative ways of carrying out the activity. For example, each person has a clothing style. Of all the many options there are in clothing, each person tends to dress in a fairly consistent and predictable way from day to day. It is relevant to note that clothing styles are learned and can be changed, if desired. Likewise, each programmer has a programming style. From all the millions of ways there are to put programming statements together, each programmer tends to consistently choose certain patterns of statements to carry out certain actions. Programming style is learned. Sometimes programming style is actually taught, but typically programmers pick up a style by observing and imitating different examples of source code, usually in textbooks or from in-class examples.

It is not easy to define what is meant by good style. Probably the two most important qualities related to good style are *simplicity* and *readability. Simplicity* is the opposite of complexity. Simplicity refers to clarity and ease of understanding. If a unit of source code takes a lot of mental effort to understand, if testing the code is difficult, or if modifying the code is a hard task, then the code is not simple. *Readability* refers to ease of scanning or reading the source code. Certainly readability is enhanced by simplicity, but factors related to the syntactic structure and to the format of the source code are important, too. There are no hard and fast rules that can be followed to produce simple, readable code, but some general guidelines can be given.

Much of the simplicity of source code is related to how well the system is designed. If the designers achieve the goals of modularity, high cohesion, and low coupling, then each module may achieve simplicity. Assuming the system structure is well designed, how can individual modules be made simple? Here are some guidelines:

1. Shorter is simpler.

2. Fewer decisions is simpler.

3. Nested logic should be avoided.

Let us look at each of these guidelines separately. (For a more complete discussion of programming style guidelines, see Kernighan and Plauger, 1978; Schneyer, 1984).

6.6.1   Style Guideline 1: Shorter Is Simpler

In general, the less code there is to read, the less complex a piece of software is. One area of software engineering research has studied *software complexity*. Many studies have been done trying to isolate factors that relate to complexity in software (for example, Halstead, 1977; McCabe, 1976). Although factors such as the number of operators and operands in a module, the number of decisions, and the number of loops have all been shown to have significant effects, the most powerful factor is simply the length: the longer a piece of software is (typically measured as lines of source code), the more complex it is. Consider the two examples shown in Figure 6.7. Each example is a Pascal function to calculate the power function from 1 to 8 for some base value and store the answers in an array, Powers. From the standpoint of logic, version A is simpler. It has no loops and no decisions. But version A is clearly longer than version B. Not only is the number of lines greater in version A, but each line is longer. Notice that version A is also less readable than version B. Visually, version A is confusing and requires the eye to move back and forth and up and down in wide swathes while you are reading. Version B is visually compact. Version A also has the serious defect that it is difficult to modify. If the requirements were changed so that powers from 1 to 20 were

Version A:

```
procedure FillPowersArray (var Base: integer;
                             var Powers:  array of integer);
begin

    Powers[1] := Base;
    Powers[2] := Base*Base;
    Powers[3] := Base*Base*Base;
    Powers[4] := Base*Base*Base*Base;
    Powers[5] := Base*Base*Base*Base*Base;
    Powers[6] := Base*Base*Base*Base*Base*Base;
    Powers[7] := Base*Base*Base*Base*Base*Base*Base;
    Powers[8] := Base*Base*Base*Base*Base*Base*Base*Base

end {procedure FillPowersArray};
```

Version B:

```
procedure FillPowersArray (var Base; integer;
                             var Powers:  array of integer);
var Index: integer;

begin

    Powers[1] := Base;
    for Index := 2 to 8 do
        Powers[Index] := Powers[Index-1] * Base;

end {procedure FillPowersArray};
```

Figure 6.7 Two Different Pascal Modules to Calculate the Power Function; Version A Is Longer and More Complex than Version B

desired, 12 more lines of code would have to be added to version A. Furthermore, each successive added line would be longer and longer. As a programmer, you no doubt feel that *you* would never produce anything as bad as version A. The example was chosen to be obvious, but you should be alert to the problem nonetheless. Just ask any programming instructor how many advanced students they have seen take the long way around to solve a programming problem. You will be surprised how often it occurs.

In general, shorter is simpler, but there are exceptions. Consider the two Pascal functions in Figure 6.8. Each function accepts a single character representing a one-digit hexadecimal value and returns the corresponding decimal integer value. In version A, the conversion is based on the ASCII code value of the character and uses the built-in function CHR. A programmer reading version A must first be aware that the target machine for the module uses ASCII character code and, second, must know about the purpose and operation of the CHR function. Although version B is much longer, it is easier to understand. There is no reference to an obscure built-in function and no need to know anything about ASCII codes. In

Version A:

```
function IntegerFromHex (HexDigit: char): integer;

var ASCIIValue: integer;

begin

    ASCIIValue := chr(HexDigit);
    if ASCIIValue < 58 then IntegerFromHex := ASCIIValue - 48
    else IntegerFromHex := ASCIIValue - 55

end;
```

Version B:

```
function IntegerFromHex (HexDigit: char):  integer;

begin

    case HexDigit of
        '0' :   IntegerFromHex := 0;
        '1' :   IntegerFromHex := 1;
        '2' :   IntegerFromHex := 2;
        '3' :   IntegerFromHex := 3;
        '4' :   IntegerFromHex := 4;
        '5' :   IntegerFromHex := 5;
        '6' :   IntegerFromHex := 6;
        '7' :   IntegerFromHex := 7;
        '8' :   IntegerFromHex := 8;
        '9' :   IntegerFromHex := 9;
        'A' :   IntegerFromHex := 10;
        'B' :   IntegerFromHex := 11;
        'C' :   IntegerFromHex := 12;
        'D' :   IntegerFromHex := 13;
        'E' :   IntegerFromHex := 14;
        'F' :   IntegerFromHex := 15
    end {case}

end {function IntegerFromHex};
```

Figure 6.8 Two Different Pascal Functions to Convert a Hexadecimal Character into Its Corresponding Integer Value; Version A Is Shorter, but Less Clear than Version B

fact, a feature that version B has that version A does not is *portability*. Version B can be run successfully on any machine that supports any standard version of Pascal; version A is restricted to machines that support ASCII and to versions of Pascal that implement the CHR function. Portability is a desirable feature in software. The point these two examples make is that, while brevity is an important component of simplicity, clarity is more important. Version B is more readily understandable—is clearer—than version A, in spite of its greater length.

Another exception to the "shorter is better" rule relates to efficiency. Back in the "good old days" of programming, computers were hundreds and even thousands of times slower than they are these days, and memories were fractions of the size they are today. A good programmer was one who could write code that executed quickly and that could be shoe-horned into the tiny memory space available. Writing a new routine that shaved a few milliseconds from the execution time and/or used ten fewer machine-level instructions than an older version was an admirable accomplishment. Unfortunately, code written with such goals in mind tended to be almost unreadable and was very difficult to modify. These days, with the advances in hardware, the issues of speed and memory use are not nearly so important. Software developers now realize that software should typically be written with the primary goal of enhancing modifications. As mentioned earlier, modifications to make code efficient should be done after the code has been written and integrated, not during the detailed design or coding stages.

In spite of the advances in hardware, some of the old attitudes remain with us today and interfere with the clarity of the code. For example, while reusing a variable within a module is a way to save a line or two of declarations and some small amount of memory, it may make the code less clear. Using obscure but slightly more efficient algorithms is another common mistake. Consider the two Pascal procedures shown in Figure 6.9. Both procedures find the modal value (the most common or frequently occuring value) in a sorted array. Version A uses a clever but nonobvious algorithm. Version B uses a method that is more obvious. Version A is shorter than version B, and somewhat more efficient (although both algorithms are of order n), but version B will be easier to debug and to maintain.

6.6.2 Style Guideline 2: Fewer Decisions Are Better

Both logically and psychologically, the more decisions a module contains, the more complex it is. Every decision statement in a module results in at least two different pathways that can be taken during execution. As each of these pathways is traversed, additional decisions might be encountered, resulting in new pairs of pathways, and so on. It has been shown that the number of decisions relates directly to the mathematical complexity of a module (McCabe, 1976). Furthermore, research has shown that the psychological difficulty of a module increases with the number of decisions. When possible, the number of decisions within a module should be kept to a minimum. As an example, consider the two Pascal procedures in Figure 6.10. Both procedures compare two measurements, Distance1 and Distance2, to determine which is longer. Clearly, version B, which involves many fewer decisions, is simpler. If a module contains an excessive number of decisions, it is possible it was not well designed. Organizing the decisions to be made within the module in a decision table (see Section 2.4) might help to clarify the module's design and reduce the number of decision statements needed to implement the module.

6.6.3 Style Guideline 3: Nested Logic Should Be Avoided

Version A in Figure 6.10 is also a good example of the complexity that can be caused by excessively nested logic. Even with the indentation as a guide, it is difficult to sort out the different levels of *if . . . else*'s. As a general guideline, the

Version A:

```
procedure Mode1 (A:  array [1..N] of integer;  N:  integer;
             var Mode, ModeFrequency:  integer);

var I, TempFreq:  integer;

begin

    Mode := A[1];
    ModeFrequency := 1;
    TempFreq := 1;
    for I := 2 to N do
        begin
            if A[I] <> A[I-1] then TempFreq := 1
                else TempFreq := TempFreq + 1;
            If TempFreq > ModeFrequency then
                begin
                    ModeFrequency := TempFrequency;
                    Mode := A[I]
                end
        end { for }

end { procedure Mode1 };
```

Version B:

```
procedure Mode2 (A:  array [1..N] of integer;  N:  integer;
             var Mode, ModeFrequency:  integer);

var I:  integer;

begin

    Mode := A[1];
    ModeFrequency := 1;
    for I := 2 to N do
        begin
            if A[I] = A[I-ModeFrequency] then
                begin
                    Mode := A[I];
                    ModeFrequency := ModeFrequency +1
                end { if }
        end { for }

end { procedure Mode2 };
```

Figure 6.9 Two Different Pascal Procedures to Find the Modal Value and Its Frequency in a Sorted Array; Version A Uses a More Straightforward Algorithm than Version B and Is Simpler than Version B

module constructs should not be nested more than three or four levels deep. Excessive nesting is an indication of poor design, and any module requiring more than three or four levels of nesting should be redesigned. Sometimes it is possible to use a series of *if-then*s rather than nested *if-then-else*s. However, this solution

Version A:

```
DistanceRecord = record
    Yards:  integer;
    Feet:  integer;
    Inches:  integer
end;


function DlisLonger
    (Distance1, Distance2: DistanceRecord):boolean;

begin

    DlisLonger := false;
    if Distance1.Yards > Distance2.Yards then DlisLonger := true
    else
        if (Distance1.Yards = Distance2.Yards) and
            (Distance1.Feet > Distance2.Feet)
            then DlisLonger := true
        else if (Distance1.Feet = Distance2.Feet) and
            (Distance1.Inches >  Distance2.Inches)
            then DlisLonger := true

end {function DlisLonger};
```

Version B:

```
function DlisLonger
    (Distance1, Distance2: DistanceRecord):  boolean;

var TotalDistance1, TotalDistance2:  integer;

begin

    TotalDistance1 := (Distance1.Yards * 36) +
        (Distance1.Feet * 12) + Distance1.Inches;
    TotalDistance2 := (Distance2.Yards * 36) +
        (Distance2.Feet * 12) + Distance2.Inches;

    DlisLonger := TotalDistance1 > TotalDistance2

end {function DlisLonger};
```

Figure 6.10 Two Different Pascal Functions to Determine Which of Two Distances is Longer; Version B Is Simpler

will not always work. Version A in Figure 6.10 could not easily be recoded this way. Neither could the following situation:

> if CondA and CondB then Action1
> else if CondB or CondC then Action2
> else ...

Notice that if this segment were recoded as a series of *if-then*s both Action1 and Action2 would be executed if both CondA *and* CondB were true—probably not what the designer intended. By using *goto*s, this complexly nested *if* could be coded into the form of a simpler to read *case*-type statement, as follows:

```
if CondA and CondB then
      begin   Action1;goto Out end;
   if CondB or CondC then
         begin   Action2; goto Out end;
      if CondD then .....
Out: ...
```

In addition, routines should not be defined (nested) within routines more than one level deep in order to avoid excessive complexity. The exception is the main module, if any, which encompasses all of the lower level routines.

6.7   Data Structure Considerations

Although the major data structures are designed in the preliminary and detailed design, the coder may still be required to make decisions concerning the implementation of data structures and the definition of local data structures. Data structures should be chosen that result in simple, clear code and that aid in testing the module. For example, subranges of globally declared types can be used when appropriate. Locally declared user-defined types or subranges should also be used when appropriate. As a simple example, suppose a procedure needs to declare an integer to be used as an index value in searching an array passed to the procedure as a parameter. The coder could simply declare the index variable to be of type integer. However, a better choice is to define the variable to be a subrange of integers, where the range covers the allowable indexes of the array. The coder may also choose to declare a locally defined array or string to simplify the coding of an algorithm. For example, a table of tax brackets and their associated tax rates might prove a simpler, clearer way to implement an algorithm to compute taxes than a series of *if* statements.

In languages that do not require a standard order of data declarations, it is a good idea to impose a standard order. For example, all simple variables might be declared first (ordered by type), followed by arrays (ordered by number of dimensions and by type), followed by files. Within each category, variable names should be alphabetized. Comments should be added to any declarations of complex or unusual data structures.

6.8   Source Code Documentation

The source code documentation is an extremely important component of the software product. If the project is successfully completed initially, there is no doubt that the software will be modified at some time in the future. The major source of information for the programmer assigned to carry out the modification is the source code documentation. To the extent that the documentation was well done, his or her job will be that much easier. If the documentation was poorly written, then the programmer must resort to understanding the system solely by reading the code— an extremely difficult task.

Three different types of program documentation are included in the source code for a single program: (1) *program header comments,* (2) *module header comments,* and (3) certain types of *line comments.*

A *program header comment* is a block of information that appears at the very beginning of a program. It contains general information concerning the entire program. *Module header comments* accompany the source code of each individual module in the program. The module headers are created during the detailed design phase and give specific information about the purpose and use of the individual procedure, function, or subroutine (see Section 4.6). During the detailed design phase, a description of the algorithm to be coded is added to the module header (see Section 5.5). *Line comments* are associated with individual lines of source code. They provide detailed information concerning some short block of instructions or statements contained in a module.

Because specific types of comments go with specific sorts of program structures, it is important to understand what these structural components are. A good way to think of the structure of a program is to compare it to the structure of a book. The total program is equivalent to an entire book, and the source code is similar to the words and sentences contained in that book. Following this analogy, we can see that the program header is similar to a brief abstract of the contents of a book. What is the title of the book? What is the book about? What can this book help the reader accomplish? Each program module is analogous to a chapter in a book. The chapters divide the material of the book into smaller, more understandable units. Each chapter deals with a particular topic. Module headers are brief descriptions of the contents of one "chapter" in the program. What does this module do? How does it fit into the overall purpose of the program?

Like chapters in a book, modules may be subdivided into sections. Just as section headings break text into sets of paragraphs that deal with a single idea, modules can be broken into sets of program statements that deal with a single idea or problem. These sets are called *blocks.* Modules are broken into blocks by inserting a line comment at the beginning of the block. Line comments are also used to document single program statements, in which case they are more like the footnotes, boldface phrases, or marginal annotations found in books. Each type of comment will be discussed in detail next.

6.8.1 Program Header Comment

A program header gives general information concerning the purpose, design, and structure of the program. It provides a general introduction to what follows. Specifically, the program header should include the following information:

Title of the program: This should be descriptive of the purpose of the program. For example, "Widget Inventory Control Program" might be a good title for a program that keeps track of the inventory of widgets. Take note that in certain languages the program also has a working name, but this is not what is meant by "title of the program." The working name might be an abbreviation of the title.

Authorship: The author or authors of the program are identified. If any portion of the code was borrowed from other sources, the original source should be acknowledged. In the case of large systems with multiple authorships, the authorship section might be eliminated from the program header, and each author name included in the module headers of the modules each wrote.

Date and version: The date of the final release of the program and a version number should be indicated.

Purpose: Describe in general terms the overall purpose of the program. What function or functions is the program performing for the user? Write these sentences so that anyone can understand them, even if he or she is not a programmer.

Structure and design: Describe in general terms how the program accomplishes the functions described in the Purpose section. If the program is not too large, this section will include a list of the modules comprising the program and a brief phrase describing what each module does. For a larger program, the design document can be referenced as a source of structure and design information.

Global variables: List any global variables used by the program. Indicate for each its type and how it is used within the program.

Files used: Describe any files used by the program. Name the file and briefly describe its format and contents.

External references: List all modules, routines, or programs used by the program that are external to the entire program.

The program header in Figure 6.11 illustrates the use of these guidelines. While this example describes a small program, the same format can be used for larger programs.

6.8.2 Module Headers as Comments

As discussed in Chapter 5, the module header for each module is created as part of the detailed design process. Although the module header serves as a design document for the coder, it is important to remember that the header is also part of the program documentation. It is up to the coder to make sure that the information in the module header is updated as design and coding changes are made. The module header is also a good place to keep historical records of such changes, including dates the changes were implemented and the personnel involved.

```
{ *****************************************************************
-
-    EXAM SCORE SUMMARY PROGRAM
-    WRITTEN BY :  A. Lovelace
-    RELEASE DATE:   April 1, 1990
-    VERSION:  1.5
-
-    PURPOSE:  This program produces a variety of statistics on a
-    group of student's exam scores.  For each score that is entered,
-    the score and a row of stars representing the magnitude of the
-    score is printed out.  In addition, the number of scores, the
-    average score, the highest score and the lowest score are
-    printed out.
-
-    DESIGN:  The program is composed of the following modules:
-        Main Module - The Main, controlling module
-        Validate Input - Gets and validates the user's input
-        Process Valid Score - Prints score and row of stars for one
-            score
-        Update Statistics - Updates global statistics
-        Print Summary Report - Prints summary statistics
-
-    MAJOR VARIABLES:
-        SumOfScores (subrange of integer, 0..2000) -
-            The sum of all scores entered
-        NumOfStudents (subrange of integer, 0..100) -
-            The total number of scores entered
-        LargestScore (subrange of integer, 0..20) -
-            The largest score in the set of scores
-        SmallestScore (subrange of integer, 0..20) -
-            The smallest score
-
-    FILES USED:
-        Input - contains integer scores, one to a line
-        Output - contains a one-line histogram for each score read,
-            followed on the next line by the number of students and
-            their average score,then on the next line by the top
-            score, and concluding on the next line with the lowest
-            score.
-
-    EXTERNAL REFERENCES:  None
*************************************************************** }
```

Figure 6.11 Sample Program Header

6.8.3 Line Comments

Line comments are inserted within the source code of a module to provide detailed information on exactly what individual program statements or sets of statements are doing. Line comments break up a module into small logical components and describe what each component does. If we consider a module to be similar to a short paper on a specific and limited topic, then each component represents one paragraph in that paper. The line comment then serves as a topic sentence for the paragraph.

How small should these logical components be? One important factor is the level of the source code language. In a high-level language such as Pascal, the logical component might be a group of, say, a dozen lines. In a low-level language such as assembler language, comments might be needed for every group of 4 to 12 statements and a brief comment for every individual statement in that group. A second factor affecting the need for line comments is identifier length. A language that allows longer identifiers will probably need fewer line comments. Whatever the level of the language and whatever the identifier length, two sorts of lines should always be commented: lines that are implementation dependent and lines that use "magic numbers." For example, obscure constants from mathematical equations are "magic numbers," which should always be commented.

Figure 6.12 is an example of the use of line comments within a Pascal procedure. Only the body of the procedure is shown. The purpose of the procedure is to read in a word of variable length as it is typed in by the user and to store it in the array variable, Instring, padded with blanks. Notice how the comments and vertical white space break up the procedure into logical blocks. One block reads in characters as they are entered. The second block flushes the *eoln* character, and the last block pads the string variable, Instring, with blanks. Also, notice the use of a brief comment following the *end* statement to identify which structure the *end* statement belongs with.

An important point to remember in writing line comments is to avoid simply repeating what the source code statements says. For example, suppose we are documenting the following Pascal statement:

Total := Total + Value;

Appending the comment "Add Value to Total" to this source code statement does absolutely nothing to increase our knowledge of what the program is doing. The comment simply reinterprets the Pascal statement in English. However, if we append the comment "Add cost of item to total expenses," we are giving the reader an idea of how the statement relates to the goal or logic of the program. (Note that

```
begin

    { Read in characters until a return is typed }
    Next := 1;
    while (not eoln) and (Next <= Maxlength) do
        { "Maxlength" is implementation dependent }
        begin
            read (Instring[Next]);
            Next := Next + 1
        end;

    {Flush  the <eoln> character}
    readln;

    { Blank out the remaining spaces in "Instring" }
    for Next := Next to Maxlength do
        Instring[Next] := Blank

end {procedure ReadString};
```

Figure 6.12 Use of Line Comments with a Pascal Procedure

in this case we would have avoided the need for a line comment if the variables had been more carefully named.)

6.9   Source Code Format and Identifier Naming

In addition to the comments added to the source code as program documentation, the source code itself is part of the documentation. Specifically, the format of the source code and the identifiers (module, variable, and constant names) that are used are important factors in the readability of a program. The readability and understandability of source code can be greatly enhanced by using the right format and identifier names (Kesler and others, 1984; Miara and others, 1983).

In some languages, such as IBM 370 Assembler and other assembler languages, the horizontal format of the source code statements is fixed to a great extent and cannot be altered. However, empty comment lines or assembler instructions such as SPACE and EJECT can still be used to improve readability by introducing vertical white space into the listing. In higher-level languages, arbitrary numbers of blank lines can be used for vertical spacing. For horizontal spacing, blocks of code can be indented like sections of an outline. Many installations have *pretty-print routines,* which accept source code in any format and reformat it according to some standard. Some pretty-print routines also insert blank lines and borders around comments. In other installations, *language-sensitive editors* are available. A language-sensitive editor is an editor designed specifically to be used in the creation and editing of source code for a particular programming language. For example, some language-sensitive editors designed to be used with Pascal automatically provide an *end* when a *begin* is entered and indent any code that is inserted between the *begin* and *end*. Such editors will also standardize the style of the reserved words and variable names. If formatting is to be done manually, a standard should be agreed upon and adhered to by all programmers.

To make identifiers more nearly self-documenting, constants, types, variables, and modules should have carefully and creatively chosen names that are close to English and long enough to be meaningful in terms of the function the identifier is performing. In other words, just by looking at the identifier the reader should be able to make a good guess about what it does. For this reason, TestScores is a much better name for an array than IntegerArray, and ComputeMeans is a better name for a module than DoCalculations. Be advised that some languages do not support identifiers as long as these, in which case it may not be possible to coin identifiers that are close to English words. Try anyway.

As a final comment on comments, it is important that correct spelling and good grammar be used throughout the documentation. Remember that the comments are more likely to be read than the code itself. Pride of work and a regard for quality should be reflected in the documentation, as well as in the code itself.

An example of the complete source code for a module is shown in Figure 6.13. When coding has been completed, the source code will include not only the pro-

```
{**********************************************************************
- TITLE:   SortItemSizes
- PURPOSE:  This module sorts a list of sizes, in ounces, that
- a particular grocery item is available in into ascending order.
- METHOD:  A Selection Sort is used, based on the following
-   pseudocode:
-
-       select the smallest item in the array and put it in the
-           first position, creating a sorted array with N = 1
-       while there are unsorted items in the arrary do
-           select the smallest item from the unsorted items
-           place it at the end of the sorted items stored at the
-           front of the array
-       end-while
-
- USAGE:  GetItemSizes
- EXTERNAL REFERENCES:  Swap
- CALLING SEQUENCE:
-     Sizes - (I/O)  An integer array of sizes to be sorted.
-     Count - (I)  An integer indicating the number of items in
-         Sizes.  Count must be > 0 and < = 25.
- INPUT ASSERTION:  The input array must contain 1 to 25 integer
-     values, in any order.
- OUTPUT ASSERTION:  The items in the array will be ordered such
-     that item1 < = item2 ... < = item N.
- VARIABLES:
-     Smallest - An integer that points to the smallest item in the
-         unsorted portion of the array
-     I, J - Integers used as array indices
- AUTHOR(S):  K. Nuth.  The algorithm used was adopted from one
-     which appeared in Wool Wirth's Collected Algorithms (1979),
-     p. 234.
- REMARKS:  Selection sort is an N square (quadratic) sort, and
-     is not very efficient.  However, it was used in this case
-     because the maximum number of items to be sorted is 25.
 **********************************************************************}

procedure SortItemSizes (var Sizes: Sizearray; Count: Countrange);

var Smallest, I, J:  integer;

begin
   if Count > 1 then
      begin { I points to first item in unsorted portion of array }
         for I := 1 to Count-1 do
            begin
               { Find the smallest item in the unsorted portion }
               Smallest := I;
               for J := I to Count do
                  if  Sizes[J] < Sizes[Smallest] then Smallest := J;

               { Swap the Smallest item with the first item in the
                 unsorted portion of the array }
               Swap (Sizes[Smallest], Sizes[I]);
            end { for }
      end  { if }
end { procedure SortItemSizes };
```

Figure 6.13 Example of the Complete Pascal Source Code for a Procedure, Including the Module Header and Line Comments

gram statements, but the comments and the module header, as well. Notice the use of borders to separate the module header visually from the actual source code. Blank lines and spaces are used to break up the source code into its logical units.

6.10   Importance of Coding Standards

In the issues of programming style and documentation, there are no hard and fast rules. The discussion of these topics in this chapter is intended to provide some general guidelines and some specific suggestions. Certainly, particular aspects of each project will influence which of these guidelines and suggestions are adopted. In particular, the types and extent of documentation required will vary depending on the choice of programming language.

No matter which standards are used, it is important that some set of standards should be drawn up and adhered to by those coding the system. Standards are important for several reasons. First, they provide a means of focusing the coders' creativity and providing an important uniformity of the code. Although individuals work on different aspects of the software, it is important to remember that the project is a *group* project. Guidelines help to foster communication among the members of the group and set quality standards. The code one person writes will be read and used by other members of the team. A similarity of standards facilitates this process. Second, standards are a great aid in the maintenance of software. Because maintenance represents two-thirds of the cost of owning software, anything that can be done during the creation of software to reduce maintenance costs should be encouraged. Well-written, up-to-date documentation and simple, clearly written code make maintenance much less of a chore.

6.11   Case Study: Coding and Integrating the Rev-Pro System

In the Rev-Pro system three components of the system, each representing one major activity, appeared to be good candidates for early coding and integration. These were the Scale-the-Hall, Tabulate-Costs, and Tabulate-Non-Ticket-Revenues. Each of these components stands alone in that it does not depend upon any other component for data. It was decided that the complete Scale-the-Hall activity would be coded and integrated first, including all the lower level modules it uses. The main module, Rev-Pro, was to be created only in the form of a driver at the same time. The Tabulate-Costs and Tabulate-Non-Ticket-Revenues components, including all of their lower level modules were to be coded and integrated in the second stage of integration (see Figure 6.14.)

The other three major components—Produce-Master-Pricing Grids, Estimate-Demand and Produce-Estimated-Revenue-Table—all require information from the first three components. Furthermore, they must be executed sequentially in the order given for the user to produce meaningful output. For these reasons, the order

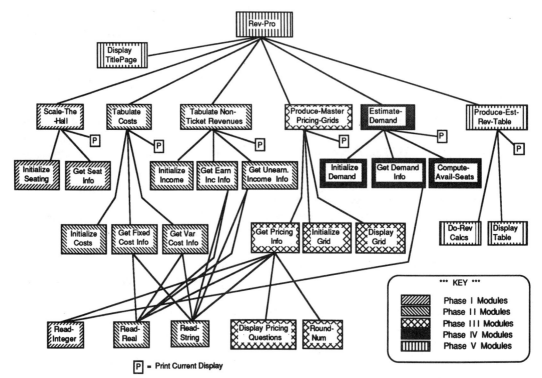

P = Print Current Display

Figure 6.14 Phases of Integration of the Rev-Pro System Case Study

of integration was to follow the potential execution order. The module Display-Title-Page was to be added in the last integration stage. Display-Title-Page was designed to signal to the user that the Rev-Pro system was functional by presenting the name of the system on the screen.

The order of coding and integration had to be determined within each of these major components, as well. For example, in the Tabulate-Costs component, it made sense to write the Initialize-Costs module first. This was because the other two modules depended on its activities, and because it would have been difficult to write a stub to simulate its actions. Likewise, it was decided to create Read-String before Get-Variable-Costs-Info and Get-Fixed-Costs-Info because these modules and many others use Read-String. The development of the Tabulate-Non-Ticket-Revenue component was scheduled to be concurrent with Tabulate-Costs due to the similarity of the two components, and the lack of dependency between the two components.

Different members or pairs of members of the Rev-Pro team were assigned to each of the integration components. One member was designated the coordinator and was responsible for overseeing the coding and integration process. Copies of the units coded and tested early in the coding phase were available to all team members, so that the style and methods used in the early units could be copied in the later units. This provided a uniformity of style that is useful in debugging and maintaining a system.

An example of a coded module is given in Figure 6.15. This figure shows the complete source code for the Get-Fixed-Costs module. Notice that the module

```
{*****************************************************************
- TITLE:  Get-Fixed-Costs-Info
- MODULE ID:  C.2
- PURPOSE:  Accept fixed-costs information entered by the user and
     update the display screen as appropriate.  Includes error
     checking features.
- METHOD:
     repeat
        ReadString (Fixed-Costs-Category)
        ReadReal   (Fixed-Costs)
        if (user presses a function key) or (user entered only
           a carriage return)then user wishes to exit
        else if category entered but no cost then
           signal error
           ReadReal (Fixed-Costs)
        else if cost entered but no category then
           signal error
           ReadString (Fixed-Costs-Category)
        else if all fixed-costs are full then
           get ready to read first variable-cost category
        else get ready to read next fixed-cost category
     until (user wishes to exit) or (all fields are full)

- USAGE:  Tabulate-Costs
- EXTERNAL REFERENCES:
     ReadReal
     ReadString
     ErrorMessage
- CALLING SEQUENCE:
     Costs (I/O):  a record containing the cost variables
     Position (I/O):  the relative location of the cursor on the
        Cost table
     Xpos,  Ypos (I/O):  The exact location of the cursor on the
        screen.Xpos is the horizontal location, Ypos is the
        vertical location.
     Return-Code (O):  the type of keypress entered by the user,
        e.g.,a function key code
- INPUT ASSERTION: The Costs record contains initialized cost
     values
- OUTPUT ASSERTION: The Costs record may contain zero or more
     changed values upon exiting the procedure.
- VARIABLES:
     errorfound:  a flag to signal the occurence of an error
        (missing data)
- AUTHOR(S):  Sandy Honken
- REMARKS:  The Return-Code is read as part of the actions of
     Read-Real and Read-String.  Each function key sets Return-Code
     to a particular value, and the Return key sets it to a
     different unique value.  Possible values of the Return-Code are
     defined as constants in the main program.
*****************************************************************}
```

Figure 6.15 Complete Pascal Source Code for the Get-Fixed-Costs-Info Procedure of the Rev-Pro System Case Study

```
PROCEDURE GetFixedCosts(VAR Costs: CostsRecord; VAR Position,
    Xpos,Ypos: integer;  VAR Return-Code:  char;);

VAR
    error-found:  boolean;
    message: string;

BEGIN
WITH Costs DO
    errorfound := false;
    REPEAT
        {get fixed cost category name}
        Read-String (Xpos, Ypos, 10, Fixed-Costs[position].name,
            Return-Code);

        {get fixed cost category amount}
        IF Return-Code = CR THEN
            Read-Real (Xpos+12, Ypos, 7,Fixed-Costs[Position].amount,
                Return-Code);

        IF (Fixed-Costs[Position].name = ' ' )AND
            (Fixed-Costs[Postion].amount = 0.0) AND
            (Return-Code = CR OR Return-Code = Calculate OR
            Return-Code = Print OR Return-Code = Exit-Back OR
            Return-Code = Exit-Front)
        THEN { User is done entering fixed costs }
            BEGIN
                Position := 11;  {ready to enter first Variable Cost}
                Xpos := 56;  Ypos := 9;
                errorfound := false;
            END

        ELSE IF Fixed-Costs[Position].name = ' ' THEN
            {Error - no name entered for category}
            BEGIN
                errorfound := true;
                message := 'PLEASE ENTER A TITLE FOR COST CATEGORY';
                ErrorMessage (message);
            END

        ELSE IF Fixed-Costs[Position].value = 0.0 THEN
            {Error - no value entered for category}
            BEGIN
                errorfound := true;
                message :='PLEASE ENTER AN AMOUNT FOR COST
                    CATEGORY';
                ErrorMessage (message);
            END

        ELSE {move on to next cost category}
            BEGIN
                errorfound := false;
                IF Position = 10 THEN {all fixed categories filled}
                    BEGIN
                        Postion := 11;
                        Xpos := 56;  Ypos := 9
                    END
```

Figure 6.15 continued

```
            ELSE {Go to next entry}
                BEGIN
                    Position := Postion + 1;
                    Ypos := Ypos +1
                END:
            END {else};

        UNTIL (errorfound = false) AND (Position = 11);
    END {with Costs}
    END; {procedure Get-Fixed-Costs-Info}
```

Figure 6.15 continued

header is now completed, with all remaining information filled in. Notice also that a new procedure, ErrorMessage, is called from Get-Fixed-Costs-Info and was, therefore, added to the design. The team chose to use an identifier-naming convention for variables not in the data dictionary. Global identifiers and formal parameters were to have at least the initial letter capitalized, while local variables were to be in all lowercase letters.

Summary

Coding involves creating the source code for the system based on the detailed design documents. A systematic approach, called an integration strategy, should be used for deciding the order in which the modules of the system are coded, tested, and put together. A number of different approaches to integration can be used, including Big-Bang, top-down, bottom-up, and threads. Factors that affect the choice of an integration approach include the amount of test harness needed, the location of critical parts of the system, the availability of hardware, and scheduling concerns. The Big-Bang method, where all modules are coded and then the entire system is integrated in one step, is not recommended. The bottom-up approach, where modules are coded from the bottom levels of the system structure first, is appropriate in situations where some of the lower-level modules are judged to be critical or questionable components of a system. However, the bottom-up approach delays evaluation of the structure of the design and does not make skeletal versions of the system available for testing. In the top-down approach, the upper-level modules are coded first. This allows the evaluation of the structure of the higher levels and can result in skeletal versions being available for evaluation. The drawback of the top-down approach is that input and output are usually performed by low-level modules, making testing difficult. In general, the threads approach is best. In this approach, a minimal set of modules that performs some primary function in the system is selected for coding and integration. The modules may come from a number of levels in the system structure. Additional threads can be coded in parallel and separately. Early skeletal versions of the system evolve naturally from this approach. An integration plan should be created that outlines the integration approach to be taken, assigns duties to personnel, and sets up a schedule of activities.

Factors that affect the quality of source code include the use of structured coding techniques, good coding style, well-chosen data structures, good source code format and documentation, and identifier naming. Structured coding techniques involve the avoidance of *gotos,* the use of top-down flow of control, and the use of single-entry, single-exit constructs. The primary guideline for good coding style is to make source code simple and readable. Three ways to attain this goal are to strive for shortness (but not at the expense of clarity), use fewer decisions, and avoid nested logic. Data structures should be chosen that result in simpler, clearer code and aid in testing. Documentation consists of program headers, module headers, and line comments. Headers should be written according to a standard format and should provide useful information for testing and maintenance. Line comments should be used to break up the source code into logical units and identify the function of these units. The right source code format and good identifier names can aid the readability of source code. Coding standards are important in producing a quality product, in facilitating communication among the developers, and in maintaining the system.

Checklist of Project Activities

_____ Begin reading Chapter 7 as soon as possible to gain an understanding of unit and integration testing. Coding and testing are carried out in parallel, so a knowledge of testing is needed during the coding phase.

_____ Decide on an integration approach. The threads approach is recommended, but special circumstances might indicate an alternate approach.

_____ Using the preliminary design document, decide on the exact progression of integration.

_____ Assign personnel to coding and testing duties.

_____ Set up a schedule of coding, integration, and testing activities. Do not neglect to include time for building test harnesses, creating test cases, updating documentation, and various evaluation activities (see Chapter 7).

_____ Document the integration plan. Text, Gantt charts, tables, and other sorts of charts or graphs can be used.

_____ Evaluate the integration plan.

_____ Establish a set of coding standards. These standards should relate to coding techniques, coding style, internal comments, source code format, and identifier naming. In some cases a department standard may be available. In other cases a standard can be adopted from a good programming text for the target language or from a text on programming style.

_____ If possible, obtain a pretty-print routine to be used to standardize source code format.

_____ If a language-sensitive editor is available, plan to use it.

Terms and Concepts Introduced

system integration	Gantt chart
integration strategy	single-entry, single-exit constructs
Big-Bang strategy	simplicity (of code)
top-down strategy	readability (of code)
bottom-up strategy	software complexity
threads strategy	program header
incremental development	line comments
test harness	blocks (of code)
driver	pretty-print routines
stub	
language-sensitive editor	

Exercises

1. Look through some of your own programs or a programming text and find some examples of situations where the use of a *goto* might produce clearer and more efficient code. (Situations where errors in the input are encountered during processing are likely candidates for *gotos*.)

2. Consider the use of recursion in programming. Some argue that a recursive solution is shorter and more natural than an iterative solution. What do you think? Is recursion easier or harder to read? Easier or harder to understand? What about the run-time efficiency of recursion? Does the cost of recursion justify its use?

3. Find one of your own programs that you have not looked at for a number of months or get a program from a friend that you have not seen before. Pick out one or two sections of the code and read these sections. How easy or hard is it for you to follow the code? Was the code well documented? Did the documentation help you in understanding the code? Imagine what it would be like to read a program that is a year or two old and many, many times larger. Would good documentation be an advantage?

4. Obtain a set of source code documentation standards from your department or a programming organization. What style of documentation is recommended? Explain the reason for each recommendation.

5. (a) This book has suggested that routines should generally contain 10 to 30 lines of executable code. What are the reasons for this recommendation?
   (b) What are some of the costs of having 10- to 30-line routines as opposed to longer ones? Do the benefits outweigh the costs?
   (c) Give some reasons for or situations when routines of less than 10 lines might be needed. Give some reasons for or situations when routines of more than 30 lines might be needed.

6. Determine what the following Pascal procedure does. Rewrite the procedure using good variable names and adding comments. Improve the indentation and add vertical white space. Add additional variables if necessary for clarity. Rewrite the instructions and output to the user, as well, to make them more meaningful.

```
procedure Compute (In: char);
const Multiplier = 3.14;
var A, B, C :  real;
begin
   case In of
      'T','t' :  begin
         writeln ('Enter the height of the figure.');
         readln (A);
         writeln ('Enter the base of the figure.');
         readln (B);
         C := (A*B)/2.0
         end;
      'C','c' :  begin
         writeln ('Enter the radius of the figure.');
         readln (A);
         C := Multiplier * (A * A);
         end;
      'S','s' :  begin
         writeln ('Enter the length of one side.');
         readln (A);
         C := A * A;
         end;
   writeln ('The answer is:'  C)
end;
```

7. The following two Pascal procedures each convert a decimal number between 0 and 50 to binary and display the binary form of the number. Which procedure is stylistically better? Which is quicker to understand? Which would be easier to modify? Defend your answers.

```
procedure Convert1;
var DecimalNum, PowerOf2:  integer;
begin
   writeln ('Enter a whole number between 0 and 50.
      The binary form of the number will be displayed.');
   readln (DecimalNum);
   writeln ('The binary form of the number entered is:');
   PowerOf2 := 32;
   while PowerOf2 > 0 do
      begin
         if DecimalNum > PowerOf2 then begin
               write ('1');
               DecimalNum := DecimalNum - PowerOf2
                     end
         else write ('0');
         PowerOf2 := PowerOf2 div 2
      end {while};
end {Convert1};
```

```
procedure Convert2;
var DecimalNum:  integer;
begin
    writeln ('Enter a whole number between 0 and 50.  The binary
        form of the number will be displayed.');
    readln (DecimalNum);
    writeln ('The binary form of the number entered is:');
    if DecimalNum > 32 then begin
        write ('1');   DecimalNum := DecimalNum - 32
        end
    else write ('0');
    if DecimalNum > 16 then begin
        write ('1');   DecimalNum := DecimalNum - 16
        end
    else write ('0');
    if DecimalNum > 8 then begin
        write ('1');   DecimalNum := DecimalNum - 8
        end
    else write ('0');
    if DecimalNum > 4 then begin
        write ('1');   DecimalNum := DecimalNum - 4
        end
    else write ('0');
    if DecimalNum > 2 then begin
        write ('1');   DecimalNum := DecimalNum - 2
        end
    else write ('0');
    if DecimalNum > 1 then write ('1');
    else write ('0');
end {procedure Convert2};
```

7. Testing

One of the most surprising facts students of software development encounter is the proportion of time, effort, and cost spent on testing. It has been estimated that approximately 50 percent of the elapsed time and over 50 percent of the total cost of the development of a system are spent on testing (Myers, 1979). Yet testing is a skill the typical computer science student has little or no training in. Why is testing such a well-kept secret? Furthermore, testing is not a trivial skill to learn. Many call the ability to test a system well an art. Like any skill, learning to do testing well takes practice and experience. However, this chapter will introduce some basic techniques that are not difficult to learn and, if carefully applied, will go a long way toward producing a sound, well-tested system.

7.1 Testing Defined

Testing is defined as "The process of exercising or evaluating a system by manual or automatic means to verify that it satisfies specified requirements or to identify differences between expected and actual results" (IEEE, 1983). Every student is only too familiar with tests and has a pretty good idea of what testing in a school environment is about. The idea of school tests is to evaluate the student's knowledge and to ascertain that that knowledge meets some specified level. The same concept applies in testing software. Before a piece of software is turned over to the sponsor, the software should be evaluated to make sure it meets the sponsor's requirements. These requirements might be either implicit or explicit. Explicit requirements are those actually given in the requirements and specification document. Does the system do what the sponsor specified that it should do, and does it follow any guidelines or restrictions the sponsor specified? Implicit requirements might include, for example, reliability and robustness. The sponsor does not expect the delivered system to have too many bugs in it. And they probably expect

274

the system to react well to unusual or unanticipated conditions. (A well-written requirements and specification would include specification of these quality factors.)

Testing is typically assumed to be those activities that take place after the code is written. However, the definition given above can easily be interpreted to cover all activities that have to do with evaluating the system in its various guises. This broader definition of testing (used by Hetzel, 1988, among others) has the advantage of emphasizing the fact that testing must be interwoven with all facets of system development. (In other software engineering literature, testing in the sense used here might be called "validation," "verification," or "quality assurance.")

Testing in the way it is defined here should begin as soon as the requirements and specification have been written. The techniques described in Chapter 2 for evaluating the requirements and specification and in Chapter 4 for evaluating the preliminary design were testing techniques. The formal reviews and walk-throughs described there are commonly used testing techniques that can be applied to other phases of the software development cycle. Likewise, the use of a system prototype, as described in Chapter 3, is also a testing technique. Prototyping has gained popularity recently because it has been shown to be a very effective testing method. The techniques to be described in this chapter are used for testing code, including individual modules, components of software systems, and entire software systems.

All testing involves the following five steps:

1. **Select what is to be measured by the test.** Before designing a test or set of tests, the tester must determine what the goal of the test is. Are the requirements to be tested for completeness? Is the code being tested for reliability? Is the design being tested for cohesion? What exactly *is* being tested for?

2. **Decide how whatever is being tested is to be tested.** Once the tester knows what is to be tested, he or she must decide how to test for the quality being tested for. A wide variety of test approaches are available, including inspection, proofs, black-box and white-box testing, and automated methods. The tester must decide what kind of test is to be used to measure the chosen quality and what sort of test items should be used.

3. **Develop the test cases.** Once the type of test has been decided on, the actual test cases must be created. A *test case* is simply a set of test data or situations that will be used to exercise the unit being tested or reveal something about the attribute being measured.

4. **Determine what the expected or correct result of the test should be and create the test oracle.** It is extremely important that the tester know what the correct output should be and write it down *before* the actual testing takes place. It is too easy to look at the results of a trial run when the output has not been predicted and say "That looks fine," when, in fact, the output contains an error. The predicted results for a set of test cases are called a *test oracle*.

5. **Execute the test cases.** The next step is to carry out the tests. In some cases this may necessitate writing software that allows the tester to exercise just the one portion of the system being tested. Such software is called a *test harness*. Once testing is complete, the test harness is set aside and does not become part of the final system.

6. **Compare the results of the test to the test oracle.** The final step is to carefully, character by character, compare the results from the execution of the test case to the test oracle. Any discrepancy between the predicted results and the actual results signals an error. The source of the error must then be tracked down. Typically, the error is in the system being tested. But it is possible that an error is the result of some aspect the testing process itself or is in the test oracle.

7.2 Levels of Testing

In most organizations, at least three basic levels or stages of testing are carried out: *unit testing, integration testing,* and *acceptance testing*.

In *unit testing*, individual modules are tested. Usually, the person who implements the module designs and executes the unit tests for that module. The primary goals of unit testing are to confirm that the module is correctly coded and that it carries out the functions it is supposed to carry out. Both *black-box* and *white-box tests,* as discussed later, are conducted. The records kept during unit testing may be somewhat casual.

Integration testing involves testing groups of integrated modules (subsystems) or the entire system. The goal is to determine if the system or subsystem meets the system requirements and functions properly and to test the interface among the modules. Integration testing is typically more formal than unit testing. A record of testing is carefully maintained, and discovered errors are logged.

Acceptance testing is carried out to evaluate the finished product. The object is to demonstrate that the system is ready to use. Acceptance testing is often carried out by the sponsor and may involve executing typical transactions or using the system on site on a trial basis. The system's documentation is also tested at this time. The degree of documentation of acceptance testing varies greatly among different organizations, but a wise sponsor approaches acceptance testing systematically and keeps careful records.

Many of the testing techniques and methods used for integration testing and acceptance testing are the same. These techniques are sometimes referred to together as "testing in the large." The techniques used on units are somewhat different and are sometimes referred to as "testing in the small." In this chapter, the techniques for testing in the small will be covered first, followed by techniques for testing in the large. First, however, several principles of testing need to be discussed to provide a foundation for testing methods and techniques.

7.3 Principles of Testing

Experience with testing has shown that testing has certain characteristics or principles, some of which may seem surprising to you. Each principle provides insight into testing, and all are important cornerstones in the design and execution of code tests.

Testing is the process of executing a program with the intention of finding errors. This definition of testing is taken from Myers (1979) and makes a very important point about code testing. A more naive view of testing is that it is done to show that a program or system works. The problem with the naive view of testing is that it leads to poor testing. It is usually easy for a tester to come up with sample input that executes correctly. The trick is coming up with sample input that does *not* work. Part of what makes this difficult is that testing to find errors is basically destructive. Creating a quality program takes great skill and effort. To turn around and "destroy" a carefully crafted piece of work by looking for flaws seems distasteful. Consider how you would feel if you gave a hand-knit sweater to someone as a gift and she or he examined it for skipped stitches. However, a sweater with a skipped stitch will still keep the wearer warm while software with a "skipped" statement may not function correctly and will thus be useless. To overcome this psychological block against testing, it is extremely important that the tester have the correct attitude: a successful test is one that finds an error; an unsuccessful test is one that does not find an error.

It is impossible to completely test any nontrivial module or any system. Here is a real shocker. We are just beginning on a chapter about testing. You might well have expected to read that, with a little skill and patience, any module or system can be tested into a state of perfection. Now you are being told that it is impossible. Why undertake testing at all if it is impossible to do it completely? It is true that testing cannot be done completely. There are both practical limitations and theoretical limitations on testing that make this true. In the sections on black-box and white-box testing, exactly what these limitations are will be explained. To get an idea of why there are limits to testing consider, for example, a test that a college student might take to determine her or his vocabulary level. It is estimated that the average college student has a working vocabulary of 8000 words. Would it make sense to test each student on 10,000 or more different words to assess their vocabulary level? Yes, it would, if you wanted a complete, reliable, and accurate test. But obviously there are practical limits. The time and cost involved in developing and administering such a test would be enormous. It makes more sense to carefully select a subset of the vocabulary and include only those items on the test. Some items should be selected from different levels of vocabulary, possibly based on their frequency of appearance in literature or in the spoken language. Whatever the details, it is possible that a vocabulary test could be developed that would take a reasonable amount of time and effort to administer and that most people would agree provided a good test of vocabulary level. The same basic problems apply to testing software. In many cases it is possible to enumerate all the test cases that would have to be run to completely test the software. But the time and cost involved are prohibitive. A less complete but still effective test can be developed. In other cases, the number of possible test cases is infinite. A subset of test cases *must* suffice. In such circumstances, it is important to chose the best possible subset of test cases.

Testing takes creativity and hard work. In the past, testing often was viewed as dirty work, on the same level, or possibly on a lower level, as maintenance. As noted in Chapter 1, two-thirds of the time and effort involved in creating and owning a piece of software is in maintenance. And 50 percent of the time and effort in developing software is involved in testing. If testing and maintenance are dirty work, then there are many, many people spending many, many hours doing dirty work. In fact, testing and maintenance both demand much creativity and present interesting challenges to software professionals. To develop effective tests, the person involved must have a detailed understanding of what the system is supposed to do *plus* a knowledge of testing techniques *plus* the skill and creativity to apply these techniques in an effective and efficient manner.

Testing can prevent errors from occurring. The traditional view of testing was that it was something done after the code had been written. The modern approach, however, is to view testing as an activity that is planned for right from the beginning and that proceeds as a continuous activity throughout the development cycle. If testing is done as the last step in the development cycle, it is similar to a teacher who gives only a final exam in a course. There is no chance for the student to gauge his or her progress during the semester or term. Testing spread at intervals throughout the term, on the other hand, allows both the teacher and student to monitor and control the learning process, to note when misunderstandings have occurred, and to detect problems. The sooner such misunderstandings and problems are detected, the easier it is to rectify them. Furthermore, detecting and treating small problems early often prevents the occurrence of larger problems later. The situation is exactly analogous in software development. Tests should be made throughout the cycle to obtain early recognition of any deficiencies. Early recognition permits less costly correction of the problem and often averts more serious later problems.

Testing is best done by several independent testers. Anyone who has learned to program knows, deep down inside, that someone else will do a more thorough job of testing a program than the author of the program. Novice programmers struggle for hours to get a program to handle the sample data provided by the teacher or the few sample input items created by themselves. When the sample data pass correctly through the system one time, resulting in more or less the correct output, the programmer heaves a sigh of relief and rushes to have the final copy printed before something happens to make the program stop working. Under no circumstances does the programmer try an alternate set of data. It might "mess up" the working program! As programmers become more sophisticated, they are willing to take more risks with the sorts of data they try out, and they understand that even working programs always need some fine-tuning. Nonetheless, when a supposedly finished program is executed by someone else, or with an alternate set of data, it very often does not work entirely correctly. The author simply cannot view his or her own creation from the same objective framework as an outsider. What may seem perfectly obvious to the author may not appear so obvious to another user. What seemed to the author to be a completely thought-out piece of logic may actually contain a gaping hole that is only discovered with input the author did not think to test.

It is best if testing of anything other than single units is carried out by someone other than the author or authors of the system or subsystem. In some cases an independent testing or quality control unit within the organization is used. In other cases, a completely independent organization may be hired to carry out the testing. At the least, team approaches and a series of reviews can be used to foster objectiveness.

7.4 Testing in the Small

Testing in the small involves the techniques and methods that are used for unit testing—the testing of individual modules. In general, the person who codes the module is responsible for designing and carrying out the unit tests. Some techniques that are used for testing in the small are informal and are known by every experienced programmer. For example, a technique that is particularly suited for interactive systems is *incremental coding*. In incremental coding a small portion of the module is written and some simple test data are used to test it. The portion is modified as necessary, and then additional portions are coded, tested, and added on. *Desk checking* or *hand execution* can also be used. Desk checking involves simply reading the source code, scanning for possible errors in either syntax or logic. Hand execution involve "playing computer." To play computer, the coder reads successive lines of source code and carries out the appropriate activities by making notations on paper. Hand execution is particularly useful for finding logic errors.

Desk checking and hand execution are examples of what is called *static analysis* (Fairley, 1985). Static analysis is testing done directly on the source code of a program, without executing the program. It can be done informally by the coder, formally in an inspection or walk-through, or by using an automated tool. Automated static analysis can produce lists of errors, highlight questionable coding practices, and signal departures from coding standards. An example of an error that a static analyzer might find is a variable that is declared but never initialized or used. This is poor coding practice. The use of backward transfer of control or modules that are too long or contain too many decisions are examples of possible departures from coding standards. In addition, static analyzers can provide information about the structure of the code, including symbol tables, call graphs (what modules are called by each module), logic flow graphs (see Section 7.5.1), lists of parameters passed to each routine, line counts, and so on.

The opposite of static analysis is *dynamic testing*. Dynamic testing tests the behavior of a unit or program during execution. The three major dynamic testing approaches used in unit testing are *black-box testing, white-box testing,* and *data-structure-based testing.* The term black box has already come up in the discussion of module design. A module is supposed to be like a black box: a component whose function is understood, with predictable output occurring for given input. The internal workings of the box are not visible and are not of interest. In *black-box testing,* we say that, if for any given input to a module we can correctly predict the output, then the module has passed our tests, and it does not matter what went on inside the module. Black-box testing is functional testing. The tests are designed to check the functions of the module. Does it do everything it is supposed to do? In white-box testing, the approach is just the opposite. *White-box testing* focuses on the logic of a module to determine what tests to run. A more apt name for white-box testing would be "glass-box" testing. The idea of white-box testing is to look at the internal workings and operations of the module, as though the box containing the function were transparent. White-box testing is structural testing. The logical structure of the module is systematically explored by white-box tests. In *data-structure-based testing,* the nature and dimensions of the data structures are examined to develop test cases.

A limitation of white-box testing is that, while it may show that the code that is present works logically, it does not detect missing functions. A limitation of black-box testing is that it may not discover extra functions that are included in the code, but that were not included in the requirements. As an analogy, consider an otherwise functional typewriter that has no hardware to produce the letter x. White-box tests, derived by examining the hardware of the typewriter, would give the typewriter passing marks. After all, all the keys that are on the keyboard work. However, a black-box test, based on a complete description of what a typewriter is supposed to do, would discover the missing function. As another example, suppose there were a perfectly sound typewriter with a faulty instruction manual. The instruction booklet neglected to tell the user that there was a little switch inside the cover that allows the user to adjust the strength with which the keys strike the paper. The typewriter would pass all the black-box tests based just on the instruction manual. However, a careful look at the internal workings of the machine (using white-box testing) would discover the little switch. The lesson to be learned here is that both types of testing are necessary.

7.5   White-box Testing in the Small

White-box testing is based on the idea of *coverage. Coverage* is a measure of how much of a module or system has been exercised (executed) by a test or series of tests. A simple way to obtain coverage is to make sure every statement in the source code being tested is executed at least once. Unfortunately, this simple approach does not test the logic of the source code. To test the logic, it is useful to think of source code as consisting of *segments, decisions,* and *loops. Segments* are a group of one or more actions that are always executed together, in sequence without any decisions or loops. Examples, in pseudocode, might be:

action1   or   action1
                             action2
                             action3

In Nassi–Shneiderman charts, segments are represented as boxes without decision outcome triangles, for example,

```
action1
```

```
action1
action2
action3
```

In white-box testing of a module, every segment in a module should be covered (executed) at least once.

Decision coverage includes segment coverage, but adds the requirement that each possible outcome from a decision be tested at least once. Thus, an *if-then-else* statement must be tested twice: once with data that cause the *if* to evaluate to *true,* and once with data that cause the *if* to evaluate to *false.* A *case* statement must be tested once for each of the possible *case* outcomes. In some instances, a decision results in no action taking place. For example, when an *if-then* evaluates to *false,* no action is executed. The concept of a *null segment* is useful here. A *null segment* is simply a segment with no actions. The execution of the *false* outcome of an *if-then* statement results in the "execution" of a null segment. Some *case* statements may also include null segments for certain outcomes. In Nassi–Shneiderman charts, null segments are represented as empty boxes.

A final criteria for coverage is *loop coverage.* Because loops contain decisions (see Section 7.5.1), complete segment and decision coverage results in the coverage of loops. However, loops are a common source of errors in programs; they are often executed one too many times or one too few times. To test out loops more completely, then, loop coverage requires that each loop be tested once with data that cause execution of the loop to be skipped completely, once with data that cause the body of the loop to be executed exactly one time, and once with data that cause the body of the loop to be executed more than one time. *Repeat* loops require a slight modification of the loop coverage rules. The actions in the body of a *repeat* loop cannot be skipped. However, *repeats* should be tested with data that cause one pass through the loop, and data that cause more than one pass through the loop. *For* loops with a constant number of repetitions are a special case for loop coverage. Because they are always executed a fixed number of times, they should be treated as simple segments.

7.5.1   Representing Module Structure Using Logic-Flow Diagrams

To really understand the object of white-box testing and to understand the limits of white-box testing, it is helpful to learn about logic-flow diagrams. A logic-flow diagram is a graph of the possible paths of flow of control throughout a module. Every segment in the module is represented as a small circle, a node in the graph. Every decision is also a node in the graph and is represented as a small diamond. The flow of control between segments and decisions is represented by arrows or arcs in the graph. Start and Exit nodes are added for clarity. Note that logic-flow diagrams are *not* flowcharts. Flowcharts are a program design notation and include enough detail to be used in creating source code. Logic-flow diagrams are an abstraction of the logic flow in a piece of source code and hide the details of the code not related to logic flow.

```pascal
procedure FindMean (var Mean: real;  var ScoreFile:  file of real);

{ Procedure which reads in a series of real values from a file, sums the values
and computes their mean.  The mean is computed by dividing the sum of the
scores by the number of scores read in.}

var Score, SumOfScores, NumberOfScores:  real;

begin
    {Initialize SumOfScores and NumberOfScores to zero}
    SumOfScores := 0.0;
    NumberOfScores := 0.0;

    {Read in and sum the scores and count the number of scores}
    while not eof (ScoreFile) do
        begin
            read (ScoreFile, Score);
            if Score > 0.0 then
                begin
                    SumOfScores := SumOfScores + Score;
                    NumberOfScores := NumberOfScores + 1.0
                end;
        end;

    {Compute the mean and print the results.}
    if NumberOfScores > 0.0 then
        begin
            Mean := SumOfScores/NumberOfScores;
            writeln ('The mean score is ', Mean)
        end
    else  writeln ('No scores were entered.')
end;
```

Figure 7.1 Pascal Module to Find the Mean of a Series of Scores

The body of a simple Pascal procedure that computes the mean of a set of scores is shown in Figure 7.1. The Nassi–Shneiderman chart for the procedure is shown in Figure 7.2. It is probably easiest to derive logic-flow diagrams from Nassi–Shneiderman charts, although it can be done directly from code or pseudocode. To begin, each of the segments and decisions in the procedure is assigned a unique, identifying number. The order in which the numbers are assigned does not really matter, but a reasonable convention is to assign the numbers from top to bottom and left to right. Numbers, in circles, have been added to the diagram in Figure 7.2. Notice that the first four executable statements in the procedure form one segment, numbered 1. The *while* statement is a decision — Are there more scores to be read in (*true* or *false*)? — and is assigned number 2. The *if* statement is also a decision and is given the number 3. The two statements that are executed if the *if* condition is *true* form segment 4. No statements are executed if the *if* condition is *false*. Nonetheless, the null segment is numbered with a 5. The same sort of reasoning is used to assign numbers to segments 6, 8, and 9 and to decision 7.

Figure 7.3 shows the logic-flow diagram derived from the Nassi–Shneiderman chart in Figure 7.2. Notice that any segment can only have one arc coming out of

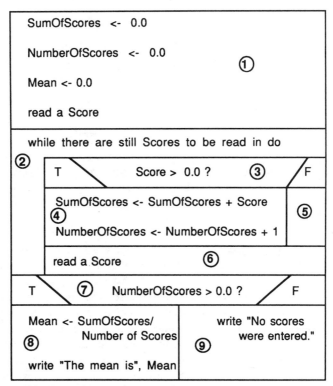

Figure 7.2 Nassi-Shneiderman Chart for the Pascal Procedure in Figure 7.1

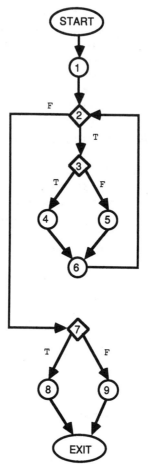

Figure 7.3 Logic-flow Diagram for the Pascal Procedure in
Figure 7.1 and the Nassi-Shneiderman Chart in Figure 7.2

it (for example, segment 1), but can have more than one arc coming into it (for example, segment 6). Decisions have a minimum of two arcs originating from them, one for the *true* path and one for the *false* path. The *true* path is labeled with a capital letter **T**, and the *false* path with an **F**. A *case* statement would have multiple arcs, one for each possible case. The arcs coming from decisions can terminate at segments (for example, the two arcs from decision 3) or can terminate at another decision (for example, the arcs from decision 2).

Figure 7.4 illustrates some special situations that can arise in drawing up logic-flow diagrams. Figure 7.4a shows a *for* loop. When diagrammed in a logic-flow diagram, they are indistinguishable from *while* loops. In Figure 7.4b, a *repeat-until* construct is diagrammed. In *repeat-until* loops the body or segment part of the loop comes before the condition or decision part of the loop; therefore, the node

Program Text	Diagram	Decision Being Tested

(a) for J = 1 to X do
    [Segment 2 actions]
   end {for}

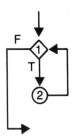

Is J >= 1 and J <= X?

(b) repeat
    [Segment 1 actions]
  until [Condition 2]

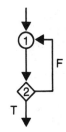

Has Condition 2 been met?

(c) if X > 0 and X < 101 then
    [Segment 3 actions]
  end-if

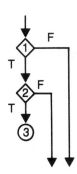

Decision 1: X > 0?
Decision 2: X < 101?

(d) if X > 0 or Y < −1 then
    [Segment 3 actions]
  end-if

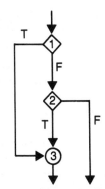

Decision 1: X > 0?
Decision 2: Y < −1?

Figure 7.4 Some Special Cases in Logic-flow Diagramming

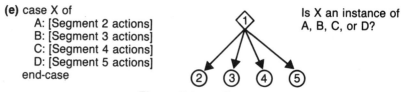

(e) case X of
  A: [Segment 2 actions]
  B: [Segment 3 actions]
  C: [Segment 4 actions]
  D: [Segment 5 actions]
  end-case

Is X an instance of A, B, C, or D?

Figure 7.4 continued

representing the body of the loop must come above the node representing the decision part of the loop in the logic-flow diagram. Figures 7.4c and d illustrate the diagramming of conditional statements that involve compound logical conditions. Figure 7.4c shows the diagram of a condition involving a logical *and*. Notice that each component of the logical statement represents a separate decision. Only if both decisions are *true* is segment 3 executed. In Figure 7.4d, the condition involves a logical *or*. Notice that the labels **T** and **F** on the arcs coming from decision node 1 are not in the typical order. Typically, the *true* arc comes straight down out of a decision arc, and the *false* arc goes to the left or right. With the *or*, however, the labels are reversed. Finally, Figure 7.4e shows the diagram of a *case* or multiway decision structure. The number of nodes below the decision node varies with the particular module being diagrammed. The example diagrammed involves a four-way decision; therefore, four segments are shown below the decision node.

7.5.2 White-box Testing Is Achieved by Covering All Arcs in a Logic-flow Diagram

Once a module has been reduced to a logic-flow diagram, it is easier to see exactly what is meant by achieving coverage during testing. Coverage is achieved by testing the module with sets of data that force flow of control to travel at least once along every arc in the logic-flow diagram. Thus, if the diagram includes at least one decision, a minimum of two test cases will be necessary, one to test the *true* arc and one to test the *false* arc. Most modules will include multiple decisions. Fortunately, the total number of test cases needed to obtain coverage of a module is *not* two times the number of decision nodes. Typically, one test case will pass through multiple decision nodes and thus will cover arcs from more than one decision node.

To see how a set of white-box tests that achieves segment, decision, and loop coverage is constructed, let us return to the FindMean example. Figure 7.5 shows the same logic-flow diagram as Figure 7.3, but lowercase letters have been added to the arcs as aids in the discussion. It is also helpful to refer to the Nassi–Shneiderman chart in Figure 7.2 while constructing the test cases. Beginning at the first node of the logic-flow diagram, node 1, notice that any data given to the system will result in coverage of that node and of arc **a**. Node 2 is a decision: Is there a score to be read in? The diagram shows that we need to find data that will cause arc **b** to be traveled and other data that will cause arc **c** to be traveled. To cause arc **b** to be traveled, the

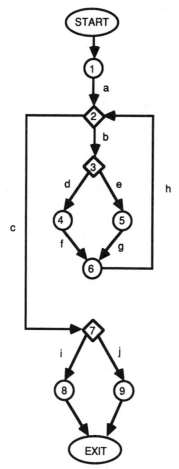

Figure 7.5 Logic-flow Diagram from Figure 7.3 with Labels Added to the Arcs

input data set must contain at least one value. To cause arc **c** to be traveled, the input data set must be empty, either because there were no items to read in or because one or more previous items have been read in and the input file is now empty. For efficiency, we might decide to use a data set of exactly one value, for example, 89.0, to achieve coverage of arcs **b** and **c**. We can note that test case 1 will be 89.0. Node 2 is also a loop as well as a decision, however. Loop coverage requires that we test each loop by skipping the body of the loop altogether one time, by executing it exactly once, and by executing it more than one time. Test case 1 takes care of executing it exactly once. To cause the loop body to be skipped, test case 2 will be a null set of input — an empty data set. To cause the loop body to be executed more than one time, test case 3 will need to include at least two values: for example, 53.41 and −77.0.

Node 3 is a decision: Is the entered score greater than 0.0? To cause both arcs **d** and **e** to be traveled out of node 3, we need one test value greater than 0.0 and one less than 0.0. Looking at the test cases we have already created, we note that test case 3 consists of exactly two such values, one greater than 0.0 and one less than 0.0, so we do not need to create additional test cases to cover these arcs. Node 6 and arc **h** will be covered if either node 4 or 5 is reached. We just saw that test case 3 reaches both nodes 4 and 5, so we need not devise a special test case to cover node 6 and arc **h**.

Node 7 is another decision: Is NumberOfScores greater than 0.0? Node 7 has two arcs, **i** and **j**, that must be covered. To cover arc **i**, a test case must include at least one positive score. Both test cases 1 and 3 meet this requirement. To cover arc **j**, a test case must consist of either no values or a set of nonpositive values. Test case 2 fills this need, because it consists of null input.

These three test cases are all that are necessary to obtain complete coverage of the module, including segment, loop, and decision coverage. Although separate test cases could have been constructed to test each arc in the logic-flow diagram, it is much more efficient to consolidate the test cases into the smallest number possible. The initial testing will take less effort, and each time the module is modified, the time needed to execute the test cases will again be minimized.

7.5.3 Why White-box Testing Cannot Be Complete

It is impossible to completely test a nontrivial module. Now that logic-flow diagrams have been introduced, it will be easier to demonstrate why this is true. On the surface, it would seem to be a reasonable goal for a set of white-box tests to exercise all possible paths through a module. Let us define what is meant by a path. A *path* is a traversal of a logic-flow diagram from the start node to the exit node, following the directed arcs in the diagram. The path is defined by listing the nodes visited during the traversal. As an example, consider the logic-flow diagram in Figure 7.5. One path would be defined by visiting the nodes 1, 2, 7, 8, in order. Another path would consist of visiting nodes 1, 2, 3, 4, 6, 2, 3, 4, 6, 2, 7, 8. In this case the path included two loops through the central *while* loop. Another unique path would be defined by passing through the central loop three times (1, 2, 3, 4, 6, 2, 3, 4, 6, 2, 3, 4, 6, 2, 7, 8). And still another unique path results if the loop were passed through four times. You are probably getting the picture by now. If a logic-flow diagram contains a loop, then an *infinite* number of paths can be defined. If white-box testing demanded that all possible paths be tested, it would never be possible to completely exercise any module containing a loop. As an alternative to complete testing, white-box testing settles for coverage of all segments, decisions, and loops.

7.5.4 Carrying Out White-box Testing

The steps involved in carrying out tests were outlined in Section 7.1 and should be followed in handling white-box testing. Because white-box testing is being used, steps 1 and 2 have already been taken care of. What is being measured by white-box testing is the integrity of the logic flow of the module. The method of white-box testing is to obtain coverage of the module being tested. The remaining steps are:

3. **Develop the test cases.** The next step is to develop the test cases using the techniques discussed. If the code does not exist yet, the Nassi–Shneiderman charts or pseudocode documents drawn up in the detailed design phase can be used as guides in designing the test cases. Logic-flow diagrams do not need to be drawn if you are able to follow the logic flow from the code or the design document and create the correct test cases.

4. **Determine what the expected or correct result of the test should be and create the test oracle.** As the test cases are being developed, the test oracle containing predicted, correct outcomes should also be created.

5. **Execute the test cases.** In most cases, a driver and/or one or more stubs will have to be written to allow the testing of the unit being assessed. Drivers and stubs were discussed in Section 6.2.1. The driver will feed the necessary input to the module being tested and call or activate the module. The driver module will also be responsible for displaying, dumping, or printing out the results of the test when control returns from the module being tested. If the module being tested calls other modules that have not been tested or integrated into the system yet, it is necessary to create stubs to simulate the activities of the called modules.

6. **Compare the results of the test execution to the test oracle.** If a discrepancy is noted, the source of the error must be found and corrected. If the fixes made on the software alter the flow of control in any way, the white-box tests must be reviewed for accuracy and completeness and revised as necessary. The tests are then executed again. Executing test cases again after changes have been made to software is called *regression testing*. The need for regression testing brings out the special need for documenting test cases, creating test oracles, and keeping careful records of the testing process. A lot of effort involved in regression testing can be saved by having the testing information at hand. The entire cycle of testing and fixing is repeated until no new errors are found in regression testing.

A suggested format for documenting white-box testing is given in Figure 7.6. One sheet containing the printed information in Figure 7.6 is created for each module in the system. When the white-box test cases are initially designed, they can be entered on the sheet by hand. Notice that the heading contains the name of the module and the module ID as they are given in the module header created during detailed design. The module ID, if you recall, relates the module to its location in the system structure chart. The module's author and the name of the tester should also be noted. The rest of the top two-thirds of the sheet contains a grid with three major columns. The first column will be filled out with one label for each of the decisions or loops in the module, for example, "if A>B" or "case MemberType" or "while not eof." The second column, headed Possible Out-

Module name _____   Module ID _____

Author _____   Tester _____

Decision or Loop	Possible Outcomes	Test Cases											
		1	2	3	4	5	6	7	8	9	10	11	12

Test Cases:

Case #	Values	Expected Outcome	Actual Outcome
1.			
2.			
3.			
4.			
5.			

Figure 7.6 Suggested Format for a White-box Test Worksheet

comes, will contain a list of the possible outcomes for each decision. For example, if the decision being tested is an *if*, then two possible outcomes exist: *true* and *false*. With a *case* decision, the number of possible outcomes matches the number of cases. If a loop is being tested, possible outcomes include those specified for loop coverage: skip, execute exactly once, and execute more than once. Once each possible outcome has been listed for a decision or loop, it is convenient to draw a heavy horizontal line completely across the grid to separate the information associated with one decision or loop from others. The last major column represents the coverage obtained by the test cases. Each subcolumn represents one test case. A check is made in each cell in the column that corresponds to a decision path covered by that particular test case. Remember that a test case originally created to cover one path of a decision may cover paths of other decisions as well.

The bottom third of the white-box test worksheet contains the actual test cases (data) to be used in testing the module. Notes concerning the dates of test runs and their results can also be made in this space. Figure 7.7 shows a white-box test worksheet filled out for the FindMean example.

Module name _Find Mean_   Module ID _B.17_
Author _Frieda Falcon_   Tester _I. N. Quisition_

Decision or Loop	Possible Outcomes	Test Cases											
		1	2	3	4	5	6	7	8	9	10	11	12
while not eof	skip		✓										
	once	✓											
	> 1			✓									
if Score > 0	T	✓											
	F			✓									
if NumberOf- Scores > 0.0	T	✓		✓									
	F		✓										

Test Cases:

Case #	Values	Expected Outcome	Actual Outcome
1.	89.0 <eof>	Mean = 89.0	
2.	<eof>	"No scores were entered."	
3.	53.41, -77.0, <eof>	Mean = 53.41	
4.			
5.			

Figure 7.7 Example of a Filled-in White-box Test Worksheet

7.6   Black-box Testing in the Small

Black-box testing focuses on the most important aspect of a module: how well the module meets its requirements. Black-box testing is *functional* testing. Does the module perform the functions it was intended to perform as stated in the requirements? In black-box testing, the module is looked at from the outside. The basic approach is to focus on the input to and output from the module, with an eye toward the functions that are to be carried out by the module.

When unit testing, extensive black-box testing is necessary only for those modules that receive raw or unedited input from outside the system. This is because the black-box testing of single modules that do not involve the processing of raw input is typically redundant with the white-box tests. However, the noninput modules should be checked to ensure that no black-box tests have been skipped by the white-box tests. To do this, begin with the requirements for the module. The test cases should cover each possible input and output. For example, have all the parameters, either import or export, been exercised at least once? Have all the different output options (for example, one, two, or three copies of some report) been exercised? If not, appropriate test cases should be created.

Black-box tests are created using the technique of *equivalence partitioning*. To use equivalence partitioning, every input condition specified is divided into a number of *equivalence classes*. Each equivalence class consists of a class or set of data items all of which are similar to each other on some relevant dimension. To create test cases, test data are chosen that include at least one piece of data from each equivalence class. When these test cases are executed, it is assumed that, if the module performs correctly on the test item from a particular equivalence class, the module will perform correctly for any other item from the same equivalence class. The goal of equivalence partitioning is to reduce the number of necessary test cases to a manageable number. For example, if a module is supposed to accept a negative number as input, equivalence partitioning assumes that testing one negative number is logically just as good as testing 10 or 20 or 1000 negative numbers.

Unfortunately, there are no rules for deciding what all the appropriate equivalence classes are. However, some guidelines can be followed. Looking at examples is also very instructive. Here are two guidelines:

> *If an input is supposed to be valid across a range of values, there are a minimum of three equivalence classes: one below the range, one within the range, and one above the range.*

For example, in the public television membership system example, suppose AmountOfContribution had been specified as being a value from $0.01 to $99,999.99. The three equivalence classes are:

1. Values from $0.01 to $99,999.99 (valid)

2. Values less than $0.01 (invalid)

3. Values greater than $99,999.99 (invalid)

If an input is valid only if it is a value from a set of discrete or nominal values, there are two equivalence classes: one class consisting of the valid, discrete values, and another class consisting of any other input values.

Using the public television example again, suppose Member-Status were to be input into some module. The two equivalence classes are:

1. Values from the set of Member-Status values, that is, Regular, Student/Retiree, or StudioClub (valid)
2. All other input (invalid)

As a more extensive example, consider a module that is designed to accept the name of a grocery item and a list of the different sizes the item comes in, specified in ounces. The specifications state that the item name is to be alphabetic characters 2 to 15 characters in length. Each size may be a value in the range of 1 to 48, whole numbers only. The sizes are to be entered in ascending order (smaller sizes first). A maximum of five sizes may be entered for the item. The item name is to be entered first, followed by a comma, then followed by the list of sizes. A comma will be used to separate each size. Spaces (blanks) are to be ignored anywhere in the input.

(Note that the design of the human interface being described here is poor and is *not* a recommended model for input format. The use of commas to separate the items is inconvenient and not very natural to the user. Separating the items with one or more blanks would be better. An alternate strategy would be to use a form-driven format, with each entry terminated by a carriage return. A double carriage return could signal the end of the list. Finally, there is no compelling reason to have the user enter the weights in ascending order. This can only lead to frustration and errors on the user's part. If there is one thing computer scientists know how to do, it is sorting! Why not let the computer do the dirty work?)

To create the black-box test cases, the specifications given are examined phrase by phrase. Starting with the name of the grocery item, we see that it is to be alphabetic characters. Thus there are two equivalence classes for this dimension of the input:

1. Item name alphabetic (valid): AbcDef
2. Item name not alphabetic (invalid): A2X?/

In addition, the item name is to be 2 to 15 characters in length. There are three equivalence classes for the length dimension:

3. Item name less than 2 characters in length (invalid): A
4. Item name 2 to 15 characters in length (valid): AbcDef
5. Item name greater than 15 characters in length (invalid): abcdefghijklmnopqrstuvwxyz

Each size is to be a value in the range 1 to 48 and is to be a whole number. There are some hidden dimensions here. The range of the value is important, but it must also be a whole number (no fractions or decimals) and must contain only numeric characters. Thus a total of seven equivalence classes emerges, as follows:

6. Values less than 1 (invalid): −1

7. Values in the range 1 to 48 (valid): 24

8. Values greater than 48 (invalid): 127

9. Whole number values (valid): 24

10. Fractional values (invalid): 5.3 or 7 1/2

11. Numeric characters (valid): 24

12. Nonnumeric characters (invalid): 5%

Notice that the sample test item for the three valid dimensions is the same for every partition. This will make it easy to test the valid cases. Notice, too, that classes 6 and 10 are actually covered by the broader dimension, number 12, because a minus sign, a decimal point, and a / are all nonnumeric. In the final set of test cases, just the broader dimension of nonnumeric characters can be used. Nonetheless, it is a good idea to be as complete as possible in initially listing the classes to be tested.

The sizes are to be entered in ascending order. There are two equivalence classes for this dimension:

13. Items in ascending order (valid): 1, 2, 3

14. Items in nonascending order (invalid): 2, 1, 3

A maximum of five sizes may be listed. A minimum of one size is implied, producing three classes:

15. No size entered (invalid)

16. One to five sizes entered (valid): 1, 2, 3

17. More than five sizes entered (invalid): 1, 2, 3, 4, 5, 6

The item name is to be entered first, followed by the list of sizes. There are two classes to cover this dimension:

18. Item name is first (valid): AbcDef, 1, 2, 3

19. Item name is not first (invalid): 1, AbcDef, 2, 3

The item name is to be followed by a comma, and each size is to be followed by a comma. The following equivalence classes result:

20. A single comma separates each entry in the list (valid): AbcDef, 1, 2, 3

21. A comma does not separate two or more entries in the list (invalid): XYZ 1, 2, 3

Finally, blanks are to be ignored anywhere in the input. An "invalid" dimension cannot be created for this partition, but two alternate test cases can be produced:

22. The entry contains no blanks (valid): AbcDef,1,2,3

23. The entry contains blanks (valid): A bcDef, 1, 2, 3

Once all the classes to be tested have been listed, the actual test cases to be used in the black-box testing can be created. With a little careful planning, many of the dimensions can be covered simultaneously with a single test case.

Before compiling a final list of test cases for the example, there is one more guideline to be considered. This guideline is *boundary testing*. Experience has shown that data from the boundaries or edges of dimension ranges are more likely to turn up errors than data from the middle of the range. *Boundary testing* says that one test value should be taken from just below (or above) a boundary and another from just on the boundary. Dimensions indicated by equivalence classes 4, 7, and 16 should each be tested at both their lower and upper boundaries. For example, each size is to be in the range of whole numbers from 1 to 48. The boundaries of this range, 1 and 48, should each be tested. In addition, a value just below the range, 0, and a value just above the range, 49, should also be tested. Table 7.1 lists the complete set of dimensions discovered in the input specifications. Table 7.2 shows the final set of test cases created from the 23 dimensions, including the boundary test cases. Study each test case and the classes covered to make sure you understand how they were derived.

An added advantage to designing black-box tests is that they often make it clear that the module to be tested has not been completely and thoroughly specified. For example, it is common for the specification to neglect to state the range or size of acceptable values. It may be specified that valid input is "any integer." Unfortunately, most programming languages will not accept just any integer. On microcomputers, for example, integers may be limited to the range of $-32,768$ to $+32,767$. Similarly, the specifications may state or imply that strings of any length may be input. Again, some languages have a built-in length limitation (for example, 256 characters). If such missing specifications are discovered, they should be discussed with the designer of the module, and possibly even with the sponsor. The module may need to be redesigned and/or recoded before the final set of black-box tests can be derived.

7.6.1 Why Black-box Testing Cannot Be Complete

Now that you are familiar with the techniques of black-box testing, you will be able to readily understand why black-box testing cannot be complete. One way that black-box testing could be complete would be to test all possible input values to a certain module. As a simple example, suppose a module is designed to accept alphabetic strings that are three characters long. Only capital letters are valid in the input string. This means there are 26 times 26 times 26 or 17,576 valid test cases. How about the invalid cases? There are a total of 128 standard, valid ASCII

Table 7.1 Complete List of Numbered Equivalence Classes for the Grocery Items Example

1. Item name is alphabetic (valid)
2. Item name is not alphabetic (invalid)
3. Item name is less than 2 characters in length (invalid)
4. Item name is 2 to 15 characters in length (valid)
5. Item name is greater than 15 characters in length (invalid)
6. Size value is less than 1 (invalid)
7. Size value is in the range 1 to 48 (valid)
8. Size value is greater than 48 (invalid)
9. Size value is a whole number in range 1 to 48 (valid)
10. Size value is a fraction (invalid)
11. Size value is numeric (valid)
12. Size value includes nonnumeric characters (invalid)
13. Size values entered in ascending order (valid)
14. Size values entered in nonascending order (invalid)
15. No size values entered (invalid)
16. One to five sizes entered (valid)
17. More than five sizes entered (invalid)
18. Item name is first (valid)
19. Item name is not first (invalid)
20. A single comma separates each entry in list (valid)
21. A comma does not separate two or more entries in the list (invalid)
22. The entry contains no blanks (valid)
23. The entry contains blanks (valid)

characters. If the module were to run on a machine that used ASCII code for characters, there would be 102 times 102 times 102 or 1,061,208 invalid, three-character sequences to test. Then there are 128 one-character invalid test cases, plus 16,384 two-character invalid sequences to test plus 2.68×10^8 four-character invalid sequences, and so on and on and on. Time, money, and patience would run out long before these tests could be run. Equivalence partitioning is a much more reasonable alternative.

7.6.2 Carrying Out the Unit Black-box Tests

Just as was the case with white-box testing, test harnesses in the form of drivers or stub modules may have to be written to allow the tester to exercise modules for the purpose of black-box testing. The driver module will call the module and may be responsible for dumping or printing out the results of the test cases. If the mod-

Table 7.2 Final Set of Black-box Test Cases for the Grocery Item Example, Based on the Equivalence Classes Shown in Table 7.1

Test Case	Expected Outcome	Classes Covered*
a. Xy, 1	Valid	1, 4(LB), 7(LB), 9, 11, 13, 16(LB), 18, 20, 22
b. AbcDefghijklmno, 1, 2, 3 , 4, 48	Valid	1, 4(UB), 7(LB), 7(UB), 9, 11, 13, 16(UB), 18, 20, 23
c. A2x?, 1	Invalid	2
d. A, 1	Invalid	3
e. abcdefghijklmnop	Invalid	5
f. Xy, -1.5	Invalid	6, 10, 12
g. Xy, 0	Invalid	7 (BB)
h. Xy, 49	Invalid	8, 7 (AB)
i. Xy, 2, 1, 3, 4, 5	Invalid	14
j. Xy	Invalid	15
k. Xy, 1, 2, 3, 4, 5, 6	Invalid	17
l. 1, Xy, 2, 3, 4, 5	Invalid	19
m. Xy 1, 2, 3, 4, 5	Invalid	21

*LB = tests the lower boundary of the dimension indicated
 UB = tests the upper boundary of the dimension indicated
 BB = tests just below the boundary of the dimension
 AB = tests just above the boundary of the dimension

ule being tested calls other modules, stubs may have to be created. The test cases, along with predicted outcomes, should be completely recorded before testing begins. A format such as those in Tables 7.1 and 7.2 could be used. A heading could be added that includes the name of the module, the module ID, the author's name, and the name of the tester. After the tests are carried out, the results should be carefully compared to the test oracle. Any errors should be noted and repaired and the tests rerun, as necessary, until no new errors are found. A record of the testing activities should be kept with the sheet listing the tests and the predicted outcomes.

7.7 Testing in the Small: Data-structure-based Testing

A final type of testing in the small is data-structure-based testing. The development of data-structure-based tests involves looking at the data structures used by the module with an eye toward errors that might be related to the structure being used. For example, if an array or linked list of values is being passed to the module being tested, four test cases should be designed to properly exercise the module, based on the number of elements in the array, as follows:

1. Zero elements in the array or list (an empty array or list)
2. Exactly one element in the array or list
3. One less than the maximum number of elements in the array or list as given in specifications
4. Maximum number of elements in the array or list

Notice that these tests involve the same philosophy as boundary testing. Similar tests can be developed by looking at the structure of files, including fields within each record and total records in the file. Whatever the data structure being used (multidimensional array, queue, stack, graph, etc.), it should be examined and suitable tests developed. Data-structure-based tests are generated by treating the data structures as though they were white boxes. However, the tests developed in this manner should be carefully compared to the specifications for the module being tested. Any discrepancies between the design of the data structures and the module specifications should be noted as errors and corrected.

A table summarizing the steps involved in unit testing is presented in Table 7.3.

Table 7.3 Summary of the Steps Involved in Unit Testing

1. Begin creating the unit tests when the detailed design has been completed.
2. Working from the detailed design (pseudocode or Nassi–Shneiderman chart), draw the logic-flow diagram of the module. Check the diagram for any obvious errors (e.g., unreachable code).
3. Create the white-box tests based on the logic-flow diagram.
4. Create the black-box tests based on the requirements for the module.
5. Create the data-structure-based tests.
6. Cross-check the white-box, black-box, and data-structure-based tests to eliminate duplicate test cases.
7. Expand the detailed design into source code. Desk check the source code.
8. Compile the source code. Informally test the module and clean up any discovered errors. Revise the black-box and white-box test cases, if necessary, based on changes made in the structure or design of the module.
9. Create any test harness needed to execute the unit tests.
10. Execute the black-box, white-box, and data-structure-based tests. Check the results against the test oracle.
11. Make any necessary changes and do regression testing.
12. Maintain records of the testing activities.

7.8   Problem of Error-prone Modules

A surprising fact has emerged from records kept concerning the location and distribution of errors in systems. If a fixed amount of unit testing has been carried out on some set of modules, then presumably a distribution of errors will occur across the modules tested. That is, in some of the tested modules only a few errors will have been found. In other modules, many errors will have been found, and still other modules will be somewhere in between. The number of errors found will vary from module to module. Now, if more testing is carried out, a surprising effect is noted. The modules that were shown to have many errors in them in the first round of tests will probably be shown to have many more errors. Conversely, the modules that had few detected errors in the first round of tests will probably have few detected errors in the second round of tests (Myers, 1979). This relationship is graphed in Figure 7.8. The horizontal axis is the number of errors that have been found in some module to date. The vertical axis is the probability that additional errors will be discovered in that module.

There is an important lesson to be gained from understanding this relationship: if a module gives indications of being error prone, it cannot be tested into being an error-free module. The best idea is to scrap the module and start over. Make sure the design of the module meets the specifications. Review the design of the module and redesign it, as necessary. Perhaps two or three modules are needed to handle the functions of the error-prone module. Have a different programmer code and test the redesigned module or modules. The old adage "You cannot make a silk purse out of a sow's ear" applies well here. If you discover a module that is a

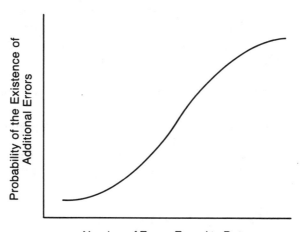

Figure 7.8 Probability of Additional Errors Given the Number of Errors Found So Far (Adapted with permission from G. J. Myers, *Software Reliability: Principles and Practice*. New York: John Wiley & Sons, Inc., 1976, p. 193)

sow's ear, it is better to pay the price and exchange it immediately for a silk purse than it is to try to transform it.

7.9   Testing in the Large

Testing in the large refers to the testing of groups of modules, up to and including the entire system. The first level of testing in the large is *integration testing*. Integration testing begins by testing small groups of modules and ends with the testing of the entire system. Integration testing has two broad purposes: (1) to test the interfacing and integration of the modules in the system, and (2) to test the functional performance of the system. *Acceptance testing* is the second level of testing in the large. In acceptance testing, the sponsor tests the entire system. The goal of acceptance testing is to make sure the system meets the sponsor's requirements.

7.9.1   Testing in the Large: Integration Testing

In Chapter 6, various integration strategies were discussed. Of the strategies covered, the preferred integration strategy was the threads approach. In the threads approach, modules are selected for coding according to the function they perform. The goal is to select a minimal group of modules that performs some basic function and thus forms a subsystem or thread. Typically, this group will include modules from different levels of the system structure chart, and a diagram of the modules being coded takes the form of a small tree. Once the subsystem has been coded and tested, additional modules can be added to it in an incremental way.

Both unit testing and integration testing are natural parts of the threads integration approach. As the individual modules are coded, unit testing is performed on them. No module should be integrated into a subsystem until it has been thoroughly unit tested. As soon as the individual modules from a thread have all been coded and tested, they can be integrated. The modules should then be tested in an informal way to get the basic function of the thread running. The next phase is to begin formal integration testing.

Integration testing includes four sorts of tests: *structure tests, functional tests, performance tests,* and *stress tests.*

The approach taken in *structure testing* is essentially the same as the white-box approach used for unit testing. The tests exercise the logic of the integrated modules, including:

- Exercising all input and output parameters of each module
- Exercising all modules and all calls, including calls to utility routines (if any)

Just as white-box unit testing covers all paths in the logic-flow diagram of a module, structure testing covers all paths in the structure chart and calling graph of the subsystem or the system. Specifically, coverage is obtained if every module is called at least once and if every called module is called by all possible callers.

One way of building structure test cases that achieve coverage is through the use of *transaction-flow diagrams*. A *transaction* is the set of activities associated with a particular class of input. These activities include the processing of the input and any output produced. A transaction-flow diagram is a diagram representing the sequence of steps or activities associated with the processing of the transaction. The diagram shows what happens to the input functionally and does not show details of the logical processing. A list or diagram of the modules called during the processing of the transaction, in the order in which they are called, is one way to create a transaction-flow diagram. In simple cases, a transaction-flow diagram might look like a subtree of the system structure chart. In other cases, many more nodes would be included in the diagram, as some modules are called repeatedly. As an alternate format, a table showing a list of calls might be used. To achieve coverage of the subsystem being tested, a series of transaction test cases are created, which, taken together, exercise all the input and output parameters of each module and exercise all modules and all calls.

As an example of the use of transaction-flow diagrams, consider the costume shop system partially diagrammed in Figure 7.9. The costume shop system is an on-line system for handling various bookkeeping duties for a university costume shop. The costume shop is in charge of building costumes for theatrical and musical productions at the university. In addition, it maintains and stores a warehouse of costumes. The warehoused costumes can be used in theater productions or can

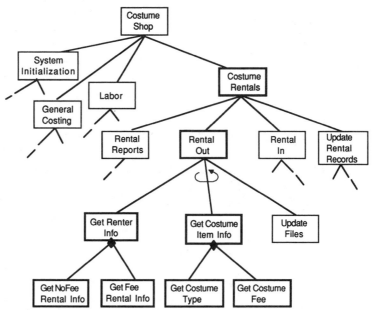

Figure 7.9 Partial Structure Chart for the Costume Shop System

be rented by other colleges and universities or by private individuals. The costume shop must keep track of costs involved in building and maintaining the costumes, the labor costs for running the costume shop, and the numerous details associated with renting out the costumes. Reports and summaries must be made available at various time intervals. The portion of the system shown in Figure 7.9 is the portion related to costume rental activities.

Suppose the integration plan called for the modules related to the activities of checking out a rental costume to be coded first. These modules are shown with darkened outlines in Figure 7.9. A brief description of the functions of these modules is given in Table 7.4. Assume these modules have been coded and unit tested. To create structure tests for these modules, we derive a series of transactions that exercise all the modules, all calls, and all input and output parameters of each module. In creating the tests, it is useful to keep in mind the lessons learned in

Table 7.4 List of the Coded Modules and Their Functions from the Costume Shop System Example in Figure 7.9

Module ID	Module Name	Description
IV	Costume Rentals	Displays a menu asking the user to choose among Rental Costume Out, Rental Costume In, Update Rental Information, or Create Rental Reports options.
IV.B	Rental Out	Controls activities associated with checking out a costume. Calls Get-Renter-Info. As a costume may consist of several items, repeatedly calls Get-Costume-Item-Info until all items are entered.
IV.B.1	Get Renter Info	Uses form fill-in interface to allow user to enter renter information. Some information varies if the rental involves fees or not. Therefore, calls either Get-No-Fee-Rental-Info or Get-Fee-Rental-Info.
IV.B.1.1	Get No Fee Rental Info	Uses form fill-in to get information pertinent to no-fee rentals.
IV.B.1.2	Get Fee Rental Info	Uses form fill-in to get information on fee rentals.
IV.B.2	Get Costume Item Info	Gets Item#, ItemName, Condition, and Remarks from user. Calls Get-Costume-Type and, optionally, Get-Costume-Fee.
IV.B.2.1	Get Costume Type	Uses a menu to allow a user to enter the type of costume being rented.
IV.B.2.2	Get Costume Fee	Uses a menu to allow the user to select the appropriate fee category for the costume item being rented.

creating unit tests. Specifically, the ideas of decision coverage and loop coverage apply at the intermodule level as well as at the intramodule level. To begin, we might derive a transaction that involves a nonfee renter renting a costume consisting of one item, test case 1. This transaction involves calling all but two of the newly integrated modules. The two modules that would not be called are the Get-Fee-Rental-Info module and the Get-Costume-Fee module. Another test involving a fee for the rental will also be needed, test case 2. These two tests taken together will cover both arcs of both of the decisions indicated on the structure chart (the choice of calls coming from the Get-Renter-Info module and from the Get-Costume-Item-Info module.) Notice that the Get-Costume-Item-Info module involves iteration, as indicated by the curved arrow surrounding the arc leading to it. It may be called multiple times. Following the ideas of loop coverage, one test should involve skipping the call, one test should call the module exactly once, and one test should involve more than one call to the module. In this design, the iteration is a *repeat..until* structure, and it is not possible to skip the call completely. Test case 1 involves exactly one call to Get-Costume-Item-Info, so test case 2 should involve more than one call. We will make the transaction for test case 2 involve renting three costume items, invoking three separate calls to Get-Costume-Item-Info.

To document the tests and create a transaction-flow diagram, a format such as that shown in Figure 7.10 can be used. The form includes five columns. The first two columns describe the test case. The first column lists the name of all modules that should be called or returned to during the execution of the test case, in the exact order they are called or returned to. The second column indicates the input or user action that is to take place while each module is active. The next two columns are the test oracle. They predict the effects the test case will have on the data structures in the system and any output that should occur. The final column is used to indicate the actual results of running the test case. If the actual results match the test oracle, checkmarks can be entered in this column. If the results do not match, notes concerning the problem can be made. Figure 7.10 has been filled out with test case 1 for the costume shop example.

Notice that to run test cases 1 and 2 will require the writing of a driver to call Handle-Costume-Rentals and a stub for Update Files. The Update Files stub can be used to show what values the affected data structures have after the test case is executed.

Functional testing is the second sort of integration testing. The goal of functional testing is to demonstrate that all the functions specified for the system in the requirements and specification document are operational. Just as structure testing in the large parallels white-box unit testing, functional testing parallels black-box unit testing. In functional testing, an integrated subsystem or the entire system is treated as a black box. No knowledge of the internal, logical structure of the system is used in designing the test cases. Instead, the tests are best designed by working from the user manual. The same principles and guidelines that apply to the generation of unit black-box tests apply to the generation of system functional tests. However, instead of focusing on a single module, functional testing focuses

Subsystem: ___Rental-Out Modules___   Test Case #: ___1___
Tester: ___   Date: ___

Name of Module Called or Returned To	Input or User Action	Expected Effects on Data Structures	Expected Output	Test Run Results
Handle Costume Rental	User selects "Rental Costume Out"	None	Display of Rental Menu	
Rental Out	User selects "Non-fee Rental"	None	Display of Fee/NoFee Menu	
Get No Fee Rental Info	User enters- Renter Name: Frieda Falcon Organization: Athletic Department Campus Address: Hayes Hall SS#: 415-74-8857 DateOut: 3/27/90 ExpectedDateIn: 4/2/90 Puller: M. Lintner	Fields in NewRenterRecord become: RenterName <- Frieda Falcon Organization <- Athletic Dept. CampusAddress <- Hayes Hall SS# <-415-74-8857 DateOut <-3/27/90 ExpectedDateIn <-4/2/90 Puller <- M. Lintner	Echo-print of data entered by user	
Rental Out	(none)	None		
Get Costume Item Info	User enters- Item#: X319 Item Name: leghorn hat Condition: good Remarks: (none)	Fields in NextCostumeItem record become: Item# <-X319 ItemName <- leghorn hat Condition <- good Remarks <- none	Echo-print of data entered by user	
Get Costume Type	User selects "Period" type	NextCostumeItem.Type <- Period	Display of Costume-type Menu	
Rental Out	User selects "No more costume items to be entered"		Display of More-Items? Menu	
Handle Costume Rental	User selects "Return to Main Menu"		Display of Rental Menu	

Figure 7.10 Transaction-flow Form for Structure Testing of the Rental-Out Thread of the Costume Shop System

on the functions of subsystems of the system (threads) or the entire system. This implies that the system must be tested to ensure that all classes of valid input are accepted, all classes of invalid input are rejected, and all functions operate correctly.

Although some test cases developed during unit testing may be used again during functional testing, many new cases will have to be developed. Because a subsystem or the whole system is being tested, many test cases will be quite large and may even require several pages to specify. The designing of test cases for functional testing can be organized around the requirements or around key functions. In either case, the idea of test cases based on transactions is useful for functional tests as well as for structure tests. However, in the case of functional tests, no predictions need be made concerning which modules will be activated. Only the input and output need be specified in the test case design and test oracle. The transactions that are created should include a variety of typical ones as well as atypical transactions. Both valid and invalid transactions should be included. See Figure 7.14 for a sample functional test case. The example is taken from the Tabulate-Costs thread of the Rev-Pro case study.

An excellent source of black-box tests is the decision tables, if any, that were created during system analysis. Decision tables partition the input into unique classes and specify the outcomes that are to be associated with each class. Each column of a decision table should be used as a basis for one test case. As an example, consider the decision table shown in Figure 7.11 (taken from Figure 2.8), which diagrams a simple billing system. The output from the system is determined by two pieces of information: whether a payment was made or not and whether a balance is owed or not. There are four different combinations of outcomes based on the information given. In testing this system, separate functional test cases should be created to exercise each of these four outcomes.

In addition to structure and functional tests, integration testing involves *stress tests*. Stress testing involves pushing an integration unit to its limits. Testing the load the integration unit can handle is one type of stress test. If the unit is supposed to handle 1,000 items, try it out with 1,000 items. Test it out with 1,001 items, too. The unit should handle an overload gracefully (without crashing). For example, suppose the costume shop has set a limit of ten costume items per customer. A test should be designed in which exactly ten costume items are entered, and another test should attempt to enter eleven items. Check the system's response to large volume. What happens when data structures, such as files, are filled to their capacity? Does the system handle attempts to overload it in a reasonable manner? Integration testing also includes *performance tests*. Performance tests assess the amount of execution time spent carrying out different functions. Does the subsystem or system handle typical cases in a timely fashion? If the system is faced with an unusual load, does it handle it in a reasonable amount of time? If not, perhaps the efficiency of one or more of the modules needs to be reconsidered.

All these types of tests used for integration testing should be designed with the goal of trying to break the unit. Do not always use typical transactions or average

Payment	Made	X	X		
	Not Made			X	X
Balance Owed	Yes	X		X	
	No		X		X
Send Receipt		O	O		
Send Bill		O		O	
Send Flyer			O		O

Figure 7.11 Decision Table for a Simple Billing System

loads. Try unusual orders of performing tasks. See if the system will allow unusual orders when the order does not matter and if it will block the performance of out-of-sequence tasks when the order does matter. Perhaps you have seen television advertisements that show products being subjected to tests. There are, for example, ads in which watches are dropped from airplanes, luggage is thrown about by gorillas, and trucks are dropped from cranes onto the ground 20 feet below. Try to keep this sort of approach in mind when designing integration tests. What is the most fiendish, abusive thing you can think of to do to the system? Try it out. Then gloat if the system bombs. You have been successful!

Table 7.5 summarizes the steps involved in integration testing. Note that the steps involved in documenting the testing are not included in this figure. The documentation of integration testing will be discussed next.

7.9.2 Documenting Integration Testing

A large part of integration testing is based either directly or indirectly on the requirements and specification. One approach to designing integration test cases is to work directly from the requirements and specification. Another approach is to work from the user manual. The user manual is the user's gateway to the functions of the system. If the system has a function that is not documented in the manual, the user will probably never know it exists. If the user manual describes a function that is not actually present in the system, that lack will surely be discovered. In a

Table 7.5 Summary of the Steps Involved in Integration Testing

1. Based on the integration plan, select a subsystem to be implemented. Code and unit test all the modules in the subsystem.

2. Put the modules in the subsystem together and do any preliminary fix-up necessary to make the unit functional.

3. Do structural testing. Test the integration of the subsystem by exercising all input and output parameters of each module and by exercising all modules and calls. One approach is to use a series of transaction tests that obtain interface coverage and include decision and loop coverage at the call level.

4. Do functional testing. Use test cases developed from the user's guide. One approach is to create a series of transactions that exercise all the functions of the system. Both typical and atypical transactions should be used. Test to see that all classes of valid input are accepted and all classes of invalid input are gracefully rejected.

5. Execute performance and stress tests. Test the load and response times of the subsystem.

6. Make it the primary goal of the tests to attempt to break the subsystem. Remember that successful testing is testing that discovers errors. Unsuccessful tests are those that discover no errors.

7. Keep records of the test cases and the testing activities.

8. Based on the integration plan, integrate the next set of modules and repeat steps 2 to 7.

sense, the user manual rewrites the requirements, showing the user how the system embodies the requirements. It makes sense to design test cases based on the user's view of the system—from the user manual.

The requirements and specification is the first document produced in the development life cycle. The user interface design and the user manual are the second set of documents developed. It is recommended that the integration tests be designed as soon as possible after the completion of these two key documents. This may seem somewhat surprising at first. However, there are several reasons why integration test development should start so soon. First, the effort involved in producing the integration tests is large and should not be put off until the tests are needed. Second, by having the integration tests designed early, an estimate can be made of the effort that will be involved in executing them. A more realistic estimate can be made of the time to allow in the development schedule for the integration testing activities. Finally, and perhaps most importantly, the integration tests can be used as a check of the completeness and accuracy of the requirements by both the developer and the sponsor. The proposed integration tests help to pinpoint exactly what the proposed system will and will not be capable of doing. Issues of error handling and default are highlighted. They also bring quality and performance issues to the foreground. The developers are forced to ask themselves what will happen to the system under unusually large loads or under stressful situations. In addition, the integration tests can form the basis of the acceptance tests. Acceptance tests are tests that are carried out by the sponsor and, if passed, indicate that the sponsor finds the operation of the system acceptable. In other words, the criteria that the sponsor feels the system should meet should be spelled out in both the acceptance tests and integration tests.

Integration tests should be thoroughly documented. As the tests are designed, they should be organized and labeled in some way. Hetzel (1988) suggests using test folios organized around specific requirements or key functions. Each folio contains an identification for the test case or group of test cases included in the folio. The objectives of the test should also be included, along with the test data and the expected results. As the tests are executed, information concerning the actual results of the execution and subsequent activities (for example, fixes or changes in the design) should be noted. The results of the tests can be actual printouts from the system. Each folio, then, becomes a historical record and can be extremely useful when tracing the history and source of a bug or when modifications to the system are undertaken.

In a student project it may not be possible to create the integration tests as soon as the requirements and specification and the user manual are complete. The location of this chapter on testing in the book reflects this fact. In most cases, the integration tests will be developed in parallel to implementation.

7.9.3   Testing in the Large: Acceptance Testing

The purpose of acceptance testing is to demonstrate that a system is ready for operational use. Normally, the acceptance test is performed by the sponsor or by the sponsor's agent and not by the developer. Acceptance testing commences when the developers are confident that the system is ready to be used. It is *not* a good idea to give the sponsor a system the developer knows has problems with the idea that the problems will be ironed out as they are discovered. In such a situation, the sponsor is bound to be very dissatisfied with the system. Two facts about software development suggest this is a bad strategy. First, even well-written unit-tested software has error rates in the range of 2 to 5 percent, based on lines of code (Beizer, 1984). In other words, for every 100 lines of executable source code in a system, there will be two to five errors discovered. Second, the majority (around 50 percent) of all errors in software is typically found by the sponsor after the system is in use, not by the developers and testers. These facts make it obvious that developers start out with the odds of giving the sponsor a quality system decidedly against them. The sponsor will certainly have enough errors to handle even if they are given a thoroughly tested system. Why make the sponsor even more unhappy by delivering a poorly tested system?

The choice of tests to be used in acceptance testing should be made by the sponsor. The sponsor, however, should have expert help in choosing the tests. If a good job was done in reviewing the requirements for the system, the acceptance tests can be developed from them. The user manual should be the main source of acceptance tests. In fact, most of the acceptance tests can be taken from the integration tests. The major difference is that the tests will be executed in the sponsor's environment. The actual software, hardware, personnel, and procedures that the system was designed to work with are used. One typical approach is to use data that have already been processed under the old system (possibly a manual system) as test data for the new system. The results from the new system can be compared to the results from the old system and repairs made as necessary. Another typical approach is to use the old and new systems in parallel for a certain amount of time. Again, output from the two systems can be compared. Performance and stress tests should also be carried out during acceptance testing. (See Section 8.9 for a discussion of system delivery and installation.)

When software is being developed for distribution to a number of customers rather than a single sponsor, an approach commonly used in acceptance testing is *alpha* and *beta testing*. In *alpha testing,* the sponsor or selected sponsors use the software at the developer's site. The software is used in a controlled setting, with the developers on hand to monitor errors and problems the user has. *Beta tests* are conducted at one or more customer sites. The developer is not present, and the software is used in its target setting. The customer must record all problems that are encountered and report them to the developer. The developer modifies the software, conducts additional tests, and finally releases the software to the customers. The advantages of using alpha and beta testing are that the software gets a realistic workout by actual potential users of the system, and the software is tried out in its target environment. Users are always able to find errors that systematic testing has missed. A disadvantage of this approach is that potential customers for the software may be discouraged from buying the software if the testing turns up too many errors. The developers must make sure that the version released for alpha or beta testing has been reasonably well tested.

7.10   Case Study: Testing the Rev-Pro System

Members of the Rev-Pro project team had been assigned to code and develop different threads of the system. Each coder was also responsible for creating the unit tests and integration tests for his or her own thread, executing the tests, making changes, and doing regression checking. The integration coordinator was responsible for integrating the coded modules and running the higher level integration tests. When errors were discovered in the components, it was the responsibility of the coder to remedy the errors.

In creating the unit tests, black-box testing was made simpler by the fact that only three modules—Read-Integer, Read-Real, and Read-String—took direct input from the user. These modules required thorough black-box testing, but the procedures that used these modules required only white-box unit testing. The white-box unit tests were created using the detailed design and were modified as necessary once the code had been written. Each coder documented the tests using the white-box test form shown in Figure 7.6. Multiple copies of the form were created and filled in by hand. An example is shown in Figure 7.12. Figure 7.12

Module name ___Get-Fixed-Costs-Info___   Module ID ___B. 2___

Author ___Yew Chian Teh___   Tester ___Cathy Frankfather___

Decision or Loop	Possible Outcomes	Test Cases						
		1	2	3	4	5	6	7
IF ReturnCode = CR	T	X	X	X				
	F	X	X	X				
If Name = '' and Amt = 0	T	X	X					
	F	X	X	X				
If Name = ''	T	X						
	F		X	X				
If Amt = 0	T		X					
	F			X				
If Position = 10	T			X				
	F	X	X	X				
Error = F and Postion = 11	T	X	X	X				
	F	X	X	X				

Test Cases:

Case #	Values	Expected Outcome	Actual Outcome
1.	Name = " " Return Code = Print Name = "utilities" Return Code = CR Amount = "1230" Return Code = Calculate	Error message "Enter title.." Category1 = 'utilities' Cost1 = $1230.00 Exits to Calculate	
2.	Name = "utilities" Return Code = CR Amount = " " Return Code = CR Amount = "1230" Return Code = CR Retunr Code = Calculate	Category1 = 'utilities' Error message "Enter amount" Cost1 = $1230.00 Exits to Calculate	
3.	Enter 10 names and amounts with no errors. Exit to Calculate.	All categories and amounts are filled. Exits to Calculate.	

Figure 7.12 White-box Tests for the Get-Fixed-Costs Module of the Rev-Pro System Case Study

STRUCTURAL INTEGRATION TEST FORM

System: Rev-Pro   Component: Tabulate-Costs   Test Case #: SIT - 3

Tester: _____   Date: _____

Name of Module Called or Returned To	Input or User Action	Expected Effects on Data Structure(s)	Expected Output	Test - Run Results
Tabulate-Costs	none	none	Display of Costs Table with titles and empty fields	
Initialize-Costs	none	none	Cursor in first fixed-cost category	
Tabulate-Costs	none	none	Unchanged	
Get-Fixed-Costs-Info	none	none		
Read-String	User enters "utilities" and presses Return	Fixed-Cost-Cat[1] <- "utilities"	First fixed-cost category becomes "_utilities"	
Get-Fixed-Costs-Info	none	none	Cursor in first fixed-cost amount	
Read-Real	User enters "1230.00" and presses the F8 (print) key	Fixed-Cost-Amount[1] <-1230.00	First fixed-cost amount becomes "$ _ 1230.00"	
Get-Fixed-Cost-Info	none	none	Unchanged	
Tabulate-Costs	none	none	Unchanged	
PrintScreen	none	none	Image of screen is printed on printer	
Tabulate-Costs	none	none	Unchanged	
Get-Fixed-Costs-Info	none	none	Unchanged	
Read-String	User presses the F10 (go forward) key	none	Unchanged	
Get-Fixed-Costs-Info	none	none	Unchanged	
Tabulate-Costs	none	none	Execution halts	

Figure 7.13 Transaction-Flow Form Showing a Structural Integration Test for the Tabulate-Costs Component of the Rev-Pro System Case Study

shows the white-box unit tests for procedure Get-Fixed-Costs-Info. The source code for this procedure is shown in Figure 6.15.

In integration testing, transaction-flow tables were created to document the sturctural tests for each of the threads of the system. An example of a structure test of the Tabulate-Costs thread is shown in Figure 7.13. (It might be useful to view the structure chart in Figure 6.14 to see the relationship among the modules being exercised by the test.) Notice that the test provides coverage of all the modules in the component. (The "go forward to next screen" and "go backward to last screen" functions were stubbed in to result in the halting of execution.)

FUNCTIONAL TEST FORM

SYSTEM: <u>Rev-Pro</u>   COMPONENT: <u>Tabulate-Costs</u> TEST CASE # : <u>FT-3</u>

STARTING CONFIGURATION: Display of Costs table wtih field titles. Fields are empty. Cursor is in first Fixed-Cost category field.

USER ACTION	RESULT
1. Enters "utilities"	First fixed-cost category field <- "utilities"
2. Presses "return"	Cursor moves to first fixed-cost amount field
3. Enters "1230"	First fixed-cost category field <- "1230"
4. Presses "return"	Cursor moves to second fixed-cost category field
5. Presses "return"	Cursor moves to second fixed-cost amount field
6. Enters "500"	Second fixed-cost amount <- 500
7. Presses "return"	Error message displayed (missing category). Cursor moves back to second fixed-cost category field.
8. Enters "phone"	Second fixed-cost category <- "phone"
9. Presses "return"	Cursor moves to second fixed-cost amount field
10. Presses "return"	Cursor moves to third fixed-cost category field
11. Enters "Utilities"	Third fixed-cost category <- "Utilities"
12. Presses "return"	Cursor moves to third fixed-cost amount field
13. Presses "return"	Error message displayed (missing cost amount) Cursor stays in third fixed-cost amount field.
14. Enters "1200"	Third fixed-cost amount <- "1200"
15. Presses "return"	Cursor moves to fourth fixed-cost category
16. Enters "Maintenance"	Third fixed-cost category <- "Maintenance"
17. Presses "return"	Cursor moves to third fixed-cost amount field
18. Enters "$500"	"$" is not accepted. Third fixed-cost amount field <- "500"
19. Presses "F7" (calculate)	Total Fixed Cost, Total Variable Costs and Grand Total Costs are displayed
20. Presses "F10:" (go forward)	Execution halts.

Figure 7.14 Transaction-Table Showing a Functional Test Case for the Tabulate-Costs Component of the Rev-Pro System Case Study

To obtain functional testing, all functions of the subsystem must be tested to see if the requirements for the subsystem are met. Thus, in the Tabulate-Costs thread, the error checking functions and the calculate function had to be tested in addition to those functions tested by the structural test. (The "go forward to next screen" and "go backward to last screen" functions could not be fully tested until the other relevant components of the system were integrated. These functions were tested in later, higher level integration tests.) The transaction-flow table in Figure 7.14 contains transactions which, when combined with those in Figure 7.13, provide coverage of all the functions specified for the Tabulate-Costs component of the system.

Additional test cases were needed to provide stress testing. To stress the Tabulate-Costs thread, for example, the tester entered maximum values at all points and the maximum number of values allowed. Thus, the stress test involved entering ten fixed-cost category names, each with ten characters and then amounts of $99999.99. The test continued by entering ten variable-cost category names, each with ten characters, and each with amounts of $99999.99. The "Calculate" option was then selected to ensure that the totals were correctly calculated.

The same strategies and methods used in testing the threads of the system were used to test the entire system. The sponsor was able to provide some test cases for the system in the form of previous revenue projections he had performed by hand. These test cases were useful in creating structural and functional tests for the entire system. However stress tests and tests of unusual sequences and values had to be created as well.

The sponsor became involved in testing parts of the system as soon as components of the system were integrated. He also performed acceptance tests on the entire system. The sponsor had been informed from the beginning of the project that he would be required to test the system and sign off on the system. The sign-off stated that the sponsor had tested the system and accepted it in its current form. The team was able to bring in the signed acceptance form on the last day of class.

Summary

Testing is the process of evaluating software. Thus it encompasses a broad range of software evaluation procedures, including the review of documents and the assessment of quality throughout the development cycle, as well as the testing of source code. This chapter focused on the testing of code.

The principles of testing are:

- Testing is the process of executing a program with the intention of finding errors.
- It is impossible to completely test any nontrivial module or system.
- Testing takes creativity and hard work.
- Testing can prevent errors from occurring.
- Testing is best done by an independent tester.

The levels of testing include unit testing, integration testing, and acceptance testing. Unit testing is testing in the small and involves the testing of individual modules. Static methods include desk checking, hand execution, and static analysis. Dynamic methods include black-box, white-box, and data-structure-based testing. In white-box testing, the internal, logical structure of the module is examined to build the tests. The goal is to obtain segment, decision, and loop coverage of the module. In black-box testing, the module is examined from a functional standpoint. Does it perform the functions it was designed to perform? Equivalence partitioning is used to guide the creation of black-box tests. Data-structure-based tests are derived by examining the structure and the limits of the system's data structures. The goal is to exercise the boundaries of the structures.

Integration testing and acceptance testing are testing in the large. Integration testing begins by testing small groups of modules (subsystems) and ends by testing the entire system. Integration tests include structure tests, functional tests, performance tests, and stress tests. Structure tests test all modules, all calls, and all input and output parameters. Structure tests can be carried out by creating transactions. These transactions specify which modules are activated, the required input, any effects on data structures and predicted output. Functional tests test the subsystem or system against the requirements and are created by examining the requirements and specification or the user manual. Transactions specifying only input and expected effects can be used. Performance tests assess the run-time efficiency of the system. Stress tests are run to see if the system stands up to unusual loads. Integration testing is documented using test folios.

Acceptance testing is testing done on the delivered system by the sponsor. If the system is to be delivered to multiple customers, alpha and beta testing may be used.

Checklist of Project Activities

_____ Schedule unit testing activities as part of the implementation activities and assign personnel.

_____ Schedule creation of the integration tests and assign personnel.

_____ Schedule integration activities and assign personnel.

_____ Inform the sponsor of the responsibilities of acceptance testing. Schedule the delivery, installation, and acceptance testing.

_____ Work out with the sponsor responsibilities and mechanisms related to reporting and correcting errors discovered during acceptance testing.

Carry out unit testing activities, as follows:

_____ Begin creating the unit tests when the detailed design has been completed.

_____ Working from the detailed design (pseudocode or Nassi–Shneiderman chart), draw the logic-flow diagram of the module. Check the diagram for any obvious errors (for example, unreachable code).

_____   Create the white-box tests based on the logic-flow diagram.

_____   Create the black-box tests based on the requirements for the module.

_____   Create the data-structure-based tests.

_____   Cross-check the white-box, black-box, and data-structure-based tests to eliminate duplicate test cases.

_____   Expand the detailed design into source code. Desk check the source code.

_____   Compile the source code. Informally test the module and clean up any discovered errors. Revise the black-box and white-box test cases, if necessary, based on changes made in the structure or design of the module.

_____   Create any test harness needed to execute the unit tests.

_____   Execute the black-box, white-box, and data-structure-based tests. Check the results against the test oracle.

_____   Make any necessary changes and do regression testing.

_____   Maintain records of the unit testing activities.

Carry out integration testing activities, as follows:

_____   Based on the integration plan, select a thread to be implemented. Code and unit test all the modules in the subsystem.

_____   Put the modules in the subsystem together and do any preliminary fix-up necessary to make the unit functional.

_____   Do structural testing. Test the integration of the subsystem by exercising all input and output parameters of each module and by exercising all modules and calls. One approach is to use a series of transaction tests that obtains interface coverage and includes decision and loop coverage at the call level.

_____   Do functional testing. Use test cases developed from the user's guide. One approach is to create a series of transactions that exercise all the functions of the system. Both typical and atypical transactions should be used. Test to see that all classes of valid input are accepted and all classes of invalid input are gracefully rejected.

_____   Execute performance and stress tests. Test the system under different loads and the response times of the subsystem.

_____   Make it the primary goal of the tests to attempt to break the subsystem. Remember that successful testing is testing that discovers errors. Unsuccessful tests are those that discover no errors.

_____   Keep records of the test cases and the testing activities.

_____   Based on the integration plan, integrate the next set of modules and repeat the integration testing steps.

—— Continue integration until the entire system is built. Execute the final integration tests covering the entire system.

—— As soon as feasible, get the sponsor involved in testing subsystems or the entire system. Not only will this provide valuable testing of the system, but it will show the sponsor how work on the project is progressing.

Terms and Concepts Introduced

testing	data-structure-based testing
test oracle	segment coverage
test harness	decision coverage
unit testing	loop coverage
integration testing	logic-flow diagram
acceptance testing	equivalence partitioning
testing in the small	boundary testing
testing in the large	error-prone modules
incremental coding	structure tests
desk checking	functional tests
hand execution	performance tests
static testing	stress tests
dynamic testing	transaction-flow diagram
black-box testing	alpha testing
white-box testing	beta testing

Exercises

1. Write black-box test cases to test a module that is part of an automatic teller machine system. The module reads in the amount the user wishes to withdraw from his or her checking account. The amount must be a multiple of $5.00 and be less than or equal to $200.00.

2. Using the following Pascal program, do the following:

   (a) Draw a Nassi–Shneiderman chart representing the logic of the module.

   (b) Draw a logic-flow diagram of the module.

   (c) Using the white-box test worksheet from Figure 7.6, create a set of white-box tests for the module.

   (d) Create a set of black-box tests for the module.

```
program GuessTheNumber (input, output);
{Program which plays a number game.  The user has to guess a
random number between 1 and 100 in seven guesses or less.}

var Number, Guess, TryCount:  integer;
    Solved:  boolean;

{ Function RandomNumber goes here. The function returns a random
number between 1 and 100.}
```

```
begin {GuessTheNumber}

     writeln ('The computer has chosen a random number between 1
          and 100.');
     writeln ('You may have 7 tries to guess the number.');
     TryCount := 0;
     Number := RandomNumber;
     repeat
          TryCount := TryCount + 1;
          writeln ('Make a guess.  Type in a number and press the
               return key.');
          readln (Guess);
          Solved := Guess = Number;
          if Guess < Number then writeln
               ('Your guess was too small.')
          else if Guess > Number then writeln
               ('Your guess was too big.')
     until Solved or (TryCount = 7);

     if TryCount = 7 then
          writeln ('You have made 7 tries. The correct answer is
               '; Number:1)
     else  writeln ('Your guess was correct!)

end {GuessTheNumber}.
```

3. Using the design for the MakeChange module created in Chapter 5, Exercise 1, do the following:

   (a) Draw a Nassi–Shneiderman chart representing the logic of the module.

   (b) Draw a logic-flow diagram of the module.

   (c) Using the white-box test worksheet from Figure 7.6, create a set of white-box tests for the module.

   (d) Create a set of black-box tests for the module.

4. Design black-box tests for a module designed to read in a date expressed using the format MM/DD/YY, where MM is the month (1 or 2 digits allowed), DD is the day (1 or 2 digits allowed), and YY is the year (exactly 2 digits). Spaces are to be ignored. Thus valid entries might be 1/1/11, 12 /25/90, or 2 /3 / 45.

5. Devise a specific set of static tests to be performed during unit testing. Make up a checklist that could be followed to carry out these tests.

6. Apply the Static Tests Checklist developed in Exercise 5 to units from your project or to some other software.

7. Draw logic-flow diagrams for the following pseudocode fragments:

   (a) If ((A<B) or (C>D)) and (A=D), then do Action 1, else do Action2.

   (b) If ((J=0) and (K<99)) or (I>J), then do Action1, else do Action2.

   (c) If (not (X=Y)) and Z<100), then do Action1, else do Action2.

   (d) If not ((L<1) or (M=L)), then do Action1, else do Action2.

8. Develop a set of functional integration tests based on any or all of the decision tables created in Exercises 4 to 9 in Chapter 2.

9. Develop a set of functional integration tests based on the pseudocode created for Exercise 12 in Chapter 2.

10. Describe what sort of performance and stress tests might be performed to test the following systems. Be precise. Add restrictions and description to the system as necessary in defining the tests.

   (a) On-line fast-food restaurant system: The system records customer orders, relays the order to the kitchen, calculates the customer's bill and change, and maintains inventory information. Each server has a terminal.

   (b) Computerized Concordance System.

   (c) Library circulation system.

8. More About Software Engineering: Now and in the Future

Chapter 1 presented an overview of software engineering and the software life cycle, and the following chapters focused on detailed aspects of software development. In this final chapter, it is appropriate to step back and take another overview of software engineering. The approach will be to look at historical influences and trends in the evolution of software engineering and to compare what has been discussed so far to this historical picture. Wherever there is a prominent idea that has not yet been introduced, some discussion of the topic will be given. To further fill in the picture of software engineering, the topic of software maintenance will be covered in one section. Another section will survey the current status of software engineering practices and make some predictions about the future. Finally, the last steps in carrying out the project will be described. These steps include delivering the system and preparing for the operation and maintenance phase of the software life cycle.

8.1 Historical Influences and Trends in Software Engineering

Some dominant influences and trends in software engineering over the last 25 years are summarized in Table 8.1. These trends include (in order): structured programming, design methodologies, analysis methodologies, the automation of software engineering methods and the introduction of object-oriented programming, and the development of computer-aided software engineering environments. Each of the trends has come into prominence across a span of approximately five years.

In the early 1970s the ideas associated with structured programming came to the fore. Until this era, programmers were concerned more with the efficiency of their programs in terms of speed and memory usage than with the readability or maintainability of their programs. Most programmers concentrated on overcoming the

Table 8.1 Historical Influences and Trends in Software Engineering

Period	Influence or Trend
Early 1970s	Structured Programming
	• Structured coding
	• Top-down programming
	• Information hiding (Parnas)
	• Levels of abstraction (Dijkstra)
	• Stepwise refinement (Wirth)
Mid 1970s	Design methodologies
	• Structured design (Yourdon and Constantine)
	• JSP design method (Jackson)
	• Warnier–Orr design method
Late 1970s	Analysis methodologies
	• Structured analysis (DeMarco)
	• Structured analysis (Gane and Sarson)
	• SADT (SofTech)
Early 1980s	Automated techniques and object-oriented design and programming
	• PSL/PSA
	• Automatic code generation
	• Stand-alone software engineering tools
	• Object-oriented design
	• Smalltalk, Ada, and Modula-2
Late 1980s	Computer-aided software engineering
	• Interactive graphics tools for analysts
	• Framing environments
	• Programming environments
	• Integrated software engineering environments
	• User interface management systems

limitations of the hardware. However, as hardware improved, as programs became more complex, as reliability became more important, and as maintenance became more of an everyday fact of life, attitudes began to change. As Wirth (1974) states:

> The true challenge does not consist in pushing computers to their limits by saving bits and microseconds, but in being capable of organizing large and complex programs, and assuring that they specify a process that for all admitted inputs produces the desired results.

Structured programming was proposed as one way to improve the quality of programs. Although structured programming is primarily a style of programming, a structured methodology grew naturally out of structured programming. This methodology includes the ideas of modularity, stepwise refinement, top-down programming, information hiding, and levels of abstraction. All these ideas have been widely accepted and have received coverage in earlier chapters.

In the middle 1970s the concept of using a design methodology to build systems began to emerge. Organizations were discovering that systems that went from the sponsor's (often informal) requirements directly to the coder were usually not successful and presented a management nightmare. Furthermore, it began to be obvious that the source of most of the problems with these systems lay in the design and specification of the systems, not in the coding itself. The newly emerging design methodologies offered the first really systematic approach for system development. All the methods were based on the idea of functional decomposition of the system: breaking the system down into separate components, each component representing one function. The structured design technique is based on a breakdown of a system into activities with data flowing among the activities in the system. The JSP and Warnier–Orr methods are based on a different approach. In these methods, the structure of the input and output data is seen as defining the structure of the system. The structured design method was described in Chapter 4. JSP and Warnier–Orr are described in Section 8.2. All these methods rely strongly on the ideas of abstraction and the use of graphic representation to communicate information.

Analysis methodologies related to structured programming and design ideas were refined and developed in the late 1970s. These methods are based on top-down, hierarchical organization and use graphic diagrams to document the analysis. The structured analysis methods of DeMarco and Gane and Sarson (1979) are quite similar. DeMarco's structured analysis method was presented in Chapter 2. SADT is a partially proprietary analysis method developed by SofTech that is also based on the structured approach. A summary of SADT is given in Section 8.2.1.

By the early 1980s there were a number of serious attempts to automate various activities of the software life cycle. The major goal of these early efforts was to speed up the development of software, thus reducing the development costs. Another important goal of automation is to increase the reliability of the process by reducing the number of errors. Automation also has an important side effect. To automate a process, that process must be clearly understood and formally described (for example, in the form of a program). Once a process has been formalized, it often becomes possible to increase its formalization and rigor even further. PSL/PSA is one of the earliest attempts to automate a significant portion of the software development process. PSL/PSA provides a tool for creating and manipulating a database of specification and requirements information. An overview of PSL/PSA is presented in Section 8.4.1. *Automatic code generation* is another area of automation. In most cases, the development of software involves writing specifications, translating the specifications into a design, and then translating the design into program language form. Automatic code generation seeks to shorten this progression by having the specifications directly translated into code. To do this, the specification language must be highly formal and contain sufficient detail to allow the translation process. Unfortunately, no generalized code generation tool is available today. However, certain specialized tools have been developed which are capable of developing some source code. For example, the ISPF form generation package for IBM mainframes and the Panel form generation package for IBM PC's automatically generate software to support the screen designs laid out by users. One estimate is that 25 percent to 50 percent of application code can be generated using current technology, and that 40 percent to 75 percent will be possible in the near future (Fisher, 1988).

Other tools to aid in software life cycle chores were also developed in the early 1980s. These included various diagramming and graphics tools, as well as design, testing and configuration management tools. Another important development of the early 1980s was the emergence of object-oriented programming and object-oriented programming languages. The object-oriented approach to programming offers great promise for making software development and maintenance more productive through the use of abstract data types, hierarchical types, and information hiding.

A serious limitation of stand-alone tools for software engineering developed in the early 1980s is that the products they produce cannot be easily passed on to the next stage in the software development process. An integrated environment with a central database of information and a spectrum of tools is needed. *Computer-aided software engineering (CASE)* is the term used for this approach to automating software engineering processes. CASE will be discussed in detail in Section 8.4.

8.2 Other Analysis and Design Methods

Several techniques for analysis and design are presented next. These methods are in contrast to the structured analysis and structured design methods introduced in detail in Chapters 2 and 4. The techniques to be discussed include the structured analysis and design technique (SADT), Warnier–Orr, and the Jackson System of Programming (JSP).

8.2.1 Structured Analysis and Design Technique

The structured analysis and design technique (SADT) was developed by D. Ross and his colleagues at SofTech, Inc. (Ross, 1977). The method is quite similar to the structured analysis and design methods of Constantine, DeMarco, and Yourdan, as described in Chapters 2 and 4 of this text. SADT is used primarily in the requirements analysis and specification stage, but can also be used in design. It has been used on a wide variety of problem types, including business applications, real-time embedded systems, manufacturing systems, and in artificial intelligence.

SADT consists of proprietary interviewing techniques, a set of modeling principles, and a set of review principles. The goal of the technique is to produce models of the system that can be analyzed and reviewed by both the developers and the sponsors. The models are top-down, with general or more abstract components of the system at the upper levels and more detailed components at the lower levels.

The system can be diagrammed from one of three perspectives: activity diagramming, data diagramming, or behavioral diagramming. From an activity perspective, the system is seen as data flowing through the system and being transformed by activities. This is the more popular form of diagramming used. In data diagramming, activities flow through the model, and data take the place of functions. Diagramming in this way allows for consistency and completeness checks when compared to activity diagrams. In behavioral diagramming, conditions or events that are triggered by activities are passed through the system. This allows the viewing of the sequencing and concurrency of the transformation of data. Only activity diagramming will be discussed here.

An activity diagram in SADT consists of boxes, arrows, and annotations such as labels or comments. Each box represents a function or activity that transforms data. A different meaning is associated with each of the four sides of the box, as shown in Figure 8.1. The left side is where input data arrive and the right side is where output data exit the activity. The top is where controls or constraints on the activity are indicated, while the bottom is where mechanisms (that is, the means) used by the activity to accomplish its purpose are indicated. Mechanisms are optional in an activity diagram. Each diagram is bounded by a labeled box. The label is a verb or verb phrase that describes the action or function of the box. Arrows represent data and their direction of flow from activity to activity. An arrow takes on a different meaning depending on which side of a box it originates from or goes to. Arrows are labeled with nouns describing the data entity they represent. Any one diagram may contain a number of boxes, although three to six is the recommended number for one diagram.

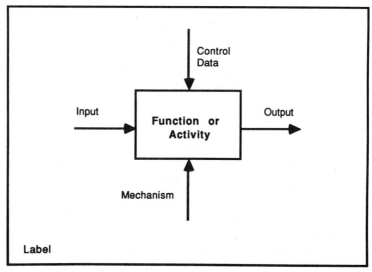

Figure 8.1 Components of a SADT Diagram

Each diagram shows all possible sources of activation of an activity. An activity is "activated" whenever the necessary data become available. A particular activity may not use all its input or controls or produce all its possible outputs for any one activation. However, at least one input and one output are necessary. Diagrams are layered, so a box in one level may be "exploded" or decomposed into a diagram at a lower level. When an activity is decomposed, the child diagram must have exactly the same inputs, outputs, and controls as the parent activity. The graphic language of SADT contains over 40 features. Aspects of the system being modeled that can be characterized are boundaries, feedback, interfaces, dominance, relevance, and exclusion. A short textual description can be included with each diagram to provide additional information.

Figure 8.2 shows a SADT diagram for a high-level view of the Handle-Cancellation activity from the noncredit courses office example used in Chapter 2. Input to the Handle-Cancellation activity is a cancellation request. Final Output is a cancellation notice (sent to the student) and an updated student account. The diagram consists of five activities and their associated input and output. For example, input to the Create-Cancellation-Forms activity consists of Invoice/2 and Blue-Form/1.

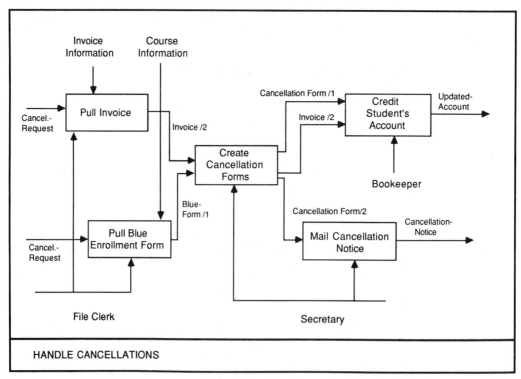

Figure 8.2 SADT Diagram of the Handle-Cancellation Activity Shown in Figure 2.7(b)

The output from this activity includes Cancellation Form/1, Invoice/2, and Cancellation Form/2. Invoice Information serves as a constraint on the Pull-Invoice activity. The File Clerk is the agent for both the Pull-Invoice and Pull-Blue-Enrollment-Form activities.

SADT provides structure for software development activities both through graphic techniques and guidelines. Proprietary training and manuals are available for teaching interviewing techniques to be used by analysts. The analysts collect the information that is diagrammed using the graphic language of SADT. The reviewing process is outlined by SADT, as well. Reviewing includes circulating a set of diagrams, called a kit, among participants in the project for comments. Once comments have been made, the comments must be acted on and the actions documented in the kit.

8.2.2 Warnier–Orr: A Data-structure-oriented Design Method

The structured analysis and structured design methods and SADT are all methods that view systems in terms of data flow and activities. In these methods, the system design is based on the relationship of the activities to one another. The structure of the system design reflects the underlying relations of the activities the system is to perform. Data structures are not emphasized in these methods, but are simply relegated to the data dictionary. The Warnier–Orr method and the Jackson System of Programming (described in the next section) both approach systems from a different aspect — the structure of the data. In these approaches, the structure of the major data entities in the system are viewed as supplying the appropriate skeletal structure of the system being designed.

The Warnier–Orr method of design involves two major steps (Warnier, 1977; Orr, 1977; Gardner, 1981). In the first step, both the input and output data structures are described using Warnier–Orr diagrams. In the second step, the design of the program is derived from the structure of the input data and documented using Warnier–Orr diagrams. Thus, systems, programs, and data structures can be represented in Warnier–Orr diagrams. Let us first look at how Warnier–Orr diagrams are constructed.

Warnier–Orr diagrams are hierarchically organized, using a one-to-many organization, and are oriented horizontally on a page. Braces are used to enclose members of a set and indicate hierarchical levels. The diagrams are read from left to right and from top to bottom within a brace. Each brace is given a name, thus naming the data structure or "procedure" (set of executable statements) that it encloses. An example of a labeled brace used to describe part of a data structure and an example of a brace used to designate an executable segment are given in the top row of Figure 8.3. Within the braces, items are listed vertically. In data structures, the vertical order represents the logical order of the items. In executable segments, the order represents sequencing. (See the second row of Figure 8.3.)

The number of times that an item occurs is indicated by a numerical expression in parentheses below the item, for example, (5) or $(1, N)$. A numerical expression

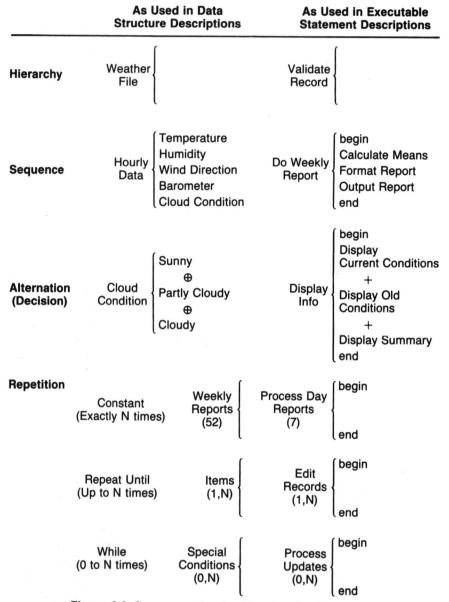

Figure 8.3 Components of a Warnier–Orr Diagram

of **(0, 1)** indicates that the item or instruction is optional (present or not present). Alternatives can be indicated through the use of what Warnier calls an *alternation structure*. If two items are separated by a plus sign, **+**, it indicates a logical *or,* and one or the other or both items may be included. A plus sign with a circle around it, ⊕, signals *exclusive or,* and indicates that one or the other but not both items are included. For example, in the third row of Figure 8.3 the data structure **Cloud_Conditions** can take on one of the states, **Sunny** or **Partly_Cloudy** or **Cloudy**. The executable segment **Display_Info** can execute one, two or all three of the following segments: **Display_Current_Conditions, Display_Last_Conditions,** or **Display_Summary_Report**. Repetition is also indicated by the use of a numerical expression in parentheses. A fixed number of repetitions (for example, a *for* loop with a constant number of repetitions) is represented by a constant or a single variable. Something that occurs at least once, and may be repeated (for example, *repeat-until*) is represented with an expression with two (nonzero) values, for example, **(1, N)**. If something may not occur at all, or may be repeated a number of times, an expression including zero is used, for example, **(0, N)**. See the last three rows of Figure 8.3 for examples.

Figure 8.4 shows the Warnier–Orr diagram for a data structure, a file. The file contains a file header and a file body. The file body consists of a series of transactions records (1 to T transactions) for library patrons who are checking out or returning books. Each record contains the patron's name, the type of transaction (check in or check out), and a block of information about each book involved in the transaction (1 to B books).

If we wished to complete the design of the library transactions system using the Warnier–Orr method, the structure of any additional input and the structure of all output would also be diagrammed. With the data structures diagrammed, the program structure could then be designed. To give the flavor of this process, Figure 8.5 shows a Warnier–Orr diagram that might be used to describe a program that handles the processing of the transaction file described in Figure 8.4. The system described does not include details on how each returned book or checked-out book is handled. Likewise, it does not detail the output from the system. Nonetheless, the example does illustrate how nicely the program structure grows out of the input structure, the major reason for using the Warnier–Orr method. (Notice that the flow of control goes from left to right across the diagram and top to bottom within each brace — a depth-first search.)

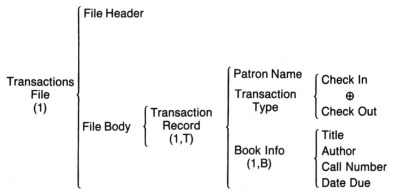

Figure 8.4 Warnier–Orr Diagram Describing a Data-Structure: A File of Transaction Records

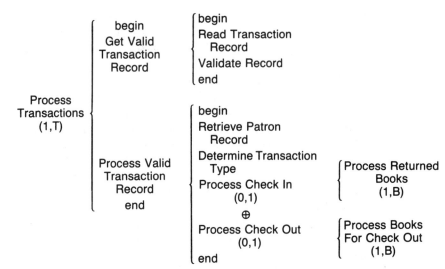

Figure 8.5 Warnier–Orr Diagram Describing a Program to Process the Transactions File Shown in Figure 8.4

The Warnier–Orr design method has several strengths. It produces designs that are both hierarchical and structured. Structured designs simplify and encourage structured coding. Its emphasis on data structures makes it a good method for designing systems that are heavily output oriented (for example, report generation) and that involve the handling of simple files. Because Warnier–Orr diagrams include procedural information, they are useful for both high-level and detailed design. There is a distinct advantage to having one method for both levels of design, as it allows the design to easily evolve from high to low levels. There are several disadvantages of the Warnier–Orr method. One minor disadvantage is that the diagrams do not show the processing of conditionals clearly. The diagram body does not contain information concerning what condition is tested to determine which function is selected. A more serious problem is that Warnier–Orr data structure diagrams are hierarchical and thus do not allow the design of nonhierarchical data structures, such as nonhierarchical databases. Another disadvantage is that, while the diagrams are structured, they do not indicate the modularization of the system.

8.2.3   Jackson System of Programming

The Jackson System of Programming (JSP) was developed by Michael J. Jackson in Great Britain in the mid-1970s (Jackson, 1975; Cameron, 1983; King and Pardoe, 1985). Like the Warnier–Orr method, the JSP method is data structure oriented. Jackson argues that what a program is to do, its specification, is completely defined by the nature of its input and output data. That is, the problem to be solved is determined by these data. From this conclusion, it is a short step to say that the structure of the program should be controlled by the structure of the input and output.

The basic method involves five steps. The first two steps build the structure of the program, including the control flow. The last three steps complete the program while checking that the program structure is correct. The steps are:

1. Draw data structure diagrams to describe the structure of streams of data input to or output from the system (typically files).

2. Derive a single program structure diagram by merging the set of data structure diagrams.

3. Write down all the elementary operations that the program will have to carry out, based on the programming language being used.

4. Associate each elementary operation with its appropriate positions in the program structure diagram.

5. Transform the program structure in its diagrammatic form into a textual form (using a structured program design language).

As in the Warnier–Orr method, both the data structure and the program structure are described graphically using the same diagrammatic components. There are three basic components: one for sequence, one for iteration, and one for selection. Figure 8.6 shows the three components, their interpretation when used to describe

Diagram Representation	Interpretation in a Data Structure Diagram	Interpretation in a Program Structure Diagram
SEQUENCE		
A / X Y Z	The data structure A is composed of element X followed by Y followed by Z.	Program step A involves executing step X followed by step Y followed by Z.
ITERATION		
A / X^*	The data structure A consists of 0 or more repetitions of element X.	Program step A consists of 0 or more repetitions of step X.
SELECTION		
A / X^o Y^o Z^o	The data structure A consists of (one of) elements X, Y, or Z.	Program step A consists of doing (one of) steps X, Y, or Z.

Figure 8.6 Components of JSP Data Structure and Program Structure Diagrams

a data structure, and their interpretation when used to describe program structure. A sequential data structure is one that consists of several parts. A sequential program structure is one that requires that each of its component steps be executed in sequence. In an iterative data structure, the data structure consists of zero or more repetitions of a data element. In an iterative program structure, the component step(s) are repeated zero or more times. A selection data structure may be composed of any one of the indicated elements, while a selection program structure involves the selection of one of two or more alternate program steps.

To see how the JSP method works, consider a simple example, the library circulation report system. Suppose a library had a file containing all the books currently checked out organized according to the patron who has the books. More specifically, the file consists of a series of packets of information. Each packet contains the information for one patron, including a record containing the patron's name, a number of records each containing information about one book in the patron's possession, and a trailer record to indicate the end of the packet of information for that patron. The library wishes to print a report about the information in the file, including the patron's name and a summary line showing how many books each patron has checked out.

Beginning with step 1 of the JSP method, diagrams of the input and output data structures are drawn. These are shown in Figure 8.7. Notice that the data structures are defined in a top-down, hierarchical manner. Each box represents a com-

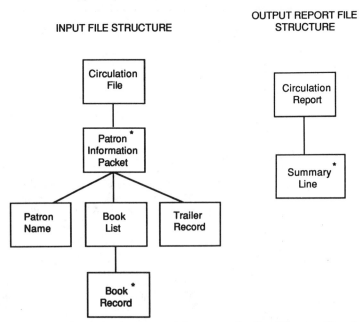

Figure 8.7 JSP Data Structure Diagrams for the Library Circulation Report System

ponent of the data structure, and any boxes below it represent subcomponents. In step 2, the program structure is derived by finding the *correspondence* between the input and output data structures and merging them into a (single) program structure diagram. Correspondence is found by matching up elements of the input structure with logically and structurally related items in the output structure. A correspondence between two elements exists if:

- there is the same number of each component,
- there is some functional relationship between the components, and
- if the functional relationship is one-to-one, with the pairs occurring in the correct matching order.

In the library circulation report example, there are two correspondences. First, the Circulation Report component corresponds to the Circulation File. This correspondence meets the listed criteria. There is one of each, a functional relationship exists (the report is to summarize information in the file), the relationship is one to one (one file, one report), and the one to one relations are in the correct order (the first and only report will summarize information from the first and only circulation file). Second, the Summary Line element of the Output Report structure corresponds to the Patron Information Packet. Again, this correspondence meets the criteria. There is the same number of each component, as there will be one summary line for each patron. The relationship is functional, because the summary line will summarize information for each patron. And the relationships are in the correct order: the order of the patron information packets in the file determines the order of the summary lines of the report. The derived program structure is shown in Figure 8.8. Notice how the data structure components are turned into processing components by simply adding the word "Process." Because the program structure reflects the data structures, the program structure is also top down and hierarchical.

The next step is to write down all the elementary operations that the program will involve. These can be written in any order. A knowledge of programming is needed to carry out this step, as the JSP method provides no guidance. For the library circulation report system, the operations include:

1. Open circulation file
2. Open output file
3. Write the patron name
4. Initialize book-record count
5. Increment count of book records
6. Write book count total
7. Close circulation file
8. Close output file

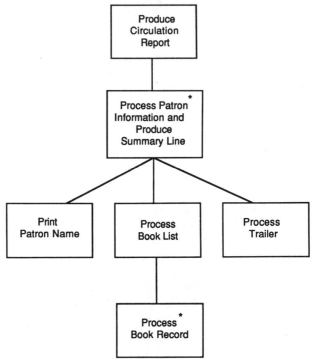

Figure 8.8 JSP Program Structure Diagram for the Library Circulation Report System

The operations are numbered for reference purposes only and need not necessarily reflect the order of execution.

Now each operation is assigned to its appropriate structure in the program structure diagram. The assignment is done by matching the operations logically and by a correspondence in the number of times the operation is to be carried out with the structure. For example, operations number 1, 2, 7, and 8 each need to be done only one time. They are thus associated with the structure "Produce Circulation Report." Likewise, operation 4 is done once for each patron and is associated with the structure "Process Patron Information and Produce Summary Line." Figure 8.9 contains a list of the elementary operations and shows each operation associated with the appropriate program structure.

In the final step, the program structure diagram, with its associated operations, is transformed into pseudocode. Although JSP has its own particular form of pseudocode, the example will be done in the same style that has been used throughout this book. The pseudocode is shown in Figure 8.10. At this point the design of the program is complete, and the programmer can create the source code for the program from the pseudocode design.

The JSP method is widely used in the United Kingdom and Europe and is less widely used in the United States. It has the advantage of being very systematic. It

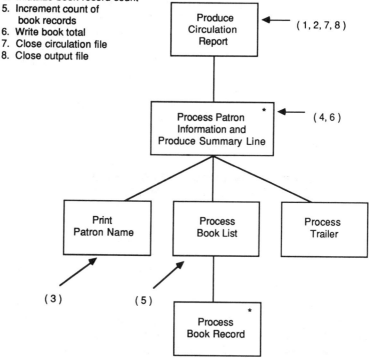

ELEMENTARY OPERATIONS

1. Open circulation file
2. Open output file
3. Write patron name
4. Initialize book-record count
5. Increment count of
   book records
6. Write book total
7. Close circulation file
8. Close output file

Figure 8.9 JSP Program Structure Diagram for the Library Circulation Report System Showing the Elementary Operations and the Program Structure Associated with Each

consists of a number of well-defined steps, each of which results in a paper product. This characteristic makes program design less based on intuition and insight and more on the systematic application of procedures. The system is also teachable, due to its stepwise nature. Likewise, the system leads to consistency: two or more people will come up with approximately the same program design. It is relatively simple and easy to use. Finally, because there is a close relationship between the data structures and the program structure, a small change in the input or output data structure should result in a correspondingly small change in the program structure.

The major disadvantage of the JSP method is that it is only a method for designing the detail of a single software program. It gives little help in designing the overall structure of a large software system, which may be broken down into several programs and components. Although Jackson claims the method is suitable for any type of application, it is clearly a file-processing-oriented approach. Fur-

```
open Circulation File
open Output File
read a record
while not end of Circulation File do
        initialize Book-record Count
        write Patron Name
        read a record
        while not Trailer-record do
                increment Book-record Count
                read a record
        end-while
        write Book-record Count
        read a record
end-while
close Output File
close Circulation File
```

Figure 8.10 Pseudocode Design of the Library Circulation Report System Derived from Figure 8.9

thermore, the literature on the JSP method contains solely examples of serial file processing. The method also sidesteps the issue of constructing the input and output data structures. It is assumed that their structures are known and understood. In many cases, however, the structure of the files may be an important design decision.

To supplement the JSP method, Jackson has proposed a method of system design called Jackson System Design (JSD). The JSD method throws out the classical model of the software development cycle, including analysis, preliminary design, detailed design, and so on. The approach includes building a model of the system that the software is to interact with. The model consists of parallel processes that interact by exchanging data (Jackson, 1983; Cameron, 1983). JSD has not been as widely used as JSP, but has been seen recently as a possible approach to object-oriented design.

8.3 Software Maintenance

Software maintenance is the term that is used to describe the various software engineering activities that occur once a software system has been delivered and installed. What makes software maintenance so important is that software systems are almost never static. Instead they continue to grow and change as they are used. Furthermore, errors uncovered during use of the system must be corrected. Software is very unlike more tangible products such as consumer goods, physical structures such as roads or bridges, or computer hardware. Once items such as these are delivered and installed, very little modification of their functional capabilities ever occurs. For example, a consumer would not expect to be able to add new features to a microwave oven to make it cook a broader range of foods or cook foods more quickly. Demands for new features or for changes in functions for software are common, however. It is really more correct to think of software as an entity that continuously evolves, rather than as a finished product delivered to a customer.

There are three basic categories of software maintenance: *corrections, adaptations,* and *enhancements.* Corrections are made to fix errors in the system. These errors may have been built into the initial version of the system, or they may be the result of later changes in the software. Some errors may require immediate attention, others may be corrected on a scheduled basis, while still others may simply be lived with ("It's not a bug, it's a feature!"). Adaptations are made as a result of changes in the environment the system is operating in. For example, the software may have to be modified to handle a different type of hardcopy format, a new disk drive, a different communications protocol, or a new operating system. These changes are not done to correct errors, nor do they add any new capabilities to the system; they simply make the software adjust to new conditions. Enhancements, on the other hand, are made to add new features and functionality to the system. Enhancements might include new capabilities, improved user interfaces, or upgraded performance.

8.3.1   The Cost of Software Maintenance

As mentioned in Chapter 1, approximately 70 percent of the total cost of owning software is related to maintenance, the other 30 percent being development costs. Furthermore, the proportion spent for software maintenance costs is actually predicted to rise in the future (Zelkowitz and Basili, 1984). Of maintenance costs, approximately 60 percent is spent for enhancements, 20 percent for adaptation and 20 percent for error correction. After doing some simple mathematics on these estimates, one can see that approximately 42 percent of the total life cycle costs of software are consumed by enhancement efforts. This figure supports the contention made above that the essential nature of software is evolutionary, not static. Furthermore, this figure once again highlights the importance of making —and keeping — software maintainable.

Software is made maintainable by developing a quality product in the first place. All of the software qualities that have been emphasized throughout this book are important. Some of the most important qualities are a good design that incorporates modularity, clear and readable code, good internal documentation, and complete, up-to-date external documentation. To keep software maintainable, the same high standards that went into its development must be used whenever any change is made to the system. There is often a lot of pressure to simply make the system work when error correction is being done, or to patch on an adaptation or enhancement for the sake of speed. Documentation and testing may be scanty. But, as the old saying goes, "Haste makes waste." While the one change to the system may be made quickly, there will be serious consequences down the line. The hastily made change may contain errors that will appear sooner or later. Furthermore, when it comes time to make the next change, the system will be a lower-quality system. It will be harder to make changes, and the chances of introducing still more errors and unnecessary complexity will be increased.

8.3.2 Configuration Management: Managerial Concerns

Software maintenance is change. Change can cause chaos unless it is carefully controlled and monitored. *Configuration management* is a term used to describe the management and control of changes made to software. Configuration management can be seen both from the management's point of view and from the technical point of view. We will focus first on the management of change.

There are typically a number of people involved in software changes, each taking on one or more different roles in the change process. These people are sometimes collectively referred to as the *configuration management team*. The team consists of:

Analysts. People who work with the users to pinpoint problems or to define what enhancements or adaptations are needed.

Programmers. People who work with the analyst to locate the source of the problems or to advise on the type and extent of change to be made. The programmers are also responsible for making any required changes.

Program librarians. People who work with the analysts and programmers to facilitate and keep track of any changes in the documentation or code.

When the user notes an error or requests an enhancement, a *change request* is created. A change request is typically a form to be filled out by the user or whoever is making the request. It asks for information such as the identity of the software to be changed, the nature of the change or error, the name of the requestor, and so on. It should describe how the system works now, what the problem is with the current system, and how the system should work if the change is made. The change request is first processed by the analyst. In some cases, the analyst may find that the reported problem can be corrected by training. Perhaps the user was entering an incorrect command or is not aware of some feature of the software. In these cases, the change request is dropped. If the analyst determines that the request needs further attention, it is directed to a *change control board* or *configuration control board* along with the analyst's recommendations.

The change control board is responsible for authorizing changes. The configuration board considers the proposed change, taking into account the expected scope of the change and the amount of time needed to implement the change, as well as staffing and cost considerations. The board then decides if the proposed change should be made. If so, a priority is given to the change process. Constraints may be placed on the change, as well. The change is then passed back to the configuration management team for implementation.

To control the effects of the change, the approved change is implemented on a test copy of the software, rather than on the operational version of the system. The analyst or programmer locates the source of the problem or the area needing change and designs the change. The change is implemented and tested. Regression tests are performed on the entire system to ensure its integrity. The change control board then makes the final decision on whether to install the new version of the system or not. If the installation is approved, the programmers work with the program librarian to perform a controlled installation of the new version of the system. Relevant documentation is updated as well. Finally, a *change report* detailing the changes made to the system is filed by the programmer.

8.3.3 Configuration Management: Technical Issues

The technical issues of configuration management have to do with tracking all changes made to a system so that the current status of the system is always known and under supervised control. Configuration management takes place during product development, as well as during the operational and maintenance phase of the software life cycle. As each phase of development progresses, certain milestones are attained. At these milestones, the deliverables for that phase, such as the preliminary design document, the test plan, or the user manual, are placed under configuration control. Any further changes to the deliverable can only be made after a formal agreement has been reached between the sponsor and the developers. During software maintenance, it is also important that all changes be authorized (for example, through the change control board) and tracked.

As a student, it may be hard to see why configuration control is so important. Working as an individual or with a small group of people, it is possible to monitor changes in versions of a program or system using verbal communication or simple written communications. However, once larger numbers of people and more complex software are involved, uncontrolled change can cause chaos. Sometimes programmers working on a system are even in physically different locations. Suppose Patty Programmer makes a change to a data structure on Monday morning without telling Fred Fixit, and Fred makes a different sort of change to the same data structure on Monday afternoon without telling Patty. On Tuesday, Patty Programmer makes additional changes based on the changes she made on Monday. The program comes crashing down, and now hoards of irate users are knocking at Patty's door. Configuration management is necessary to avoid such scenarios.

It is important to remember that the software being maintained is software that is being used. While there may be no serious effects of tinkering around with software in the developmental stage, tinkering around with installed software can produce expensive and disastrous consequences. Another advantage of configuration control is that it preserves the ability to go back to earlier, known states. It is possible that a series of small, incremental changes made to a system can result in the system suddenly becoming seriously unreliable. In such cases, an earlier version of the system with known bugs can be put back into operation while the newer version is revised. Furthermore, the historical records of changes made will help in isolating the source of the new problems.

Special software is often used to assist in configuration management. A *configuration management database* is used to provide information and reports on the current status of each software product. The information such a database should be able to provide includes (Shigo and others, 1982):

- Number of versions currently in existence
- Comparison of the structure of the different versions
- Where the different versions are being used
- Changes made to each component of each product
- Hardware support required for each version
- Which versions are affected by each error report
- Number of change requests per unit time
- Status of all change requests
- Causes of reported errors

In addition to a configuration management database, a *version control library* is useful in configuration management. A version control library tracks and controls all the files that comprise the various versions of a software product. Objects in the library might include source code, object code, job control sequences, data files, test files, and various sorts of documentation. For each object, the version number, date of creation, and identity of the person or group responsible for the version must be maintained. A version control library system that is popular with users of IBM systems is Pansophic Systems' Panvalet. Panvalet provides editing features, allowing the user to alter strings in one file or many files. Multiple versions of a file are permitted. One version, however, is designated the production file and may not be changed. To make changes, a user must create a copy of the production file and make changes in the copy. This allows the system to monitor all changes. For each version of a file there is a directory of information about the file. The directory includes information on the version of the file, access and change dates, and the types of action last taken on the file. Panvalet automatically adds the version number and date of last change to compiler listings and object code modules when a source code file is compiled. Panvalet also provides report capabilities, recovery and backup functions, and three levels of security access.

8.3.4   A Special Configuration Management Problem: Multiple Releases

When a software product is installed at many installations, the problems of configuration management and version control become more complex and more critical. In such cases, change requests may come from any of the installation sites. When a change is made in the system as a result of the request, the issue of how to distribute the new version of the software becomes important.

For small changes that fix critical problems, the customers can be sent updated source code or object code for installation at their site. However, there is no guarantee that every customer will install the new version, especially if a customer is not experiencing the problem that brought on the change. In addition, it is necessary to keep careful records of which customers have been sent the changes. Newsletters and bulletins can be useful in distributing information about the availability and use of small fixes.

When a number of changes have been implemented, the revised software can be labeled a new major release. Old customers who have a maintenance contract or for whom maintenance was a condition of the original contract should receive the new release. To avoid the expense of sending a completely new set of documentation to the customer, documentation updates can be provided. An update should contain a summary of the important differences in the new version and copies of the revised pages of the documentation with the changed sections highlighted. Of course, the documentation must have been designed to incorporate updates (e.g., using a loose-leaf notebook with independently numbered sections.) New customers should receive the latest version and a complete, revised set of documents.

8.3.5 The Role of the Maintenance Programmer

What do programmers really do? The answer is: maintenance programming. A survey of 25 data-processing installations found that 39 percent of a programmer's effort goes toward development of new software, while 61 percent goes toward maintenance efforts and user support (Fjeldstad and Hamlen, 1983). This ratio of effort is not surprising, given that about two-thirds of the cost of owning software is due to maintenance. However, these results do not imply that every programmer spends 61 percent of her or his time in maintenance activities. Some programmers may work exclusively on development, while others may work exclusively on maintenance.

The programmers assigned to do maintenance (either part time or full time) may or may not be the ones who developed the software product. There are both advantages and disadvantages of having the team that developed a product maintain it. The advantages are that they are very familiar with the design and code of the system. They understand how the system works and where the likely weaknesses in the system are. In addition, if the team building the system knows they must maintain it as well, they should be more likely to build it in such a way that maintenance is easier for them. A disadvantage is that developer/maintainers may not thoroughly document the system during development or keep the documentation up to date. Their attitude might be that they can remember a lot about the system and do not need to write it down. While this might be a somewhat valid assumption, the fact is that people forget and that programmers can move to new assignments or new jobs. If a separate maintenance team is to be assigned to a software product, the developers may be more complete and careful in their documentation efforts. Another advantage of a separate maintenance team is that they might be more objective. They can make a distinction between what the software is *supposed* to do and what it really does. This advantage is related to the same phenomenon that happens to many programmers and has probably happened to you. A programmer may spend a large amount of time looking for the source of a bug. In

Table 8.2 Kinds of Activities (by Percent) Performed by Maintenance Personnel for Modifications and Enhancements and for Correction

Maintenance Task	Enhancements and Modifications	Corrections
Define and understand change	18	25
Review documentation	6	4
Trace logic	23	33
Implement the change	19	15
Test the change	28	20
Update documentation	6	3

frustration, he or she shows the program to another person. The other person spots the bug in a matter of minutes. A disadvantage of a separate team is the start-up time needed for the team to become familiar with the design, the documentation and the source code.

One study looked at the kinds of maintenance activities maintenance personnel engage in and the proportion of time spent on each of these activities for modifications and enhancements and for correction (Fjeldstad and Hamlen, 1983). These data are shown in Table 8.2. The figures show that relatively little time is spent in actually implementing the change (15 to 19 percent). Three categories — defining and understanding the change, reviewing documentation, and tracing logic — could all be considered related to understanding the problem. These three categories together comprise 47 percent of the effort for enhancements and modification and 62 percent of the effort for corrections. Clearly, simply understanding the problem is the major effort involved in doing maintenance.

8.4 Automating the Software Engineering Endeavor

Because many activities of software engineering involve clerical and/or repetitive aspects, software engineering is a good candidate for automation. Furthermore, the continued and increasing demand for software development and maintenance has made productivity an important issue. Frenkel (1985) states, "The need for software and software engineers is growing exponentially, but productivity is only rising at a rate of about five percent a year." Bobbie (1987) summarizes the current situation as follows:

> The increasing need [for software] is a result of the proliferation of and ever-increasing reliance on computers throughout our society. The complexity and size of this new application software threatens to completely overwhelm our current ability to

produce software. Consequently, there is a gap between societal computing needs and expected software productivity rate. Achievement of significant increases in productivity will be the key to continued growth in automation (page 30).

In the past, increases in productivity have come from the introduction of software engineering techniques. Boehm and others (1984) analyzed 63 software development projects and found a strong correlation between the use of techniques and the amount of effort needed to develop software. As tool use went up, effort went down. Boehm estimated that the use of standard software engineering techniques can reduce development effort by 9 to 17 percent. He further estimated that the creation of a software engineering environment (the combination of software engineering techniques with various automated tools) could reduce efforts by 28 to 41 percent.

Besides reducing the cost of development, automating the software engineering endeavor can aid productivity in a number of other ways. These include:

- Providing better management control of the development, operation, and maintenance of computer software
- Lowering the cost of software maintenance activities
- Providing better quality and consistency control

Management is a central component of software development, operation, and maintenance. Management controls the when, why, and how of these activities. For management to succeed, managers need a clear picture of the current status of the system, historical information, and projections for the future. Automated software engineering can aid in the collecting and organizing of information by providing a database of information for the managers' use.

Automated software engineering can also facilitate standardization in development and maintenance. Standardization, in turn, makes development and maintenance activities easier. By following standardized development procedures, the developers know what to do when and how to do it. Communications are greatly facilitated by use of an agreed on format. The developers can focus on solving the problem at hand, rather than spending time establishing the rules of operation. A standardized product is easier to maintain, as well. The maintainers know what information is available, what format the information is in, and what procedures to follow. A general goal of software engineering is to provide such standardization. Automating the processes can make standardization easier to achieve and enforce.

A final reason for automation is to increase the reliability of software systems. Automation can include automated checks for consistency and completeness that are more extensive and reliable than manual checking. Automation can also increase the extent and amount of testing.

The automating of software engineering activities is referred to collectively as *CASE: computer-aided software engineering.* A software package which automates only one activity is referred to as a CASE *tool,* and a selection of tools used in a coordinated manner is called a *software engineering environment.*

The *IEEE Standard Glossary of Software Engineering Terminology* (1983) does not define a software engineering environment, but it does define a programming support environment, a precursor of software engineering environments, as follows: "An integrated collection of tools accessed via a single command language to provide programming support capabilities throughout the software life cycle. The environment typically includes tools for design, editing, compiling, loading, testing, configuration management and project management." This definition applies very well to software engineering environments designed to support programming efforts. Software engineering environments surround a user with tools that can be used in the systematic development and maintenance of software. Remember that software engineers define software in the broader sense of data and documentation from all stages of the software life cycle, as well as programs. Thus software engineering environments are intended to aid all facets of the software engineering process and are not limited to coding aids.

Software engineering environments are closely tied to the software life cycle and provide support throughout the cycle. As described in Chapter 1, the software life cycle includes the software development cycle (the focus of the majority of this book), the operational and maintenance phase, and death or retirement. Progression through the software life cycle results in numerous software products. Although many of these products have been described earlier, this text has presented a somewhat limited view of the complete range of possible products. In particular, the software development process has been scaled down to a one-term endeavor, and issues not of direct concern to students developing a project have been skipped. In this light, it is instructive to consider the full range of products suggested by the Federal Information Processing Standards (compiled by Houghton and Wallace, 1987), as shown in Table 8.3.

Not all the documents listed in Table 8.3 may be needed for all projects. Flexibility is required in determining what documents are needed. Likewise, different projects may require different approaches to development. The exact order of progression through the software development cycle may vary depending on particular situations. For these reasons, software engineering environments must provide flexibility to the software engineer. An additional complication in producing software engineering environments is that the software life cycle includes implicit iterations. Maintenance is perhaps the most obvious example of iterations. When an enhancement to a software system is requested, every stage in the software life cycle is repeated again. Errors discovered during development also result in more or less extensive iterations through earlier stages. Thus, a successful software engineering environment must support not only transitions from one phase to the next in the software life cycle, but must support iterations as well.

CASE systems can be broken down into three basic types: *framing environments, programming environments,* and *general environments. Framing environments* focus on the schematic design at the earlier stages, when the system is being "framed" by its requirements and preliminary design. The major activities involved in framing a system include creating a schematic representation of the problem and creating specifications. *Programming environments* include a variety

Table 8.3 A List of Standard Documents Which May Be Formally or Informally Required During the Software Life Cycle (based on Houghton and Wallace, 1987)

Life Cycle Phase	Documents
Initiation	• General definition of the requirements • Feasibility study • Development plan • Cost/benefit analysis
Definition	• Functional requirements document • Data requirements document • Verification, validation, and testing plan
High-level design	• System/subsystem specification • Verification, validation, and testing plan
Detailed design	• Program specification • Database specification • Test plan
Coding	• User manual • Operations manual • Program maintenance manual • Test analysis report
Operations and maintenance	• Formal change request • Updated document

of tools to aid in the creation, testing, and documenting of code. *General environments* contain basic tools that support all phases of the life cycle. Let us examine each type in more detail, and look at some examples of each.

8.4.1 CASE Tools: Framing Environments

Framing environments concentrate on the early stages of systems development. Studies and experience have shown that by focusing extra effort on the early stages great savings in resources can be made in the later stages (Boehm, 1981). This is because most problems result from errors introduced in the early stages and because the cost of fixing an error increases with the stage in the life cycle where it is discovered. Thus it is not surprising that some of the earliest and most widely used CASE tools, such as SREM and PSL/PSA, were developed to support these stages. Other examples of framing environments include Information Engineering Workbench (Knowledgeware, Inc.), Excelerator (Index Technologies), and Teamwork/PCSA (Cadre Technologies).

Earlier framing environments only helped the analyst in producing specifications and documentation. Recently, however, more capabilities have been added to aid in solving critical problems at the beginning of the life cycle. A complete framing environment today includes diagramming and graphics capabilities, tools to support prototyping, a design dictionary, and analysis capabilities for error checking of various sorts. In some cases, framing environments are designed to support a particular analysis and/or design methodology. For example, SREM supports its own particular method, while Teamwork/PCSA supports the Yourdon/ DeMarco structured analysis technique. In other cases, the tool supports a variety of methods (for example, PSL/PSA and Excelerator).

As an example of a framing tool, let us examine PSL/PSA in more detail. PSL/ PSA was developed in the 1970s by Tiechrow (Tiechrow and Hershey, 1977). The tool is not method based and is primarily concerned with providing automatic verification and various types of reports. Because it is based on an entity–relationship model, it can be used to describe a wide variety of different system models. An entity–relationship model is a model that consists of entities and relationships. An entity is a "thing" about which certain facts are known. Normally, an entity is something tangible, like a physical object; but it may also be something more abstract, such as a report, a process, or an idea. It is some part of the real world or the system being modeled. A relationship is an association between two entities. A single entity can have many associations with other entities. Furthermore, relationships can be one to one (Ian likes Andrea), one to many (Aaron plays hockey with . . .), or many to many (a telephone system).

PSL stands for Problem Statement Language. PSL is a formal language (just as a programming language is a formal language) and is used to describe the requirements of a system. The system can be described from several viewpoints, including:

- Input/output: the interaction between a system and its environment
- Structure: hierarchical relations among objects in the system
- Data structures: relationships among data entities
- Data derivations: data entities used by specified processes
- Size and volume characteristics of the system
- System dynamics: the behavior of a system
- Attributes: properties of entities
- Project management information

Each of these aspects is described in terms of objects (entities) and relationships. Each object is given a PSL name as designated by the PSL/PSA user. The language contains over 20 predefined objects. Relationships between objects are defined using one of the 50 relationships that are predefined. Examples of some of the objects and relationships are shown in Table 8.4. Attributes can also be attached to objects. Attributes describe values or properties of the objects. Figure 8.11 shows an example of a PSL problem statement that defines a process for determining the membership characteristics of a new member of a public television station. (This is the same example used in Figures 2.9 and 2.10.)

The PSL description of the requirements for a system is input into the PSA component of the tool. PSA stands for Problem Statement Analyzer. PSA is a sophisticated database manipulation/report-generation tool. It can analyze the PSL

Table 8.4 Objects and Relationships from PSL

Objects	Relationships
Input	Part of
Output	Contained
Interface	Use
Process	Derive
Set	Update
Element	Receive
Group	Generate
Relation	Consist
Entity	Consumes
System parameter	Performed by
Interval	Makes . . .
Condition	Termination
Event	Inception
	Happens
	Triggers

descriptions in over 50 different ways and provide a report for each of these different analyses. The reports can be broken down into four major types: database modification reports, reference reports, summary reports, and analysis reports. Database modification reports record changes that have been made in the database of specifications (PSL statements) and provide feedback concerning possible inconsistencies or missing elements in the specifications. The reference reports can be used to search and report on various sorts of information stored in the database. For example, the user can request a reference report of all attributes and relationships for a particular object or create a data dictionary that provides information about all data entities within the system. Summary reports can be used to provide summaries of various aspects of the system. One type of summary report provides project management information, while other types will show the system hierarchy or graphically represent data flow in the system. Finally, analysis reports can be used to validate and verify the specifications. For example, gaps in information flow or unused data entities can be detected using one sort of analysis report facility. Another type of report analyzes the dynamic behavior of the system.

PSL/PSA is not designed to support any particular analysis method. The tool provides very little guidance on how to approach the analysis problem. If it is utilized without being tied to a specific method, its usefulness is questionable. The key to its successful use lies in the thoroughness with which the system is specified in PSL. Once the system is specified, however, PSA provides powerful support for verifying completeness and consistency and for providing a wealth of documentation.

```
PROCESS:   Determine-Membership-Characteristics
DESCRIPTION:  Based on contribution amount and age-class, determine
              membership category of new member, premium (if any), and if
              the member is to receive a monthly guide
GENERATES:  Member-characteristics
RECEIVES:  Contribution-amount, Age-Class
SUBPARTS ARE:  Add-Member-to-Member-List, Add-Member-to-Studio-
               Club-List, Add-Member-to-Premium-List,
               Add-Member-to-Guide-List
PART OF:  Process-New-Member
DERIVES:  Member-Status
     USING:  Age-Class; Contribution-Amount
DERIVES:  Premium
     USING:  Age-Class; Member-Status; Contribution-Amount
DERIVES:  Guide
     USING:  Member-Status
PROCEDURE:
     1. Categorize Member by Age-Class
     2. Determine Member-Status according to Contribution-Amount
     3. Determine Premium according to Member-Status
     4. Determine if receive guide according to Member-Status
     5. Add member to appropriate lists
HAPPENS:  for each new member
TERMINATION CAUSES:  error in input data
SECURITY IS:  none
```

Figure 8.11 Example of a PSL Problem Statement Defining the Determine-Membership-Characteristics Process

8.4.2 CASE Tools: Programming Environments

Programming environments support the later stages of the software life cycle. These tools consist of any automation of the programming effort, including compilers, linkers, loaders, operating systems, and so on. This sort of tool helps mainly with clerical aspects of implementing a system. Tools that support the more creative aspects of programming are also available, and more such tools are appearing every year. One special category of programming environment tools is *code generators*. Code generators range from language-sensitive editors, to compilers based on expert systems, to systems that create code automatically from formal specifications with no programmer intervention. Still other programming environment tools aid in testing and debugging.

Language-sensitive editors are one of the more simple sorts of code generators. These editors combine features of a compiler (syntax checking) with editing. Typically, these tools are graphically oriented and are usually language specific. When using a language-sensitive editor, the programmer selects a programming language construct, such as an *if-then-else*. A visual representation of the construct is displayed on the screen as a template. The keywords of the language may be highlighted (for example, in boldface), and the operand that requires manipulations may be accented in some way. The programmer then fills in the blanks with the operands or operators desired. If the filled-in template is not syntactically correct according to the rules of the programming language being used, the programmer is immediately notified. Different editors provide different levels of checking and aid. Some editors allow execution of the incomplete code, with graphics showing the flow of execution.

Several advantages accrue from using a language-sensitive editor. One advantage is that the programmer can concentrate on the semantic aspects of implementation and does not have to worry about syntax. One study found that syntax errors occur 12 to 17 percent of the times programs are sent to a compiler (Boies and Gould, 1974). The language-sensitive editor makes syntax error detection immediate, providing an educational benefit as well as a time-saving benefit to the programmer. Due to the incremental approach allowed by some editors, unfamiliar language constructs can be tried out before the programmer decides to incorporate them into the code. Productivity is increased because the code does not have to cycle repeatedly through the editing, compiling, linking, loading, and executing steps. Examples of language-sensitive editors include LSE (Language Sensitive Editor), which runs under VMS on the VAX systems (Digital Equipment Corporation) and supports Pascal, C, FORTRAN, and COBOL programming; POE (Fischer and others, 1984); and Magpie (Delisle, Menicosy, and Schwartz, 1984), both of which support Pascal.

Other code generators are basically compilers that generate source code from detailed design specifications or from prototypes, or that translate between languages. User Interface Management Systems (see Section 8.5) generate source code for a user interface from prototypes. Another example is DEC's VAX COBOL Generator which can be used to translate programs in a high level design language into COBOL. It can be used to standardize and update old programs, or to standardize programs written by a variety of programmers. Intermetrics, Inc. has built several compilers which utilize expert system technology to produce compilers which generate high-quality code in a target language from code in a different language (Frenkel, 1985). Their goal has been to automatically generate machine language code from a high-level language that is comparable in quality to that produced manually by expert programmers. The problem requires that the system understands the structure of the high-level language and understands the target machine's architecture. For example, when code written in Pascal must be translated to run on the Intel 8086 microprocessor, it is important that the code use the microprocessor's register set and memory efficiently. In using the 8086, various computations must be performed in particular registers to fully harness the microprocessor's potential power. Code sequences must be designed so that the operands are in the right place when needed. In addition, the machine is capable of addressing only 64,000 bytes from one address register. To use the machine's entire memory space requires changing the contents of the address register. Frequent shifts in the currently accessible memory result in inefficient programs. Code should be designed to avoid such shifts. Expert programmers use a variety of programming tricks to develop good 8086 code. Intermetrics' goal was to write a compiler that used the same tricks that expert programmers use. To accomplish this, they used expert system technology. The compiler includes a set of production rules that represents a programmer's knowledge and an inference engine that selects how and when to apply the production rules during translation.

Another class of programming environment tools is automated testing tools. Automated testing attempts to reduce the clerical effort involved in conducting tests and provide more thorough testing. Some test tools provide *static analysis* of the code or test data, while others provide *dynamic analysis*. In static analysis, the source code or test data are examined without regard to their executability. In *dynamic analysis,* the run-time behavior of the code is examined. One use of *static analysis* is to determine the possible paths through the code. This information can, in turn, be used to generate white-box test cases. Static analyzers can also find such flaws as unreachable code, transfer statements that simply transfer to the next executable statement, loops that have no action parts, variables defined and never used, and so on. File comparators can be used to compare the actual output from test runs with the predicted output. Differences between the files indicate errors in the output (or possibly errors in the predicted output). File comparators are useful not only because they are faster and more accurate than manual comparison, but because they do not have the bias toward expecting the system to work that most programmers have.

Dynamic analysis is used to derive information about a system's execution behavior. Dynamic analysis tools include *debuggers, coverage analysis, assertion checking,* and *regression testing. Debuggers* are tools that are used to help a programmer in debugging a program. Debuggers monitor the status of a program while it is executing. The user can do such things as set breakpoints in the program that cause execution to halt when the breakpoint is encountered, trace the flow of execution, trace the values taken on by an indicated variable during execution, step through execution one statement at a time, and examine and alter variables during execution.

In *coverage analysis,* the amount of "action" seen by a designated program element can be assessed. For example, the analysis can indicate how many times each statement in a program or module was executed. Such an analysis indicates if certain code is unreachable or if code that was expected to be reached was in fact reached. An additional use of static analysis is in improving the efficiency of a program. By studying the coverage analysis for a variety of input, the programmer can determine which part or parts of the program are most involved during execution. These sections are then likely candidates for optimization. Optimization can be obtained by using a different or more refined algorithm or by writing the section directly in machine code. When white-box testing is being done, coverage analysis indicates if the expected paths were taken by a particular test case. Other analyses can show the minimum and maximum values ever assigned to a variable during a run, the number of times a variable takes on a particular value, the calling sequence, and so on.

An *assertion* is a formal logical expression that specifies a condition or a relation among variables in a program. To aid in checking the correctness of a program, assertions can be inserted into various points in a program. The assertions assert that a particular condition or state is assumed (by the code) to be true at that point. For instance, an assertion might state that the value of some integer variable is assumed to be greater than or equal to zero. The assertions are then checked at run time. If the assertion is met (true), execution continues. If the condition specified by the assertion is not met, a message is displayed and/or execution is halted. *Assertion checking* can be used as an aid to debugging. Assertions can also be placed in the code so that there is a mapping from each assertion to each design or requirement specification. Such assertions can be used to check the completeness and correctness with which the design or requirements were implemented.

Regression testing involves rerunning previously run test cases to detect errors created by recent changes or corrections. Regression testing takes place during system development and during maintenance. Regression testing tools provide the ability to automatically drive the program through its test data and report any differences between the current results and prior results of the test run.

8.4.3   CASE Tools: General Environments

General environments contain basic tools that support all phases of the software life cycle. The degree of integration of the environment can vary greatly, and the power of each tool can vary greatly, as well. General environments can be focused on a particular model of the life cycle and particular methods, or they can be adapted to a number of software methodologies. The basic components of a general environment are shown schematically in Figure 8.12. The five basic components include:

Graphics capabilities. The environment should include software that can pictorially represent various aspects of the software process. It should sup-

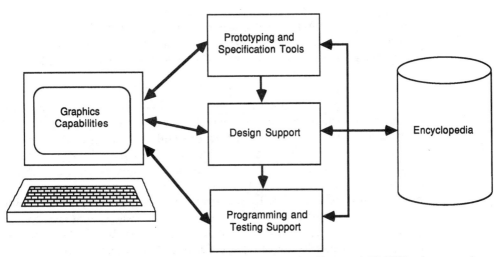

Figure 8.12 Major Components of a General CASE Environment

port the generation, editing, and displaying of different kinds of graphical representations.

Prototyping and specification tools. Prototyping tools can be used with the graphical capabilities of the system to automatically generate user interface screens, diagram a data base, or model the system. Specification tools can include diagramming techniques, as well as the storage and manipulation of textual materials. Automated checks for consistency and completeness can be included.

Design support. Design support includes tools for the creation of the design of the system and for the analysis of the design. The analysis should include checks for inconsistencies, ambiguities, and omissions in the design.

Programming and testing support. Tools for creating, debugging and testing source code are included here. In the ideal environment, source code would be generated directly from design specifications.

Encyclopedia. The encyclopedia forms the central repository of the general environment. It holds knowledge about the software enterprise and its structure, functions, procedures, data, processes, and so on. Its primary functions are to support information management, version control, and maintenance.

Examples of general environments include ITT's PSE (Redwine and others, 1984), GTE's STEP (Griffen, 1984), TRW's SPS (Boehm and others, 1984), UNIX (Ritchie and Thompson, 1974; Kernighan and Mashey, 1981), and APSE (Stoneman, 1980; Wallace and Charette, 1984). Two of these, UNIX and APSE, will be discussed in more detail.

8.4.4   Example of a General CASE Environment: UNIX

UNIX is one of the oldest and most popular environments. UNIX is somewhat different in character from most CASE environments. From one viewpoint, UNIX is an operating system that handles a wide variety of application software. From another viewpoint, it is a general CASE environment. There are interesting historical reasons for this dual nature.

UNIX was developed in 1969 by two individuals (D. Ritchie and K. Thompson) who wished to provide programmers with tools to make programming easier. They based their tools on an operating system where, for the sake of convenience, all files have the same structure. UNIX files are defined as strings of characters, so data files, user program files, and operating system program files appear alike to the system. This eliminated the need for the usual access routines and extra control structures then typical of operating systems. Because data and program files are not distinct, data produced by a program and stored in a file can be used by another program with little or no inconvenience. The basic system interfaces for input and output treat files, input/output devices, and programs in the same way. Thus, a program does not have to be concerned about where the data it uses or produces come from or go to. In addition, all operating system functions, such as listing the contents of a user's directory, are implemented as user programs. These functions are therefore open to users, who can change them at will.

UNIX interfaces with users through what is called a *shell*. The *shell* is basically an interpreter for commands from the user. All commands are seen by the shell as requests to run programs. UNIX comes with a number of system programs (over 200 in UNIX System III), called UNIX tools, that can be used to help the user create programs or documents, manipulate files, and so on. The philosophy of the UNIX system is founded on the use of these tools. By providing a variety of tools and allowing users to select which tools they care to use, a great deal of flexibility is provided. The user is not forced to use a monolithic operating system that may or may not be capable of providing the services the user wants.

Due to the nature of file handling in UNIX, output from one tool can be directed (piped) as input to another. Very high level programs can be created by stringing together a series of tools using piping. Each program can serve a particular function for the user and can consist of standard UNIX tools, modified UNIX tools, and/or user-supplied tools. The order of execution of the tools can be varied from program to program, and the programs can be very simple or very complex.

The advantages of UNIX are numerous. First, UNIX is available on many machines. This is because the number of UNIX primitives is small and easy to define. Most UNIX tools are written in C, which does require that a C compiler be available. However, C compilers are readily available for many machines. Second, the system is flexible, powerful, and conceptually simple. Programs can be rapidly created and tested, with a minimum of user-written code. The numerous UNIX tools support the power and flexibility and encourage reuse and creativity. Third, the system is based on modularity. Each tool provides one function and serves as one module in a program. Modularity aids debugging, understanding, and reusability. Finally, many of the UNIX tools can be used as aids in documentation. They provide direct support for many software engineering tasks.

There are some disadvantages to UNIX. Perhaps the greatest criticism of UNIX as a general CASE environment is its main strength — its flexibility. Each UNIX tool is a separate or stand-alone tool. Its method and place of use in the environment are not specified. The best choice of which tool to use is not obvious in every case. Thus only a sophisticated user can utilize the full power of UNIX and its tools. Furthermore, because UNIX is so flexible, it supports almost any life cycle model in general and requires substantial work to make it support a particular life cycle. UNIX provides no direct support for requirements analysis and specification, for high-level design, or for the overhead activities associated with mid-size and larger project development (for example, configuration management or use of standards). The philosophy of UNIX is very individualistic, the exact opposite of what is needed for larger project support.

A final, but very important, criticism of UNIX is its user interface. The interface is a command language. Each tool has its own command, most of which require a number of parameters. The command language is extremely terse. Feedback is nonexistent or minimal. The command language is extensive, as well. All these factors taken together produce an interface that is very difficult to learn in depth. Most users learn a minimal subset of UNIX, including just enough commands to solve most of their problems, and never tap many of the resources available to them.

A solution to the disadvantages of UNIX is to use UNIX as the basis for a CASE system. There are certain advantages to this approach (Cureton, 1988). UNIX is available on more types of computers than any other operating system, and it is estimated that more than a half-million programmers use some form of UNIX. This popularity, along with an industry-wide drive for standardization in many areas, has created a push for standardization of UNIX. Furthermore, a number of technological trends are closely tied to UNIX, which should have positive effects on the development of CASE technology. One such trend is the support of windowing and standardized user interfacing through the use of User Interface Management Systems and the communication protocol, X Window. These are discussed in more detail in Section 8.5. A second trend is in database technology. The design of database systems for CASE environments is challenging, and it appears that the relational database model has only limited usefulness in this arena. Object-oriented and associative-database technologies are receiving increased attention as possible approaches. A final trend is in the area of networking and data communications. Without the ability to communicate with other systems, a CASE system or workstation has limited use. Organizations are beginning to realize the importance of having open networking and are supporting network standards such as Ethernet, OSI, and NFS.

A number of CASE systems have already been developed that have UNIX as an intermediate level between the user level and the machine level. Examples include ARGUS (Stucki, 1983), SPS (Boehm, 1984), and USE (Wasserman, 1983).

8.4.5 Second Example of a General CASE Environment: APSE

A second example of a general CASE environment is the Ada Programming Support Environment (APSE). A set of specifications for APSE was released in 1980 (Stoneman, 1980). Since that time, the Department of Defense has funded three efforts to implement a subset of APSE called Minimal Ada Programming Support Environment (MAPSE). A MAPSE contains the minimal tools necessary to implement, debug, and manage Ada programs. Additional tools are to be added to support design, specification, testing, and integration, thereby transforming MAPSE into APSE. The three MAPSE efforts are similar. The version called ALS (Ada Language System), developed by SofTech, Inc., will be described here.

The ALS provides tools for testing, documenting, managing, and maintaining Ada programs intended for use in dedicated, embedded target computers (Wallace and Charette, 1984). Information on a project can be stored in a database throughout the life cycle. ALS is designed to accept programs written in the assembly language of the target computer as well as programs written in Ada. This allows programmers to create special subprograms that can access capabilities of the target computers that cannot be directly accessed by Ada.

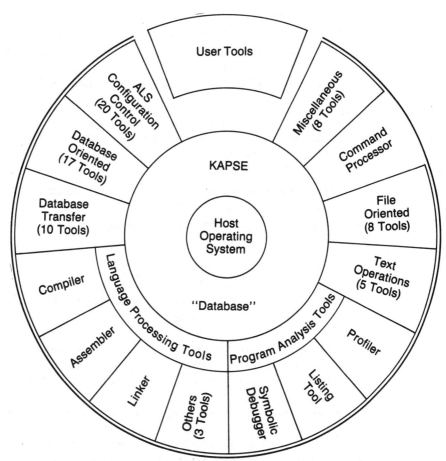

Figure 8.13 Structure of ALS (from Wallace and Charette, 1985)

Figure 8.13 shows the structure of ALS. ALS is designed to interact with a host operating system called KAPSE (Kernel APSE). The KAPSE allows the ALS tools to be host hardware and host operating system independent. The KAPSE acts as the interface between the host operating system and host tools. Additionally, KAPSE provides services for maintaining the ALS database. Over 70 different tools are included with ALS. These can be broken down into nine categories, each of which is shown in Figure 8.13. These nine categories include:

Language processing tools. These tools include compilers and linkage editors. They also provide for the examination, modification, and maintenance of the Ada program libraries.

Program analysis tools. The program analysis tools include an interactive debugger and generation support for various reports and listings without requiring recompilation, linking, or execution of a program.

Configuration management tools. These tools provide a system for describing and controlling the creation, modification, and current status of a program.

Database transfer tools. These tools aid in the creation and maintenance of the ALS database. Activities such as the archiving of files, database backup, and the flow of database information to and from other ALS tools are handled by these tools.

Database-oriented tools. Tools in this category allow the ALS user to examine and modify the contents of the ALS database. The associations, attributes, and structure of the database can be manipulated, but not the data portion of files in the database.

File-oriented tools. These tools allow the user to examine and modify the data portion of the database files.

Text operation tools. The main interactive text entry and formatting facilities are supported by the text operation tools.

Miscellaneous tools. This category of tools includes user help and tutorials.

User-supplied tools. ALS makes no distinction between system-defined and user-defined tools. Therefore, the user is able to extend the basic tools of ALS by adding tailor-made tools.

To use the ALS tools, the user issues commands through the command processor. Commands can be strung together, giving the appearance of a pipe. However, the system does not use piping in the way it is defined in UNIX.

The advantage of ALS is that it provides strong support for the implementation of Ada software and configuration management. In addition, it provides portability of user programs and tools, allowing the tailoring of the system to match an organization's practices and to enforce management policies. The disadvantage of ALS is that it does not support the entire life cycle at this point. It will be difficult to add additional support as the current system has high system overhead and uses large amounts of storage. The use of the KAPSE approach adds overhead to every operating system call.

8.4.6   Third Example of a General CASE Environment: Teamwork

As a final example of a general CASE environment, but one with a different approach than the two discussed so far, is the array of integrated CASE tools offered by Cadre Technologies, Inc., called Teamwork. Their tools include:

Teamwork/SA: a tool set for systems analysis based on the structured analysis technique of Yourdon and DeMarco

Teamwork/RT: a tool set based on Teamwork/SA for modeling real-time systems

Teamwork/IM: a system analysis tool for creating entity–relationship models (used chiefly in building database systems)

Teamwork/SD: a tool set for system design based on the structured design technique of Constantine and DeMarco

Teamwork/ADA: a design and coding tool for Ada programming

Teamwork/ACCESS: provides access to data from all Teamwork tools, creating a project database and facilitating project management, documentation, and integration with other tools

As examples of what this environment can do, let us look more closely at Teamwork/SA and Teamwork/SD.

Teamwork/SA allows a user to create, store, and update the elements of the structured analysis method, including data-flow diagrams, activity specifications (called process specifications or P-specs in their terminology), and a data dictionary. The interface is windowed and graphics oriented, allowing users to view and edit several windows simultaneously. A sample screen is shown in Figure 8.14. This screen shows a high-level data flow diagram for a Perform Laundry Tasks system. Once the user creates a data flow diagram such as the one shown, the data elements are automatically entered into the data dictionary (without definitions) and the outline of process specifications for any primitive activities (those not expanded into lower-level data flow diagrams) are automatically created. The process specification outlines include a list of all inputs and outputs as indicated in

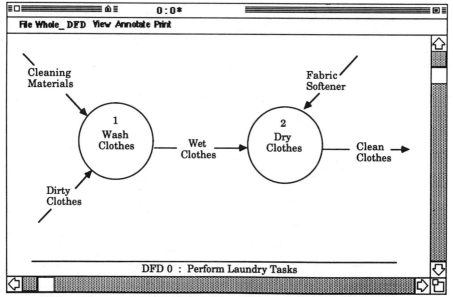

Figure 8.14 Sample Screen Showing the Use of Teamwork/SA

the data flow diagram. The user may move among the data flow diagram editor, the data dictionary editor and the activity specification editor at will.

The Teamwork/SA editor for creating the model elements is intelligent and syntax directed. The editor knows the rules for making the elements and how they should interrelate in the specification. The editor works together with a consistency checker to detect problems in the specification as it is being created. A configuration management function in the system collects models into hierarchical sets. Analysis can begin at any level, and data-flow diagrams (which define the essential structure of the analysis model) can be changed to repartition the model. Relationships can be established between the data-flow diagrams and other components, such as process specifications and data dictionaries. Versions are automatically tracked, allowing analysts to experiment with different versions of models. Once a model has been created, the consistency checker can be used to assess the model's accuracy by detecting errors in and between data-flow diagrams, data dictionary entries, and process specifications. Additional features include the ability to attach ad hoc notes to any element of the specification, to interface with document production software, to answer queries through searching, and to attach status labels to any object in the model. Status labels can be used by management to monitor project progress.

Teamwork/SD implements structured design. Thus the elements created using this tool include structure charts, data dictionaries, and module specifications. An example of a structure chart created using Teamwork/SD is shown in Figure 8.15. Like Teamwork/SA, Teamwork/SD uses an intelligent editor to notify the user of

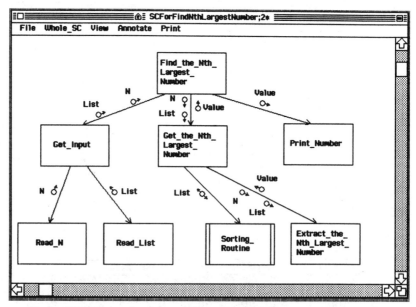

Figure 8.15 Sample Screen Showing the Use of Teamwork/SD

inconsistencies or incompleteness in the elements. In addition, the system can make higher-level analyses of the design, including checking the design against established criteria, checking and quantifying the amount of coupling, and checking the shape of the structure chart. Extensive cross-referencing facilities are included, which allow the user to see lists of modules and all modules they invoke, modules and the names of modules that invoke them, modules by type, and so on. An interface table editor allows the user to trace and list in several ways the interfacing of the modules (parameters). Ad hoc notes, query answering, and status labels are also provided.

The facilities provided by Teamwork/ACCESS are what make the Teamwork products into an integrated environment. ACCESS makes the data dictionary, project status information, and project notes available to all the tools. It also allows the interfacing of Teamwork tools to other tools such as documentation tools, project management packages, and other software development tools.

8.4.7   Status of CASE

Although CASE offers great promise for increasing productivity, organizations have been somewhat slow to adopt a software engineering environment. One estimate is that only 2 percent of potential users have bought into CASE (*Computerworld*, July 8, 1987). There are a number of reasons for this. One is that getting into CASE represents a long-term commitment to a particular method of software engineering. Developers and programmers must learn to use the tools of the environment, and the organization needs to build up a repository of information that can be used in development and maintenance. Both of these activities take time. Thus on the first project using a CASE environment there may actually be a drop in productivity compared to the old methods. Only on the later projects can the payoff be realized. The greatest success stories for CASE have come from organizations that already had a methodology in place, had a commitment from management to support CASE, and selected CASE tools to support their current methodology.

A second problem with the current status of CASE is that there is a great amount of variability in the products available. Some products are intended to support framing activities, some support programming activities, and others are intended as general environments. Because even a compiler or an editor can legitimately be called a CASE tool, the buyer must understand what is available and what goals he or she has. Some tools have been criticized as being basically "electronic Etch-a-Sketch" (*Computerworld*, July 8, 1987). Such tools are capable of drawing neat, easily edited diagrams, but they only automate some of the clerical aspects of software development. They do increase productivity to some extent, but do little to facilitate the creative aspects of development or to enhance the quality or reliability of the final product.

Probably the most important characteristic the buyer of CASE tools should look for is the degree to which they are integrated. Integration refers to the amount of information that is shared among the functions of the environment and the services automatically performed by the environment. The more information that is shared and the greater the number of automatic services, the more highly integrated the environment is. General environments are more integrated than framing or programming environments because they support more of the life cycle. However, within each category there can be variability in the degree of integration as well. For example, a framing tool such as FreeFlow from Iconix automatically creates a data dictionary based on the information provided in the data-flow diagrams, provides automatic consistency checking between the data-flow diagrams, data dictionary, and activity specifications, and creates skeletal versions of the detailed designs. (Iconix also provides additional, integrated tools for the later development stages.) Other framing tools may not provide as much integration. As an estimate of the lack of maturity and integration of CASE tools, Jones estimates that ultimately a CASE should contain about 110 tools. Most environments available today contain 30 or fewer tools.

A final barrier to the widespread adoption of CASE is the cost. Although many systems run on microcomputers or workstations, the 1988 costs range from approximately $500 for only one component of a system to $12,500 and up for more complete systems. The most widely installed system (according to the developers) is Index's Excelerator, which costs $8400. Annual maintenance fees may also be required.

8.5 User Interface Management Systems

A special category of CASE tools is *user interface management systems* (*UIMS*). Originally, UIMSs were thought of as tools that would allow each user to program a personalized interface. The capabilities that a UIMS should provide for its users include the ability to control program sequencing and the ability to organize and design screen layouts. In controlling sequencing, the user should be able to create commands that invoke a series of actions, similar to a subroutine in a programming language. After the command is executed, control returns to the user, who can then specify another command. The user should also be able to interactively create the layout for a screen and design icons, menus, and help screens. Another important capability of a sophisticated UIMS is to provide embedded help capabilities. The system stays aware of where a user is in a sequence of possible activities and can provide context-sensitive help.

Although UIMSs were originally conceived as being an end-user product, they are being most actively used in the development of software. This trend has resulted from several factors. One factor is that the user of a UIMS has to be fairly knowledgeable. The user must have some programming experience and a familiarity with computers. Another major factor is that developers have discovered that UIMSs are a powerful development tool, providing prototyping capabilities, control over interface standards, and productivity enhancements. Let us look at each of these capabilities separately.

UIMSs as Prototyping Tools. The advantages of prototyping the user interface for a system under development were discussed in Chapter 3. The basic idea behind prototyping the user interface is to design the system as it will look to the user and then test the proposed design on the user. A prototype can be more or less sophisticated. At the lower end, there are paper mock-ups of the interface. An intermediate level of sophistication would be to produce the mock-ups on the target machine, but without showing the behavior of the interface. At the upper end, the prototype accepts input and provides realistic responses. A prototyping tool might also produce source code to support the interface. UIMSs provide support at the upper end of prototyping. A UIMS is basically a high-level interface design language, allowing the user to quickly design and implement an interface without programming it in a standard programming language.

UIMSs as Interface Standards. One primary benefit of UIMSs is in standardizing the user interfaces of the various software systems running on a computer. Chapter 3 emphasized that consistency of a user interface within a piece of software makes the interface easier to learn, easier to remember, and less likely to cause errors. Consistency across applications and system domains, provided by an interface standard, can have many of the same benefits. A number of visual standards are currently in use, including the Apple Macintosh (Apple Computer,1987), MS Windows, and Interleaf. An organization can also set its own standards.

Increases in Productivity. One source of increased productivity from UIMSs stems from the ease of prototyping, as just described. While it might take all day to lay out a screen in COBOL or FORTRAN, it can be done in less than an hour with a UIMS. This, in turn, makes it easier and more feasible to realize the benefits of prototyping. A second source of increased productivity stems from the use of an interface standard within an organization. If users must use a number of different systems, their productivity will be enhanced by similar standards across the systems. The skills learned for interacting with one system will help in learning other systems, and the user will be less likely to encounter the negative transfer (interference) of skills often encountered when switching between systems (Smith, Zirkler, and Mynatt, 1985).

A second source of increased productivity comes from the fact that using a UIMS supports the creation of two-part software systems. In such systems, the software that supports the user interface is separated as much as possible from the part that supports the functional capabilities of the system. As mentioned in Chapter 3, there are a number of advantages to creating two-part systems. Because up to 70 percent of source code for systems today can be concerned with user interfacing (Shneiderman, cited in *Computerworld*, July 8, 1988), the interface is no longer simply a minor part of a system. As a major part of the system, the design of the interface is best handled as a separate design problem, independently from the functional capabilities. To the degree that the interface is independent of the functional portion, the two parts become easier to design, create, test, and maintain. Alterations in the interface, such as those brought about through changes in available input/output devices, can be made with minimal changes to the functional portion of the system. Likewise, changes in the functional portion can be made with less concern for their effects on the interface.

Two-part systems are an important step toward freeing software from hardware constraints and supporting portability. Any system has two fronts on which to face hardware concerns: (1) the hardware that the system executes on, and (2) the input and output devices directly controlled by the system. Two-part systems make these two fronts into separate concerns. While some CASE tools are designed to help with the problems of portability among different hardware that the system is to execute on, a UIMS can facilitate portability of the interface portion of a system. An even more powerful aid to portability comes from combining a UIMS and a data communication protocol, X Window, as described below.

As a final aid to productivity, UIMSs are based on the concept of reusable code. UIMSs utilize reusable code and encourage the use of such code in the application portion of the system.

8.5.1 X Window: A Communication System to Support UIMSs

The vision of many system designers today is that users will be able to move easily among applications because of the uniform user interface style used by the applications and that the user will be unaware of which host hardware is running the system they are using. To the user, the environment will be "seamless." To make this vision a reality requires three components:

- User interface standards
- UIMS
- A way to make user interfaces device independent

Two of these components, user interface standards and UIMSs, have been described. The final component is supplied by X Window. X Window is a set of network protocols developed at the Massachusetts Institute of Technology with support from a number of vendors, including Digital Equipment Corporation (Scheifler and Gettys, 1987). The goal of X Window is to make user interfacing device independent.

In most applications programs, the program directly controls what is displayed on the screen and deals directly with user input. The program must understand the requirements of the particular input and output devices it uses and service those devices accordingly. Although the program may call operating system routines or library functions to aid in these tasks, this only pushes the device dependency back one step from the application program. Such programs have limited portability. They will run only on the hardware and/or operating system they were orginally designed to run on. The approach used by X Window is to decouple the application software from the device handling. The decoupling goes to the extent that the application communicates with the devices over a network. Thus the application becomes independent of both the type and location of the display and input devices. Users may run software resident on a remote computer and make use of whatever input/output devices they have available locally.

Looking in more detail at how X Window works, it is basically an asynchronous communication protocol using a server and a client, as shown in Figure 8.16. The client is the application program, and the remote device handling is the server. (Note that this is the reverse of typical communication protocols.) The protocol can be transmitted over any network that provides reliable data transfer and is independent of the server's operating system and display hardware. The client end of the communication path includes the application program, the X Library, and X Window primitives. The X Library uses the network to communicate

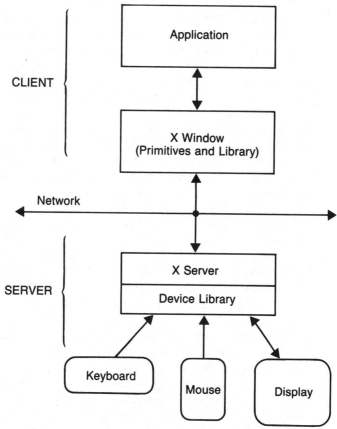

Figure 8.16 Structure of the X Window System

with the X Server. The X Server interprets the messages sent to it and manages the appropriate window and input devices.

The X system allows a client to have multiple connections to a server, multiple applications to have simultaneous connections to the same server, and one application to have simultaneous connections to multiple servers. At the server, the X Server owns a root window encompassing the entire display. Each application creates one or more windows, which become children of the root window. Each child window may have children, and so on. The client is responsible for maintaining the contents of its windows, as well as requesting icons, fonts, new windows, and the like. However, the server is responsible for creating and managing these resources when requested by the client.

X Window grew out of the need for intercommunications among workstations and is thus designed mainly to work with mainframe-to-workstation or workstation-to-workstation communication. It is not a new way to use terminals. In fact, X Window will not work with terminals, only with workstations. The development of X Window has received both financial support and encouragement from workstation vendors. There are several reasons for this enthusiasm. One major appeal of X Window is that it is in the public domain. The protocols are available to any vendor free of charge and with no obligations. All source code and documentation for a version that runs on VAX and other computer systems using Berkeley UNIX are available at low cost. A second appeal is that X Window has been implemented on a number of different systems and takes account of issues involved with handling different systems. Finally, X Window was designed for graceful expansion into new domains.

X Window is not a user interface management system. However, it does serve as a natural and very powerful platform for such systems. X Window only specifies how to do things on a screen; it does not specify how those things should be arranged or how they should behave. To get the most productivity from the X Window system, an organization needs all three components: an interface standard, a UIMS, and X Window. The interface standard provides the guidelines for how user interfaces should look and behave, the UIMS aids in prototyping and building the interface, and the X Window system aids in both building the system and making it portable to other hardware environments. Figure 8.17 consists of a modified form of Figure 8.16 showing where a UIMS fits into the total system. The application is able to pass its interfacing requests through the UIMS or to directly access X Window. The UIMS accesses the X Window system to create displays and handle input.

Graphics and windowing systems such as Apple's User Interface Toolbox and Microsoft Corporations's Windows are early forms of UIMSs. These systems are embedded in kernels working with operating systems and thus become basically extensions of the operating system command set. Some UIMSs have been developed and used in-house by companies such as TRW, Inc., Boeing Company, and Computervision Corporation. Recently, however, UIMSs have become available commercially. In 1986, Apollo Computer, Inc., released Domain/Dialogue, the first commercial UIMS product. The current version of Domain/Dialogue is based

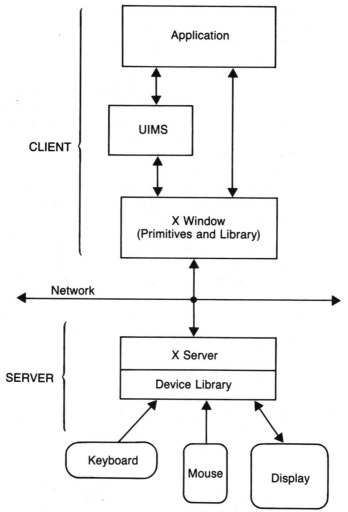

Figure 8.17 Structure of the X Window System Integrated with a UIMS

on the X Window system and is called Open Dialogue. Digital Equipment Corporation's DECwindows is also based on X Window and will probably support the MS Windows or Apple Macintosh visual interfacing standards.

8.6   Object-Oriented Development

Object-oriented development is playing an increasingly significant role in the design and implementation of software systems. Its influence has been compared to that of structured programming in the 1970s. Object-oriented development uses simulation as a design and programming paradigm. Simulating the behavior of physical objects in a real-world system on a computer is not a new idea. Object-oriented development takes this approach one step further and applies it to abstract systems as well.

An historically important example of object-oriented development was the creation of the software for the Xerox Star workstation, which was released in 1981. The Xerox Star is a personal workstation designed for use in an office environment. The system was designed to handle a wide variety of office tasks, such as document handling, electronic mail, data processing, and printing. When it was released, the system was revolutionary in two ways. First, it was one of the first workstation systems to use bit-mapped graphics, which allow high resolution and great flexibility in displays. Second, the design of the system was based on a conceptual model of how the user would function in a real office and used visual metaphors (icons) and mouse-based interaction to implement the conceptual model. The screen display represents a desktop, with electronic metaphors for the physical objects of an office also present (for example, file folders, file cabinets, mailboxes, and pages from a document). By using the mouse, activities in the system are carried out in a manner that mimics physical actions in an office. For example, to file a document the appropriate document icon is selected by pointing to it with the mouse; then the icon is dragged to the file cabinet icon. These actions mimic what might be done in a physical environment: picking up a folder, walking to a file cabinet, and putting the folder in the cabinet. The desktop metaphor has since been used in the design of other workstation and microcomputer interfaces, most notably the Apple Macintosh. The desktop metaphor in the Star system was designed and implemented in an object-oriented fashion. The abstract objects in the interface were objects in the system. To see how and why this was done, let us take a closer look at first object-oriented design and then object-oriented programming.

8.6.1 Object-oriented Design

Object-oriented design is fundamentally different than traditional design methods, which are based on decomposition and the procedural/data model of programming. In the traditional approach, the overall system is decomposed into a set of modules, each of which represents a major step in the overall system process. The modules map directly onto the subprograms (subroutines, functions, procedures, and the like) of traditional languages such as FORTRAN, COBOL, C, and Pascal. Subprograms in these languages represent procedural abstractions. That is, calling a subprogram is like using a very high level language construct to perform some action (procedure). Data, in the traditional approach, are seen as separate entities from procedures. Procedures are the actors in the system, and the data elements are passive elements in the system.

As an example of the traditional methods, consider a simple system for drawing a rectangle on a display device. For the system to draw a rectangle, it must know the desired size and placement of the rectangle. The size is determined by knowing the height and length, and the placement is determined by knowing the desired x-coordinate and y-coordinate of the upper-left corner of the rectangle on the screen. The system will then be responsible for drawing the rectangle. A simple block diagram showing inputs and output is presented in Figure 8.18, and a data-flow diagram of the system is shown in Figure 8.19. Using the structured design method (as in Chapter 4), the structure chart in Figure 8.20 is produced. Notice that the system has been decomposed into a hierarchy of modules that reflects the major functions of the overall process.

With an object-oriented approach, the design proceeds in an entirely different manner. Rather than factoring the system into modules that denote operations, the system is structured around objects that exist in the model of the system. If the objects from the problem definition are extracted and their relationships to each

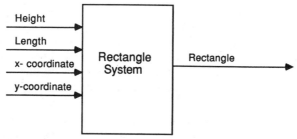

Figure 8.18 Diagram of a Simple System to Draw a Rectangle

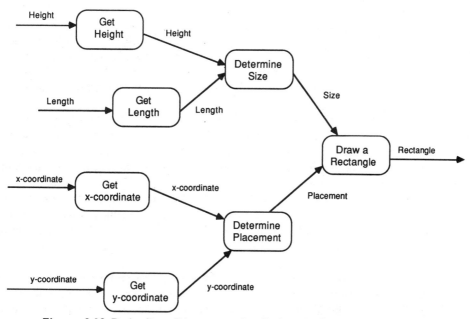

Figure 8.19 Data-flow Diagram of a System to Draw a Rectangle

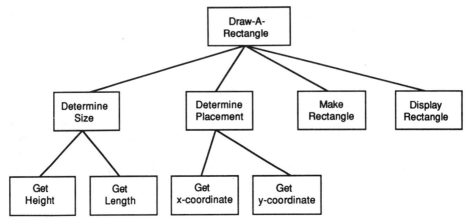

Figure 8.20 Structure Chart for a System to Draw a Rectangle

other diagrammed, the structure shown in Figure 8.21 is generated. The three-dimensional ovals in the figure represent objects, and the arrows represent the paths of messages that the objects can send to each other. The meaning of these symbols will be explained in more detail later. For now, the diagram serves to make some points concerning object-oriented design. Notice that the object-oriented design closely matches the model of the system as shown in the data-flow diagram or as abstracted from the verbal description of the system. The design based on the traditional method, on the other hand, is created only through a complete transformation of the problem space. This transformation is necessary because of the nature of the target programming languages (for example, FORTRAN, Pascal, COBOL, or C). The target languages support only procedural abstraction, so each component of the final design must represent a procedure or operation. Using object-oriented programming, the objects themselves behave (perform operations) so that a description of the objects in the problem space and their relationships to each other *is* the design of the system.

As we have seen, in object-oriented design the system is composed of objects. An *object* is an entity that behaves. The behavior of an object includes its responses to actions from outside and the actions that it elicits from or requires of other objects. An object includes both data and *methods*. The data within an object can only be modified by the methods of that object. Program execution proceeds by *messages* being passed to objects. The object then responds to the message (behaves) by producing new objects as results. Object-oriented programming and its terminology are explained in more detail later. For now, let us examine more closely how object-oriented design proceeds. The major steps are:

1. **Examine the requirements of the program and identify the objects in the system.** In this step, the major actors, agents, and servers in the problem space are defined. In general, the objects identified are derived from the nouns used in describing the problem. If several objects are similar, a class of objects may be formed.

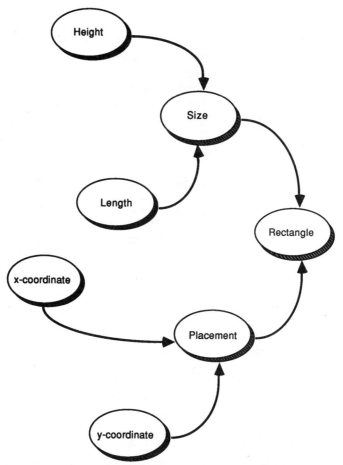

Figure 8.21 Object-oriented Design of a System to Draw a Rectangle

2. **For each object, identify the messages that can be received by the object and the messages that can be sent by the object.** Another way of stating this process is to say that the operations that may be suffered by each object and the operations required of each object must be identified. This step characterizes the behavior of each object or class of objects and defines the outside view or specification of each object.

3. **Design the appropriate data structures(s) to represent the data within the object and choose efficient algorithms for implementing the methods (operations) of the object.** In this step, the inside view of the object is defined. The inside view can be changed at any time without affecting users of the object. For example, the programmer may change the representation of a queue from a linked list to a stack. As long as the message protocol is not changed in any way, the modification will be invisible to other objects.

Systems designed by following these steps have some characteristics that it is important for large software systems to have. First, the systems are modular. Objects provide a natural way to modularize a system. Second, the interface between modules is understandable and clearly specified. The *message protocol* for each object clearly specifies its outside view. The protocol states what set of messages the object will respond to and the response the object will produce upon receiving a valid message. Third, the system is modifiable. Much of its modifiability is due to the modularity of the system. In general, the parts to be modified are localized to one or more objects and their related operations. Furthermore, objects can be readily added to the system.

8.6.2 Object-oriented Programming

Object-oriented design involves describing a system in terms of objects and their associated behaviors. In object-oriented programming, the system is implemented using an object-oriented programming language or by employing the ideas and concepts of object-oriented programming. These concepts include:

Object
Message
Class
Instance
Method
Subclasses and inheritance

This terminology grew out of Smalltalk, one of the first and most important object-oriented programming languages. The most recent version of Smalltalk makes consistent use of the object concept. All elements of the language, including control structures and data elements such as characters and integers, are treated uniformly as objects. The object-oriented concepts discussed here are based on the Smalltalk definitions.

Objects. An object is an entity that behaves. It responds to actions from outside (which are sent as messages), and it may elicit or require actions from other objects by sending messages. An object consists of both data and methods (operations or procedures). In addition, an object has the following characteristics:

- It has a state: a value plus the objects denoted by this value.
- It is characterized by the messages it responds to and the messages it is capable of sending.
- It is an instance of some class.
- It has a name.
- It has restricted visibility to and from other objects (not every object can send or receive messages from every other object).

- It may be viewed either from the outside by looking at its message protocol (interface) or from the inside by looking at its implementation detail.

Each object can be classified as an actor, an agent or a server, depending on how it relates to other objects. An actor object is one that receives no messages, but only sends messages to other objects. At the other extreme, a server object is one that only receives messages, but does not operate on other objects. An agent is an object that performs some operation on behalf of another object and may, in turn, operate on another object.

Messages. Objects communicate with one another through only one mechanism: messages. A message is a request for an object to carry out one of its operations. Each object has associated with it a message protocol that specifies which messages that object can respond to and determines what information within the object may be accessed or manipulated by other objects. The components of a message consist of the *receiver,* the *selector,* and the *arguments.* The receiver describes what object is to receive the message. The selector describes what operation is being requested, and the arguments include any extra data or information that the object needs to carry out the operation. The evaluation of a message expression results in a message being sent to the receiver.

Examples of messages include:

4 factorial The selector "factorial" is sent to the integer object "4". The result is to return the integer object "24."

8.19 + 27.5 The selector "+" is sent to the real object "8.19", along with the argument "27.5." The result is to return the real object "35.69."

TermPaper copy The selector "copy" is sent to the (user-defined) TextFile object "TermPaper." The result is to return the TextFile object "TermPaper.copy."

Class. A class is a description of a group of similar objects. It is an object that describes the implementation of a set of similar objects. It includes the set of operations that are defined for the class. To understand what is meant by a class, it is useful to distinguish between class (the description of an object) and objects that follow that description, called *instances.* For example, we may have a predefined class, *integer,* from which we create several instances (objects), for example, "1" or "−57." Or we may have a user-defined class, DollarsAndCents, from which we create a number of instances, for example, "$100.01" or "$3.99." Another example of a user-defined class might be TextFile, from which the instances "FormLetter" or "TermPaper" might be created.

Instance. An instance is an individual object in a class. Each instance has a value, but shares the methods stored with its class description. The methods described for class instances may be applied only to instances of a class and cannot be applied to the class itself. For example, it would make sense to send the selector "open" to an instance of the TextFile class, but it would not make sense to apply the same operation to an instance from the DollarsAndCents class.

Method. A method is a description of how to carry out an operation. It may specify changes to values of instances and it may specify other messages to be sent. It also specifies a value (object) to be returned.

Subclasses and Inheritance. Through the mechanisms of subclasses and inheritance, a hierarchy of classes can be created. Objects can be instances of a class, which can be a subclass of a higher class, and so on. Each subclass can inherit all the instance variables of its parent class, and it may define additional instances or contain only a restricted subset of the instances of the parent class. Each instance of a subclass inherits all the methods of its parent class, and it may define additional ones, modify existing ones, or hide methods from the parent class as well. For example, consider the TextFile class example used previously. TextFile might be a subclass of class File. The description for the class File might include the operations Open, Close, Rename, Delete, and Copy, which would all be inherited by the subclass TextFile. However, the description of the subclass TextFile might also include the operation Display, which allows the contents of the file to be displayed on a screen in text form. This operation would not be suitable for other types of files. On the other hand, if the File class description included an Execute operation, this operation would be excluded from the inheritance to the TextFile subclass.

8.6.3 Applying the Object-oriented Approach

Inheritance is an example of an object-oriented language feature that is available only in the language Smalltalk. Other languages support object-oriented programming to a greater or lesser degree. The packages feature of Ada and the module feature of Modula-2 provide considerable support. Through packages, abstract data types can be implemented, providing the class, modularity, and information-hiding capabilities of a true object-oriented language. To implement the Smalltalk message concept in Ada, procedure calls can be made on procedures encapsulated in an Ada package. Although instances can be created in Ada, they must be declared statically at compile time. They cannot be created dynamically, as in Smalltalk. Extensions of existing languages such as Pascal, Lisp and C have also been developed (for example, Objective-C, OOPC, Flavors, and Clascal). Standards for existing languages have been proposed as well (Jacky and Kalet, 1987; Isner, 1982). The drawback of these approaches, however, is that the programmer must make the style of the program object oriented. This is similar to the task facing the programmer in the late 1960s who wished to create structured programs using a nonstructured language. While the task is not impossible, it is made more awkward and difficult by the lack of appropriate language features.

It is important to note that at this time object-oriented design and programming are only partial software development methods. They focus only on the design and implementation stages of software development. Furthermore, some experts feel that object-oriented programming is more suitable for mid-sized programs (Schmucker, 1988). The steps involved in deriving an object-oriented design have not been formalized and "require a great deal of real world knowledge and intuitive understanding of the problem" (Abbott, 1983). To become a viable development method, object-oriented design needs to be associated with an appropriate requirements and analysis method. Booch (1987) suggests Jackson Structured Development might be appropriate. (Jackson's system of program development, a forerunner of Jackson Structured Design, was discussed in Section 8.2.3.) Wiener and Sincovec (1984) have proposed a design method and described how object-oriented development might proceed through all stages of software development. Given the newness of the approach and its lack of an integrated software life cycle methodology, it will probably be a number of years before object-oriented development becomes widely accepted.

8.7 Current Status of Software Engineering

There is little doubt that the demand for software and thus software engineering is strong and will increase in the future. For example, while data-processing costs in the United States were approximately 2 percent of the gross national product in 1970, they are projected to be 10 percent or more in the early 1990s. Furthermore, it has been estimated that the demand for software increases tenfold each decade, having resulted in a hundredfold increase between 1965 and 1985 (Musa, 1985). While the growth in demand for software has accelerated, software development rates have been increasing more slowly. This is due primarily to two factors: the number of software professionals available and productivity rates. A shortage of software professionals exists now and will probably continue into the future. Although there was rapid growth in the number of programmers through the 1960s and 1970s, this rate has slowed. Furthermore, the number of students choosing computer science as a major dropped by 50 percent in 1984–1985 and was continuing to drop in the late 1980s (Higher Education Research Institute, 1988). Great increases in productivity could make up for a lack of personnel; however, productivity rates have not increased fast enough to keep up with the demand for software and to overcome the lack of personnel. It has been estimated that productivity is increasing at a rate of about 4 percent per year. The overall picture has been painted as follows: personnel are increasing at a rate of approximately 4 percent per year, productivity is increasing at approximately 4 percent per year, and demand for software is increasing at a rate of 12 percent per year (Dolatta, 1976; Musa, 1985). Clearly, this creates a widening gap between demand and the ability to produce.

The primary goal of software engineering is to address one of these two major causes of the software shortage: productivity. Throughout this book, it has been stressed that software engineering techniques are aimed at producing a quality, maintainable software product. As maintenance is where two-thirds of the cost of owning software lies, a product that is easier to maintain is one that is cheaper and more productive to maintain. It is time now to ask two questions: "Do software engineering techniques work?" and "Are software engineering principles and techniques used in the actual production of software?" The answer to the first question is a definite yes. A number of studies have shown that reduced software costs and more reliable software result from the application of some software engineering techniques (Hecht and Houghton, 1982; Yeh, 1985; Card, Church, and Agresti, 1986).

The answer to the second question, concerning how widely software engineering is used, is "Not much." It is surprising to find how little software engineering technology is applied to the development and maintenance of software. A study by Zelkowitz and others (1984) surveyed in depth the software development techniques used by 30 organizations in the United States and Japan, including five IBM divisions and companies such as AT&T Bell Telephone Laboratories, Digital Equipment Corporation, Hewlett-Packard, Microsoft, Sperry Univac, TRW, and Xerox Corporation. The type of software being developed was all revenue producing and included government contract software, data-processing applications, and systems software. Figure 8.22 shows the percentage of companies actually using (on most of their projects) the listed software engineering practices. All the companies surveyed use high-level languages, and almost all have on-line access for development, technologies that came to the fore in the late 1960s and early 1970s. The next most widely used techniques are reviews and program design languages, techniques widely introduced in the 1970s. Techniques of the 1980s, including formal techniques and the use of automated tools, are infrequently or never used.

The picture of the prototypical software development process that emerged from the survey was as follows. Developers work two to seven to a terminal. Natural language is used in writing the requirements. (No company used anything except natural language.) No analysis tools, such as PSL/PSA, were ever used except on toy projects. Reviews are used to determine if the system architecture is correct, specifications are complete, the system interfaces are defined, and if the system is feasible. Designs are almost always expressed in program design language (pseudocode). Tools used for design are text processors and formatters. No tools are used to analyze the structure or completeness of the design. Coding is done in a high-level language. However, unit testing has little machine support. Most checking is done manually. Testing is done on an adversarial basis. The programmer purports to have tested a module, and the manager decides whether or not to believe the programmer. Integration testing consists primarily of stress testing.

A number of reasons can be suggested for this failure to use software engineering technology. First, there is widespread skepticism among managers in the computer industry that new software technology can really save money. They have already heard that the latest development in computing (compilers, chief programmer teams, microcode, artificial intelligence, or whatever) is the best thing since sliced bread and is bound to produce unprecedented improvements in productivity. Many have been burned before by such claims and are reluctant to get burned

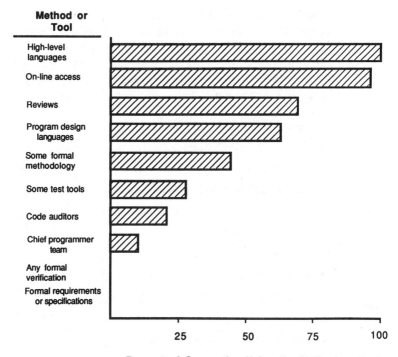

Method or Tool

- High-level languages
- On-line access
- Reviews
- Program design languages
- Some formal methodology
- Some test tools
- Code auditors
- Chief programmer team
- Any formal verification
- Formal requirements or specifications

25   50   75   100

Percent of Companies Using the Method or Tool

Figure 8.22 Software Engineering Practices Actually Used by Companies (based on Zelkowitz and others, 1984)

again. Furthermore, they can look at the cost figures. If coding is only taking 10 to 20 percent of a budget, a tool to increase programming productivity, even by a healthy 15 percent, is not going to save that much money on a substantial project. Anyway, the real cost of software development is people. A tool or technique must show itself able to permanently reduce the number of personnel needed or to at least keep staff size constant. Finally, there is the overall cost of the tool or technique itself: software costs, possible hardware costs, training costs, start-up costs, and so on. Changing to a new method usually produces an initial reduction in productivity, with benefits accrued further down the line. Most managers do not have the luxury of slowing down a current project by introducing new methods in order to speed up later projects.

A second factor holding back the adoption of software engineering methodologies and tools is the fragmentation and immaturity of the discipline. No uniform set of standards exists across the industry. Even the vocabulary of software engineering is inconsistent. Many of the tools and procedures are more or less standalone. As stated in the discussion of CASE tools, the real need in this area is for an integrated environment so that the information created and collected in one facet of a project can be readily used in another.

Finally, there is the basic problem of *technology transfer*. Technology transfer involves taking state-of-the-art ideas and moving them in an orderly, coherent fashion into day-to-day practice. It typically takes from 15 to 19 years for a method to go from an initial idea into a commercially available automated software technique (Riddle, 1984). Charette (1986) discusses a number of reasons why technology transfer is hindered in software engineering:

- Explosion in the numbers of practitioners
- Lack of management commitment to new technology
- Need for a low cost for the benefits derived from the technology
- Lack of software and computer literacy in top management
- Lack of positive experiences with other new technologies
- Lack of a well-developed technology
- Lack of standards
- Insufficient quantitative data to guide the choice of technologies
- Lack of a recognized need for a technology
- Lack of a formalism in the concepts and basic theories of software engineering
- Proprietary attitudes toward software technology

None of these issues is easy to solve. Most will require years of research, innovation, and hard work. One specific attempt that has been made to work on the problem of technology transfer has been the creation of the Software Engineering Institute at Carnegie Mellon University under the auspices of the Department of Defense. The Software Engineering Institute has as it goals "educating engineers, moving state-of-the-art software technologies into practice, and developing software engineering as a discipline" (SEI brochure).

Another hopeful avenue for technology transfer is through education. Each year more and more colleges and universities are adding software engineering to their curriculum (Leventhal and Mynatt, 1987). The students that take these courses or are exposed to software engineering concepts in other courses are the computer professionals of tomorrow. By bringing their high standards, knowledge, and expectations into the job, the technology will be slowly injected into industry and government. Gradually, engineering software will become the accepted way of developing and maintaining software.

8.8   Future of Software Engineering

As the previous section makes clear, the need for software engineers and software engineering is a real need now and will continue to be so in the foreseeable future. A bright future for software engineering, however, lies in the path of increased productivity. If software engineering can be shown to consistently produce significant increases in productivity, its acceptance will be greatly speeded. What are the chances of significantly increasing software productivity? Brooks (1987) describes the problem this way:

> The familiar software project, at least as seen by the nontechnical manager, has something of this character; it is usually innocent and straightforward, but is capable of becoming a monster of missed schedules, blown budgets, and flawed products. So we hear desperate cries for a silver bullet — something to make software costs drop as rapidly as computer hardware costs do.
>
> But, as we look to the horizon of a decade hence, we see no silver bullet. There is no single development, in either technology or in management technique, that by itself promises even one order-of-magnitude improvement in productivity, in reliability, in simplicity . . . .
>
> Skepticism is not pessimism, however. Although we see no startling breakthroughs — and indeed, I believe such to be inconsistent with the nature of software — many encouraging innovations are under way.

Brooks points out that there are two basic types of difficulties facing software technology. One set of difficulties is related to the *essence* of software. These are difficulties inherent in the nature of software. The other set of difficulties is related to *accident*. Accidental difficulties are those that accompany the production of software, but that are not inherent. The essence of software is its complexity, the fact that much of the complexity is arbitrary and by its nature can never be reduced, its changeability, and its invisibility.

Certainly, a number of breakthroughs in software development have produced great advances in productivity. These breakthroughs, however, have attacked only the accidental difficulties, and thus there is a natural limit to the effectiveness of further advances along these avenues. The three breakthroughs Brooks mentions include high-level languages, timesharing, and unified programming environments. High-level languages have done much to increase productivity, reliability, simplicity, and comprehensibility. Their impact comes from the fact that they free a program and the programmer from much of the accidental complexity associated with programming. With a high-level language the programmer can concentrate on the abstract tasks the program is to perform and can avoid concerns with registers, branching, input/output device handling, memory management, and so on. However, even though languages have evolved toward higher-level abstractions (for example, data types), the gains are increasingly smaller. At some point, a language may become more of a burden to use and to learn than a tool for freeing the programmer from complexity. Timesharing is another advance that has brought major improvements in productivity and quality. Timesharing provides the programmer with immediacy, enabling her or him to manage complexity by keeping the current task fresh in memory. No major improvements can be expected in this domain, as human responses have a certain natural limit. Unified programming environments, such as UNIX and Interlisp, seem to have had significant effects on productivity. These appear to be due to the fact that they overcome the accidental difficulties involved in making individual software units (for example, programs, files, library routines) function together as a whole.

A number of current technical developments promise hope for the future. The issue is which of these can offer real improvements in productivity by addressing the essence of software and which offer moderate help because they address only the accidental nature of software. Let us first consider some that probably offer only incremental improvements and address accidental difficulties.

Ada and other high-level languages. Ada embodies a philosophy of modulariza-tion, abstract data types, information hiding, and hierarchical structuring. Unfortunately, largely as a result of its requirements, Ada in its present form is often too elaborate and costly to use. These problems are not fatal. Working subsets of the vocabulary can be developed, and architectures to support the language can be created. Nonetheless, Ada is not the silver bullet. It is still simply a higher high-level language. Brooks predicts that Ada's biggest contribution will come from it being used to train programmers in modern software design techniques.

Object-oriented programming. Object-oriented programming offers help through the concepts of abstract data types and hierarchical types (classes, subclasses, and inheritance). These ideas allow a designer to express a program or system design in higher-order abstractions. He or she is freed from having to create large amounts of syntactic material to represent what is essentially a simple idea. The limit of object-oriented programming, however, is that, while it eases the expression of a design, it does nothing to change the essential complexity of designs.

Expert systems. Expert systems are the most widely used and advanced area of artificial intelligence. An expert system consists of a generalized inference engine and a rule base. The system takes input data, including basic assumptions, and explores the inferences derivable from the rule base. Conclusions and suggestions are produced, and the system is able to explain how it arrived at its conclusions by retracing its reasoning path for the user. In addition to purely deterministic problems, an expert system can handle probabilistic rules and inferences as well. These systems could be used in software engineering in a number of ways. For example, they could be used in suggesting interface rules, providing advice on testing strategies, and offering optimization hints. Overall, expert systems could put some of the knowledge of experts into the hands of inexperienced software developers.

Environments and tools. Brooks believes that the biggest gain to be realized from programming environments is through the use of an integrated database to keep track of the information related to the development and maintenance of software. While this goal, if obtained, will provide increases in productivity and reliability, it is not the silver bullet either.

What technological advances do hold out hope of providing large boosts in productivity? The techniques just listed attempt to reduce some of the repetitious and noncreative aspects of creating software and to provide tools for creativity. Their limitations are that they do not attack the essence of the software development process, which is formulating complex conceptual structures. Real gains in productivity will come by attacking this issue. Brooks proposes several candidates for attacks on the conceptual essence, as follows.

Buy versus build. The most radical solution to the problem of building software is not to build it at all—buy it instead. This option is becoming more and more feasible as more and better software products are being offered. Even if a software product costs $100,000, it costs only about as much as one programmer-year (including salary, benefits, and on-the-job expenses). And the product is immediately available, aiding productivity sooner than a product developed in-house. Furthermore, it tends to be better tested and better documented than in-house products. The key to making buy versus build work is the availability of suitable software. Demand should have an important role here. Demand has steadily increased for off-the-shelf software, and as the costs of software development continue to rise, the demand should increase even further. The quality and ease of use of applications packages such as word processors, spreadsheets, and simple database systems have also made the buy option more appealing and realistic. In many cases users can derive their own application using these packages, solving their problems on their own without needing to have special software developed for them. (The newly evolving area of end-user computing relates to just such users.)

Requirements refining and rapid prototyping. The most difficult part of developing software is deciding exactly what to build. No other aspect of the process is as difficult as establishing the requirements in detail, and no other part is so critical to the final success of the software. Add to this the fact that the sponsor does not know exactly what is needed or wanted, even if they think they do. Therefore, an approach to software development that offers a true breakthrough in attacking the essence of the problem is rapid prototyping. A prototype of a software system simulates the interfacing and may perform the main functions of the system, while not necessarily being bound by hardware constraints. The purpose of the prototype is to make the conceptual and functional structure of the system observable to the sponsor so that it can be tested for consistency and usability.

Incremental Development. Brooks believes that the metaphor that software is built rather than written has outgrown its usefulness. Building implies that a set of detailed blueprints exists and that the activity of building is purely skilled labor. But the software structures of today are often too complex to be specified completely in advance. It is time to take a lesson from nature. Forms in nature, such as trees, the human eye, and volcanos, are all complex beyond imitation—and all are grown, not built. Software systems should evolve the same way, starting with a miniature version or seedling form of the final system and working in incremental stages to the final product. Just as a seedling tree is truly a tree, although a miniature version, a seedling system should be truly a system. It should run, even if it does nothing very useful. The approach necessitates top-down design, as the software must be grown top-down. Early prototyping is encouraged. And revision through backtracking to an earlier version is simple. The morale of the developers is improved, too, because there is always a working version.The approach is appropriate for large systems as well as small (Boehm, 1985).

Great designers. The key to great software design is great software designers. Good design practice can and should be taught. But the talent that makes a good designer into a great designer is granted to only a few. As examples, compare UNIX, APL, Pascal, Modula-2, and the Smalltalk interface—each developed by one or a few designers—to COBOL, PL/I, Algol, and MVS/370—all developed by committees or groups. The first examples have been and still are exciting products. They inspire passion in their fans. The second examples are not as exciting, useful, or skillfully designed as they might be. Brooks advocates cultivating good designers as a priceless resource. Good designers should be recognized, nurtured, and rewarded.

8.9   Finishing Up the Project: System Delivery and the Operational/Maintenance Phase

The final stage in the development of software is system delivery. The delivery process may include a number of steps:

- Site preparation
- System installation
- Training
- Start-up

Site preparation. Site preparation includes those activities needed to get the sponsor's site ready for the new system. If only software is to be installed, this step may be unnecessary. But if the system involves combined hardware and software components, considerable effort may be necessary. In some cases a new peripheral device may be added as part of the new system, in other cases a new computer or computer network may be installed, while in still other cases a completely new hardware configuration may be created. In any of these cases, consideration must be given to the physical characteristics of the site, including access to sufficient, clean, and reliable power, space for cabling, adequate air conditioning, fire detection and control, cleanliness, and security. When peripherals are added, the physical layout is important. Most peripherals have limits on the length of cable that can be used to connect them to the computer. If the limits are exceeded, additional equipment may be necessary. Even small systems may require some site preparation. Personal computers require space and may not conveniently fit on a desk, requiring a separate desk or worktable of sufficient size. Printers and the fans on devices such as printers can be noisy and may require sound deadening.

System installation. In system installation, the system is installed at the sponsor's site. If installation is complex, the developer may be responsible for the installation. If installation is simple, the sponsor may do the installation using instructions provided by the developer. These instructions should cover:

- Information about the delivery medium (for example, disk or tape, and its characteristics)

- Description of the minimum hardware configuration needed to run the system

- Description of how to run any installation programs

- Descriptions of any permanent files, including how to install them or create them

- Information on customizing the system, if this is allowed

- How to run test cases (these should be included with the installation package)

User training. The potential users of a system include operators and end users. Operators are those who utilize supplementary or support functions of the system. For example, operators may be responsible for making backup copies, setting up security access, keeping statistics on system use, and updating parts of the system as necessary. End users are those who use the system as a tool in carrying out some other activity. These two different types of users each require different sorts of training. Training may take the form of operation manuals, user manuals, training sessions, and/or access to an expert user. Ideally, such materials provide help both for the novice and the more advanced user.

Start-up. There are a number of ways to start up use of a new system at the sponsor's site. In some cases the switchover to the new system can be immediate. As soon as the system is installed, it goes into use. This approach requires that there be no serious consequences from lack of user training or system problems. In some situations the new system is used in parallel with the old system for a while. This requires duplicating work, as the data must be entered into both systems, and the output from the new system must be compared to that from the old system. However, it provides protection for users for whom reliability is vital. Still another approach is a phased replacement. In this approach, parts of a new system may be introduced one at a time, or only part of an organization may switch over to the new system.

Once delivery is complete, the operational/maintenance phase of the software life cycle begins. The process and activities involved in maintenance were discussed in Section 8.3. The developer and sponsor must discuss at the onset of a system development project who will be responsible for each facet of maintenance: corrections, enhancements, and adaptations. No matter who is responsible, the maintainers will require access to certain documentation. Certainly they will need a source code listing, which should include module headers describing the detailed design of each module and line comments. The preliminary design document, in an updated form, is another valuable maintenance document. Test documentation including actual test cases is also needed to perform regression tests during maintenance. Finally, copies of the installation guide, user guide, and any on-line help should be provided.

Summary

Chapter 8 presents an overview of software engineering, looking at it from a historical perspective and from today's perspective. Widely known analysis and design techniques not introduced in earlier chapters were profiled. These include SADT (Structured Analysis and Design Technique), Warnier–Orr, and JSP (Jackson System of Programming).

Software maintenance, the final stage in the software life cycle, was discussed. Software maintenance includes corrections, adaptations, and enhancements. Configuration management is the management and control of changes made to software. Although configuration management is important in software development, it is perhaps the central or controlling process in software maintenance. A configuration management team, consisting of analysts, programmers, and a program librarian, is directly involved in maintenance activities. A change control board is used to oversee and authorize changes. A configuration management database provides information and reports on the current status of software products.

Automation of the software engineering endeavor is desirable to increase productivity and help keep software development and maintenance abreast of demand. Computer-aided software engineering (CASE) is the term used to describe the tools that have been developed to aid the software process and to create software engineering environments. Framing environments, such as PSL/PSA, are designed to support the early stages of software development. Programming environments, such as code generators, language-sensitive editors, and automated testing tools, aid the coding and testing of software. General CASE environments provide tools that assist across the development cycle. Examples include UNIX, APSE, and the Teamwork family of tools.

User interface management systems (UIMS) are tools that allow the user to create custom user interfaces to lay on top of application software. UIMSs provide tools for prototyping, aid in standardizing interfaces, and increase productivity. X Window is a set of network protocols that allows the user interface and device handling to be handled separately from the application over a network. X Window serves as a natural and powerful platform for UIMSs.

Object-oriented development is an influential new approach to programming and software engineering. In object-oriented design the system is structured around objects that exist in a model of the system. An object is an entity that behaves, and it includes both data and methods (operations). Objects respond to messages. In object-oriented design, first the objects in the system are identified and then the messages that can be received and sent by each object are identified. In the final step the appropriate data structures and algorithms are chosen for representing the data within each object and for implementing the methods. The concepts of object-oriented programming include object, message, class, instance, method, sub-classes, and inheritance.

The demand for software and software maintenance continues to grow, while the number of computer professionals and increases in productivity are growing more slowly. Thus the gap between supply and demand is widening. The application of software engineering principles and techniques to software activities has great potential to address the problem of productivity. Yet evidence shows that these techniques and practices are not being widely used. Possible causes are skepticism among managers concerning the efficacy of software engineering, the immaturity of software engineering and the problem of technology transfer. The education of future and present computer professionals about software engineering is one approach to solving the technology transfer problem.

While some emerging techniques offer only small hope for increasing software productivity, others offer greater hope. Ada, object-oriented programming, expert systems, and environments and tools offer only modest increases because they address just the accidental aspects of software development. Buying versus building, rapid prototyping, incremental development, and the nurturance of great designers may provide greater gains in productivity because they attack problems that are the essence of software.

The final facet of a system development project is system delivery. System delivery includes site preparation, system installation, operator and end-user training, and start-up. To support the operational/maintenance phase of the software life cycle, the maintainers of the system should receive copies of the system documentation, including the preliminary design, the documented source code, the test plan and test cases, and all user documents.

Checklist of Project Activities

_____ Discuss with your sponsor what site preparation is necessary before the system can be installed.

_____ Set up a schedule of delivery, installation, and acceptance testing activities.

_____ Decide who will be handling installation: the developer or the sponsor.

_____ Create an installation manual. The level and style of the manual should reflect who is to do the installation: the developer or the sponsor.

_____ Determine if an operator's manual is necessary. If so, create one.

———— Plan for user training. Aside from a user manual, consider training sessions, telephone or on-site experts, training programs, and the like.

———— Determine what strategy is to be used during start-up: immediate, parallel, or phased introduction of the new system.

———— Determine who is responsible for each type of maintenance activity: corrections, enhancements, and adaptations.

———— Make the development documents available to the maintainers of the system.

———— Have the sponsor officially sign off on the system once delivery and installation are complete.

Terms and Concepts Introduced

automatic code generation

computer-aided software
   engineering (CASE)

SADT

Warnier–Orr design method

Jackson System of Programming (JSP)

corrections

adaptations

enhancements

configuration management

configuration management team

change control board

change request

change report

configuration management database

version control library

software engineering environments

framing environments

programming environments

general environments

PSL/PSA

language-sensitive editor

static analysis

dynamic analysis

debugger

coverage analysis

assertion checking

regression checking

APSE

Teamwork

user interface management
   system (UIMS)

X Window

object

methods

messages

message protocol

class

instance

subclass

inheritance

technology transfer

essence

accident

Exercises

1. Create a SADT diagram for the Handle Payment Activity shown in Figure 2.7c.

2. (a) Use the Jackson method to diagram the structure of a file containing student course information for the end of a term. For each student in the file, the student's name, prior grade point average, total hours of prior credit, list of classes taken, hours of credit for each class taken, and final grade in each class are given.

   (b) Use the Jackson method to diagram an output report concerning student grades. The report consists of a list of students, their total hours of credit, grade point average for the term, and new overall grade point average.

   (c) Using the two data structure diagrams, create a program structure diagram using the JSP method.

3. Redo Exercise 2 using Warnier–Orr diagrams.

4. Create a Warnier–Orr diagram to describe the structure of the concordance of the concordance system described in Section 2.2.1. Create another Warnier–Orr diagram to describe the structure of an input file to the concordance system. An input file for the concordance system is a text file.

5. Based on the two Warnier–Orr diagrams of data structures created in Exercise 4, create a Warnier–Orr diagram describing a design for the concordance program.

6. Compare the design created in Exercise 5 to the structure chart for the concordance system shown in Figure 4.11. What similarities are there between the two designs? Compare the modularity of the two designs. Are there any natural divisions evident in the Warnier–Orr diagram that would aid in creating a modular system?

7. Do Exercises 4, 5, and 6 again, this time using the Jackson System of Programming. Compare the design created using the JSP method to the Warnier–Orr design, as well as to the structured design.

8. Interview a representative from an organization who is involved in software development concerning the organization's software development processes. What software development model does the organization use? What are the deliverables produced during development? What specific techniques, if any, do they use at each stage in the process? What sort of testing do they do? What CASE tools do they have? What CASE tools do they use on a regular basis?

9. Look in recent periodicals such as *IEEE Software* or *ComputerWorld* for advertisements and/or articles concerning CASE tools. What tools are being advertised or written about? Classify each tool according to type. What features and functions do they offer? What claims are made concerning increases in productivity?

10. Pick some consumer technology of interest to you. Examples might include compact disks, sewing machines, cars, calculators, electricity, or video games. Research the history of this technology. When was the device or tech-

nology actually invented? When did the technology first become available to the consumer? How readily was the technology accepted? How long did it take before the technology was widely accepted?

11. Take an existing piece of software and modify it in some way. Use an old program written by yourself, a program written by a friend, or one provided by your instructor. Keep track of how much time you spend on each of the maintenance task categories listed in Table 8.2. How do your times compare to the times given in the table?

12. Consider an automatic date-book system for keeping track of daily appointments electronically. Identify the objects that might exist in this system and the behaviors that would be associated with each object. Draw an object-oriented design of the system.

13. Use structured design to create a structure chart describing the automatic date-book system in Exercise 12. Compare the ease of creating the two designs and the "naturalness" of the two designs.

Appendix A
Sample Documents from the Rev-Pro Case Study

Part I: Requirements and Specification Document Excerpts

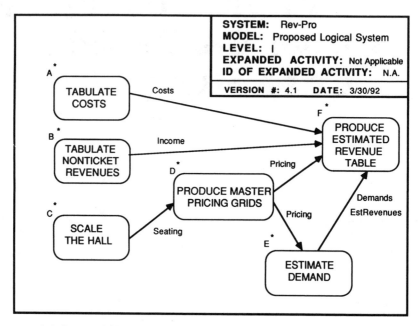

* Indicates additional detail is provided in later figures of the Rev-Pro Case Study Requirements and Specification Document excerpts.

Figure A.1 Highest Level Data-flow Diagram for the Proposed Logical System of the Rev-Pro Case Study

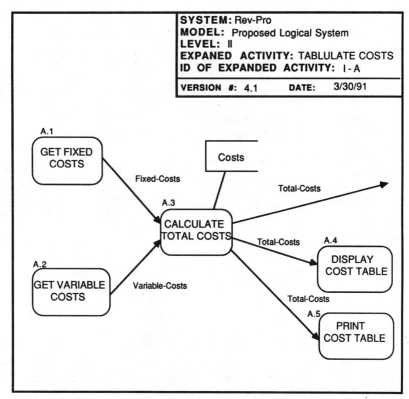

Figure A.2 Level II Data-flow Diagram of the TABULATE COSTS Activity from the Rev-Pro Case Study

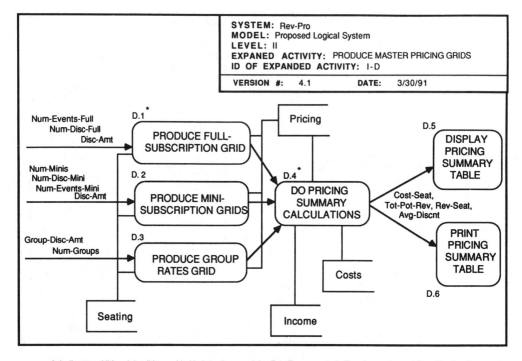

* Indicates additional detail is provided in later figures of the Rev-Pro case study Requirements and Specification document

Figure A.3 Level II Data-flow Diagram of the PRODUCE MASTER PRICING GRIDS Activity from the Rev-Pro Case Study

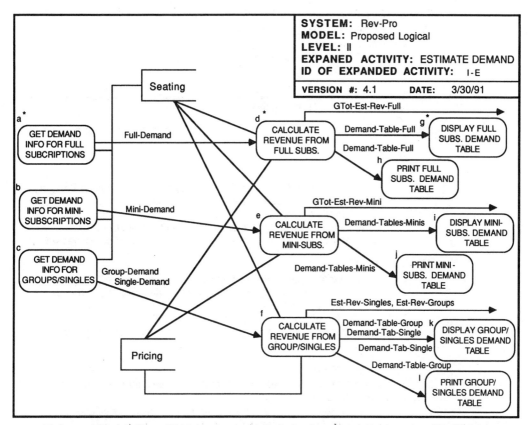

* Indicates additional detail is provided in later figures related to the Rev-Pro case study Requirements and Specification document.

Figure A.4 Level II Data-flow Diagram of the ESTIMATE DEMAND Activity from the Rev-Pro Case Study

ACTIVITY SPECIFICATION FOR:
System: Rev-Pro
Activity: TABULATE NONTICKET REVENUES
Activity ID: I.B.

===

Version: 4.1   **Date:** 3/30/92

repeat

>   repeat
>   >   get name of unearned income category (Unearned-Income-Category)
>   >   get amount of unearned income from the named category (Unearned-Income-Amout)
>   >   add amount to total of unearned income (Tot-Unearned)
>   until user indicates no more categories or the number of categories = 5
>
>   repeat
>   >   get name of earned income category (Earned-Income-Category)
>   >   get amount of earned income from the named category (Earned-Income-Amount)
>   >   add amount to total of earned income (Tot-Earned)
>   until user indicates no more categories or the number of categories = 5
>
>   compute total income base (Income-Base) by adding Tot-Unearned and Tot-Earned
>   compute target for ticket sales (Target-Sales) by subtracting Income-Base from Total-Costs
>   display a table showing all entered information and all calculations

until user wants no more changes

Figure A.5 Activity Specification for TABULATE NONTICKET REVENUES Activity of Level I of the Proposed Logical System of the Rev-Pro Case Study

---

ACTIVITY SPECIFICATION FOR:
System: Rev-Pro
Activity: SCALE THE HALL
Activity ID: I. C.

===

VERSION: 4.1   **DATE:** 3/30/92

---

repeat
    get total seats in house (Tot-Seats)
    get number of price categories (Num-Cat)
    for each price category do
        get number of seats (Num-Seats)
        get number of complimentary seats (Num-Comps)
        NetSeats = (Num-Seats) - (Num-Comps)
        get price of individual ticket (Single-Price)
    end-for
    calculate total complimentary seats (Tot-Num-Comps)
    calculate total net seats (Tot-Net-Seats)
    display all input information and totals
until user wants no more changes

Figure A.6 Activity Specification for SCALE THE HALL Activity of Level I of the Proposed Logical System of the Rev-Pro Case Study

---

ACTIVITY SPECIFICATION FOR:
System: Rev-Pro
Activity: PRODUCE FULL SUBSCRIPTION GRID
Activity ID: II. D. 1

==
Version: 4.1   **Date:** 3/30/92

```
repeat
    get number of events in full subscription series (Num-Events-Full)
    get number of discount rates (Num-Disc-Full)
    for each discount rate level do
            get title of level (Disc-Full-Level)
            get discount rate (Disc-Full-Rate)
            for each price category (Num-Cats) do
                calculate the full price for the series at the discount rate (Full-
                    Series-Disc-Price)
                calculate the single ticket price at the discount rate (Full-Single-
                    Disc-Price)
            end-for
    end-for
    display a table showing all input and calculated information
until user wants no more changes
```

Figure A.7 Activity Specification for PRODUCE FULL SUBSCRIP-
TION GRID Activity of Level II of the Proposed Logical System of
the Rev-Pro Case Study

ACTIVITY SPECIFICATION FOR:
   System: Rev-Pro
   Activity: DO PRICING SUMMARY CALCULATIONS
   Activity ID: II.D.4

==
Version: 4.1   **Date:** 3/30/92

---

calculate the average discount level
for each price category (Num-Cat times) do
   Tot-Pot-Rev-(no disc) =
         Tot-Pot-Rev-(no disc) + (Single-Price in this category *
         Net-Seats in this price category)
   Tot-Pot-Rev-(w. avg. disc) =
         Tot-Pot-Rev-(w. avg. disc) + ((Single-Price in this category *
         avg. discount) * Net-Seats in this price category)
end-for
Avg-Cost/Seat = Total-Costs / Tot-Seats
Avg-Rev/Seat-(no disc) = Tot-Pot-Rev-(no disc) / Tot-Seats
Avg-Rev/Seat-(w. avg. disc) = Tot-Pot-Rev-(w. avg. disc) / Tot-Seats

display a table showing all calculated values

Figure A.8 Activity Specification for the DO PRICING SUMMARY
CALCULATIONS Activity of Level II of the Proposed Logical System of the Rev-Pro Case Study

---

ACTIVITY SPECIFICATION FOR:
   System: Rev-Pro
   Activity: GET DEMAND INFO FOR FULL SUBSCRIPTIONS
   Activity ID: II.E.a

==
   Version: 4.1   **Date:** 3/30/92

---

for each discount rate level (Num-Disc-Full) do
   display name of category (Disc-Full-Level)
   for each price category (Num-Cat) do
         display category number
         display the number of seats available (Net-Seats)
         get the estimated demand (Full-Demand)
   end-for
end-for

Figure A.9 Activity Specification for the GET DEMAND INFO
FOR FULL SUBSCRIPTIONS Activity of Level II of the Proposed
Logical System of the Rev-Pro Case Study

ACTIVITY SPECIFICATION FOR:
  System: Rev-Pro
  Activity: CALCULATE REVENUES FROM FULL SUBSCRIPTIONS
  Activity ID: II.E.d

===

Version: 4.1   **Date:** 3/30/92

```
for each price category (Num-Cats) do
    for each discount rate level (Num-Disc-Full) do
        Tot-Full-Demand = Tot-Full-Demand + demand in this
            discount level
        Tot-Est-Rev-Full = Tot-Est-Rev-Full + (Single-Price * Tot-Full-Demand
            in this discount level)
    end-for
    Gtot-Est-Rev-Full = Gtot-Est-Rev-Full + Tot-Est-Rev-Full in this price category
    calculate the number of seats left in each price category using the
        formula:  Seats-After-Full-Sub = (Net-Seats in this price category
        -  (Tot-Full-Demand in this price category)
end-for
    Est-Series-Full-Rev = Gtot-Est-Rev-Full * Num-Events-Full
```

Figure A.10 Activity Specification for the CALCULATE REVENUES
FROM FULL SUBSCRIPTIONS Activity of Level II of the Proposed
Logical System of the Rev-Pro Case Study

ACTIVITY SPECIFICATION FOR:
System: Rev-Pro
Activity: DISPLAY FULL-SUBSCRIPTION DEMAND TABLE
Activity ID: II. E. g

===
Version: 4.1   **Date:** 3/30/92

display table title
display column headings

for each price category (Num-Cats) do
     display price category indication
     display total seats available (Net-Seats) at this price category
     for each discount rate level (Num-Disc-Full) do
         display estimated demand for this price category
     end-for
     display total demand at this price category (Full-Demand)
     display seats left at this price category (Seats-After-Full-Sub)
     display estimated revenue (Tot-Est-Rev-Full) at this price category
end-for

for each discount level (Num-Disc-Full) do
     display the total demand summed across the price levels (Tot-Full-Demand)
end-for

display the total estimated revenue per show (Gtot-Est-Rev-Full)
display the total estimated revenue for the series (Series-Est-Rev-Full)

Figure A.11 Activity Specification for the DISPLAY FULL-SUBSCRIPTION DEMAND TABLE Activity of Level II of the Proposed Logical System of the Rev-Pro Case Study

---

ACTIVITY SPECIFICATION FOR:
    System: Rev-Pro
    Activity: PRODUCE ESTIMATED REVENUE TABLE
    Activity ID: I. F.

===

Version: 4.1   **Date:** 3/30/92

```
for each series-type do
    Gtot-Est-Revenue = Gtot-Est-Revenue + Gtot-Est-Revenue for this
        type of series
    Gtot-Demand = Gtot-Demand + Demand for seats in this type of
        series
end-for
Breakeven-%-Of-Demand = Total-Costs / Gtot-Est-Revenue

display Gtot-Est-Revenue
display Total-Costs
display  Breakeven-%-Of-Demand
display Gtot-Demand
```

Figure A.12 Activity Specification for the PRODUCE ESTIMATED REVENUE TABLE Activity of Level I of the Proposed Logical System of the Rev-Pro Case Study

General Goals of the Rev-Pro Project

A vital function of an arts administrator is to ensure the health and continual growth of the organization. This can be aided by the careful monitoring of budget concerns including the projection of ticket sales revenues from performances and a comparison of actual sales to projected sales. However, the calculations involved are time-consuming and frequently done manually. This precludes analysis of "what if" situations. Thus, many administrators lack an easy method of revenue projecting and tracking.

The aim of this project is to provide a generalized software package for arts administrators that will enable them to experiment with various pricing and scaling strategies for a particular performance series. Ticket revenue projections and breakeven points can be quickly generated in table format. Information concerning ticket sales and unsold tickets will also be maintained and tracked.

In particular, the system will allow the user to:

- Make accurate estimates of revenue based on differing demands for tickets at various price levels
- Calculate different discount rates for categories such as adult, senior citizen and student-discount for both subscriptions and single tickets
- Keep account of all additional variables related to series budget and revenue projections
- Calculate how many seats are needed to be sold in each category of ticket in order to achieve breakeven
- Be able to redo all of the above calculations as new data becomes available
- Be able to do "what if" alternative projections based on different scenarios such as different price structures, different levels of ticket sales, and so on.

The system must begin by determining the amount of revenue from ticket sales needed for breakeven on a concert series. The breakeven amount is the critical concern in making decisions about ticket pricing. The breakeven revenue needed is calculated by subtracting the total income from sources other than tickets from total costs. The system will make these calculations based on input from the user, including information on fixed and variable costs, and earned and unearned income.

Next, the system will aid the user in pricing and scaling the hall. The number of price levels to be used and the number of seats to be allocated to each price level will be determined by the user and entered. The number of complimentary seats at each pricing level, for which there will be no revenue, will be entered and those seats will be excluded from further calculations. The single ticket price and the discount rate for subscription tickets will then be entered. The system will display tables of the various pricing grids, which includes information on potential revenues per show and per series if all tickets are sold. This feature will allow the user to see if the initially entered prices can reasonably result in breakeven. Finally, the system will allow the user to estimate demand for tickets in each category and review the effects of these estimates on revenue and breakeven. The process may be repeated any number of times.

The user will be able to obtain printed output of any of the various tables displayed during system execution. The system will be designed to handle up to fifteen events, with up to 3 mini-series within these events; up to 7 price categories; and up to 5 levels of subscription discounts. The system will be designed to run on an IBM/PC using a single double-sided floppy disk drive.

Figure A.13 General Goals Section of the Rev-Pro Requirements and Specification Document

Data Dictionary

Part I: Data Stores

Income = {Unearned-Income-Category + Unearned-Income-Amount} $_0{}^5$ + {Earned-Income-Category +

Earned-Income-Amount} $_0{}^5$ + Tot-Unearned + Tot-Earned + Income-Base

A data store that contains all income figures and information.

Costs = {Fixed-Cost-Category + Fixed-Cost-Amount}$_0{}^{10}$ + {Variable-Cost-Category + Variable

Cost-Amount} $_0{}^{10}$ + Fixed-Costs + Variable-Costs + Total-Costs

A data store that contains all cost figures and information.

Seating = Tot-Seats + Num-Cats + {Num-Seats + Num-Comps + Net-Seats + Single-Price}$_1{}^7$ +

Tot-Num-Comps + Tot-Net-Seats

A data store that contains all seating information for each price category, all general seating

information and the price of single tickets for each price category.

Pricing = Num-Events-Full + Num-Disc-Full + {Disc-Full-Level + Disc-Full-Rate}$_0{}^5$ +

{Full-Single-Disc-Price} $_0{}^{35}$ + Tot-Pot-Rev(no disc) + Tot-Pot-Rev (no disc) +

Avg-Cost/Seat + Avg-Rev/Seat(no disc) + Avg-Rev/Seat(w. avg. disc)

A data store that contains all pricing information and figures

Demand = {Full-Demand} $_0{}^{35}$ + Tot-Full-Demand

A data store that contains all demand information

EstRevenue = {Tot-Est-Rev-Full}$_1{}^7$ + Gtot-Est-Rev-Full + Est-Series-Full-Rev

A data store that contains information overall estimates of revenue based on demand.

Part II: Data-Items Related to Income

Unearned-Income-Amount = Dollar-Amount

The amount of income from one Unearned-Income-Category.

Earned-Income-Amount = Dollar-Amount

The amount of income from one Earned-Income-Category.

Tot-Unearned = Dollar-Amount

The sum of income from all unearned income categories.

Tot-Earned = Dollar-Amount

The sum of income from all earned income categories.

Figure A.14 The Data Dictionary for the Rev-Pro Project Requirements and Specification

Unearned-Income-Category = {character}$_1$ ^{15}

> The descriptive name of an unearned income source. There may be a range of zero to five unearned income categories.

Earned-Income-Category = {character}$_1$ ^{15}

> The descriptive name of an earned income source. There may be a range of zero to five earned income categories.

Income-Base = Dollar-Amount

> The sum of Tot-Unearned and Tot-Earned.

Target-Sales = Dollar-Amount

> Grand-Total-Costs - Income-Base. The sales total needed to achieve breakeven.

Part III: Data-Items Related to Cost

Fixed-Costs = Dollar-Amount

> The sum of the amounts of all Fixed-Cost-Amounts.

Fixed-Costs-Category = {character}$_1$ ^{10}

> The descriptive name of a fixed cost. There may be a range of zero to ten fixed-cost categories.

Fixed-Cost-Amount = Dollar-Amount

> The amount of one Fixed-Costs-Category.

Variable-Costs = Dollar-Amount

> The sum of the amounts of all Variable-Cost-Amounts.

Variable-Costs-Category = {character}$_1$ ^{10}

> The descriptive name of a variable cost category. There may be a range of zero to ten variable-cost categories.

Variable-Cost-Amount = Dollar-Amount

> The amount of one Variable-Costs-Category.

Total-Costs = Dollar-Amount

> Variable-Costs + Fixed Costs.

Part IV: Data-items Related to Scaling the Hall

Tot-Seats = {digit}$_1$ ^{4}

> The total number of seats in the house.

Figure A.14 continued

Num-Cats = 1 | 2 | 3 | 4 | 5 | 6 | 7

>　The number of price categories.

Num-Seats = {digit}$_1$^{3}

>　The number of seats in one price category.

Num-Comps = {digit}$_1$^{3}

>　The number of complimentary seats in one price category.

Net-Seats = {digit}$_1$^{3}

>　For one price category, Num-Seats - Net-Seats. The net number of saleable seats
>　in one price category.

Single-Price = Dollar-Amount

>　The price of an individual ticket in one price category.

Tot-Num-Comps = {digit}$_1$^{3}

>　The sum of Num-Comps across all price categories.

Tot-Net-Seats = {digit}$_1$^{4}

>　The sum of Net-Seats across all price categories.

Part V: Data-items Related to Producing Pricing Grids

{**Note:** Date items not related to Full Subscription have been left out for simplification }

Num-Events-Full = 1 | 2 | 3 ... | 14 | 15

>　The number of events in a full subsription series.

Num-Disc-Full = 1 | 2 | 3 | 4 | 5

>　The number of discount categories for a full subscription series.

Disc-Full-Level = {character}$_1$ ^{15}

>　The descriptive name of a discount level for a full subscription series. There may be a maximum
>　of five discount levels.

Disc-Full-Rate = digit + digit

>　The percent of discount in one discount level.

Full-Single-Disc-Price = Dollar-Amount

>　The price of a single ticket in a full subscription series at one price level and one discount level.

Full-Series-Disc-Price = Dollar-Amount

Figure A.14 continued

The price of a full subscription series ticket at one price level and one discount level.

Avg-Disc = digit + digit

The average of the discount rates across all discount levels.

Tot-Pot-Rev(no disc) + Dollar-Amount

The sum of (Single-Price * Net Seats) across price categories. Represents total potential revenue if all seats are sold at the single ticket price.

Tot-Pot-Rev(w. avg. disc) = Dollar-Amount

The sum of (Single-Price * Avg-Disc) * (Net-Seats) across price categories. Represents the total potential revenue if all seats are sold at an average discount price.

Cost/Seat = Dollar-Amount

Total-Costs/Tot-Seats.

Avg-Rev/Seat (no disc) = Dollar-Amount

Tot-Pot-Rev(no disc) / Tot-Seats. The average revenue per seat if all seats are sold at the single ticket price.

Avg-Rev/Seat(w. avg. disc) = Dollar-Amount

Tot-Pot-Rev(w. avg. disc) / Tot-Seats. The average revenue per seat if all seats are sold at the average discount price.

Full-Demand = $\{digit\}_1{}^4$

The estimated demand for a full subscription ticket at one price level and one discount level.

Tot-Full-Demand = $\{digit\}_1{}^4$

The total of all Full-Demands for all price levels and all discount levels in a full subscription series.

Tot-Est-Rev-Full = Dollar-Amount

The sum of (Single-Price * Tot-Full-Demand) for all discount levels in one price category of a full subscription series.

Part VI: Data-items Related to Revenue Estimates Based on Demand

{ **Note:** Data items not related to Full-Subscriptions have been left out for simplification }

Gtot-Est-Rev-Full = Dollar-Amount

The sum of all Tot-Est-Rev-Full across all price categories.

Figure A.14 continued

Seats-After-Full-Sub = {digit}$_1^4$

> The number of seats left after demand in one price category of a full subscription series. Calculated by subtracting Tot-Full-Demand for the price category from Nets-Sets for the price category.

Est-Series-Full-Rev = Dollar-Amount

> The grand total estimated revenue for a full subscription series. Calculated by multiplying Gtot-Est-Rev-Full times Num-Events-Full.

Part VII: General Data-Items

Dollar-Amount = '\$' + {digit}^{7} + '.' + digit + digit

> A dollar and cents value.

Figure A.14 continued

Nonfunctional Requirements for the Rev-Pro System

I. User Interface and Human Factors Considerations
a. Users will be knowledgeable intermittent users.
b. The system should be easy to learn to use and easy to remember, as usage of the system will be intermittent.
c. Users should be able to teach themselves to use the system with the aid of a manual. There will typically be only one user of the system at any installation.
d. The system will require the input of many numbers. Errors such as entering a character instead of a number should be blocked and readily corrected. Editing of entries should be easy and accessible.
e. A keyboard will be the only device for direct human input. A CRT, tones and a printer are available output media.
f. The system should be designed to allow easy printing of any table or data display shown on the screen during system execution.
g. The displays should display the input and output in readable, uncrowded formats following the guidelines of Smith and Mosier, 1986.

Figure A.15 The Nonfunctional Requirements Document for the Rev-Pro System Case Study

II. Hardware Considerations

a. The system will be designed to run on an IBM/PC with two internal floppy disk drives, 256K of internal memory and using the DOS 3.1 operating system.

b. The system will reside on one double-sided, 5 1/4 inch floppy disk capable of holding 400,000 bytes.

c. The system will support the storing of data on either of the internal disks.

d. The system will be capable of utilizing any printer supported by the DOS 3.1 operating system.

e. The system will be designed for a monochrome non-graphics display.

III. Performance Characteristics

a. The system will handle up to 15 events in one concert series.

b. The system will handle up to 3 subseries from the concert series.

c. The system will handle up to 7 pricing categories for tickets.

d. The system will handle up to 5 levels of subscription discounts.

IV. Error Handling and Extreme Conditions

a. The system should not fail if an attempt is made to exceed any of the Performance Characteristics listed above. Appropriate messages should be given to the user and the action blocked.

b. The validity of input data should be checked and any errors immediately signaled to the users. These errors might include entering characters where digits are required, entering a decimal value where a whole number is required, or failure to make a proper menu selection.

c. The user must be allowed to reenter incorrectly entered data.

d. The system will handle total dollar values up to $10,000,000.00.

V. Potential System Modifications

a. The number of concerts, number of mini-series and number of pricing levels handled by the system are likely areas of potential modifications.

b. The inclusion of graphic displays of summary data (e.g., pie charts) is another area of potential modification.

Figure A.15 continued

Part II: User Interface Design Document Excerpts

OVERALL: The major tasks for the user of the Rev-Pro system are listed below. The order in which the tasks are listed indicates the order the user will be required to follow. Although tasks B, C and D do not strictly have to go in the given order, the sponsor requested the order shown. Within each task, the subtasks are listed in sequential order.

A. Starting the system
Description: Activities related to starting up the system
1. Enter: start-up command

B. Scaling-the-Hall
Description: Activities related to scaling the hall. The hall (theater) must be divided into different sections. Each section has a different price category associated with it. The user must indicate how many categories there are, the number of seats in each category, the price of a single ticket at each price category and the number of complimentary seats that will be given away in each category. Once all the data have been entered, the user may ask the computer to calculate the total of all complimentary seats and all gate seats. The user will be given the option of changing any entries and recalculating. The user may print out the entered and calculated information.

> **Task Sequencing:**
> 1. Enter: total seats in the house
> 2. Enter: number of price categories
> 3. Observe: running total of number of seats left to assign
> 4. Enter: number of seats for each price category (up to 7 different entries)
> 5. Enter: number of complimentary seats for each price category (up to 7 different entries)
> 6. Enter: the price of a single ticket for each price category (up to 7 different entries)
> 7. Options: make any changes desired in entered data, (re)calculate totals
> 8. Observe: all information entered, total of all complimentary tickets and total of all gate seats
> 9. Option: print information
> 10. Options: quit, go to next task
>
> **Task Objects:** See "Seating" in the Data Dictionary

C. Tabulate Costs
Description: Activities related to itemizing fixed costs and variable costs for a concert series. The user will enter the name and amount of up to 10 different fixed cost items, and the name and amount of up to 10 different variable cost items. Once all entries

Figure A.16 The Semantic Design of the User Interface of the Rev-Pro System Case Study

have been made, the user may request that the total of fixed costs, total of variable costs and total costs be calculated. The user will be given the option of changing any entries and recalculating. The user may print out the entered and calculated information.

1. Enter: name of fixed cost category (up to 10 different entries)
2. Enter: amount of fixed cost category (up to 10 different entries)
3. Enter: name of variable cost category (up to 10 different entries)
4. Enter: amount of variable cost category (up to 10 different entries)
5. Options: make any changes desired in entered data, (re)calculate totals
6. Observe: all information entered, total of fixed costs, total of variable costs and grand total costs
7. Option: print information
8. Options: go back to prior task, go to next task

Task Objects: see "Costs" in the Data Dictionary

D. Tabulate-Nonticket-Revenues

Description: Activities related to itemizing earned income and unearned income for a concert series. The user will enter the name and amount of up to 10 different earned income items, and the name and amount of up to 10 different unearned income items. Once all entries have been made, the user may request that the total of earned income, total of unearned income and total income base be calculated. The user will be given the option of changing any entries and recalculating. The user may print out the entered and calculated information.

Task Sequencing:

1. Enter: name of unearned income category (up to 10 different entries)
2. Enter: amount of unearned income category (up to 10 different entries)
3. Enter: name of earned income category (up to 10 different entries)
4. Enter: amount of earned income category (up to 10 different entries)
5. Options: make any changes desired in entered data, (re)calculate totals
6. Observe: all information entered, total of unearned income, total of earned income, total income base, total costs, target for ticket sales
7. Option: print information
8. Options: go back to prior task, go to next task

Task Objects: see "Income" in the Data Dictionary

E. Produce-Master-Pricing-Grids

Activities related to producing a master pricing grid for each type of series. (Note: Only the full subscription series is discussed here, for purposes of brevity.) The user will enter the number of events in the series, the number of discount levels and the title and rate for each discount rate level. Once all entries have been made, the user may request that the system compute the full price for the series at the discount rate and at the single-ticket rate. The user will be given the option of changing any entries and recalculating. The user may print out the entered and calculated information.

1. Enter: Number of events in the full series
2. Enter: Number of discount levels
3. Enter: Title of discount level (up to 5 different entries)
4. Enter: Discount rate (up to 5 different entries)

Figure A.16 continued

5. Options: make any changes desired in entered data, (re)calculate totals
6. Observe: all information entered combined into a pricing grid
7. Option: print information
8. Options: go back to prior task, go to next task

Task objects: see "Pricing" in the Data Dictionary

F. Produce-Master-Pricing-Grid-Summary-Table

Description: The user may request the display of master pricing grid summary information. This information includes the total potential revenue (with no discount) for each price category, the total potential revenue (with an average discount) for each price category, the average cost per seat, the average revenue per seat (with no discount) and the average revenue per seat (with average discount). The user may print out the displayed information.

Task Sequencing:

1. Observe: master pricing grid summary table
2. Option: print information
3. Options: go back to prior task, go to next task

Task Objects: see "Pricing" in the Data Dictionary

G. Estimate-Demand

Description: The user enters the estimated demand for each discount level within each price category. A running total of the number of seats available is kept. The user will be given the option of changing any entries and recalculating. The user may print out the entered and calculated information.

Task Sequencing:

1. Enter: Estimated demand for each price-category/discount-level combination (up to 35 different entries)
2. Observe: Estimated demand table, estimated revenue price per level, estimated revenue per show, estimated series revenue
3. Option: print information
4. Options: go back to prior task, go to next task

Task Objects: See "Demand" in the Data Dictionary

H. Produce-Estimated-Revenue-Table

Description: The user may request the display of the estimated revenue table. This table includes information on the grand total estimated revenues based on demand, total costs, breakeven percent of demand and grand total demand. The user has the option of printing the information. The user may go back to a previous task, or quit.

Task Sequencing:

1. Observe: Estimated revenue table
2. Options: go back to prior task, quit

Task Objects: See "EstRevenue" in the Data Dictionary

Figure A.16 continued

```
                        TOTAL COST TABLE

            FIXED COSTS                      VARIABLE COSTS

     A. space rent   $ _1200.00      A. -hall rent   $ _1800.00
     B. -----phone   $ _ 600.00      B. artist fee   $ 40000.00
     C. -utilities   $ _1230.00      C. -----promo   $ _2000.00
     D. ---mainten   $ _ 500.00      D. -advertise   $ _6000.00
     E. --salaries   $ 20000.00      E. production   $ _1000.00
     F. --security   $ _ 600.00      F. -----wages   $ _ 600.00
     G. -----other   $ _ 200.00      G. -royalties   $ _ 300.00
     H. ----------   $ -----.--      H. -----other   $ _ 200.00
     I. ----------   $ -----.--      I. ----------   $ -----.--
     J. ----------                   J. ----------   $ -----.--


 TOT FIX. $  24300.00   TOT VAR. $  51930.00 GR. TOT $  76200.00

      F7: Calculate     F8: Print       F9: <--      F10: -->
```

Figure A.17 Design of User Interface of Rev-Pro System: Total Cost Table Display Prototype

```
                MASTER PRICING GRID I (Full Subscription)

Number of Events:   6

                         PRICING LEVELS
Adult 20%         1         2         3         4
    Full Price   $72.00    $62.00    $53.00    $43.00
    DST          $12.00    $10.40    $ 8.80    $ 7.20

Fac/St 25%
    Full Price   $68.00    $59.00    $50.00    $41.00
    DST          $11.25    $ 9.75    $ 8.25    $ 6.75

Sr Cit 33%
    Full Price   $60.00    $52.00    $44.00    $36.00
    DST          $10.05    $ 8.71    $ 7.37    $ 6.03

Stu 50%
    Full Price   $45.00    $39.00    $33.00    $27.00
    DST          $ 7.50    $ 6.50    $ 5.50    $ 4.50

     F8:  Print Screen          F9:  <--        F10:   -->
```

Figure A.18 Design of User Interface of the Rev-Pro System: Master Pricing Grid Display Prototype

Appendix B
Writing a User's Manual

Katherine Nell Macfarlane

Whatever sort of software an organization is designing, one of the most crucial parts of the user interface is the user's manual. No matter how intuitive the software interface is, it simply cannot make allowances for the sort of detailed instructions users need when they are learning to use a new product. Moreover, the familiar book format, which requires no special training to operate, is convenient to novice and expert user alike. In it the novice can easily find concise, understandable instructions for performing a task, and the expert can use it to look up information quickly and accurately.

It Ain't Necessarily So

Unfortunately, a large percentage of software manuals are part of the problem, not the solution. However well-intentioned and capable the author and editor may be, manuals generally turn out to be an uneasy compromise between what ought to be and what has to be. This is true whether they are the work of a professional technical writer operating as part of a software production team, or a developer whose job includes documenting her or his own product.

One perennial problem for a writer of software manuals is determining who is going to be using the manual. Although some software is designed for specific users to meet defined specifications, a great deal is intended for the mass market and users who could be anyone: the greenest beginner who wants to be told in words of one syllable where to find the switch to turn on the computer or the expert who wants to push the system to the limit; and all levels in between. Trying to be all things to all users is one of the biggest problems a technical communicator must deal with.

Another problem is understanding exactly what the product does (and to some extent how it does it), so the writer can, in turn, explain these things to the user. Ideally, of course, technical writers should be in on the project from the start, designing the specifications and developing the manual as the programmers develop the software. In fact, the writer is often on his or her own.

Given these difficulties, is it possible for you as a technical writer to produce a sound, informative, readable software manual that will help the user make effective use of a product? To be sure, a great deal depends on individual circumstances; nevertheless, there are certain rules that any good technical communicator follows that can aid in producing a good manual and can make it very good indeed.

Audience

However vague the developers may be about their end user, it is your responsibility as a technical writer or editor to come up with some idea of who your readers are going to be so that you can write a manual geared to their particular needs. In many cases, you can tell from the nature of the product how sophisticated the user is likely to be. You can probably assume, for example, that users of a C compiler will have a fair amount of technical knowledge; users of a word processor, on the other hand, may be literate but not necessarily computer literate.

The projected user's level of expertise should determine not only the style in which you write and the terminology you will use, but even the kind of manual you design.

The Reference Guide. If you are addressing an audience of sophisticated technical experts, you will probably meet their needs most effectively with a *reference guide*. These people will already be veteran computer users, and you can usually assume that they are also familiar with the general type of product you are documenting. What they need is a reference manual in which they can easily look up specific items of information, particularly features of your product that may be new, or different in some important way from those of other, similar software packages. For example, if you are writing the manual for a new language compiler, you will want to include sections describing built-in procedures and functions, data types, and special utilities that may be included. (A utility is a special program that is used by the product to perform some task. For example, a spelling checker might be a utility for a word processor.)

A reference guide must also include a detailed index, and this poses special problems for you. First, you must familiarize yourself with the product to the extent that you are comfortable with the technical terminology that it involves. An experienced user will know that terminology, and will expect to be able to look under it in the index to reference information; you must be able to anticipate where such a user will look to find a particular item of information. Second, you must know how to design a good index, which involves a complex process of cross-referencing and choosing primary and secondary topics.

The Tutorial. If you anticipate, on the other hand, that most of your users will be rank beginners, you will be better off to provide them with a manual designed as a *tutorial*. This sort of manual contains very little technical information, which would only confuse a novice. It should be written in a very simple, straightforward style and consists, for the most part, of step-by-step instructions on how to use various features of the product. A good tutorial will make extensive use of illustrations, charts, and simplified checklists of instructions.

The User's Guide. The *user's guide* falls somewhere between these two extremes, and contains elements of both the reference guide and the tutorial. It is a good format to adopt if you are writing for a broad, general readership, or if you anticipate that most of your users will be people with intermediate experience who will need a certain amount of basic instruction in the special features of the product, but will then be able to proceed on their own, referencing information as needed.

Note that, if you anticipate that your product is going to be used by people with a wide range of experience, it is a good idea to ship one manual of each sort with it. This requires a lot of initial effort from you and is more expensive for the developer, but it will save a great deal of frustration and revising once the product ships.

Back to Basics

There are also a number of basic techniques that any good technical writer will always apply, regardless of audience, because they make a manual easier to read and understand.

K.I.S.S. (Keep it Simple, Stupid). Whatever your users' level of expertise, you should adopt a style that is simple and straightforward. Not even expert users enjoy having to wade through long, involved sentences full of compound verbs and subordinate clauses.

A good rule of thumb to follow is that simple equals short. You don't have to adopt a style so terse that it feels choppy, but it is a good idea to confine yourself to no more than one subordinate clause per sentence and hold paragraphs down to three or four sentences. Your readers will always find it easier to digest information that is given to them in small bites. The same applies to sections and chapters: It is better to have many small sections that can be assimilated a little at a time than one long chapter that is not broken down into units of information. (Edmond H. Weiss, in his excellent guide, *How to Write a Usable User Manual,* proposes doing away with chapter divisions altogether, and breaking the information down instead into short modules no more than two pages long. This allows all the information on a particular topic to be displayed on two facing pages; the user can see all the instructions for a given task without having to turn the page.)

Try at all times to keep your language *task oriented* and *user oriented:* In other words, keep your attention on the user and what the user is supposed to be doing. One very good way to do this is use the *active voice* and the *imperative mood,* especially when you are writing the instructions for a task. Here are some examples:

- Put the disk labeled "Installation Program" in the internal drive.
- Type INSTALL, then press the Return key.
- To save your file, select Save from the File menu.

Even in situations where the imperative is not appropriate, concentrate wherever possible on writing sentences that are about somebody *doing* something.

Unless you are certain that you are writing exclusively for experienced users, it is also a good idea to stick as much as possible to standard English instead of specialized technical language. You will always be faced with the dilemma of how much jargon is too much jargon. Specialized terminology offers the advantage of allowing you to say exactly what you want to say to the experienced user, but at the risk of losing and confusing the less sophisticated members of your readership. A good rule of thumb for avoiding the overuse of technical language is, "Never use a technical term unless you have first explained what it means." If you find yourself explaining every second word, you are using too much technical language.

A Picture is Worth . . . . Never underestimate the value of graphics such as pictures, charts, and diagrams in getting your point across. Humans are intensely sight-oriented creatures, and they will assimilate information from a visual illustration much more quickly and easily than they will from the most straightforward verbal description.

The less experienced the user, the more valuable graphics become. It does you no good, for example, to tell someone to put Disk B in the external drive if he or she doesn't know an external drive from a numeric key pad. A set of simple, clearly drawn illustrations accompanying your instructions can be invaluable to someone who is just getting started. (See the example in Figure B.1.) Pictures and

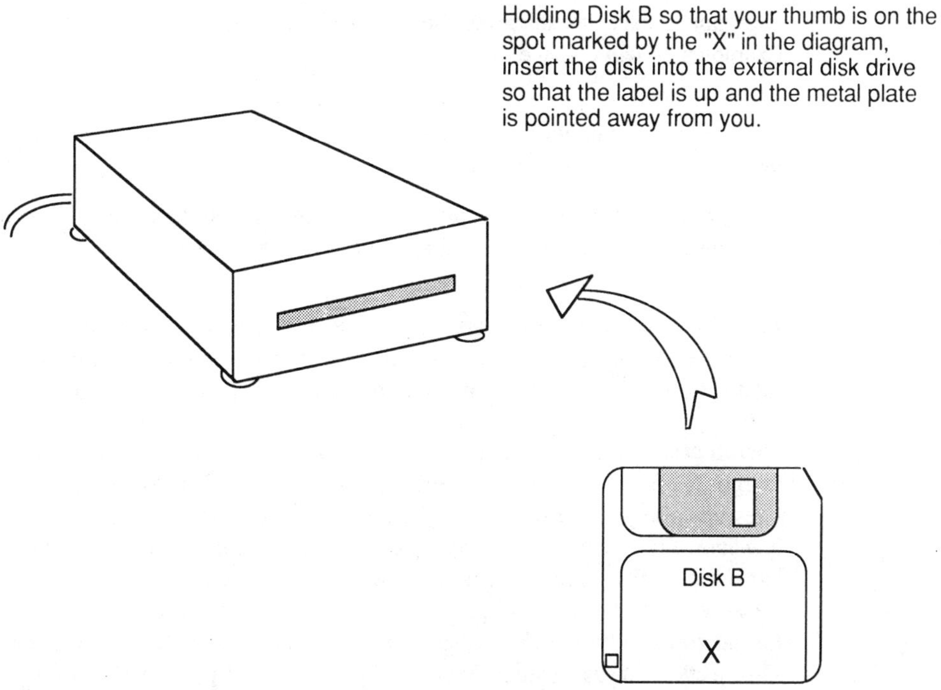

Holding Disk B so that your thumb is on the spot marked by the "X" in the diagram, insert the disk into the external disk drive so that the label is up and the metal plate is pointed away from you.

Figure B.1 An Example of an Illustration that Might Be Used in a User's Manual.

diagrams also have the effect of breaking up the text into smaller chunks, which makes it less intimidating to the user.

Illustrations have one drawback: They are expensive, both to produce and to reproduce. For this reason, many firms are reluctant to include them, even though doing so would make their manuals much easier to understand and use. Some companies avoid the expense of hiring a technical illustrator by having the writer or editor produce the illustrations. This is not terribly difficult if they are done using a computerized graphics package, and illustrations produced this way can often be copied directly into the word-processed text. This saves the company the expense of doing a *pasteup,* in which a professional layout specialist pastes text and illustrations onto the page.

There is another sort of illustration, however, that is not expensive and that users find extremely helpful. This is the "word picture," or example. Tutorials use examples a great deal: Walking your users step by step through one fairly typical task will build their confidence and give them specific information that they can extend to other similar tasks.

Layout. Layout is a powerful tool for making a manual easier to read and understand. Layout is related to how a page looks visually. There are a number of facets of layout that can be manipulated to make the manual better. These include:

- **White space.** Together with shorter paragraphs and chapter sections and frequent illustrations, white space (just what its name implies) breaks up the page and makes it easier for the user to isolate and absorb information. Examples of white space are:

  Wide margins. The wider the margin, the narrower the column of text, and the easier for the reader to scan across.

  A blank line between paragraphs. This isolates the paragraph for the reader and makes it easier for her or him to focus attention on it.

  Like illustrations, unfortunately, extensive use of white space does tend to make manuals longer and therefore more expensive to produce. But use it in moderation and you will greatly improve the quality of your product.

- **Justification.** Justification governs the way your text lines up along the margin. Most books, including this one, are *full justified;* that is, the text lines up evenly along both the right and left margins. Some formatters, however, favor using *left justification,* in which the text lines up along the left margin only, creating what is known as a *ragged right* margin. Because the lines on the page are of different lengths, the ragged right format supposedly makes it easier for the reader to keep his or her place. This section on justification is an example of ragged right justification.

- **Lists.** Try not to embed sequences of instructions or series of related ideas in your text. This makes it difficult for the reader to find them. If you put such items into a list, you will make it much easier for the reader to:

  1. Follow a sequence of instructions.
  2. Identify a series of related ideas.

  This example is the familiar *enumerated (numbered) list.* A popular variation on the enumerated list is the *bullet chart,* in which each item is marked with a bullet (•) instead of a number. This list of formatting techniques is an example of a bullet chart.

- **Section titles.** You should always break down your chapters into sections, and give each section a *section title.* Section titles make it easy for the reader to keep his or her place in the text, and also to recognize at a glance the key idea that you are discussing in the section. If your word processor allows you to use a variety of fonts (type styles), you can also use these to identify different section levels:

  Primary section:

  Secondary section:

  Third-level section:

  An even better way to identify section levels is to number them, using a hierarchical numbering system (1, 1.1, 1.1.1, 1.1.2, 1.2, and so on.)

- **Fonts.** Most word processors offer you at least **boldface**, *italic,* and <u>underline</u> fonts (typefaces), and some also allow you to use alternate type, such as appears on a computer monitor. Using special fonts of this sort lets you:

  Introduce *important new ideas.*

  Highlight **key vocabulary words** that you want your reader to remember.

  Identify examples of computer code embedded in your text.

The Index and the Table of Contents. The index and the table of contents are two vitally important parts of any manual, and particularly a reference guide, since they enable the user to find information quickly and easily. Whether or not your word processor handles the alphabetizing of the index and the format of the table of contents, it is your responsibility as writer or editor to determine what items will appear and how they are worded.

Your table of contents should reflect the organization of the manual itself. If your chapter sections are arranged in *hierarchical order* (that is, some are subsections of other, more general sections), you should reflect this in the table of contents, either by numbering the entries hierarchically, or by indentation level, or both:

1. Primary section

    1.1. Secondary section

        1.1.1. Third-level section
        1.1.2. Third-level section
        1.1.3. Third-level section

    1.2. Secondary section

2. Primary section

Although the table of contents is useful for locating general topics that rate a section heading, a manual generally requires an index as well to handle cross-references, topics that are related to one another ("See also . . ."), and detailed references. This appendix is too brief to explain in detail how to set up an index; whole books have been written on the subject. At the very least, you should refer to a style guide (the *Chicago Manual of Style* is a good place to start) to give yourself some idea of how to go about it. Some publications departments consider indexing important enough that they employ a professional indexer.

When Is a Manual Not a Manual? In addition to the hard-copy (printed) manual, there is another kind of informational software intended to be accessed *on line* — that is, via the computer. Two common instances of on line information are:

- **Help file.** This is a file that the user can access while the product itself is executing in order to get information about various features of the product: what a particular menu item does, for example, or what type of data a particular function must be given.

- **README file.** One of the most frustrating facts of life for a manual writer is that software continually undergoes changes. A manual must go to press generally from two weeks to a month before the product ships, and during that interval you may be sure that the developers will be busy tracking down last-minute bugs, adding new features, and changing the old ones. Consequently, most products ship with a special file on the distribution disk that contains important last-minute information that did not get into the manual. This is traditionally called the README file, in the hope that the user will do so.

References

Chapter 1

Agresti, W. W. (1986). *New Paradigms for Software Development*. Washington, DC: IEEE Computer Society Press.

Alavi, M. (June 1984). An assessment of the prototyping approach to information systems development. *Communications of the ACM, 27*(6), pp. 556–563.

Basili, V. R., and Perricone, B. T. (Jan. 1984). Software errors and complexity: An empirical investigation. *Communications of the ACM, 27*(1), pp. 42–52.

Boehm, B. (May 1973). Software and its impact: A quantitative assessment. *Datamation*, pp. 48–59.

——— (1981). *Software Engineering Economics*. Englewood Cliffs, NJ: Prentice-Hall, Inc.

——— (Mar. 1983). The hardware/software cost ratio: Is it a myth? *IEEE Computer, 16*(3).

——— (Jan. 1984). Verifying and validating software requirements and design. *IEEE Software*, pp. 75–88.

——— Gray, T. E., and Seewaldt, T. (May 1984). Prototyping versus specifying: A multi-project experiment. *IEEE Transactions on Software Engineering, SE-10*(3), pp. 290–302.

——— (June 1984). A software development environment for improving productivity. *IEEE Computer, 17*(6).

Brooks, F. (1975). *The Mythical Man-Month: Essays on Software Engineering*. Reading, MA: Addison-Wesley Publishing Co.

Brooks, F. P. (Apr. 1987). No silver bullet: Essence and accidents of software engineering. *IEEE Computer*, pp. 10–19.

Burton, K. (1984) Cost, cancellations impair software quality. *ComputerWorld*, July 8.

Carey, T. T., and Mason, R. E. A. (Aug. 1983). Information system prototyping: Techniques, tools and methodologies. *INFOR — The Canadian Journal of Operational Research and Information Processing, 21*(3), pp. 177–191.

Comptroller General. (1979). Contracting for computer software development. *General Accounting Office Report*. (FGMSD-80-4). Washington, D.C.

Constantine, L. L., and Yourdon, E. (1979). *Structured Design*. Englewood Cliffs, NJ: Prentice-Hall, Inc.

DeMarco, T. (1978). *Structured Analysis and System Specification*. New York: Yourdon Press.

Endres, A. (June 1975). An analysis of errors and their causes in system programs. *IEEE Transactions on Software Engineering, 1*(2), pp. 140–149.

Fairley, R. (1985). *Software Engineering Concepts*. New York: McGraw-Hill Book Co.

Hamilton, M. (Mar. 1986). Zero-defect software: The elusive goal. *IEEE Spectrum*, pp. 48–53.

Hecht, H., and Houghton, R. (1982). The current status of software tool usage. *IEEE Computer Society's 6th International Computer Software and Applications Conference*. Washington, DC: IEEE Computer Society Press.

IEEE (1983). *IEEE Standard Glossary of Software Engineering Terminology*, IEEE Standard 729-1983. New York: IEEE Society Press.

Jones, C. (1986). *Programming Productivity*. New York: McGraw-Hill Book Co.

Jones, T. C. (1978). Measuring programming quality and productivity. *IBM Systems Journal, 17*(1), pp. 39–63.

———— (1981). Program quality and programmer productivity, T. C. Jones (ed.), *Programming Productivity: Issues for the Eighties* (pp. 130–161). Washington, DC: IEEE Computer Society Press.

Leavitt, H. J. (1951). Some effects of certain communication patterns on group performance. *Journal of Abnormal and Social Psychology, 8*(1), pp. 38–50.

Leventhal, L. M., and Mynatt, B. T. (1987). Components of typical undergraduate software engineering courses: Results from a survey. *IEEE Transactions on Software Engineering, SE-13*(11), pp. 1193–1198.

Lientz, B., and Swanson, E. (1980). *Software Maintenance Management: A Study of the Maintenance of Computer Application Software in 487 Data Processing Organizations*. Reading, MA: Addison-Wesley Publishing Co.

Lipow, M. (July 1982). Number of faults per line of code. *IEEE Transactions on Software Engineering*, pp. 437–439.

Mantei, M. (Mar. 1981). The effect of programming team structure on programming tasks. *Communications of the ACM, 24*(3), pp. 106–113.

McCue, G. M. (1978). IBM's Santa Teresa Laboratory: Architectural design for program development. *IBM Systems Journal, 17*(1), pp. 4–25.

Mills, H., Dyer, and Linger, H. (Sept. 1987). *IEEE Software*, pp. 20–.

Musa, J. (Jan. 1985). Software engineering: The future of the profession. *IEEE Software, 2*(1), pp. 55–62.

Palmer, B. C., and Palmer, K. R. (1983). *The Successful Meeting Master Guide for Business and Professional People*. Englewood Cliffs, NJ: Prentice-Hall, Inc.

Parikh, G., and Zvegintzov, N. (1983). *Tutorial on Software Maintenance*. Silver Springs, MD: IEEE Computer Society.

Parnas, D. L. (1985). Software aspects of strategic defense systems. *American Scientist, 73*, pp. 432–440.

Pfleeger, S. L. (1987). *Software Engineering: The Production of Quality Software*. New York: Macmillan, Inc.

Porter, L. W., and Lawler, E. E. (1965). Properties of organization structure in relation to job attitudes and job behavior. *Psychological Bulletin, 64*, pp. 23–51.

Posten, R. M. and Bruen, M. W. (Sept. 1987). Counting down to Zero Software Failures. *IEEE Software*, pp. 54–61.

Pressman, R. S. (1988). *Software Engineering: A Beginner's Guide*. New York: McGraw-Hill Book Co.

Sackman, H., Erikson, W. J., and Grant, E. E. (1968). Exploratory experimentation studies comparing on-line and off-line programming performance. *Communications of the ACM, 11*(1), pp. 3–11.

Shaw, M. E. (1971). *Group Dynamics: The Psychology of Small Group Behavior*. New York: McGraw-Hill Book Co.

Spector, A., and Gifford, D. (Apr. 1986). A computer science perspective of bridge design. *Communications of the ACM, 29*(4), pp. 268–283.

Suydam, W. (Jan. 1, 1987). CASE makes strides toward automated software development. *Computer Design*, pp. 49–70.

Tropman, J. E., and Morningstar, G. C. (1985). *Meetings: How to Make Them Work for You*. New York: Van Nostrand Reinhold Co.

Wileden, J. C., and Dowson, M. (Aug. 1986). Introduction to International Workshop on the Software Process and Software Environments. *ACM SIGSOFT Software Engineering Notes, 11*(4), pp. 1–4.

Yeh, R. Software requirements: New directions and perspectives, C. Vick and C. Ramamoorthy (eds.) (1984). *Handbook of Software Engineering*. New York: Van Nostrand Reinhold Co.

Yourdon, E. (1975). *Techniques of Program Structure and Design*. Englewood Cliffs, NJ: Prentice-Hall, Inc.

Chapter 2

Basili, V. R., and Perricone, B. T. (Jan. 1984). Software errors and complexity: An empirical investigation. *Communications of the ACM, 27*(1), pp. 42–52.

Boehm, B. W. (1981). *Software Engineering Economics*. Englewood Cliffs, NJ: Prentice-Hall, Inc.

——— (Jan. 1984). Verifying and validating software requirements and design specifications. *IEEE Software*, pp. 75–88.

Brooks, F. P. (1975). *The Mythical Man-Month*. Reading, MA: Addison-Wesley Publishing Co.

——— (Apr. 1987). No silver bullet: Essence and accidents of software engineering. *IEEE Computer*, pp. 10–19.

DeMarco, T. (1978). *Structured Analysis and System Specification*. New York: Yourdon Press.

Fagan, M. E. (July 1986). Advances in software inspection. *IEEE Transactions on Software Engineering, SE-12*(7), pp. 744–751.

Fagan, M. E. (1979). Design and code inspections to reduce errors in program development. *IBM Systems Journal, 15*(3), pp. 182–211.

Fairley, R. (1985). *Software Engineering Concepts*. New York: McGraw-Hill Book Co.

Freedman, D. P., and Weinberg, G. M. (1982). *Handbook of Walkthroughs, Inspections and Technical Reviews* (3rd ed.). Boston: Little, Brown & Co.

Gilbert, P. (1983). *Software Design and Development*. Chicago: Science Research Associates, Inc.

Hetzel, W. (1988). *The Complete Guide to Software Testing* (2nd ed.). Wellesley, MA: QED Information Sciences, Inc.

Hurley, R. B. (1983). *Decision Tables in Software Engineering*. New York: Van Nostrand Reinhold Co.

Jones, T. C. (1978). Measuring programming quality and productivity. *IBM Systems Journal, 17*(1), pp. 39–63.

Vessey, I., and Weber, R. (Jan. 1986). Structured tools and conditional logic: An empirical investigation. *Communications of the ACM, 29*(1), pp. 48–57.

Yeh, R. Software requirements: New directions and perspectives, C. Vick and C. Ramamoorthy (eds.) (1984). *Handbook of Software Engineering.* New York: Van Nostrand Reinhold Co.

Yourdon, E. (1978). *Structured Walkthroughs* (2nd ed.). New York: Yourdon Press.

Chapter 3

Billingsley, P. A. (1982). Navigation through hierarchical menu structures: Does it help to have a map? *Proceedings of the Human Factors Society, 26th Annual Meeting,* pp. 103–107. Santa Monica, CA: Human Factors Society.

Brown, C. M. (1986). *Human–Computer Interface Design Guidelines.* Norwood, NJ: Ablex Publishing Co.

Brown, J. W. (July 1982). Controlling the complexity of menu networks. *Communications of the ACM, 25*(7), pp. 412–418.

Cohill, A. M., and Williges, R. C. (1982). Computer-augmented retrieval of HELP information for novice users. *Proceedings of the Human Factors Society, 26th Annual Meeting.* Santa Monica, CA: Human Factors Society. pp. 79–82.

Dwyer, B. (Sept. 1981). A user friendly algorithm. *Communications of the ACM, 24*(9), pp. 556–561.

Foss, D., Smith-Kerker, P. L., and Rosson, M. B. (1987). On comprehending a computer manual: Analysis of variables affecting performance. *International Journal of Man-Machine Studies, 26*(3).

Gould, J., and Grischkowsky, N. (Jan. 1983). *Doing the same work with hardcopy and with cathode ray tube (CRT) terminals,* IBM Research Report RC 9849. IBM Research Center, Yorktown Heights, NY 10598.

Green, T. R. G., and Payne, S. J. (1984). Organization and learnability in computer languages. *International Journal of Man-Machine Studies, 21*, pp. 7–18.

Hutchins, E. L., Hollan, J. D., and Norman, D. A. (1986). Direct manipulation interfaces. D. A. Norman and S. W. Draper (eds.), *User Centered System Design: New Perspectives on Human-Computer Interaction.* Hillsdale, NJ: Lawrence Erlbaum Associates.

Jones, T. C. (Sept 1984). Reusability in programming: A survey of the state of the art. *IEEE Transactions on Software Engineering, SE-10*(5), pp. 488–493.

Jorgensen, A. H. (1987). The trouble with UNIX: Initial learning and experts' strategies. H.-J. Bullinger and B. Shackel (eds.), *Human-Computer Interaction — INTERACT '87.* Stuttgart, Germany, pp. 847–859. Amsterdam: North-Holland.

Kiger, J. I. (1984). The depth/breadth trade-off in the design of menu-driven user interfaces. *International Journal of Man-Machine Studies, 20*, pp. 201–213.

Landauer, T. K., and Nachbar, D. W. (1985). Selection from alphabetic and numeric menu trees using a touch screen: Breadth, depth and width. *Proceedings of the Human Factors in Computing Systems Conference,* pp. 73–78. New York: Association of Computing Machinery.

———, Calotti, K. M., and Hartwell, S. (July 1983). Natural command names and initial learning. *Communications of the ACM, 23*, pp. 495–503.

Magers, C. S. (1983). An experimental evaluation of on-line help for non-programmers. *Proceedings of CHI '83 Conference: Human Factors in Computing Systems,* pp. 277–281. Baltimore, MD: Association of Computing Machinery.

McDonald, J. E., Stone, J. D., and Liebelt, L. S. (1983). Searching for items in menus: The effects of organization and type of target. *Proceedings of the Human Factors Society, 27th Annual Meeting*, pp. 834–837.

Mosteller, W. (1981). Job entry control language errors. *Proceedings of SHARE 57*, pp. 149–155. Chicago: SHARE, Inc.

Musa, J. (Jan. 1985). Software engineering: The future of the profession. *IEEE Software*, 2(1), pp. 55–62.

Muter, P., and others. (1982). Extended reading of continuous text on television screens. *Human Factors, 24*, pp. 501–508.

Norman, D. A. (Apr. 1983). Design rules based on analyses of human errors. *Communications of the ACM, 26*(4), pp. 254–258.

Ogden, W. C., and Boyle, J. M. (1982). Evaluating human–computer dialog styles: Command vs. form fill-in for report modification. *Proceedings of the Human Factors Society, 26th Annual Meeting*, pp. 542–545. Santa Monica, CA: Human Factors Society.

Pakin, S. E., and Wray, P. (July 1982). Designing screens for people to use easily. *Data Management*, pp. 36–41.

Perlman, G. (1984). Making the right choices with menus. *INTERACT '84: First IFIP International Conference of Human-Computer Interaction*, pp. 291–295. Amsterdam: North-Holland.

Potosnak, K. (May 1988). Do icons make user interfaces easier to use? *IEEE Software*, pp. 97–99.

Price, J. (1984). *How to Write a Computer Manual*. Reading, MA: Addison-Wesley Publishing Co.

Prieto-Diaz, R., and Freeman, P. (Jan. 1987). Classifying software for reuse. *IEEE Software, 4*(1), pp. 6–16.

Roberts, T. L. (1980). *Evaluation of Computer Text Editors*. Unpublished doctoral dissertation, Stanford University, Stanford, CA.

Rosson, M. B. (1983). Patterns of experience in text editing. *Proceedings of CHI '83, Conference on Human Factors in Computing Systems*, pp. 171–175. Baltimore, MD: Association of Computing Machinery.

Schneider, M. L. (1984). Ergonomic considerations in the design of text editors. Y. Vassilou (ed.), *Human Factors and Interactive Computer Systems*, pp. 141–161. Norwood, NJ: Ablex.

Shneiderman, B. (1982). System message design: Guidelines and experimental results. A. Badre and B. Shneiderman (eds.), *Directions in Human/Computer Interaction*, pp. 55–78. Norwood, NJ: Ablex.

——— (1987). *Designing the User Interface: Strategies for Effective Human-Computer Interaction*. Reading, MA: Addison-Wesley.

Smith, S. L., and Mosier, J. N. (1986). Guidelines for Designing User-Interface Software (ADA177198). Alexandria, VA: National Technical Information Service.

Spiliotopoulos, V., and Shackel, B. (1981). Toward a computer interview acceptable to the naive user. *International Journal of Man-Machine Studies, 14*, pp. 77–90.

Standish, T. A. (Sept. 1984). An essay on software reusability. *IEEE Transactions on Software Engineering, SE-10*(5), pp. 494–497.

Teitelbaum, R. C., and Granda, R. (1983). The effects of positional constancy on searching menus for information. *Proceedings of CHI '83, Human Factors in Computing Systems*, pp. 150–53. Baltimore, MD: Association of Computing Machinery.

Weiss, E. H. (1985). *How to Write a Usable User Manual*. Philadelphia, PA: ISI Press.

Chapter 4

Agresti, W. W. (1986). *New Paradigms for Software Development*. Washington, DC: IEEE Computer Society Press.

Baker, F. (Jan. 1972). Chief programmer team management of production programming. *IBM Systems Journal, 11*(1), p. 58.

Booch, G. (1987). *Software Engineering with Ada*. Menlo Park, CA: Benjamin/Cummings Publishing Co.

Cox, B. (1986). *Object Oriented Programming*. Reading, MA: Addison-Wesley Publishing Co.

Hetzel, W. (1988). *The Complete Guide to Software Testing*. 2nd Ed. Wellesley, MA: QED Information Sciences, Inc.

Jackson, M. A. (1975). *Principles of Program Design*. New York: Academic Press, Inc.

Liskov, B., and Guttag, J. (1986). *Abstraction and Specification in Program Development*. New York: McGraw-Hill Book Co.

Martin, J., and McClure, C. (1985) *Diagramming Techniques for Analysts and Programmers*. Englewood Cliffs, NJ: Prentice-Hall, Inc.

Miller, G. (1956). The magical number seven, plus or minus two: Some limits on our capacity for processing information. *Psychological Review, 63*, pp. 81–97.

Parnas, D. (1971). *Information Distribution Aspects of Design Methodology*. Pittsburgh, PA.: Carnegie-Mellon University Technical Report.

——— (April 1972). On criteria to be used in decomposing systems into modules. *Communications of the ACM, 14*(1), pp. 221–27.

Warnier, J-D. (1974). *Logical Construction of Programs*. New York: Van Nostrand Reinhold Co.

——— (1981). *Logical Construction of Systems*. New York: Van Nostrand Reinhold Co.

Weinberg, G. (1971). *Psychology of Computer Programming*. New York: Van Nostrand Reinhold, Co.

Wirth, N. (Apr. 1971). Program development by stepwise refinement. *Communications of the ACM, 14*(4), pp. 221–227.

Yourdon, E., and Constantine, L. (1979). *Structured Design*. Englewood Cliffs, NJ: Prentice-Hall, Inc.

Chapter 5

Bell, D., Morrey, I., and Pugh, J. (1987). *Software Engineering: A Programming Approach*. Englewood Cliffs, NJ: Prentice-Hall, Inc.

Bohm, C., and Jacopini, G. (May 1966). Flow diagrams, Turing machines and languages with only two formation rules. *Communications of the ACM, 9*(5), pp. 366–371.

Brooke, J., and Duncan, K. (1980). An experimental study of flowcharts as an aid to identification of procedural faults. *Ergonomics, 23*(4), pp. 387–399.

Department of Defense (Oct. 1982). *Reference Manual for the Ada Programming Language*. Washington, DC: Ada Joint Program Office.

Knuth, D. E. (1971). An empirical study of Fortran programs. *Journal of Software Practice and Experience, 1*, pp. 105–133.

——— (1973a). *The Art of Computer Programming, Vol. 1: Fundamental Algorithms* (2nd ed.). Reading, MA: Addison-Wesley Publishing Co.

——— (1973b). *The Art of Computer Programming, Vol. 3: Searching and Sorting*. Reading, MA: Addison-Wesley Publishing Co.

Nassi, I., and Shneiderman, B. (Aug. 1973). Flowchart techniques for structured programming. *ACM SIGPLAN Notices, 8*(8), pp. 12–26.

Shneiderman, B. (Jan. 1982). Control flow and data structure documentation. *Communications of the ACM, 25*(1), pp. 55–63.

—— and others, (1977). Experimental investigations of the utility of detailed flowcharts in programming. *Communications of the ACM, 20*(5), pp. 373–381.

Wirth, N. (1976). *Algorithms + Data Structures = Programs*. Englewood Cliffs, NJ: Prentice-Hall, Inc.

Chapter 6

Bohm, C., and Jacopini, G. (1966). Flow diagrams, Turing machines and languages with only two formation rules. *Communications of the ACM, 9,* pp. 366–371.

Gifford, D., and Spector, A. (July 1984). The TWA Reservation System. *Communications of the ACM, 27*(7), pp. 649–665.

Halstead, M. (1977). *Elements of Software Physics*. New York: Elsevier North-Holland.

Kernighan, B. W., and Plauger, P. J. (1978). *Elements of Programming Style* (2nd ed.). New York: McGraw-Hill Book Co.

Kesler, T. E., and others, (1984). The effect of indentation on program comprehension. *International Journal of Man-Machine Studies, 21,* pp. 415–428.

McCabe, T. J. (Dec. 1976). A complexity measure. *IEEE Transactions on Software Engineering,* pp. 308–320.

Miara, R. J., and others, (1983). Program indentation and comprehensibility. *Communications of the ACM, 26,* pp. 861–867.

Schneyer, R. (1984). *Modern Structured Programming: Program Logic, Style and Testing*. Santa Cruz, CA: Mitchell Publishing.

Chapter 7

Beizer, B. (1984). *Software System Testing and Quality Assurance*. New York: Van Nostrand Reinhold Co.

Hetzel, W. (1988). *The Complete Guide to Software Testing,* 2nd ed. Wellesley, MA: QED Information Systems, Inc.

Howden, W. E. (1987). *Functional Program Testing and Analysis*. New York: McGraw-Hill Book Co.

IEEE (1983). *IEEE Standard Glossary of Software Engineering Terms,* IEEE Standard 729-1983. New York: IEEE Society Press.

Myers, G. J. (1979). *Software Reliability: Principles and Practice*. New York: John Wiley & Sons, Inc.

Chapter 8

Abbott, R. (Nov. 1983). Program design by informal English descriptions. *Communications of the ACM, 26*(11), pp. 884–891.

Apple Computer, Inc. (1987). *Human-Interface Guidelines: The Apple Desktop Interface*. Reading, MA: Addison-Wesley Publishing Co.

Bobbie, P. O. (Apr. 1987). Productivity through automated tools. *ACM SIGSOFT Software Engineering Notes, 12*(2), pp. 30–31.

Boehm, B. (1981). *Software Engineering Economics*. Englewood Cliffs, NJ: Prentice-Hall, Inc.

Boehm, B. W. (1985) A spiral model of software development and enhancement. *TRW Technical Report #21-371-85*. TRW, Inc., 1 Space Park, Redondo Beach, CA 90278.

————, and others (1984). A software development environment for improving productivity. *IEEE Computer, 17*(6), pp. 30–44.

Boies, S. J., and Gould, J. D. (1974). Syntactic errors in computer programming, *Human Factors, 16*(3), pp. 253–257.

Booch, G. (1987). *Software Engineering with Ada*. Menlo Park, CA: Benjamin/Cummings Publishing Co.

Brooks, F. P. (Apr. 1987). No silver bullet: Essence and accidents of software engineering. *IEEE Computer*, pp. 10–19.

Cameron, J. R. (1983). *JSP & JSD: The Jackson Approach to Software Development*. Los Angeles, CA: IEEE Computer Society.

Card, D. N., Church, V. E., and Agresti, W. W. (Feb. 1986). An empirical study of software design practices. *IEEE Transactions on Software Engineering, SE-12*(2), pp. 264–271.

Charette, R. N. (1986). *Software Engineering Environments: Concepts and Technology*. New York: McGraw-Hill Book Co.

Cureton, B. (Mar. 1988). The future of Unix in the CASE renaissance. *IEEE Software*, pp. 18–22.

Delisle, N. M., Menicosy, D. E., and Schwartz, M. D. (1984). *Proceedings of the ACM SIGSOFT/SIGPLAN Software Engineering Symposium on Practical Software Development Environments*. New York: Association of Computing Machinery.

Dolatta, T. (1976). *Data Processing in 1980–1985*. New York: John Wiley & Sons, Inc.

Fischer, C. N., and others (1984). The Poe language-based editor project. *Proceedings of the ACM SIGSOFT/SIGPLAN Software Engineering Symposium on Practical Software Development Environments*. New York: Association of Computing Machinery.

Fjeldstad, R. K., and Hamlen, W. T. (1983). Application program maintenance study: Report to our respondents. G. Parikh and N. Zvegintzov (eds.), *Tutorial on Software Maintenance*. Silver Springs, MD: IEEE Computer Society Press.

Frenkel, K. A. (June 1985). Toward automating the software development cycle. *Communications of the ACM, 28*(6), pp. 578–589.

Gane, C., and Sarson, T. (1979). *Structured Systems Analysis: Tools and Techniques*. Englewood Cliffs, NJ: Prentice-Hall, Inc.

Gardner, A. C. (1981). *Practical LCP*. New York: McGraw-Hill Book Co.

Griffen, W. (Nov. 1984). Software engineering in GTE. *IEEE Computer, 17*(11), pp. 66–73.

Hecht, H., and Houghton, R. (1982). The current status of software tool usage. *IEEE Computer Society's 6th International Computer Software & Applications Conference*. New York: IEEE Society Press.

Higher Education Research Institute: *The American Freshman: National Norm for Fall, 1985*. Los Angeles: UCLA Graduate School of Education.

Houghton, R. C., and Wallace, D. R. (Jan 1987). Characteristics and functions of software engineering environments: An overview. *ACM SIGSOFT Software Engineering Notes, 12*(1), pp. 64–84.

Hurst, R. (July 8, 1987). CASE systems near fruition. *Computerworld*, pp. 27–29.

IEEE (1983). *IEEE Standard Glossary of Software Engineering Terms,* ANSI/IEEE Std 729-1983. New York: IEEE Society Press.

Isner, J. F. (Oct. 1982). A Fortran programming methodology based on data abstraction. *Communications on the ACM, 25*(10), pp. 686–697.

Jackson, M. (1975). *Principles of Program Design.* New York: Academic Press, Inc.

—— (1983). *System Development.* Englewood Cliffs, NJ: Prentice-Hall, Inc.

Jacky, J. P., and Kalet, I. J. (Sept. 1987). An object-oriented programming discipline for standard Pascal. *Communications of the ACM, 30*(9), pp. 772–776.

Kernighan, B., and Mashey, J. (Apr. 1981). The UNIX programming environment. *IEEE Computer, 14*(4), pp. 12–24.

King, J. J., and Pardoe, J. P. (1985). *Program Design Using JSP.* New York: John Wiley & Sons, Inc.

Kolodziej, S. (July 8, 1987). User interface management systems. *Computerworld,* pp. 31–34.

Miller, E. (ed.) (1979). *Tutorial: Automated Tools for Software Engineering.* New York: IEEE Computer Society.

Musa, J. (Jan. 1985). Software engineering: The future of the profession. *IEEE Software, 2*(1), pp. 55–62.

Leventhal, L. M., and Mynatt, B. T. (1987). Components of typical undergraduate software engineering courses: Results from a survey. *IEEE Transactions on Software Engineering,* SE-13(11), pp. 1193–1198.

Orr, K. T. (1977). *Structured Systems Development.* New York: Yourdon Press.

Redwine, S., and others (1984). DoD related software technology requirements, practices and prospects for the future, IDA Paper P-1788.

Riddle, W. (1984). The magic number eighteen plus or minus three: A study of software technology maturation. *DoD Related Software Technology Requirements, Practices, and Prospects for the Future,* IDA Paper P-1788.

Ritchie, D., and Thompson, K. (July 1974). The UNIX time-sharing system. *Communications of the ACM, 17*(7), pp. 365–374.

Ross, D. T. (Jan. 1977). Structured analysis (SA): A language for communicating ideas. *IEEE Transactions on Software Engineering,* SE-3(1), pp. 16–34.

Scheifler, R. W., and Gettys, J. (Apr. 1987). The X Window system. *ACM Transactions on Graphics, 5*(2), pp. 79–109.

Shigo, O., and others. (1982). Configuration Control for Evolutional Software Products. *Proceedings of the Sixth International Conference on Software Engineering.* Tokyo.

Smith, K. H., Zirkler, D., and Mynatt, B. T. (1985). Transfer of training from introductory computer courses is highly specific . . . and negative! *Behavior Research Methods, Instruments & Computers, 17*(2), pp. 259–264.

Stoneman (Feb. 1980). *Requirements for Ada Programming Support Environments:* DoD Ada Joint Project Office.

Stucki, L. G. (1983). What about CAD/CAM for software? The ARGUS concept. *Proceedings of SoftFair. IEEE Order No. 83CH1919-0.* New York: IEEE Society Press.

Teichroew, D., and Hershey, E. A. (Jan. 1977). PSL/PSA: A computer-aided technique for structured documentation and analysis of information processing systems. *IEEE Transactions on Software Engineering,* SE-3(1), pp. 41–48.

Tucker, M. (July 8, 1987). Software engineering's frontiers. *Computerworld,* pp. 35–38.

Wallace, R., and Charette, R. (Dec. 1984). *Architectural Description of the Ada Language System (ALS).* (JSSEEEARCH01). Joint Service Software Engineering Environment Report.

Warnier, J. D. (1974). *Logical Construction of Programs*. New York: Van Nostrand Reinhold Co.

Wasserman, A. I. (1983). The unified support environment: Tool support for the user software engineering methodology. *Proceedings of SoftFair. IEEE Order No. 83CH1919-0*. New York: IEEE Society Press.

Wiener, R., and Sincovec, R. (1984). *Software Engineering with Modula-2 and Ada*. New York: John Wiley & Sons, Inc.

Wirth, N. (Dec. 1974). On the composition of well-structured programs. *Computing Surveys, 6*(4), p. 247.

Zelkowitz, M. V. and others. (June 1984). Software engineering practices in the US and Japan. *IEEE Computer*, pp. 57–66.

Index

Abstract data types
    see Data abstraction
Abstraction
    in system design, 146
    in systems analysis, 53–54
Abstraction by specification, 170–175
Acceptance testing, 276, 308–309
Activity specifications, 62
    using decision tables, 66–70
    using prose, 62
    using pseudocode, 62–66
Ada, 174, 203–204, 208–230, 370, 376
Agenda, 36–39
Algorithm
    efficiency, 193, 194–197
    order of, 194–196
    selection of, 193–197
Analysis,
    see Requirements analysis
ASPE, 352–354
Assertions, 181, 348–349
Automatic code generation, 320–321, 346–348

Big bang, 239–243
Black box, 149–150
Black-box testing, 276, 280, 292–297
Blueberry muffin factory example, 28–30, 50–52
Bottom up integration, 239–240, 243
Boundary testing, 295–297, 298

CASE, 322, 340–363
    framing environments, 342–346
    general environments, 342, 349–358

programming environments, 342, 346–349
Chief programmer team, 34–35
Class, 29–30, 368–369
Coding, 239–270
Coding style, 251–258
Cohesion, 147–148
Command languages, 99, 106–109
Computer Aided Software Engineering
    see CASE
Computerized concordance example, 29–31, 52–53, 162–165, 244–248
Configuration management, 336–339
Control item, 29
Costs
    maintenance, 20–21, 335
    software development, 17–21
    software ownership, 17–21
Coupling, 148–149
Coverage, 280–291, 348
Current logical system, 55
Current physical system, 55

Data abstraction, 169–175, 204, 224–229
Data dictionary, 60–62, 87–88, 177
Data flow diagram
    defined, 49–53
    examples, 55–60, 86–87
    system models, 53–56
Data item, 29
Data sink, 30, 50–51
Data source, 29
Data store, 30, 50–51